The Temptation of Graves in Salafi Islam

The Temptation of Graves in Salafi Islam
Iconoclasm, Destruction and Idolatry

Ondřej Beránek and Pavel Ťupek

EDINBURGH
University Press

To our children: Jakub and Ruben – Bertik and Barunka

Edinburgh University Press is one of the leading university presses in the UK. We publish academic books and journals in our selected subject areas across the humanities and social sciences, combining cutting-edge scholarship with high editorial and production values to produce academic works of lasting importance. For more information visit our website: edinburghuniversitypress.com

© Ondřej Beránek and Pavel Ťupek, 2018

Edinburgh University Press Ltd
The Tun – Holyrood Road
12 (2f) Jackson's Entry
Edinburgh EH8 8PJ

Typeset in 11/15 Adobe Garamond Pro by
IDSUK (DataConnection) Ltd

A CIP record for this book is available from the British Library

ISBN 978 1 4744 1757 0 (hardback)
ISBN 978 1 4744 1758 7 (webready PDF)
ISBN 978 1 4744 1759 4 (epub)

TherightofOndřej Beránek and Pavel Ťupek to be identifiedasauthorsofthisworkhasbeenasserted in accordance with the Copyright, Designs and Patents Act 1988 and the Copyright and Related Rights Regulations 2003 (SI No. 2498).

Contents

List of Figures	vi
Acknowledgements	vii
Introduction	1
1 Graves and Shrines in Medieval Islam: From Pre-Islamic Times to Ibn Taymiyya's Legacy	18
2 Early Wahhabism and the Beginnings of Modern Salafism	70
3 Saudi Arabia between pan-Islamism, Iconoclasm and Political Legitimacy	126
4 Following Current Paths of Destruction: ISIS and Beyond	172
Conclusion	220
Bibliography	228
Index	253

Figures

1	The destruction by ISIS of a Muslim cemetery in Ninive Province, northern Iraq	2
2	The cenotaph of Imam al-Shafi'i in Cairo. Undated; turn of the nineteenth/twentieth century	32
3	The Mamluk graves, Cairo. Undated; turn of the nineteenth/twentieth century	33
4	Funeral architecture, Damascus. Undated; turn of the nineteenth/twentieth century	38
5	The grave, near Mecca, of the last of the nine wives of the Prophet Muhammad, Maymuna, *c.* 1888	82
6	An advertisement by ISIS for Ibn 'Abd al-Wahhab's book: *The Clarification of Doubts* (*Kashf al-shubuhat*)	83
7	The al-Baqi' cemetery, Medina, the first Islamic cemetery	106
8	A current image of the al-Baqi' cemetery, Medina	107
9	The al-Mu'alla cemetery, Mecca	112
10	Khadija's shrine at the al-Mu'alla cemetery	133
11	Shrine of John the Baptist in the Umayyad Mosque, Damascus. Undated; turn of the nineteenth/twentieth century	137
12a	The mosque and shrine of Jirjis: before its destruction, 15 November 2013	182
12b	The mosque and shrine of Jirjis: after its destruction, 21 August 2014	183
12c	The mosque and shrine of Jirjis: approximately one year after its destruction, 29 November 2015	183
13	The destruction by ISIS of Qabr al-bint, Mosul, 2014	185
14	The destruction by ISIS of Imam al-Muhsin shrine in Mosul	186
15	The grave of Eve, Jeddah	187
16	The destruction of graves in Yemen in 2016	188

Acknowledgements

This book began as an article that we wrote together almost a decade ago.[1] We would therefore like to express our gratitude to the Crown Center for Middle East Studies at Brandeis University, both for supporting and publishing our initial research, and for giving us permission to use parts of that article in this book. Since the article was published in 2009, our ideas have continued to develop and we have carried on sifting through some extremely rich material. The wave of uprisings in the Arab world, followed by increasing levels of destructive activities by various Salafi groups, from Mali to Libya and, most prominently, the rise of ISIS, gave our research new meaning and impetus.

The final manuscript has been written at our home institutions: the Oriental Institute of the Czech Academy of Sciences and the Institute of Near Eastern and African Studies, Charles University, Prague. Both institutions deserve our sincere gratitude for supporting our research. Parts of our research have also been presented at several international conferences and workshops: the Zentrum für interdisziplinäre Forschung (Centre for Interdisciplinary Research), Bielefeld University, Bielefeld (2014); the international conference of the German Middle East Studies Association (DAVO), Bochum (2015); the international workshop 'Islamism and the State: Contested Normativities in the Muslim World', organised by the Cluster of Excellence 'Formation of Normative Orders', Goethe University, Frankfurt (2015); and most recently, the annual conference of the Middle East Studies Association, Boston, United States (2016). We wish to express our thanks to all those who attended these events and provided us with useful advice, criticism or suggestions.

We further acknowledge the support of various libraries, without whose assistance and resources it would have been impossible to finish this book: besides our two home libraries, the Oriental Institute of the Czech Academy of Sciences and the Institute for Near Eastern and African Studies at Charles

University, Prague, thanks are particularly due to Harvard University Library, the University of Edinburgh library and the Universitätsbibliothek Leipzig for their incredible and seemingly inexhaustible collections. Finally, we gratefully acknowledge financial support for our research from the Crown Center for Middle East Studies at Brandeis University, the Royal Society of Edinburgh and the Czech Science Foundation (GAČR) under grant project No. 14-16520S ('Death, Graves, and the Hereafter in Islam: Muslim Perceptions of the Last Things in the Middle Ages and Today').

Furthermore, we owe our sincere gratitude to the editors at EUP, Nicola Ramsey in particular, for their great patience and help with the manuscript. We also wish to thank Stefano Taglia, who read parts of the manuscript and provided much needed feedback, and Steven Patten and Anna M. Barton, who helped us to make the language more accessible. We also owe our gratitude to those anonymous readers who provided us with many great ideas and suggested improvements. Needless to say, all the potential shortcomings or mistakes that might appear in the text are entirely our own.

Ondřej Beránek: I particularly wish to thank Naghmeh Sohrabi, who has supported my research from the very onset and become a great friend. Last, but certainly not least, I wish to thank my wife, without whose endless support and presence in my life I would never have found the time and energy to accomplish this project, and our sons Jakub and Ruben, who have had to endure my occasional absent-mindedness. It is to them, and their constant innocent question 'Why?', which should really form the underlining methodology of any scholarly work, that I dedicate this book.

Pavel Ťupek: there are really no words that could express my thanks to my wife for her sacrifices while I have been working on this book and for her patience with me and our children.

Notes

1. Beranek and Tupek, 'From Visiting Graves to their Destructions'.

If given the opportunity, we will destroy the domes and buildings on graves and shrines and annihilate the sources of polytheism.

> From Islamic State's proclamations

For whatever cause a country be devastated, these buildings should be spared which are an honour to the human race and which do not add to the strength of the enemy, such as temples, tombs, public buildings and all edifices of remarkable beauty. What is gained by destroying them?

> Emmerich de Vattel, *Le droit des gens* (1758)

Destroying graveyards and monuments is a way of carrying out ethnic cleansing retroactively.

> Robert Bevan, architecture critic

I reflected on entering his sitting room and catching sight of a large picture of a bearded man who might have been his father or grandfather! Photographs were at that time considered next to mortal sin . . . I kept staring at the picture without crossing the threshold . . . Didn't the angels abandon a place where pictures were hung to devils and demons? . . . One day I ventured to ask him how it was permissible to hang a forbidden image in his house. Instead of answering my question directly he, in turn, asked me if I had ever thought of worshipping that picture. Then he said nothing more on the subject.

> Hamza Bogary, *The Sheltered Quarter*, pp. 49–50

Introduction

In various parts of the Islamic world over the past years and decades virulent attacks have targeted Islamic funeral and sacral architecture. These attacks, which have destroyed graves and other artefacts in the Islamic world should not be viewed as random acts of vandalism, but as acts associated with 'performing one's religious duty'. The requirement to level graves (*taswiyat al-qubūr*), is attested in the Wahhabi–Salafi tradition and texts, and is quite often invoked by Saudi religious scholars and bodies. According to their belief, mosques, mausoleums and domes containing graves must be levelled to the ground, especially when they are used as places of worship. In the Salafi understanding, worshipping a human being, whether dead or alive, is a kind of polytheism (*shirk*) and, as such, is tantamount to idolatry. Even the mere fear of idolatry associated with graves, the so-called temptation to worship and venerate graves (*fitnat al-qubūr*), justifies their removal.[1] The motivation to destroy statues and sculptures also stems from this same fear.

Two seemingly independent phenomena of the contemporary Islamic world demonstrate our central argument. First, let us consider the risks posed by the so-called Islamic State (henceforth ISIS) and its ongoing intentional destruction of erected monuments (tombs, shrines, mosques) and other sites and artefacts, often deemed by them to be polytheistic and to represent a return to the veneration of saints and idolatry. Over the past few years, such incidents have mostly taken place in and around Mosul, al-Raqqa, Nineveh, and Dabiq, although some have also occurred in other areas. These acts of iconoclasm on the part of ISIS indicate a pattern evocative of the Taliban destruction of artefacts in Afghanistan. ISIS seems, in particular, to be systematically targeting aspects of Shi'i cultural heritage, with Sufi and Yazidi sites also included, in addition to pagan heritage (Palmyra, Nimrod). However,

Figure 1 The destruction by ISIS of a Muslim cemetery in Ninive Province, northern Iraq

(An image grab taken from a video, 'Izalat mazahir al-shirk', released by ISIS in February 2015, see at: https://www.youtube.com/watch?v=EEhWzVBqX-c.)

many Sunni monuments have also been targeted, including those of the Prophet Muhammad's Companions.

Second, a number of recent reports[2] have mentioned Saudi efforts to destroy the tomb of the Prophet Muhammad, which is part of the Prophet's Mosque in Medina, and remove his remains to an anonymous grave at the nearby al-Baqiʿ cemetery. This is not a new demand – the Saudi Ministry of Islamic Affairs has previously called for the demolition of the dome over the Prophet's Mosque and for the graves of Muhammad and the first two caliphs Abu Bakr and ʿUmar to be levelled. The Saudis have proved in the past that where cultural heritage is concerned, they are not averse to sanctioning the destruction of monuments, whether in the name of doctrinal issues or to make way for developmental plans. Hence, most of the old buildings and sites in Mecca have been destroyed and replaced with luxury hotels and shopping malls.

In books on Islamic theology and jurisprudence, the sacred geography of Islam is quite simple: Muslims should pray towards the Kaʿba in Mecca and undertake the *ḥajj* (pilgrimage) there. The position of Mecca, however, is not uncontested, and many areas of the Islamic world have gradually developed a special emphasis upon other shrines. Across the Middle East and North Africa and central, south and southeast Asia, many, much smaller, sites have become established, to which pilgrimage is sometimes even prioritised over to that to Mecca. The tombs of dead saints, be they former miracle-workers, ulama (*ʿulamāʾ*, religious scholars) or local heroes, are transformed into shrines and are often attached to a mosque. These saints' shrines tend sometimes to serve as a social space for women, rather than as the religious space of a mosque.[3] The special status given to saints stems from the fact that people attribute special powers to them and believe that they are in a direct relationship with God, which makes them particularly well positioned to serve as a means of intercession and to transfer God's grace (*baraka*) to ordinary people. This belief in saints' miraculous powers, together with the tradition of visiting their shrines (*ziyāra*), is widely spread across the Islamic world, and is a feature shared with other religions.[4]

While the *ḥajj* is a universal rite in Islam, *ziyāra* is also universally popular but lacks the authority of the Qurʾan. In a narrower sense, this term specifically designates grave visiting (*ziyārat al-qubūr*), which is recorded in the hadiths (*ḥadīth*, pl. *aḥādīth*), the Prophetic traditions. However, some scholars have rejected the authenticity of several of these hadiths, and the meaning of others has been interpreted in many different ways. In many instances, the beliefs and rituals associated with *ziyāra* have led to tension with the ulama who condemned the visits to graves. A huge gap appeared in the early history of Islam between purist ideals and the daily reality of burials and local burial practices. There has always been near-uniform agreement that the resting place of the dead must be honoured and about the form of graves below the ground, but disagreements emerged regarding the parts above ground. Some religious scholars feared that visiting graves might lead to their veneration, which in turn some viewed as polytheism and apostasy. Vigorous debates and divisions emerged over the legality of building domes over graves; whether it is permissible for women to visit graves; what kind of utterances, such as prayers and supplications, are allowed in graveyards; whether it is proper to pray directly to the dead and to seek their intercession; whether physical contact with a grave is permissible; and how high a grave can be built up without becoming an idol. These debates mirror the perennial struggle for spiritual purity and other disputes among Muslims over issues of doctrine and orthodoxy.

Vigorous opposition to certain well-established funerary practices can be confidently traced to Hanbali scholarship, and especially to Ibn Taymiyya (1263–1328), one of the most famous – and controversial – medieval Islamic jurists and theologians, whose influence is still palpable in current Sunni discourse. Ibn Taymiyya spent a large portion of his life in prison for his teachings; his last imprisonment was a result of him issuing a legal opinion in which he reportedly denounced the practice of visiting the Prophet Muhammad's grave.[5] Ibn Taymiyya was defeated by the ulama of Egypt and Syria, and died in prison. Although his views were quashed in his lifetime, Ibn Taymiyya left an influential legacy for subsequent generations, who engaged in similar debates over the following centuries both in refutation of his arguments and in defence of them.

Still, the suspicion surrounding veneration of saints and their shrines that had emerged in the Islamic Middle Ages concerned only a small fraction of ulama and was entirely academic, theoretical and, save to say, highly unpopular. This is probably the feature that mostly distinguishes the phenomenon of *ziyāra* in medieval times from the contemporary Islamic world. Ordinary believers were barely affected by the ulama's legal opinions, and continued their usual practices regardless. A frequently mentioned anecdote, according to which Ibn Taymiyya's burial was attended by crowds of people, who then came to regard him as a saint and visit his grave, is quite indicative of this. Only the coming of the modern age, with its reinterpretation, reformulation and reorientation of religious experience and an obsessive emphasis on scripturalism, shed new light on centuries-long habits. With the advent of printing, the rise of mass media, urbanisation and the spread of education, traditional forms of religious expression slowly began to be eradicated. Finally, the systematisation of the religious establishment and its better funding and staffing enabled the spread of textually based orthodoxy among the mass population.

All this meant that the issue of visiting graves and the question of their precise structure became a highly contested area of religious practice. The 'idolatrous' custom of visiting graves quite often elicited condemnation or – under the right historical and social conditions – provoked violent reactions. Ibn Taymiyya's spiritual legacy, oversimplified and whether justifiably or not, found fertile ground in the person of Muhammad ibn 'Abd al-Wahhab (1703–92) and has been appropriated by today's Salafis. Their harsh stance against certain traditional Muslim practices, including *ziyāra*, which had always constituted an important part of Islam, has also been supported to a large extent by various Wahhabi institutions, most notably the Saudi Permanent Committee, which is charged with providing Islamic rulings on a wide range of issues and, consequently, with influencing Muslims all around the world. These, together with several non-Saudi scholars who either studied or taught in Saudi Arabia, and their contacts in other Muslim countries, have helped to create a very strict viewpoint on the treatment of graves, tombs and shrines, which has been disseminated to many parts of the contemporary Islamic world. And so, nowadays, under different social and political contexts that allow these doctrines to be translated into action, we witness graves and shrines being destroyed in places as diverse as Mali, Tunisia, Pakistan, Iraq and Syria.

Our Aim: Following Iconoclasm and the Destructive Path

The overarching argument of this book is that certain Islamic movements, most specifically Salafism, both in its broader meaning and its narrow interpretation as Wahhabism, try to control and uproot various local interpretations of Islam and annihilate religio-political opponents. They do so by oversimplifying certain traditional aspects of medieval Islamic theology and law, in this case iconoclasm. To demonstrate this, we explore the formation and context of these theological and legal aspects, as well as their relevance to current religio-political discussions and events in various Muslim countries, most of which are rooted in the political realities of global modernity. We also argue that views on grave destruction have shifted over the course of Islamic history and that today's iconoclastic tendencies form part of the Saudi state's overall strategy to act as the protector of Ibn 'Abd al-Wahhab's reformism in order to strengthen the legitimacy of its regime.

Needless to say, a study of this vast topic cannot be exhaustive and it is not our intention to describe the broader phenomenon of iconoclasm in Islam.[6]

Neither are we interested in damage caused by casual vandalism or neglect. Lastly, we do not deal with the phenomenon of the saints in Shiʻi Islam,[7] which has always recognised the importance and merit of visiting the tombs of Shiʻi imams. What we want to explore here is the systematic destruction of religious monuments – and the desire to destroy them – within Sunni Islam.

The popularity of visiting shrines in the contemporary Islamic world is a far cry from what it was in medieval times; such habits have very evidently decreased.[8] In modern times, this practice has been often regarded as superstitious, and the global rise of Salafism accompanied by the proliferation of religious education and tendencies towards literalism among some individuals, pamphleteers and groupings, have spread this view. This process has provided the issue of iconoclasm aimed at graves with a new twist, which can be seen not only from the ongoing fight between those in favour of visiting graves and those opposed to the practice, but also by the fact that not only are shrines being destroyed, but new ones are emerging.[9]

In order to better understand this phenomenon, we will examine the evolution of debates related to *ziyāra* and the construction of tombs, and show how opponents of these practices understood them differently at different times – and how the issue of visiting graves was gradually simplified and turned from a nuanced and multifaceted legal issue into a key matter of doctrine, examined by many religious scholars and thinkers. We will look in particular at the positions of those for whom building structures over graves and visiting the saints frequently were practices amounting to innovation and idolatry. We will not aim to focus on all scholarly views on these practices, however. Rather, we will highlight the most significant and influential thoughts, trends, figures and movements related to these issues. Less attention will be devoted to more peripheral figures whose legacy has not yet reached the arena of contemporary mainstream debate.

Chapter 1 provides an overview of the broader context within which debates regarding graves, funeral architecture and *ziyāra* have taken place. The early Islamic interdictions against certain funerary structures and grave-related rites did not arise in a vacuum. Therefore, we have contextualised these debates and the gap that began to emerge between the traditionalists' (*Ahl al-hadith*) vision of ideal Islam and the reality of popular Islam. We offer a detailed focus on the teachings of Ibn Taymiyya, as it was his narrative of

Islamic history and the ideal Islamic community that inspired later Sunni reformists, among them the Salafis, who sought to defend Islamic identity against the incursion of foreign influences and impurities, be they elements of Christianity, Judaism, syncretism or modernity.

In Chapter 2, we contextualise Ibn Taymiyya's influence on modern Salafis and their mutual interaction. An emphasis is placed on Wahhabism during the period of the first Saudi state, as this provides us with the most influential sources of iconoclastic ideas. The teachings of Ibn ʿAbd al-Wahhab and his disciples constitute the core part of current Salafi thought, appearing in a variety of mutated forms. The purpose of this chapter is twofold. First, it expounds on classical Wahhabi doctrine, as excerpted from early texts, within the context of its historical development and observed in relation to the stages of *jāhilīya* (the barbarian pre-Islamic age): *daʿwa* (Islamic proselytism), *hijra* (migration) and jihad. In doing so, we explore the origins of antipathy towards grave veneration as a form of *shirk*. Ibn ʿAbd al-Wahhab's call contains a dichotomist theory of the world, where believers are obliged to love and help each other, while hating all forms of *shirk* and *mushrikūn* (polytheists). We focus on this because it has a strong – both social and doctrinal – impact on the later development of the doctrine referred to as *al-walāʾ wa al-barāʾ*, meaning 'loyalty and disavowal' (not yet attested in this formulation in the works of Ibn ʿAbd al-Wahhab). Second, as Wahhabism, or indeed Hanbalism, were not the only strongly iconoclastic trends, this chapter also aims to identify other influential movements, especially those of Yemeni, Syrian, Iraqi and Indian traditionalists, with Muhammad al-Shawkani, Ibn al-Amir al-Sanʿani, Mahmud Shukri al-Alusi and Siddiq Hasan Khan in the forefront of developments. To trace the transition between theory and practice, we also provide a description of the two waves of destruction committed by Wahhabis after their conquest of the Hijaz, first in the early nineteenth century and then again in the first quarter of the twentieth century.

Chapter 3 explains the process of Wahhabism institutionalisation that occurred during the period of the third Saudi state, as well as the proselytic mechanism that has been part of Saudi-led pan-Islamism since the 1960s. It focuses mostly on the opinions of Muhammad ibn Ibrahim Al al-Shaykh, Ibn Baz and Muhammad Nasir al-Din al-Albani, especially with regard to funeral architecture and the legality of visits to graves by women. In the case of al-Albani, we focus on the methodology he advocated in relation to the fulfilment of Salafi goals. We also identify some of the patterns regarding opposition to the Saudi regime, such as those associated with Juhayman al-'Utaybi and Abu Muhammad al-Maqdisi, both of whom were influenced by the Saudi propagation of *tawḥīd* and iconoclasm. They, in turn, were probably responsible for influencing the ideological contours of ISIS, another manifestation of serious opposition directed at the Saudi state. While those movements have questioned Saudi legitimacy, they have also drawn on Wahhabi–Salafi sources propagated by Saudi proselytism. This chapter also describes the internal mechanisms and structures of the official Saudi religious establishment, especially its *fatwā* institutions.

In Chapter 4, we outline the context within which various iconoclastic incidents have taken place in various parts of the Islamic world in recent years. After focusing on ISIS and the massive destruction of funerary monuments for which they have been responsible in Iraq and Syria, we deal with similar incidents, especially in the Arabian Peninsula, parts of Africa and central and south Asia.

Our research is based on a critical analysis of the vast textual data sources that are available in both classical and modern Islamic literature. All translations of texts originally in Arabic or other languages, unless otherwise indicated, are our own. When translating from the Qur'an or hadith, we have at times slightly modified the phrasing of existing English translations if we deemed it appropriate to more accurately reflect the original Arabic. In order to make the final bibliography more comprehensible, we have not included some resources referenced in the text, especially online materials; full information about these resources can be found in the chapter notes. The transliteration of non-English terms follows the guidelines provided by the publisher.

Terminology: Wahhabism–Salafism and Iconoclasm

The terms 'Salafism' and 'Wahhabism' can be confusing because they refer to a plethora of interpretations.[10] However hazardous it is to use these terms, we still prefer to do so for the lack of better labels. Wagemakers offers the following definition: 'Salafism is a branch of Sunni Islam whose modern-day adherents claim to emulate "the pious predecessors" (*al-salaf al-ṣāliḥ*; often equated with the first three generations of Muslims) as closely and in as many spheres of life as possible.'[11] Accordingly, we use the term Salafism to refer to the specific tendency within Islam that places particular emphasis on a return to the piety and principles of the Prophet Muhammad and the *salaf* as the only true understanding of Islam. Although all Muslim scholars look to the first generations of Muslims as role models, the majority believe that the institutions and historical developments that scholars have accepted within their thinking and practice over the centuries also represent legitimate expressions of Islam.

A distinct feature of Salafi Islam is its specific and discernible theology, which is largely derived from the Hanbali *madhhab* (school of law), and particular legal methodology. The term 'Salafi' is attested even before Ibn Taymiyya; he uses it very rarely, usually only when speaking about the theological understanding of God's attributes and names. More frequently, Ibn Taymiyya refers to a 'methodology of the Salaf' (*madhhab al-salaf, ṭarīqat al-salaf, manhaj al-salaf*), both in the context of theology, and of the law.[12] As this methodology is based on hadith, it seems that the terms 'Salafi' and 'methodology of the Salaf' are nearly synonymous with Hanbali theology, as opposed primarily to Muʿtazila and Ashʿarism. It is important to bear in mind the duality of the Hanbali school (a term used by M. Watt and G. Makdisi), which was both a legal and theological school based strongly on hadith, without making a clear distinction between the two. In the spheres of dogma and theology, traditionalism finally triumphed in the Hanbali creed, defeating the teachings of theologians who depended primarily on reason (Muʿtazila) – whereas the Hanbalis were, with some exceptions, literalists, subjecting reason to the Qur'an and Sunna. Salafis claim that this particular methodology, based on a literal understanding of the scripture, can be applied even to ambiguous or potentially ambiguous texts to which other theologians, such as Ashʿaris, prefer to assign metaphorical and allegorical meanings. It was particularly within Hanbalism, being the only school that was both legal and theological, that a Salafi creed was formed. Hanbalism has also significantly influenced the creed of contemporary Sunni Muslims, who oppose innovative – and to them, therefore, heretical – religious practices. The Hanafi, Maliki and Shafiʿi schools were solely legal schools, and in theological matters they usually followed Ashʿarism or Maturidism, a theological school very close to Ashʿarism and popular especially within the Hanafi school.

Ibn Taymiyya, the most influential figure in later Salafism, was not the first by far to refer to the early Muslim community (*salaf*) as an ideal model to be emulated.[13] Yet the legacy he left behind inspired later generations of Salafis in several ways. First, he coined the term 'Salafi methodology' (*al-manhaj al-salafī*) in the theology of God's names and attributes, whose proper understanding and interpretation was a criterion of orthodoxy. With regard to a proper understanding of the character of God's sitting on the throne (*al-istiwā'*) and transcendence (*fawqīya*), Ibn Taymiyya even used, albeit very rarely, the term *salafīya* to designate those of proper methodology. In this respect, his teachings were at variance with Ash'arism, the prevalent form of orthodox theology of his time. Second, Ibn Taymiyya stressed the idea of *ijtihād* (use of individual reasoning and personal effort in questions concerning the Shari'ah), both in absolute and lesser degrees, for those who had the capacity to adopt it instead of blindly following (*taqlīd*) an institutionalised school of law (*madhhab*). Ibn Taymiyya considers absolute *ijtihād* superior and more legitimate than adherence to the established *madhhab* system. As all eponyms of the four schools were Salaf by definition, being at the same time absolute *mujtahid*s, Ibn Taymiyya claimed the superiority of the early Muslim community over any partisanship in favour of the established schools. However, he does not refuse *taqlīd* absolutely, since it is a convenient method of guidance for those who do not have the intellectual capacity and scholarly erudition of a *mujtahid* (one capable of *ijtihād*). In a similar vein, Ibn Taymiyya challenged Ash'arism, arguing that al-Ash'ari himself had denounced his rationalist doctrine in order to follow Ahmad ibn Hanbal in terms of his theological position. Despite Ibn Taymiyya's efforts to challenge the status quo of his day, he has been regarded in most cases as an ardent adherent of the Hanbali school, since it was unthinkable at that time to assert institutional independence from the established system of four legal *madhhab*s promulgated by the Mamluks. Third, and most relevant to our subject of study, he put emphasis on the application of Islamic law, and took a strong stance against heretical and illegal practices. He was harshly critical of those seeking aid or intercession from the dead and of the related issue of illegal *ziyāra*, necrolatry and rituals and cults linked with popular Islam, Sufism and Shi'ism. He considered some of these practices outright polytheism, and some as having the potential to lead to it. Some of these views were later reflected in Salafi thought.

The roots of Salafism can thus be found in medieval times. However, as Lauzière,[14] who calls Salafism 'a conceptual chimera that exists only in our modern scholarship', rightly observes, one of the mechanisms that enable scholars to circumvent the problem of conflicting interpretations of Salafism and the fact that it refers to completely different types of movements and individuals, consists 'in positing the existence of parallel and at times unrelated strands of Salafism throughout history'. In his opinion, some scholars commit a lexical anachronism when they ascribe to Muslims of the past an understanding of the word Salafism similar to that of today.

In general, the growth of Salafi tradition involved two concomitant processes: the (re)invention of tradition and the (re)appropriation of the intellectual heritage of classical Hanbalism.[15] These processes resulted in many different streams of Salafi Islam. However, a common denominator is the reverberation of the thoughts of Ibn Taymiyya, whose teachings have become a source of inspiration for modern Sunni reformism/Salafism. The religious belief (*'aqīda*) common to today's Salafis is one that facilitates the application of religious tenets to contemporary issues. It is based on a fervent adherence to the concept of *tawḥīd* (the belief that God is one and unique), and a strict rejection of human reasoning that is not based on revelation. By following the Qur'an and the Sunna, Salafis aim to eliminate the mistakes caused by human bias (which is thought to threaten the clarity of *tawḥīd*) and accept only the one truth of God's commandments. From this point of view, they maintain that there is only one legitimate religious interpretation of the Qur'an, and hence that Islamic pluralism (let alone political pluralism) is inadmissible. Salafis advocate a strict adherence to traditional Islamic values, and uphold religious orthopraxy as well as religious orthodoxy.[16]

As already emphasised, Salafism is far from being a coherent movement. Some Salafi movements adopt very extreme religiosity and reject the social and political institutions of their states. Instead, they aim to radically change them and create a unified doctrine within their communities, while preserving the purity of religion and distancing themselves from anything that could contaminate their beliefs and principles. Wiktorowicz recognises three major Salafi factions: purists, that is, those who are primarily focused on maintaining the purity of Islam; politicos, those who are willing to engage in the sphere of politics, criticising incumbent regimes; and jihadis (also called

Jihadi-Salafis), those who support the use of violence to overthrow supposedly apostate regimes in the Islamic world and establish Islamic states.[17]

In contemporary usage, the term 'Salafism' is predominantly associated with the interpretation of Islam prevalent in the Gulf region. This interpretation is also known as 'Wahhabism', a term that emphasises the political agenda of this ideology and refers only to the institutionalised, pro-regime religious establishment in Saudi Arabia. The term Wahhabism was first coined by the movement's opponents to underline the fact that it was an extreme interpretation of Islam based on the teachings of Muhammad ibn ʿAbd al-Wahhab. There is no sound evidence of any intellectual continuity connecting early Wahhabism to broader Sunni thought, despite efforts to create such a narrative in Wahhabi/Saudi historiography. By early Wahhabism we mean what scholars have referred to as 'the imams of the Najdi call' (*aʾimmat al-daʿwa al-najdīya*). Wahhabi scholars have also tried to connect themselves with the broader movement of *Ahl al-hadith*, the partisans of traditions, which emerged in the second century of Islam and that came to be considered by the Sunni majority as a non-extremist interpretation of Sunni Islam.

Judging by its intellectual status, Wahhabism was only a marginal ideology when compared with the much more developed centres of Salafi thought. Very important Salafi movements originated – independently of Wahhabism – within the boundaries of the Ottoman Empire, first in Baghdad and perhaps somewhat later in Damascus. Their emergence is usually connected with the circulation of works by Shah Waliullah (1703–62) of Delhi and, especially, Muhammad al-Shawkani (1760–1834) from Yemen, with whose help the modern Salafis rediscovered Ibn Taymiyya. Another significant movement within Salafi Islam was the so-called 'Enlightened Salafism' of Jamal al-Din al-Afghani (1838–97), Muhammad ʿAbduh (1849–1905) and, to some extent, Rashid Rida (1865–1935). This movement followed the path of rational Salafism in Damascus that was represented by figures such as ʿAbd al-Razzaq al-Baytar (1837–1917), Tahir al-Jazaʾiri (1852–1920) and Jamal al-Din al-Qasimi (1866–1914), who focused on the harmony between reason and revelation. In Baghdad a similar trend evolved, which was largely promoted by members of the al-Alusi family. These early Salafis were frequently denounced for their connections with Wahhabism with which, however, they shared very little besides their interest in Ibn Taymiyya. For example, Muhammad ʿAbduh was influenced by the idea of the rigidity of the *madhhab* system and was critical of Sufism if it was in disagreement with the Shariʿah; however, his *Book of Monotheism* (*Kitab al-tawhid*) is regarded as excessively rationalist, and so he was labelled as a Muʿtazili. This rationalist line of Salafism was of limited influence and the term Salafi was gradually appropriated and adopted by traditionalist Salafis, who upheld Ibn Taymiyya's theological opinions.

The spread – and simultaneous ideological fragmentation – of Salafism was further accelerated by the process of decolonisation, which removed the common goal of many Islamic reformers. While the political struggle for independence was over, purist Salafis started to focus almost entirely on the purity of the creed and turned their attention to the finer theological and legal aspects of Islam. This process, in turn, created dissension in the Salafi ranks and sometimes quite fierce and open rivalries.[18] As a result, Lauzière distinguishes between two paradigmatic conceptions of Salafism: 'modernist Salafism', that is, the multifaceted movement that tried to reconcile Islam with the social, political and intellectual ideals of Enlightenment, which was active mostly through the late nineteenth century to the mid-twentieth century and was represented by figures such as al-Afghani or ʿAbduh; and 'purist Salafism', whose proponents have managed to impose their interpretations based on their claim of following the only true, 'pure' Islam.[19]

In the 1970s, thanks to its oil revenues and geopolitical position, Saudi Arabia started to build a network of transnational outreach programmes and proselytism. Around the same time, purist Salafism, a trend that had hardly existed before, gained the upper hand over the modernist (rationalist or enlightened) Salafi trend. Eventually, the modernists lost their claim to Salafism. By the 1990s, a vast number of publications from purist Salafi circles had begun to circulate elucidating the meaning and origins of Salafism. The second half of the twentieth century thus saw Salafism become a total ideology, subsuming all topics, concepts and ways of behaviour, and turn itself into all-encompassing and comprehensive 'method' (*manhaj*) and the ultimate expression of Islamic cultural authenticity (*aṣāla*).[20] This line of Salafism built its existence on a profoundly purist presentation of Islam based on a strict system of prescriptions and proscriptions, which provided believers with a simplified approach to both orthodoxy and orthopraxis. Its proponents, therefore, consider Salafism to be an ideal tool preventing dangerous and corrupting innovations, such as Sufism, Shi'ism and various Western influences (from secularism to communism). Of these, Sufism tends to be the primary target of disputes and attacks from Salafism/Wahhabism.[21]

Our terminology difficulties do not stop at Salafism, however: one also needs to find an appropriate way of referring to the main phenomena we deal with. To begin with, the use of the terms 'monument', 'cultural object' and 'historical (cultural) site' is problematic, as these are fluid labels.[22] That the monuments we refer to have varying value might be obvious, but it is not obvious how that value should be measured and who can measure it. Monuments might have historical, antique, cultural, artistic or memorial value.[23] The latter is the most interesting for us. The next question is how to refer to the Arabic term *taswiyat al-qubūr*, which is most usually used to refer to one of our key phenomena, and literally means 'levelling of graves'. To the best of our knowledge, there is no technical term that encapsulates this. In any case, it is not easy to borrow terms that are already burdened with their own specific cultural or historic meanings. Vandalism is too broad a term and usually denotes barbarous acts of destruction devoid of meaning. Therefore, we feel more inclined to borrow the term 'iconoclasm'. Of course, this term also has its own specific connotations, as it usually refers to the destruction of religious icons, idols and images for both religious and political reasons (think of the Byzantine 'Quarrel of the Images'). Its semantic meaning, however, widened during the nineteenth century, such that it can also be applied to venerated institutions or monuments that are regarded by an opposing group to be fallacious or superstitious. In a general sense, the term refers to 'the destruction of and/or suspicion against physical representations of the divine, the sacred, the transcendent',[24] and can thus describe not only the destruction of images but also other physical objects, including statues, tombs, shrines, buildings or even natural objects.

We do not here claim that iconoclasm or the destruction of religious sites is exclusively symptomatic of Islam. History is replete with evidence of blatant destructive behaviour by winning parties. Some of the most obvious examples include the Conquistadors' annihilation of Aztec culture, the Nazi destruction of German synagogues, Stalin's destruction of churches, China's demolition of Tibet's monasteries, or the destruction of both religious and non-religious monuments in Bosnia and Kosovo. Whether this was done in the name of the Conquistadors' fight against idolatry and primitivism, of Nazi racial ideology, of Soviet Bolshevik hostility towards religion, of Chinese revolutionary zeal, of Serbian expansionism or the state-building efforts of others, the purpose was always similar: to eradicate the opponents' collective memory and identity. This kind of destruction often has other similar features, too, including the habit of turning the religious sites of others to different purposes (such as into garages, depots, stables, granaries or even public toilets). The conquering Nazis turned the old Sephardic synagogue in Sarajevo into a garage, and Islamic graveyards in the Balkans were often cleared for parks. Hundreds of Armenian churches and monasteries met the same destiny, while religious buildings were systematically turned to new agrarian uses in Central Asia under the Soviets or in Cambodia under Pol Pot and the Khmer Rouge. ISIS, as we will see, does exactly the same.

The destruction of cultural or religious artefacts belonging to an enemy people, in order to subjugate, dominate or terrorise them, has been part of wars and conflicts since time immemorial. Conquerors have also always had a tendency to rewrite history. As Bevan notes, architecture and monuments in this case take on a 'totemic quality: a mosque, for example, is not simply a mosque; it represents to its enemies the presence of a community marked for erasure.'[25] The selection of the structures to be erased is not haphazard; it is not mere collateral damage. On the contrary, the very systematic destruction of a cultural heritage serves to enforce the collective identity of the local population and tie it together through shared experience and common tradition. Religious identification can be a very strong sentiment, and may supersede an individual's identification with their nation-state. Despite this, the destruction of cultural or religious sites and its role in changing the social landscape of a given locality has been largely understudied.

Notes

1. As David Cook aptly points out, the word *fitna* is the most vexatious word to translate. He refers to E. W. Lane's *Arabic–English Lexicon*, where the word has all of the following meanings: 'a burning with fire, a melting of (metals) in order to separate or distinguish the bad from the good, a means whereby the condition of a man is evinced in respect of good or evil, punishment, chastisement,

conflict among people, faction and sedition, discord, dissension, difference of opinions, a misleading, causing to err, seduction, temptation'. See Cook, *Studies in Muslim Apocalyptic*, p. 20. We prefer to translate it either as 'temptation', or 'riot' and 'discord'.

2. Johnson, 'Saudis Risk New Muslim Division with Proposal to Move Mohamed's Tomb'.
3. Cf. Mernissi, 'Women, Saints, and Sanctuaries', p. 105.
4. Cf., for example, the study of a Moroccan pilgrimage centre in Eickelman, *Moroccan Islam*, p. 71.
5. See Ibn Rajab, *al-Dhayl ʿala tabaqat al-hanabila*, vol. 4, p. 518.
6. A good introduction may be found in King, 'Islam, Iconoclasm, and the Declaration of Doctrine', pp. 267–77, or Grabar, 'Islam and Iconoclasm', pp. 45–52. Cf. also Noyes, *The Politics of Iconoclasm*, who attempts to demonstrate the relationship between the destruction of images and the construction of political order and control, and argues that throughout history iconoclasm has tended to go hand in hand with political centralisation.
7. For the topic of *ziyāra* in the Shiʿi context see, for example, Suleman, *People of the Prophet's House*; Khosronejad, *Saints and their Pilgrims in Iran and Neighbouring Countries*; Meri, *The Cult of Saints*, pp. 157–61; Aghaie, *The Martyrs of Karbala*; Penault, *The Shiites*; or Takim, 'Charismatic Appeal or Communitas?', pp. 181–203.
8. This is not, however, universally valid. For example among the Negev Bedouins the practice of visiting graves and shrines has become more popular in recent generations, possibly as a result of a lack of mosque networks and persistent unfamiliarity with the appropriate Muslim rituals. Cf. Kressel, Bar-Zvi and Abu-Rabiʿa, *The Charm of Graves*.
9. This can be observed, quite naturally, mainly in the Shiʿi areas. One of the recent cases involves a mausoleum of the late Rafiq Hariri (1944–2005), the Lebanese business tycoon-turned-politician and former prime minister of Lebanon, who was assassinated in 2005. His mausoleum draws many visitors every year. Cf. Vloeberghs, 'Worshipping the Martyr President', pp. 80–92.
10. For the debate about the usage of these terms, see especially Commins, 'From Wahhabi to Salafi', pp. 151–66, or Lauzière, *The Making of Salafism*, esp. the introduction, pp. 1–25.
11. Wagemakers, 'Salafism'.

12. Salaf are very rarely also called *salafiya*. See, for example, Ibn Taymiyya, *Darʾ taʿarud al-ʿaql wa al-naql*, vol. 2, p. 8.
13. For example, the term 'Salafi' is attested two centuries before Ibn Taymiyya in *Kitab al-ansab* by ʿAbd al-Karim al-Samʿani (d. 1166/67), to give just one example.
14. Lauzière, *The Making of Salafism*, pp. 12–17.
15. Mouline, *The Clerics of Islam*, p. 43.
16. Beránek, 'The Sword and the Book', p. 2.
17. Wiktorowicz, 'Anatomy of the Salafi Movement', pp. 207–39. This division has since been followed by many other specialists. Cf., for example, Wagemakers, 'Salafism'.
18. Lauzière, *The Making of Salafism*, p. 168.
19. Ibid., pp. 4–6. As Lauzière puts it, 'given the difficulty of defining purity in absolute terms, contemporary Salafis often must define it negatively – that is, by elaborating on all the things they deem contrary to the pristine Islam of the pious ancestors'.
20. Ibid., pp. 199–202, 222–4. Cf. also Haykel, 'On the Nature of Salafi Thought and Action', p. 47.
21. For a general account of these disputes throughout modern history see Sirriyeh, *Sufis and Anti-Sufis*. It is perhaps worth mentioning what the influential religious scholar Yusuf al-Qaradawi has to say on these matters. In an interview he stated his wish to 'making Sufism into Salafi and making Salafi into Sufi. The Sufi takes from the discipline of Salafi in not following the fabricated Hadith, polytheist rites, and tomb-side rites, and we want the Salafi to take from the Sufi tenderness, spirituality, and piousness. From this mixture we get the required Muslim.' See 'A Conversation with Sheikh Yusuf Al-Qaradawi', *Asharq al-Awsat*, 26 December 2010, available at: http://english.aawsat.com/2010/12/article55248123/a-conversation-with-sheikh-yusuf-al-qaradawi, last accessed 6 September 2016.
22. As shown by Gamboni, *The Destruction of Art*, introduction.
23. Cf. ibid., p. 219.
24. Van Asselt et al., *Iconoclasm and Iconoclash*, p. 4. Cf. also *The Oxford English Dictionary*.
25. Bevan, *The Destruction of Memory*, p. 8.

1

Graves and Shrines in Medieval Islam: From Pre-Islamic Times to Ibn Taymiyya's Legacy

> The Bedouins know of no communion with the saints. In the whole inner desert there is not a single holy grave or shrine erected in honor of a saint. In fact they have no saints whatever.
>
> Musil, *The Manners and Customs of the Rwala Bedouins*, p. 417

The Pre-Islamic Era and Early Islam

The Sunni legal stance on the issue of graves and funerary structures, and visiting them, has gone through a long evolution. The practice of visiting graves certainly did not emerge only with the rise of Islam: pre-Islamic Arabs were also familiar with the cult of the dead, which suggests that *ziyāra* was most likely an ancient practice. However, describing the pre-Islamic Bedouin society in general, not to mention its funerary practices in particular, has never been an easy task. The classical literature (be it in the cuneiform, Greek or Latin) provides us with only very limited textual evidence about life in Arabia. The first Western scholar to attempt to describe the old Arabian religion was Edward Pococke.[1] A few more attempts then followed, with varying degrees of success,[2] before the arrival of the first serious scholars, in particular Ignaz Goldziher (1850–1921) and Julius Wellhausen (1844–1918). The late nineteenth and early twentieth centuries saw south Arabian and proto-Arabic epigraphic inscriptions come into use (especially by Ditlef Nielsen, although often in a rather speculative manner). In 1947, Gonzague Ryckmans used the growing corpus of epigraphic material in his *Les Religions arabes préislamiques*.[3]

Ignaz Goldziher, more than anyone else, described the clashes between ordinary popular practices and religious orthodoxy when it came to funerary rituals and habits.[4] Using a broad range of materials (from the Qur'an and hadith to pre-Islamic and early Islamic poetry), Goldziher documented how many pagan practices survived under Islam disguised as true piety, despite efforts to put an end to them for their 'barbaric features' on the part of the religious establishment, supported by the authorities at the time. In an essay titled 'On the Veneration of the Dead in Paganism and Islam', Goldziher deals specifically with the practice of building various objects above graves,[5] spending one's time there or seeking asylum there while being prosecuted, sacrificing people, animals[6] or locks of hair[7] at the graves of esteemed figures, or wailing in an exaggerated manner. He concludes that the religious establishment's efforts to eradicate these pre-Islamic habits failed and many of the practices continued to survive at that time.

As Goldziher shows, in pre-Islamic times ancestral graves appear to have held a solemn significance. The cult of the dead was coupled with the cult of ancestors, with only a minor distinction between the two: the former focused on the memory of more recent generations, whereas the latter looked for objects of veneration in the distant past. Some Arab tribes maintained traditions related to ancestral graves even in later periods. The graves of deceased heroes and saints in particular were believed to benefit people who were in need of protection or help. The Qur'an mentions *anṣāb* (5:90, alt. *nuṣub*, 5:3, 70:43) as a cult object for the pagan Arabs. This term refers to upright stones that were honoured by pagan Arabs as part of a cult, and were erected in particular at the graves of venerated heroes.[8] The pagan Arabs preferred to mark such graves by erecting memorials of durable and elevated construction, be they cairns, houses or other structures. A number of individual shrines in the form of temples or simple houses (referred to as *bayt* or *kaʿba*), as well as enclosed and protected spaces (*ḥaram* and *ḥimā*), existed in Hijaz and were associated with polytheistic worship. Some of these sites probably commanded a certain level of inter-regional devotion and attracted pilgrims from near and far.[9] Such places were considered to possess a special nature and constituted protected areas. Another common practice was that of erecting a tent (*khayma, fusṭāṭ, miẓalla* or *qubba*, which later became the word for a dome or mausoleum) over a deceased person's grave and spending some time there after the burial. Families also used to repeat this wailing ceremony annually, together with the sacrifice of a camel for their deceased loved ones.

The sacred awe inspired by graves venerated in this way was also connected with the belief that the grave provided a safe and inviolate sanctuary. *Anṣāb* were also connected with some manifestations of religious feeling or real cultural practices. Hence the pre-Islamic Arab poets used to swear oaths 'by the *anṣāb*'. Sacrifice for the dead was another of these cult acts that survived until Goldziher's day among the Bedouins and was transplanted – with Islamic reinterpretation – into proper Islamic rituals. These sacrifices did not only involve animals; hair was also used to honour the dead.

With the emergence of Islam, the building of *anṣāb*, their veneration and sacrifice by them were forbidden, as is evident from the Qur'anic verse: 'O you who have believed, indeed, intoxicants, gambling, stone altars (*anṣāb*), and divining arrows are but defilement from the work of Satan, so avoid it that you may be successful' (5:90). Similar instructions also appear in early Islamic poetry, as in this verse from al-Aʿsha panegyric on Muhammad: 'Do not sacrifice to the raised *nuṣub* – do not pray to the high places, worship God alone.'[10] Wailing for the dead (*niyāḥa*), a tradition among female relatives for their deceased loved ones, but also practised by professionals, also belongs in the same category of reprehensible acts. In place of the widespread cult of the dead, with all its accompanying practices, the early Islamic ulama tried to establish a ritualised funerary prayer (*ṣalāt al-janāza*).

The continued practice of many of the pre-Islamic habits was confirmed by many others who travelled to the Middle East in Goldziher's times. Alois Musil (1868–1944), a famous Czech theologian and Orientalist, visited the Levant and the Arabian Peninsula at the turn of the twentieth century. In the Hijaz, he witnessed a Bedouin funeral and reported that after it, the women 'tore the garments on their bosoms, scratched their faces and scattered dust over themselves' and that 'the sister or daughter sometimes cut either all of their hair, or at least one lock, which they hung or laid on the grave'.[11] Musil also confirmed the habit of sacrificing a camel in commemoration of the dead, spilling the blood of the sacrificed animal, erecting stones on the graves of the dead[12] and ascribing a special significance to locks of hair from the forehead.[13]

The largest amount of evidence about the survival of ancient funerary and mourning rituals in modern times comes, however, from North Africa.[14] Of all the pre-Islamic customs that were connected with graves and burials, women's wailing for the dead proved to have the strongest roots: they would express their grief (known as *ndīb* in North Africa) by groaning loudly, scratching their faces and cutting their hair. Professional wailers (*ḥazzāna*) operated both in the urban centres and in the countryside.[15] The women's habit of gathering at cemeteries was also observed throughout the centuries. Louis Massignon (1883–1962), a renowned French scholar of Islam, stated in his study of Cairo's cemeteries that their main function was to serve as a gathering place for women during Friday prayers, while the men attended mosques.[16]

It is worth mentioning that Muslim jurists were not alone in their struggle against pagan rituals. Their efforts, motivated by a desire to root out all pre-Islamic features from Islam and help to distinguish their religion from the other monotheistic faiths, mirrored similar tendencies in Judaism. Old Jewish habits similarly included accompanying the dead with lamentations, crying, tearing of clothes and scattering dust over one's head (Joshua 7:6 and elsewhere), and these acts were quite often performed by professional female wailers. As for men, they would cut their hair and shave their beards (Job 1:20), although Leviticus (19:27) considers these habits to be a remnant of paganism and forbids them.[17]

The Time of Muhammad

> He who performs the pilgrimage and does not visit me, has shunned me.
> Whoever visits my grave must ask me for intercession.
> My mediation is assured for whoever visits my grave.
> The Messenger of Allah forbade us from wailing.
> The Messenger of Allah said: 'The deceased is tormented because of his family's weeping for him.'
> One of the oaths which the Messenger of Allah received from us about the virtue was that we would not disobey him in it (virtue): that we would not scratch our faces, nor wail, nor tear the front of our garments nor dishevel our hair.
> It was narrated that Umm ʿAtiyya said: 'We were forbidden to follow the funerary procession, but this was not emphasised.'

The Messenger of Allah cursed women who visited graves, those who built mosques over them and erected lamps (there).

The Prophet forbade sitting on graves, plastering them with gypsum, and building any structure over them.

May Allah fight the Jews and Christians who make the graves of their prophets into places of worship; do not imitate them.

The saddles shall not be fastened except for the three mosques: the Sacred Mosque [in Mecca], my mosque [the Prophet's Mosque in Medina], and al-Aqsa Mosque [in Jerusalem].

The Messenger of Allah visited his mother's grave and wept and caused those around him to weep. The Messenger of Allah then said: 'I asked my Lord's permission to pray for forgiveness for her, but I was not allowed. I then asked His permission to visit her grave, and I was allowed. So visit graves, for they make one mindful of death.'

Do not leave any statue without destroying it nor any raised grave without levelling it.[18]

As far as we can gather from the Islamic tradition, Muhammad himself was accustomed to visiting the graves of his deceased Companions and interceding with God on their behalf.[19] Yet the ambiguity of both his practice and of the traditions ascribed to him in later times bequeathed a legacy of uncertainty to the following generations. Attempts to bring some clarity, by either transforming pre-Islamic funeral customs into Islamic Sunna or eradicating them entirely, can be found in hadith collections, embodied in often contradictory rules. For example, due to the changing political situation and specific needs of the moment, the hadith collections contain hadiths that both favour and forbid visiting tombs and performing prayers at graves and at cemeteries. Some of the reports suggest that Muhammad feared that Muslims would imitate other monotheistic religions in venerating the dead and thus did not urge his followers to build monuments over the tombs of distinguished Muslims. The later hadith material also implies that the same fear led him to order tombs to be levelled so that they did not become places of idolatry and polytheism. From the very outset, he – according to some interpretations – also discouraged and prohibited any tendencies towards building funerary monuments. That is why, for instance, the Prophet himself – according to hadiths recorded by al-Tirmidhi, Muslim and others – sent out ʿAli to destroy elevated graves, and later ʿAli, during his rule, sent out one Abu al-Hayyaj al-Asadi on the same mission with the words: 'Do not leave any statue without destroying it nor any raised grave without levelling it' (*lā tadaʿ timthālan illā ṭamastahu wa lā qabran mushrifan illā sawwaytahu*).

According to the Muslim narrative, Muhammad's death brought with it an immediate controversy as to the proper means of burial and the appropriate structure of a grave.[20] From Ibn Ishaq's biography of the Prophet, we learn that Muhammad suddenly became ill and died shortly afterwards (incidentally, this happened after he had returned home from Medina's cemetery, where he had offered prayers for the dead). Following this, some of his Companions argued that prophets should be buried precisely where they die, while others wanted Muhammad's corpse to be taken to his mosque or to the al-Baqiʿ cemetery in the vicinity of Medina, where some of his relatives were already buried. Eventually, the first approach gained the upper hand, so a grave was dug immediately beneath his bed and Muhammad was buried in the room where he died, which belonged to his wife ʿAʾisha. A partition wall was built to divide the space into two rooms. It was said that after the Prophet's burial, ʿAʾisha continued to occupy the same room, without even a curtain between her and the tomb. Only later on, when she became vexed by the crowds of visitors, did she allow a wall to be built around the grave, which she then continued to visit unveiled. After ʿUmar's corpse was added, she always covered her face.

Even today, purists are unable to countenance the gradual reconstruction of Muhammad's grave, whose form and features have always been the subject of disputes and have been seen by many traditionalists as violating their 'pure' ideals. According to various reports, Muhammad's grave was either completely level or only slightly elevated by about one or two spans (*shibr/shibrayn*), while some report that the whole grave or at least its rear section was *musannam*, that is, raised higher or had a mound over it. These mixed reports may have led to the intermediate position claiming that the tombs of Muhammad, Abu Bakr and ʿUmar were 'neither elevated (*mushrifa*) nor wholly flat (*lāṭiʾa*)'.[21]

What is certain is that what had originally been a humble site was frequently demolished and reconstructed, and at some points even decorated with gold and mosaics.²² During the Marwanid period (684–750) of Umayyad rule, the mosque was enlarged and Muhammad's wives' chambers, including 'A'isha's, were incorporated into the mosque. Muhammad's grave was covered up and a funerary monument was built in its place. At some point, an inner stone wall was built to physically separate visitors from the inner sanctum. Outer walls served as a second barrier. These barriers only accentuated the overwhelming feeling that visitors to the grave inevitably experienced, that within the walls there lay a holy presence. A major reconstruction took place in 706/7–709/10 under the caliph al-Walid ibn 'Abd al-Malik (r. 705–15), who had the Medina mosque significantly expanded and splendidly decorated. The caliph, who was also a patron of costly building projects elsewhere, is reported to have written to his governor in Medina, 'Umar ibn 'Abd al-'Aziz, ordering him to demolish the old mosque and the neighbouring houses, including those of the Prophet's wives, and to incorporate them into the new edifice. It is also reported that the people of Medina, when hearing this order to demolish the houses of the Prophet's family, were disappointed. 'Ata' al-Khurasani said on that occasion: 'I have never seen a day with more sore weeping than there was among the people that day.' Sa'id ibn al-Musayyab, a well-known scholar of Medina, added: 'I wish, by Allah, that they would leave them alone just as they are.'²³ The original mud-brick burial chamber was thus replaced with stone walls and the mosque, probably for the first time, then incorporated Muhammad's grave.²⁴

Nevertheless, Muhammad's grave and the mosques associated with his post-hijri activities were not the only structures that helped to turn Medina into an important site. The grave landscape was typical for early Islamic Medina. Some rules even seem to have existed regarding the most appropriate burial sites for various individuals and their families: the Baqi' al-Gharqad cemetery was described as the Banu Hashim family cemetery. The graves of the martyrs of the Battle of Uhud (625), in particular Muhammad's uncle Hamza ibn 'Abd al-Muttalib, were another important site. By the early ninth century a mosque stood over Hamza's grave. Several miracle stories mention the uniqueness of these martyrs' graves. According to some, if a passer-by were to greet those in the graves, they would return his greeting.²⁵ Moreover, many of the mosques in Medina must have been highly regarded by early Muslims, as a number of hadiths equate visiting them for prayer with making a pilgrimage to Mecca, or report that praying in them is more meritorious than doing so in Jerusalem. The literary evidence provided by the hadith and *fiqh* compilations suggests that pilgrimage to various sites in Medina, and Muhammad's grave in particular, was commonplace from the eighth century onwards.[26]

Medina thus underwent a significant change in status and was promoted into an important pilgrimage site and sacred landscape.[27] This promotion into an identifiably Islamic holy city was a natural result of the ever-increasing importance of Muhammad as the ultimate source of legitimate political, religious and legal authority, mainly from the eighth century. This change attracted harsh opposition from some Muslim scholars who, at least from the eighth century onwards, debated the permissibility of visiting graves and conducting rituals at them.

Eighth–Fourteenth Century: Between Purist Ideals and Reality

The Prophet's death and the events that immediately followed set an example for the times to come. Performing funeral ceremonies and seeking God's forgiveness for the sins of fellow believers played central roles in defining Muslim piety during the first century of Islam, although their origins were rooted in different religious traditions. These Islamic rituals thus very soon began to be contested and consequently underwent fundamental transformations.

Early Islamic law came to contain many anti-funeral prescriptions celebrating modesty and austerity. Inscribing tombstones[28] and wailing for the dead are examples of practices that were popular and widespread in geographic and social terms but, at the same time, were despised by traditionalists. Hadith also included material prohibiting the plastering of tombs or the building of structures over graves. This opposition was built on the egalitarian principle of levelling the graves (*taswiyat al-qubūr*), meaning that all grave mounds should be low.[29] Jurists argued that the dead had no need for any kind of grave embellishment and that such embellishment was abhorrent.[30] Besides the egalitarian principle, the objection of early Muslim purists to tomb-building probably also arose from their desire to clearly separate graves from places of worship and to prevent the practice of praying at grave sites.

Religious rules regarding graves also appear in later, thematically classified collections of hadiths in special chapters titled 'Funerals' (*janā'iz*).

These chapters seek to precisely regulate the procedures to be followed when an individual in the Muslim community dies. However, the exact position of the eponyms of the legal schools (*madhhab al-fiqh*) is impossible to discern as their writings usually contain few opinions – and those are quite often contradictory ones. Perhaps the need to reconcile religious requirements with the reality of contemporary funeral customs led the majority of jurists to decide not to broadly stigmatise all funerary architecture as prohibited (*ḥarām*) under Islamic law; instead, they resigned themselves to simply frowning upon the glorification and veneration of the dead through funerary monuments and commemorative architecture, including elevated graves or plastered and painted tombs.[31] Buildings over graves were therefore often classified as reprehensible (*makrūh*), a weaker designation that did not convey a strict prohibition. Al-Shafi'i (767–820), Malik ibn Anas (715–96) and Ahmad ibn Hanbal (780–855), three of the four eponyms, all belonging to *salaf*, of the Islamic schools of religious jurisprudence, are all reported to have agreed that buildings over graves should only be categorised as *makrūh* and not as *ḥarām*. The fourth, Abu Hanifa (699–767), is reported to have regarded structures over graves as legal and not reprehensible at all.[32]

The establishment and development of legal schools added further specific legal features to these debates. One of these, for example, revolved around the distinction between building funerary structures on private and public property. This distinction was most likely introduced by Shafi'i legal tradition. While structures on private property were deemed indifferent, their construction was forbidden in communal cemeteries (*maqbara musabbala*). When such a structure was built on communal land, many Shafi'is considered it the ruler's obligation to destroy it (as, for instance, in the case of the mausoleum of al-Shafi'i himself in Cairo).[33] However, this is not to say that their statements necessarily led to the destruction of the monuments. In fact, within the same legal tradition we can find quite different interpretations, for instance a view that negative attitudes towards building mosques over graves are in order to prevent the grave becoming a *qibla* and a place of prayer. According to this interpretation, the obligation to take down such structures in communal spaces is due to their illegality and the fact that they occupy public spaces and restrict other people from using them. As a famous

Shafiʿi scholar Ibn Hajar al-Haytami (1503–66) succinctly concluded in his *al-Fatawa al-kubra*, Shafiʿi imams have taken various positions regarding building structures over graves, ranging from unconditionally forbidding them to unconditionally permitting them.[34]

What was probably unanimously agreed upon by most of scholars of the various *madhhab*s was that it was permissible to visit Muhammad's grave. Religious scholars did not try to keep believers from visiting other shrines and graves altogether, either; quite the contrary: the general attitude was that visiting tombs is at least permissible, if not outright beneficial. In general, jurists did not consider visiting shrines to be problematic and accepted the practice as permissible as long as it was done for the purpose of remembering God, the dead, the Prophet Muhammad or the Day of Judgement.[35]

What sometimes became more hotly contested, from the juristic point of view, were the rituals connected with these visits, the issue of women visiting graves and the question of whether it was permissible to visit infidels' graves. Proscriptive guidelines existed about the appropriate behaviour for visitors to graves. The most fundamental issues addressed by jurists and theologians regarding the legality of shrine visits included journeying[36] to pilgrimage sites and partaking in pilgrimage festivals; praying for the dead; praying for rain at tombs; supplicating and seeking intercession on behalf of oneself or others; asking the dead to work miracles; making physical contact with the tomb, such as kissing it or collecting dust from it to rub it on oneself (in the belief that this is curative or somehow beneficial[37]); and also circumambulating the tombs, prostrating oneself before or walking and sitting on them. These proscriptions might be taken as an indication that these types of physical contact with tombs regularly featured during *ziyāra*.

Some of these proscribed activities were contained in a literary genre of books against innovations (*kutub al-bidaʿ*).[38] Novelties or innovations (sing. *bidʿa, ibtidāʾ*) are things or modes of action the like of which has not formerly existed or been practised. In this respect, the *bidʿa* is the exact opposite of *sunna* – in the narrowest sense precedents of the Prophet. It is important to distinguish between innovation (*bidʿa*) and disbelief (*kufr*). *Bidʿa* is an innovation in Islam, while disbelief (*kufr*) is denial of Islam. According to this logic, Shiʿis are innovators/heretics (*ahl al-bidaʿ*), but they remain Muslims.

Nevertheless, in some interpretations of Sunni Islam, this distinction has been blurred, so that one who claims to adhere to Islam but commits innovations could be accused of being a non-Muslim.

As for the typology of innovations themselves, there were two approaches: moderate and purist. As far as we are aware, the prevalent view in medieval times was the moderate one. To give just one example of such an approach, we can take a closer look at *The Instigation into Reprehensibility of Heresies and Innovations* (*al-Baʿith ʿala inkar al-bidaʿ wa al-hawadith*). Its author, Shihab al-Din Abu Shama al-Maqdisi (d. 1267/8), was a Shafiʿi lawyer and traditionalist, known also as a chronicler of the Crusader and Ayyubid periods in Syria, who died at the beginning of the Mamluk era. Abu Shama divides innovations into commendable (*mustaḥsana*) and repugnant (*mustaqbaḥa*) based on the account of al-Shafiʿi, who said: 'There are two kinds of *bidʿa* – praiseworthy (*maḥmūda*) and blameworthy (*madhmūma*). Praiseworthy is that which is in agreement with Sunna, while blameworthy is in discordance with Sunna.' Al-Shafiʿi argued using the words of ʿUmar ibn al-Khattab about the performance of Ramadan: 'Blessed be this innovation' (*niʿmat al-bidʿa hādhihi*).[39] As for the advocates of the strictest, intolerant position, their argument is based on the famous saying of the Prophet Muhammad, which makes each *bidʿa* tantamount to heresy: 'Beware of novelties (*muḥdathāt al-umūr*), since every novelty is a *bidʿa*, and every *bidʿa* is an aberration (*ḍalāla*), and every aberration leads to hell-fire.' In other words, according to this approach, there is no such thing as a good innovation, since all innovations are wrong.

Another author of a book against innovations, the Maliki scholar al-Turtushi (d. 1126), prohibited prostrating oneself over Muhammad's grave and touching it (*lā yutamassaḥ bi-qabr al-nabī wa lā yumass*). He also opined that any invocation offered should be performed facing the *qibla*, with one's back turned to Muhammad's grave, so that there is no confusion regarding the object of prayer. Al-Turtushi also mentions women's participation in funeral processions and lamentation over the deceased as innovations in the eyes of the ulama (*wa min al-bidaʿ al-munkara ʿinda jamāʿat al-ʿulamāʾ khurūj al-nisāʾ li-ttibāʿ al-janāʾiz*).[40]

Treatises against innovations thrived in the Mamluk period. The Middle East had experienced threats from the Crusaders, followed by the Turkic and

Mongol invasions, culminating in a continual stream of immigrating Mamluks themselves. It seems that the challenge posed by these immigrants and conquerors was at the root of a feeling of vulnerability and decay that fuelled the frustration of the rigorous traditionalism represented by men such as Ibn Taymiyya and Ibn al-Hajj (d. 1336). In Western scholarship, the ardent traditionalist view has usually been attributed to the Hanbalis, but it is in fact not so straightforward. There is no doubt that the Hanbalis advocated this strict position on the whole, especially in doctrinal issues. However, ardent advocates of hadith from other schools have also shared such views (for example, the Maliki scholar Ibn al-Hajj, who seems to be concerned by rather mundane practices). Indeed, scholars such as Ibn Taymiyya and Ibn al-Hajj perceived themselves as 'tolerant moderates', in contrast to those who denied the legitimacy of the *ziyāra* altogether. For example, Muhammad ibn Isma'il al-Bukhari (810–70), the eponym of the al-Bukhari's collection of hadiths, failed to mention the traditions most widely accepted as abrogating the Prophet's initial prohibition against visiting graves.[41]

As far as women's participation in rituals involving funerals and graves was concerned, while some scholars did not differentiate between sexes at all, as long as both behaved properly, the issue became rather hotly contested among others. Because women were substantially excluded from communal prayers, the practice of *ziyāra* represented an attractive form of religious practice for them, as it was both a social event and a spiritual undertaking. Graveside rituals were, and still are, occasioned by personal life crises, and a person observing them typically asks the deceased holy person for intercession with God on their behalf.[42] Although it has often been controversial, the practice of women visiting graves is amply substantiated in Muslim tradition. Key Muslim women associated with the cult of the dead include Muhammad's own daughter Fatima, who used to pay regular visits to Hamza's grave, which was clearly marked by a gravestone. Another example was set by the Prophet's wife 'A'isha. During her funeral, held in 678 – which in many ways represented the antithesis of the later Islamic ideal – huge crowds of both men and women came to offer her homage without any protests from the jurists. Furthermore, a famous hadith related by Umm 'Atiyya and recorded by al-Bukhari, Ibn Maja and others – 'We were forbidden from following biers, yet it was not enforced' – might be taken to show that during the life of the

Prophet women were not excluded from gravesite ceremonies. Muhammad did, however, as we are told, curse hired female mourners.[43]

A particularly misogynistic campaign against women and their public roles in funerary and grave culture was launched during the eighth century, mainly in the garrison cities of Kufa and Basra in today's Iraq, and later became part of canonised hadith collections. Some Kufan traditionalists narrated that the ancestors 'used to padlock women indoors' before the men departed for funerals, because if women attended them, they might be a source of temptation and heretical innovations and lead the Muslim community astray. It is interesting to compare these Kufan traditions with those originating in Medina, as the latter differed markedly in tone and reflected a relatively sympathetic attitude towards women. However, owing to the influence of Ibn Hanbal and others who endorsed the stricter interpretation, it was the Kufan traditions that succeeded in transforming Muslim funerary norms.[44] The wailing nevertheless proved to be hard to eradicate. Muhammad is even reported to have predicted that wailing would be one of the four uncivilised habits that Muslims would not be able to abandon (besides glorifying the deeds of one's own ancestors, calumniating the pride of another's genealogical descent and seeking rain by the configuration of the stars).[45]

Despite these legalist stances, women could and did become saints. Their participation in shrine visits, however, was problematised even by staunch defenders of the practice of visiting graves. Thus, the Shafi'i scholar Taqi al-Din al-Subki (d. 1355) opined that 'a distinction between men and women is that men possess restraint and strength, in as much as they do not weep and they do not become saddened in contrast to women'.[46] Besides the issue of female visits, scholars also agreed that kissing the tomb (*taqbīl*) and indulging in loud wailing (*niyāḥa*) should be avoided, both of which were popular practices among the masses.

The purist ideals, however, were shattered with the emergence of spectacular funeral and commemorative architecture. Mausoleums and shrines for martyrs were built very early on. Raghib's research has revealed that the history of monumental funerary architecture dates not to the ninth century, as Creswell and Grabar had both suggested, but was present in Islam from the very start, perhaps even before the death of the Prophet Muhammad. To give an example, according to early Muslim historian al-Waqidi (d. 822) when

Abu Basir, one of the Companions of the Prophet, died in 628/9 a mosque was built over his grave.[47] The earliest surviving domed structure, the Qubbat al-sulaybiyya, was built in the Iraqi city of Samarra in 862 by the Greek mother of the ʿAbbasid caliph al-Muntasir.[48] By the eleventh century, built tombs had become quite common throughout the Middle East. However, until the thirteenth century, descriptions of funerary architecture in Islamic literature and their position in Islamic law were still of secondary interest.[49] Debates about the proper style of funeral architecture and visits to graveyards intensified in the twelfth and thirteenth centuries, when the monumental tombs of the Ayyubids (who ruled Egypt, Syria and other regions of the Middle East in the twelfth and thirteenth centuries) and the Mamluks (who ruled Egypt and Syria between 1250 and 1517) in Damascus and Cairo sprang up.

The state participated in the establishment of shrines and mausoleums, as building funerary architecture represented a significant means of attaining legitimacy. From the rule of the Fatimids (the Shiʿi dynasty that controlled varying areas of Egypt and the Maghrib in 909–1171) onwards, rulers tried to manifest a claim to descent from the Prophet Muhammad. The Fatimids, for instance, buried their dead in Cairo, but also built a congregational mosque at the al-Qarafa cemetery (which is now known as the City of the Dead) and created a multifunctional funerary and residential complex where they re-interred their dead brought with them from the Maghrib, the western part of the Islamic world. The subsequent dynasty of the Ayyubids followed the same tradition: Salah al-Din al-Ayyubi (1137–93) built a madrasa in the eastern part of the cemetery around the tomb of imam al-Shafiʿi, a founder of the *madhhab* to which the Ayyubids mostly adhered. The Ayyubid sultan al-Kamil (1180–1238) built a dynastic tomb for his dynasty above al-Shafiʿi's grave, which was previously venerated by the Fatimids because the imam was of the Prophet Muhammad's lineage and had taken a moderate position towards the Shiʿa (*tashayyuʿ*).[50] In a similar vein, Salah al-Din al-Ayyubi converted the Church of St. Anne in Jerusalem into a religious school, known as al-Madrasa al-salahiyya. There, he imparted Ashʿari dogma and Shafiʿi law, the two most important constituents of the Sunni creed officially espoused by the Ayyubids. He also built the Dome of Yusuf on the Temple Mount, the southern side of the platform of the Dome of the Rock in Jerusalem, and had his name engraved on it.

Figure 2 The cenotaph of Imam al-Shafiʻi in Cairo. Undated; turn of the nineteenth/twentieth century

(From Alois Musil's (1868–1944) collection of photographs held by the Institute of Near Eastern and African Studies, Charles University, Prague.)

The Mamluks, who ruled in Egypt and Syria after the Ayyubids, also endeavoured to build magnificent monuments of religious and funerary architecture to legitimise their rule.[51] They also used to visit the tombs and mausoleums not only of their predecessors, but also those of deceased Sunni scholars and pious individuals. Such visits provided the rulers with an opportunity to demonstrate their piety and served as a means of legitimising them by highlighting their connection to a respected deceased sultan.[52] Like the Ayyubids, the Mamluks propagated Sunni Islam in the sense of law together with Sufism and its institutions. The Mamluks were the first to introduce a broad system of four law schools, which was partly caused by migrants and the need to accommodate their different legal backgrounds. In doing so, they had madrasa complexes built that included the four schools. Each of them were treated equally; however, the Hanbali school was the least popular at the time. Their unequal positions in terms of their overall number of followers was expressed in the architectonic character of the madrasa complexes: the Shafi'i part of the complex was the most developed of the four in terms of its proportions, layout and position.

Figure 3 The Mamluk graves, Cairo. Undated; turn of the nineteenth/twentieth century (From Alois Musil's (1868–1944) collection of photographs held by the Institute of Near Eastern and African Studies, Charles University, Prague.)

Another source of motivation for building funerary architecture is seen in the Zengid dynasty (1127–1250) in Syria, who attempted to create important centres based on Prophetic authority and pilgrimage rituals. This practice grew to the extent that certain cities were turned into centres for the display of Prophetic tradition. The authenticity or accuracy of such sites was not as significant as their well-publicised patronage.[53]

In addition to the general ambiguity regarding funerary edifices, a further paradox was added by the discrepancy between the opinions of the founders of the legal schools, on the one hand, and the historical reality, on the other. A case in point is that of the resting places of the *madhhabs*' eponyms. The mosque of Abu Hanifa in Baghdad, built around his grave during Buwayhid rule (934–1062), is nowadays one of the most venerated Sunni sites in Iraq. It was turned into a shrine under the Seljuqs, when Sharaf al-Mulk Abu Sa'd Muhammad ibn Mansur, head of Seljuq sultan Alp-Arslan's tax bureau (*mustawfi*), was sent on a mission to the caliph in 1066–7. When he saw the Nizamiyya madrasa that the vizier Nizam al-Mulk had begun to build to promote the Shafi'i school of law, he gave instructions for a building to be constructed over the tomb of Abu Hanifa and a madrasa for the Hanafis at Bab al-Taq, in order to outshine Nizam al-Mulk.[54]

The construction on Abu Hanifa's grave led to a serious dispute with Hanbali scholar Ibn 'Aqil, because it necessitated excavation for the mosque's foundations. While digging, the story has it, the workers unearthed many human bones, which they re-buried in a nearby field. Ibn 'Aqil was outraged, even more so because the doors and other woodwork for the building were plundered from churches and synagogues in Samarra. He pointed out that there was a good possibility that the workers had excavated the bones of Abu Hanifa himself, which he found absurd. If Abu Hanifa's bones had been excavated and re-buried elsewhere, there was no reason for the shrine.[55]

In the Ottoman period, Abu Hanifa's mosque became a place of worship that was ceremonially visited on many occasions. Ottoman sultans were attentive to the shrines of Sufis and saints, due to their great importance as vehicles of political legitimation. As Peirce points out, it was for this reason that acts of patronage typically occurred at the moment of conquest. When the sultan Selim (1470/1–1520) extended Ottoman authority to the holy cities of Mecca and Medina, one of his first gestures towards his newly conquered domain was to restore the tomb of Ibn ʿArabi (1165–1240), renowned as the greatest master of the Sufis and buried in Damascus. When Selim's son Suleyman the Magnificent (1494–1566) took the traditional residence of the Sunni caliphate Baghdad from the Safawids in 1535, he discovered the tomb of Abu Hanifa and had it rebuilt, together with other tombs belonging to prominent historical and religious figures, such as ʿAbd al-Qadir al-Jilani. For the Ottomans, Abu Hanifa and ʿAbd al-Qadir al-Jilani were of particular significance: the Hanafi legal school constituted the official Ottoman *madhhab* in this period, and the discovery of his tomb provided crucial support for Ottoman claims to the leadership of Sunni Islam. The Qadiriyya was one of the most popular and influential Sufi orders at that time. A similar miraculous discovery took place when the Ottomans conquered Constantinople in 1453 and found a grave belonging to Eyyup, the Prophet's companion and standard-bearer.[56]

The Ottomans rebuilt Abu Hanifa's shrine after this had been destroyed by the Shiʿi Safavids, who had conquered Baghdad in 1508 and smashed many tombs there. Shiʿi theologian Yunus ibn Ahmad al-Bahrani (d. 1772) reports the circumstances of the destruction of Abu Hanifa's shrine from a polemical perspective and mocks the charismatic powers (*karāmāt*) of the four imams, because only Safawids claimed to possess such power. Al-Bahrani writes that people witnessed a most powerful miracle at the grave of Abu Hanifa when the greatest sultan Shah Abbas I conquered Baghdad and ordered that Abu Hanifa's grave be turned into a public toilet. He donated two mules and ordered them to be placed at the entrance of the market so that whoever needed to go to the toilet could ride them to go and relieve themselves at Abu Hanifa's grave. One day, al-Bahrani recounts:

> Shah ʿAbbas called for a servant from Abu Hanifa's grave and asked him: 'Why are you serving at this grave when Abu Hanifa is already in the deepest pits of the Hellfire?' The servant replied: 'There is a black dog in this grave, your grandfather Shah Ismaʿil buried it when he conquered Baghdad and tossed out Abu Hanifa's bones from his grave and made it a resting place for the black dog. I am serving that dog.' He was truthful in what he said as the late Shah Ismaʿil really did so.[57]

Besides Abu Hanifa's grave, the grave of imam al-Shafi'i has also held great significance,[58] while the graves of Ahmad ibn Hanbal and Malik ibn Anas were of rather minor importance. According to Ibn Khallikan, Ahmad ibn Hanbal was buried in Haribiyya street in Baghdad, and his tomb was a well-known and visited site in that burial ground.[59] The Hanbali scholar Ibn al-Jawzi mentions in his book on the virtues of Ahmad ibn Hanbal that it is beneficial to be buried near him or to visit his grave, especially on a Wednesday.[60] However, the tomb was destroyed by flooding from the Tigris in the thirteenth century and veneration shifted to his son 'Abdullah. It is not known how many times the cemetery was affected by flooding; however, rumours suggest that after another flood in 1937, Ibn Hanbal's remains were transferred to the 'Arif Agha Mosque.[61]

The grave of Malik ibn Anas in Baqi' al-Gharqad has never been a popular place of worship. According to Ibn Jubayr (d. 1145), a traveller and geographer from al-Andalus, who paid attention to various domes and mausoleums during his visit to Medina, Malik's grave had only a small and very simple cupola (*qubba ṣaghīra mukhtaṣarat al-binā'*). This was in sharp contrast to the elevated graves of 'Abbas ibn 'Abd al-Mutallib and al-Hasan ibn 'Ali, which were adorned with copper roofs and nails, as well as the grave of Ibrahim, son of the Prophet Muhammad.[62] Nowadays, Malik's grave is very modest indeed: just a mound of dirt.

Medieval Islam: A Religion of Tombs

The veneration of saints at their tombs and shrines was a prevalent phenomenon throughout the Middle East for many centuries, despite opposition from some Muslim theologians and jurists.[63] Pilgrimage sites proliferated mainly from the twelfth and thirteenth centuries. The process was accelerated for multiple reasons, including the political context and the spread of Sufism.[64] At these times, everyday religiosity sought guidance and blessing from miracle-working saints and turned their tombs into venerated sites. The importance of this phenomenon was such that some scholars speak of medieval Islam as 'a religion of tombs', which can help us to remove the façade of official religion and reveal much older and broader layers of worship.[65] What is even more striking and makes the terms 'popular', or 'folk' religion, or the dichotomy between 'low' and 'high', or 'popular' and 'orthodox' Islam quite problematic, is that nearly all Muslims participated in this phenomenon, including the ulama and those in power.

The medieval religion was much more porous than it is today, and at the centre of the medieval Islamic cosmos stood a saint (*walī*) who did not belong to any specific religious denomination.[66] It was particularly during the modern era that Muslims, Christians and Jews monopolised their faith and made it a reason for national disputes. With this process, harmonious site-sharing seems to have vanished. By the last quarter of the twentieth century scholars had begun to report that there is no such thing as a mutually respected understanding of sacred sites and that competing discourses prevail in the claims of different religious groups.[67]

In medieval times, however, the veneration of saints provides us with a picture of relatively harmonious relations among various denominations. These were characterised by a disregard for sectarian controversies to such an extent that Muslims regularly attended the shrines of Christian saints or sought blessing from monks. It was not unusual for the venerated sites to have much older roots from pre-Islamic times; the occupants of the graves were later incorporated into the Islamic tradition as Muslims with new sets of legends surrounding their origins.[68] The attitude of Christians and others towards Muslim sacred sites was similar, such that at the level of popular practice one can hardly speak about clearly distinct religious traditions established along sectarian lines. This was particularly the case in the Levant, which was full of Jewish and Christian religious memories. Many of their venerated sites were adopted by Muslims. The lines were also blurred when it came to Sunni–Shi'i relations, as can be seen from the non-sectarian veneration of the 'Alids. The Shi'i shrines had been built, maintained and perpetuated mainly by Sunni elites.[69] The medieval religious environment did not require a clear religious affiliation, but rather a humble approach. As Grehan puts it, 'beneath all the superficial differences between Islam, Christianity, and Judaism lay a vibrant folk religiosity which, in practice, had no qualms about trampling over formal religious boundaries. It provided a common vocabulary for prayer and supplication, and created the framework for a communal calendar of observances.'[70]

Figure 4 Funeral architecture, Damascus. Undated; turn of the nineteenth/twentieth century

(From Alois Musil's (1868–1944) collection of photographs held by the Institute of Near Eastern and African Studies, Charles University, Prague.)

As we have already mentioned, most religious scholars displayed no antagonism towards the veneration of saints across the religious spectrum. Strikingly, sainthood was open to anyone regardless of their origin: men and women, Muslims and non-Muslims. Still, most shrines were at the tombs of famous religious figures from the past (especially prophets,[71] Muhammad's Companions, folk saints and other righteous individuals who were seen to have acted with God's grace: *walī*, pl. *awliyā'*). Many of these places were 'rediscovered', quite often through the medium of dreams, while some were of more recent origin.[72] The graves of these pious people either stood alone or served as a cornerstone around which a cemetery was formed, because it was considered beneficial to be buried near a righteous person's grave. Such places also served to strengthen the local identity or pride.

The spread of the cult of saints was aided by a lack of official religious infrastructure (mosques). Rural believers in particular had little access to mosques and so looked for an alternative place to focus their religious practice. Most Muslims could not afford to undertake a pilgrimage to Mecca. Visiting the shrines of local saints was therefore, for many, an affordable substitution for *ḥajj*, and, as we will see, this remains true today. Moreover, local shrines did not need to be authorised by the official establishment, either religious or lay. Hence, saints' shrines served as the true centres of most believers' religiosity, and their veneration was an integral part of orthodox religious life. This does not mean, however, that the veneration of saints was only typical of the countryside; the domes of shrines formed a familiar panorama in towns as well. These sites were visited throughout the year, although certain times were considered particularly good for visiting the dead (for example, on a Friday,[73] Saturday morning, Wednesday – due to a hadith mentioning that God created light on this day – *ʿid al-aḍḥā* or *ʿid al-fiṭr*, and several more sophisticated calculations of the best occasions).

In general, visiting saintly shrines served various purposes:[74] believers went to seek the strength to deal with disease, war or personal tragedies, or expected that any prayers they offered at these sites had a better chance of being answered. Prayers at some shrines were even believed to be directly accepted in heaven. Some graves or shrines served purely tribal interests (for instance, as places where tribal warriors came to seek advice before going into battle or on a raid); some were seen to be patrons of the weak or protectors of the well-being of herds; some were visited in order to settle inter-tribal scores, restore health or increase fertility. Probably the most common reason for visiting a shrine was to seek the sanctity of the place and obtain the saint's spiritual intercession. The graves' occupants were believed to have the power to bless, reward or curse those who came near them. While most of the normative religious aspects were almost exclusively the domain of men, Muslim women also commonly visited saints' shrines and developed separate practices from those of men. This was especially true of places or saints associated with childcare and birth.[75] As Meri succinctly puts it: 'Saints brought good fortune and plenitude, imparted knowledge, blessings, hope, comfort, solace, and protection from evil. They were God's agents on earth.'[76]

The sacred topography was composed of various types of shrines, and different authors used different terms when speaking of various funerary structures. The most generic term used for pilgrimage sites was *mazār* (pl. *mazārāt*, lit. a place that is visited), or simply *ziyāra*. The most frequently recurring type of pilgrimage site was a tomb (*qabr*, pl. *qubūr*), often synonymous with *ḍarīḥ* (pl. *ḍarā'iḥ*). *Qabr* might also refer to the building over a grave. The shrine might contain a cenotaph (*tābūt*, *ṣundūq*). Domed shrines or mausoleums are known as *qubba* (pl. *qibāb*, *qubab*), while for a place of assembly or the location where a saint was believed to have been martyred the term *mashhad* (pl. *mashāhid*) was used. *Mashhad*, however, did not always contain a tomb. Finally, a tomb complex was called *turba* (pl. *turab*); this was usually a large space in a cemetery where one or more people were buried.[77] An even more specific type of architectural complex was a 'tomb-college'. The tombs of great prophets constituted an entirely unique category of their own.[78]

Devotees identified many places as holy and sanctified them by building various commemorative structures, including tombs and shrines. Those places then acquired further characteristics and were considered supernatural sites, where the pilgrims could see lights, smell pleasant odours emanating from the graves, experience visions and seek blessings (*baraka*). They were also connected with rituals consisting, for example, of lying on the tombs, circumambulating them, touching or rubbing against them, and collecting soil from their confines, which was later used as a cure. The performance of miracles was attributed both to saints and their tombs and shrines. Besides, some believed that by sleeping at a shrine or a grave they had a better chance of communicating with the dead through dreams in which the saint might give them advice or information.

We do not have exact historical records that enable us to assess the number of Muslims visiting shrines in this period, yet the sheer quantity of monuments indicates the pervasiveness of this phenomenon, and it is further attested to by the existence of the specific literary genre of *faḍā'il* (lit. merits) describing the excellent qualities of sacred sites, as well as popular pilgrimage guides (*kutub al-ziyārāt* or just *ziyārāt*) that describe the sacred topography and provide the biographies of the holy dead.[79]

Ibn Taymiyya, Legal Schools and Theology

The role of the dead in medieval Islamic society, the independence of the shrine culture, the unbound nature of popular religiosity, rulers' exaggeration in building funeral monuments, and the cults and practices of Shi'i Islam induced negative attitudes among some religious scholars who had a fear of innovations (*bidaʿ*). However, debates about what was correct practice were almost exclusively confined to legal treatises and collections of *fatāwā* and had close to no impact on the realities of Muslim cemeteries, the proliferation of shrines and the rituals associated with visiting them. The overwhelming majority of people simply knew almost nothing about the ongoing debates over Islamic law and doctrine. This was especially the case in the countryside, which had high rates of illiteracy and only limited oversight of orthodox religious observance by the religious establishment. Most believers simply did not look to texts and scholars for religious guidance. However, over time the issue of visiting graves, performing funeral rituals and constructing funerary architecture became critical in Sunni Islam. The question of visiting the grave of the Prophet, as well as the graves of other prophets and pious men, was of utmost importance. The issue of visiting private graves was also discussed, although it was of considerably less significance.

If we leave aside the traditionalist movement in Medina in the very early period of the emergence of Islam, the first concerted opposition to shrine visits crystallised among the Hanbali scholars. Despite some Mamluk rulers' efforts to treat all schools of law equally, there existed certain animosity or rivalry between the schools, and especially between Hanbalis, on the one hand, and Hanafis and Malikis, on the other. The Hanbali school adhered to the hadith literature most closely and was also distinguished by its duality: it was not merely a school of law, but also a school of theology. Its theological school was known as Hanbali, Salafi or traditionalist (*ahl al-ḥadīth, atharī*). The Shafiʿi, Maliki and Hanafi schools had no such duality and were merely schools of law. Their followers preferred Ashʿari theology, with the exception of Shafiʿi school, which was divided into traditionalist and Ashʿari fractions. This is relevant because it meant that the Hanbalis constituted a minor voice in what we may call a Sunni orthodoxy, the majority being the Ashʿaris. This also explains why the majority of Ibn Taymiyya's followers came from the Hanbali as well as the traditionalist part of the Shafiʿi school, while his rivals were Malikis and Hanafis. It also indicates why we can trace the origins of the strong opposition against *ziyāra* and the cult of the dead in the *Ahl al-hadith* movement to the Hanbali and – to a lesser extent – Shafiʿi legal schools.[80] The Hanbali and *Ahl al-hadith* opposition against *ziyārat al-qubūr* has been significant throughout Islamic history.

The most serious opposition first emerged in ninth-century Iraq, and rose up again in eleventh-century Syria. The reason for this is that Baghdad was a bastion of the Hanbali school of law until it was conquered by the Mongols in 1258, after which Damascus became the established centre of Hanbali jurisprudence. As the religious texts were not explicit about visiting saints' graves, the Hanbalis came to consider the practice an heretical innovation (*bid'a*). Furthermore, the practice attracted women and thus encouraged intermingling of the sexes, which they deemed to be 'un-Islamic' and offensive to 'proper' morality. As Ibn Taymiyya later argued, 'much of the imitation of the holiday customs of the People of the Book is due to women (*kathīr min mushābahāt ahl al-kitāb fī a'yādihim wa ghayrihā, innamā yad'ū ilayhā al-nisā'*)'.[81]

Ibn Hanbal himself, however, was not concerned with the practice of *ziyāra*; rather, this emerged among subsequent generations of his disciples. One of the first Hanbali condemnations came from the Baghdadi scholar Ibn 'Aqil (1039/40–1119); he did not completely reject the practice of visiting graves, as according to certain traditions the Prophet himself had urged believers to do so. Instead, Ibn 'Aqil simply insisted that it should be done in accordance with Sunni tradition, wherein certain limitations regulating *ziyāra* existed. He specifically criticised making special journeys to graves; gathering in shrines at night time, because 'beardless youths and women [would mix] together with wanton men'; and exalting graves or revering them, for example, by kindling fires, kissing the tombs and perfuming them.[82] His attitude is that of a moralist terrified by the possible consequences of visiting a distant uninhabited place, combined with a theologian's fear that such a place could be the focus of practices that ought to be restricted only to God himself. The purists considered that praying at a grave or facing towards a grave in prayer constituted idolatry and violated the principle of the unicity of God (*tawḥīd*). In later times, the Hanbali scholar Ibn Qudama al-Maqdisi (d. 1223) formulated that attitude as follows: 'The special treatment of graves by means of praying by them is similar to the veneration of idols (*aṣnām*) by prostrating (*sujūd*) oneself before them and wishing to draw near to them.'[83]

The centrality of the Shari'ah and the orthopractic emphasis of the Islamic tradition make texts of Islamic jurisprudence (*fiqh*) an invaluable source of historical evidence about many aspects of medieval life and thought, including *ziyāra*.[84] Taqi al-Din Ahmad ibn Taymiyya (1263–1328), a Syrian[85] polymath, theologian and jurist affiliated with the Hanbali school of law and theology, was probably the foremost critic of what he deemed heretical practices in Sunni Islam. He also contributed significantly to the legal debate about *ziyāra*, helping to define its meaning and function.[86]

The historical setting is important for contextualising Ibn Taymiyya's religious opinions. His were times when the numbers of Christian and Jewish pilgrims from Europe had multiplied compared with previous centuries, largely owing to the Crusaders' conquest of the Holy Land, securing the pilgrimage and trade routes. It is also important to repeat that Jews, Christians and Muslims quite often followed the same rituals when visiting graves, and sometimes even venerated the same sites. These were also times when the 'Abbasid influence was long gone and the power vacuum in the Islamic world in general was filled by various local dynasties, which undertook to restore many shrines and considered the devotional culture to be an effective means of establishing their presence and legacy. Ibn Taymiyya spent a substantial part of his life in Damascus, together with many other refugees, seeking shelter against the Mongol invasion of the eastern parts of the Islamic world. He also spent some time in Cairo, the capital city of the Mamluk state, of which Syria was a part. In his lifetime Cairo achieved its widest expansion to date and community activities in the growing graveyards were extensive.

In the Sunni intellectual tradition, Ibn Taymiyya's advocates extol him as the killer of heresies (*mumīt al-bida'*)[87] and a revivalist of Sunna (*muḥyī al-sunna*), who sought to strip Islam of all its heresies and return it to its pristine form. This form was idealised in the beliefs and practices of the early Muslim community, for whom the term *salaf* is used. Ibn Taymiyya stressed the importance of following the *salaf* and imitating their example by strict adherence to sound and true hadiths, hence, he undoubtedly ranks among the most ardent advocates of the traditionalist movement (*Ahl al-hadith*) within Sunni Islam. Although all Sunni Muslims revere hadith literature to some extent and all Sunni religious scholars of the classical age respect the Qur'an and Sunna (the latter being a more frequent term for hadith in legal terminology) as two primary sources of God's law, they nevertheless ascribe varying importance to hadith in legal matters. Traditionalists called for legal reasoning (*ijtihād*) directly from the Qur'an and Sunna, and were harshly critical of blindly imitating (*taqlīd*) legal authorities. Ibn Taymiyya was one of these traditionalists who stressed the importance of *ijtihād*. Different levels of *ijtihād* existed, depending on the jurist's knowledge and intellectual capacity. The ability to perform absolute *ijtihād* was, according to many traditionalists and Ibn Taymiyya in particular, superior to the established system of legal schools (Hanafi, Shafi'i, Maliki and Hanbali) that had developed during the Mamluk period since the thirteenth century.

Ibn Taymiyya represented rather a minor, yet very important tendency of Sunni Islam at the time. The majority of Sunni scholars have always shown great respect for the legal and religious legacy of later generations of Muslim scholars, for whom the term *khalaf* is coined in opposition to *salaf*. Now, the previous statement regarding Ibn Taymiyya's affiliation with the Hanbali school must be specified. It is well known that he came from a renowned Hanbali religious family. However, this affiliation was only because at the time legal opinions could not be expressed outside the system of legal schools. Ibn Taymiyya himself claimed to be an absolute interpreter (*mujtahid mutlaq*), based on his enormous religious knowledge of Islamic literature and the methodology of the early Muslim community. Although disagreement among individual jurists over interpretation has been frequent, he became convinced that the methodology of the *salaf* in law was superior to that of his colleagues and contemporaries. As a result, he advocated certain unconventional legal opinions.

In theology, too, Ibn Taymiyya insisted on the crucial roles of hadith and the Qur'an (both termed *naql*) and their superiority over reason (*'aql*). He was convinced that the way of the *salaf* in theology, and especially in the theology of God's name and attributes, was to understand and interpret them literally without embarking on allegory and metaphor. The limits of this approach were that certain of God's anthropomorphic attributes were affirmed, while human understanding was restricted in the sense that one was not allowed to qualify them in order not to commit anthropomorphisation (*tashbīh*), corporalism (*tajsīm*) and likening or exemplification (*tamthīl*). In this regard, Ibn Taymiyya's theological view was contrary to Ash'arism, the mainstream theology of his day. Its eponym, Abu al-Hasan al-Ash'ari (d. 936), tried to avoid anthropomorphism by admitting a certain degree of metaphorical interpretation, achieving a compromise between the two extremes of harsh anthropomorphism and pure allegory. However, Ibn Taymiyya criticised the Ashʿaris claiming that only the way of the *salaf* is true and is superior to Ashʿarism. His arguments were certainly not feeble: he argued that even al-Ashʿari himself in later life abandoned the Ashʿari compromise and returned to the methodology of the *salaf* and that the Ashʿaris were therefore wrong to advocate it.

When it comes to committing *shirk* by worshipping things besides God alone, Ibn Taymiyya did not distinguish between statues (*timthāl*) and pictures (*ṣūra*), both being images. In Arabic, there are many words for idols, be it *ṣanam*, *wathan*, *ṭāghūt*, *naṣab* or *rijz*. Although some exegetes and lexicographers tried to define what is the precise difference between them, stating, for example, that a *wathan* is an idol made of stone, while *ṣanam* is made of wood, silver or copper, these opinions are not reflected and worked with in our study and we use *wathan* as a more general term (hence, a venerated grave is *wathan*).[88] For Ibn Taymiyya and all traditionalists mentioned in our work (such as Ibn Qayyim al-Jawziyya, Ibn ʿAbd al-Wahhab, Nasir al-Din al-Albani), both *ṣūra* (picture, form) and *timthāl*, a generic word for a statue derived from the same radix as the Qurʾanic *mithl* (likeness) or theological principle of *tamthīl*, means the same. This is evidenced by Ibn Taymiyya's interpretation of Muhammad's depiction of idolatry in Abyssinia: 'When a pious person amongst them dies they build a place of worship on his grave, and then decorate it with such images (*ṣawwarū fīhā tilka al-ṣuwar*). They would be the worst of creatures before God.' For Ibn Taymiyya, this hadith points to two temptations combined: the temptation of graves and the temptation of images/statues (*tamāthīl*).

Speaking of God's names and attributes, we must introduce the theological conception of God's unicity that Ibn Taymiyya used, which is based on a tripartite classification of theology. The theology of God's names and attributes is considered the third aspect of monotheism, which divides Sunnis into two camps: Ashʿaris and Salafis. The first aspect is called 'monotheism of Lordship' (*tawḥīd al-rubūbīya*) and is derived from the idea that the Lord (*rabb*) is the Creator of all things. This idea is common to Christians and Jews, too, and is shared by most philosophers, who suppose that in causality there must be a primary cause (*ʿilla*).

The second aspect is 'monotheism of cult' (*tawḥīd al-uluhīya*, *tawḥīd al-ʿibāda*). This is crucial for the identity of true Islam as it makes a distinction between 'true monotheism of Islam' and polytheism (*shirk*). Ibn Taymiyya sometimes considers the third aspect, 'monotheism of God's names and attributes', to be part of monotheism of cult. In all likelihood, the reason for this is that God must be worshipped by his own names – by the names and attributes by which He described himself – as to do otherwise would be to commit a *shirk* by associating him with improper ideas.

Ibn Taymiyya's animosity to heretical practices regarding *ziyāra* must be viewed in the context of his terminological classification of God's monotheism, and monotheism of cult in particular. As already mentioned, he lived at a time of huge proliferation of pilgrim sites and shrines, inhabited among others by devout Muslims of various Sufi orders who flagrantly violated, in their opponent's eyes, the principle of monotheism of cult. During his lifetime, Ibn Taymiyya also witnessed the golden age of intellectual Sufism, when Sufis occupied positions in the state apparatus and some exercised significant influence over political leaders. The Sufi teachings of the 'unity of being' (*waḥdat al-wujūd*) of Ibn 'Arabi and Ibn Sab'in (d. 1271) were a spiritual and intellectual alternative to dogmatism and legal aridity. However, to Ibn Taymiyya these teachings were nothing more than a violation of monotheism and of the strict dichotomy between the Lord and his servants.

Ibn Taymiyya and Ibn Qayyim al-Jawziyya: The Master and his Pupil

The opinions of Ibn Taymiyya and Ibn Qayyim al-Jawziyya (1292–1350)[89] about *ziyāra* stemmed from Hanbali tradition and became both the most controversial and the most influential on later Sunni reformism. Their names very often occur together: Ibn Qayyim al-Jawziyya has been traditionally perceived as no more than his master's student and is not seen as an independent scholar.[90] An anecdote cited by Hanbali biographer Ibn Rajab (d. 1393) reports that shortly before his death Ibn Qayyim al-Jawziyya saw Ibn Taymiyya in a dream. He asked about his master's rank (*manzila*) in Heaven. Ibn Taymiyya replied that it was higher than that of some elites (*akābir*) and said to Ibn Qayyim al-Jawziyya: 'You have almost reached us, but you are in the stratum (*ṭabaqa*) of Ibn Khuzayma, may God have mercy upon him.'[91] This anecdote illustrates how Ibn Qayyim al-Jawziyya was perceived shortly after his lifetime.

Ibn Qayyim al-Jawziyya came under the influence of Ibn Taymiyya in his twenties. At that time, Ibn Taymiyya and his followers were destroying relics and tombs, especially in the cemeteries around Damascus. Despite their efforts to appear relatively moderate, both scholars were persecuted by the ulama in power and the authorities, and both were imprisoned several times. Ibn Taymiyya's final persecution was the result of a treatise on the visiting of graves, which he had been writing for nearly sixteen years. He was unjustly accused by his opponents of belittling the Prophet Muhammad by allegedly forbidding visits to his grave, and was put in prison for this. Ibn Qayyim al-Jawziyya was imprisoned with his teacher, allegedly for criticising a religious pilgrimage to Hebron. He was released shortly after his master's death.

Muhammad al-Shawkani (d. 1839), a famous Yemeni traditionalist and reformer, describes Ibn Qayyim al-Jawziyya in his biography of renowned scholars as 'a student of Ibn Taymiyya who loved his teacher so much that he did not disagree with any of his opinions and was always on his side'. However, it is important to note that although the two were received as master and pupil, al-Jawziyya also had his own significant role in the later development and spread of Salafi thought. As al-Shawkani notes: 'It was him [Ibn Qayyim al-Jawziyya] who spread Ibn Taymiyya's ideas by writing accessible and fitting works. He was sent to prison with him, humiliated, whipped and paraded on a mule.'[92] Ibn Taymiyya was an enormously influential author, however, his complicated writing and erudition makes his work very difficult to read at times. Henri Laoust aptly notes that the eloquence of Ibn Qayyim al-Jawziyya contrasts with the incisive dryness of his famous master's succinct prose.[93]

Indeed, it was not only their writing styles that differed. The same can be said about their personalities. While Ibn Taymiyya was a rather impatient, choleric man, whose aggressive character made him many an enemy, Ibn Qayyim al-Jawziyya was mild and more tolerant. While they both shared a harsh and relentless criticism of heresy (*bidʻa*), Greek-influenced Muslim philosophy, Shiʻa and Sufism in its 'deviant forms', be they popular 'heretic' practices or the intellectual doctrine of the 'unity of being', Ibn Qayyim al-Jawziyya's writings stood apart from those of his master not only for their more eloquent prose, but also their milder tone: Ibn Qayyim al-Jawziyya was more ready than his teacher to be indulgent to those with whom he differed. Furthermore, Ibn Qayyim al-Jawziyya had a great interest in Sufism, and some of his major works are almost entirely devoted to Sufi themes. The latter, as well as terminology, can be found in nearly all his writings; for example, human beings' natural inclination to God and the maladies of the heart.

Ibn Taymiyya's (and Ibn Qayyim al-Jawziyya's) Opinions on Pilgrimage to Jerusalem and Palestine

In 1322/3, Ibn Taymiyya went on a pilgrimage to Mecca from which he brought back the subject matter of his treatise *Proper Rituals of the ḥajj and ʿumra (Manasik al-ḥajj wa al-ʿumra)*. This was his contribution to a common genre of Islamic religious literature that dealt with the proper rituals (*manāsik*) of journeys to Mecca and Medina. From the perspective of Sunni law, going on an annual pilgrimage to Mecca (*ḥajj*) in certain months of the Muslim calendar is one of the five pillars of Islam. The *ʿumra*, a shorter form of the pilgrimage, can be undertaken at any time of the year, but in contrast to the *ḥajj* is generally only considered a recommendation not an obligatory duty. Visiting the Prophet's Mosque in Medina is also recommended, and would often follow either the *ḥajj* or the *ʿumra*.

The purpose of Ibn Taymiyya's treatise was to set out briefly the proper rules for pilgrims to Islam's most venerated holy sites. This was probably the first treatise in which Ibn Taymiyya denounced a certain number of innovations in the rituals of the *ḥajj*, *ʿumra* and occasionally other pilgrimages.[94] He warned against touching and kissing sites close to the Kaʿba, such as the supposed image of a foot of the Prophet Abraham (*maqām Ibrāhīm*, petrosomatoglyph), the graves of prophets and pious men, the Prophet Muhammad's room (called variously *ḥujrat al-nabī*, *al-ḥujra al-sharīfa*, *al-qabr al-sharīf* or simply *al-rawḍa*, the garden), the Cave of the Patriarchs (*maghārat Ibrāhīm*) in Hebron and the Rock in Jerusalem (*ṣakhrat bayt al-maqdis*).[95] According to Ibn Taymiyya, one of the gravest heresies was circumambulation of these places and whoever made this their religion was to repent, otherwise he would be put to death.

Neither Ibn Taymiyya nor Ibn Qayyim al-Jawziyya attempted to belittle the role of the prophets and holy men in Islam as such, although it might seem so to an uninformed beholder. In fact, the opposite is true; Ibn Taymiyya openly admitted the existence of saints and their power to perform miracles. In his *Wasitian Dogma* (*al-'Aqida al-wasitiyya*) he writes: 'Among the fundamentals of the Sunnis is belief (*taṣdīq*) in the miracles of the saints (*karāmāt al-awliyāʾ*) and the supernatural acts which God performs through them in varieties of knowledge, illuminations (*mukāshafāt*), power, and impact.'[96] It is significant that the passage mentioning the miracles of the saints is omitted from some of the manuscripts used in the critical edition, including the one authorised by Ibn Taymiyya himself.[97]

The concepts of *ḥajj* and *'umra* are associated with Prophet Abraham, who is depicted in the Qur'an as a true monotheist. Ibn Taymiyya promoted the proper cult of Allah, according to which only Allah himself may be worshipped, not any human being, such as Prophet Muhammad or Abraham. The blurred limits between proper Islamic rules and popular beliefs and practices represented a challenge for Ibn Taymiyya, which he approached from the standpoint of a jurist, using precise, well-defined language. Accordingly, he distinguishes between long-distance journeys, undertaken with the object of paying a visit to graves or other religious places, and *ziyāra* as a shorter-distance visit.

In defining destinations for long-distance journeys, Ibn Taymiyya relies primarily on the following hadith mentioned in the *Sahih* of Muslim and *Sahih* of al-Bukhari: 'The saddles shall not be fastened except for the three mosques: the Sacred Mosque [in Mecca], my mosque [the Prophet's Mosque in Medina], and al-Aqsa Mosque [in Jerusalem].'[98] Ibn Taymiyya interprets this hadith to mean that undertaking a long-distance journey for religious purposes to places other than those indicated is prohibited. It is therefore permissible and recommended to travel to these mosques in order to perform legal worship, including ritual prayer (*ṣalāt*), invocational prayer (*duʿāʾ*), remembrance of God's names (*dhikr*), reading the Qur'an and spiritual retreat (*iʿtikāf*); in other words, worship of the kind practised in the Prophet's Mosque and other mosques, with the exception of the al-Haram Mosque in Mecca. Here, some additional worship practices are legal, namely circumambulation of the Kaʿba (*tawāf fi al-kaʿba*), touching the Yemeni corners of the Kaʿba (that is, those facing Yemen), and kissing the Black Stone.[99]

As for a long-distance journey to the al-Aqsa Mosque, Ibn Taymiyya sets precise rules because by popular Muslim belief the al-Aqsa Mosque was identical to another Muslim religious site, the Dome of the Rock (*Qubbat al-ṣakhra*), which is actually situated in the middle of the same compound as the al-Aqsa Mosque. This confusion may be attributed to the fact that the Dome of the Rock was built in 691 by the Umayyad caliph ʿAbd al-Malik in place of the Temple of Solomon. It is only legal to travel to the al-Aqsa Mosque, which is crucial for Islam as such, since it is mentioned both in the Qurʾan and hadith, although it does not usually rank among the very holy places (*ḥarām*) alongside the *ḥaramayn* of Mecca and Medina. The status of the al-Aqsa Mosque is certainly not equal to the Kaʿba sanctuary in Mecca. Therefore, the al-Aqsa Mosque must not be visited during periods such as the Sacrifice feast (*ʿīd al-aḍḥā*), which might lead to confusion with the *hajj*. Ibn Taymiyya harshly criticised any attempt to equate the Dome with the Haram Mosque in Mecca. He said that those who pray facing the Rock instead of the Kaʿba are unbelievers and renegades, and if they do not repent they are to be killed.[100] On the other hand, Ibn Taymiyya did not object to visiting the dead after going on a pilgrimage to al-Aqsa or elsewhere. It was the custom of the Prophet Muhammad and his Companions, when they passed by graveyards, to greet deceased believers and ask God for his Mercy upon them (*taraḥḥum*).[101]

It can be inferred from Ibn Taymiyya's opinions that he was afraid that vibrant religious centres, to which pilgrimage was deeply rooted in both the Jewish and Christian traditions, could also attract Muslims, and that this would weaken the religious importance of the Holy cities of Mecca and Medina. Indeed, Ibn Taymiyya was afraid that imitation (*muḍāhāt*) of Jews and Christians in their customs and habits could result in a loss of Muslim identity.

Hence, Ibn Taymiyya was an example of an individual who opposed the exaggerated popular views of the sanctity of Jerusalem and Palestine, which had also become places of prominence in Islam. This was, first, because Jerusalem had been set by the Prophet Muhammad as the first direction (*qibla*) that should be faced during ritual prayer, although he later altered this *qibla* in favour of Mecca, which became the holiest place in Islam. However, in early Islamic historiography, the al-Aqsa Mosque mentioned in the Qurʾan was linked with Jerusalem, which became the third holiest place in Islam after Mecca and Medina. We know that as early as the first part of the second century of Hijra, the biographer of the Prophet, Ibn Ishaq, connected Muhammad's night journey (*al-isrā'*) with his ascension (*mi'rāj*) into Heaven, where he met earlier prophets. It was the caliph 'Umar who built a mosque there, knowing the site's significance in Jewish tradition. What made both Mecca and Jerusalem so holy is the religious narration of the Abrahamic religion according to which the Ka'ba was built by Adam and then rebuilt by Abraham and his son Ismael to become a proper place of worship after it had been filled with idols. In Jerusalem, in turn, the Rock and the surrounding area acquired mystical significance and became associated with a series of legends involving major figures of the Biblical tradition, especially Abraham and Isaac.

According to some authors, Jerusalem's prominence was developed by the religious and political policies of the Umayyad caliph 'Abd al-Malik, who wanted to divert pilgrims from Hijaz as a result of rivalry with his counterpart 'Abdullah ibn al-Zubayr in Mecca and Hijaz. It has been also asserted that the plan of the Dome of the Rock, with two ambularies around the rock itself, originated with the liturgical requirements of the *ṭawāf*.[102] Its religious importance was heightened by the presence of Crusaders and the temporary loss of the territory of Palestine. As Grabar convincingly demonstrates, 'Abd al-Malik intended to Islamise the holy place in Jerusalem and chose the one symbol associated with it that was equally holy to Jews and Muslims – that of Abraham – while emphasising the superiority of Islam in Muslim eyes, since in the Qur'an Abraham is neither a Christian nor a Jew, but a *ḥanīf*, a pure monotheist, and the first Muslim.[103]

In Ibn Taymiyya's times, legends surrounding the holy places in Jerusalem and Palestine were very popular. A special genre of literature known as the merits of Jerusalem (*faḍā'il al-quds, faḍā'il bayt al-maqdis*) came into existence. Because of the merits of Jerusalem and Palestine, the rites there, such as prayer, fasting and alms-giving, were desirable to such a degree that pilgrimages to Jerusalem instead of the *ḥajj* to Mecca were not unheard of. Ibn Taymiyya was afraid of these syncretic tendencies, which tended towards incorporating Jewish and Christian holy sites and traditions into Islam more than he deemed appropriate given the Judaeo-Christian origin of Islam. Hence, based on proper legal and theological argumentation, he forbade visits to all unbelievers' cult places, such as Bethlehem (Bayt laḥm), Sion (Sahyun) and Christian churches.[104] He devoted his short, well-known treatise *Rules for Visiting Jerusalem* (*Qaʿida fi ziyarat bayt al-maqdis*) to this topic, and declared that it was also forbidden to travel to the grave of the Prophet Abraham in Hebron, as well as to other graves such as the grave of the Prophet Muhammad.[105]

Ibn Taymiyya's (and Ibn Qayyim al-Jawziyya's) Opinion on Pilgrimage to Medina

As far as Jerusalem and Hebron were concerned, Ibn Taymiyya was worried about the possible impact of religious confusion on Islamic identity. However, this was not the case for Medina. To Judaism and Christianity, the city was totally unknown as a site of religious significance. Of course, according to the Muslim narrative Jewish tribes lived there, nevertheless the city became a holy place only with the emergence of Islam. Both Muhammad's mosque and his grave are situated there. Insofar as Ibn Taymiyya was occupied with Medina, it was not because of possible confusion, but because of Muhammad's grave becoming a place of worship and seeking the mediatory role (*shafāʿa*) of the Prophet Muhammad.

Although Ibn Taymiyya acknowledged that Medina was a place of pilgrimage that had been legalised by the Prophetic utterance 'The saddles shall not be fastened except for the three mosques,' in reality Medina was often visited because of Muhammad's grave. According to another hadith, the Prophet was aware of the fact that people would venerate him excessively after his death. When he was close to death, he is reported to have said: 'May Allah curse the Jews and Christians who make the graves of their prophets into places of worship; do not imitate them.'

Muhammad's grave, however, was a common destination for religious pilgrims to Medina, who sought his assistance or intercession. Ibn Taymiyya acknowledged Muhammad's role as a mediator in two separate instances: first, Muhammad's right to mediate between man and God during his lifetime – in theological parlance this is 'minor intercession' (*al-shafāʿa al-ṣughrā*); and, second, intercession on Judgement Day, which is part of Sunni eschatological imagery: the Prophet will intercede for those who are awaiting (*ahl al-mawqif*) God's judgement after they have asked the prophets Adam, Noah, Abraham, Moses and Jesus, who in turn cede the right to intercede to Muhammad. This is 'major intercession' (*al-shafāʿa al-ʿuzmā*). In an eschatological sense,

Muhammad also has the right to intercede for those who deserve to enter Paradise. Besides this, all prophets (including Muhammad) and pious men (*ṣiddīqūn*) possess the right to intercede on behalf of those who deserve to enter Hell or, if they have already entered it, to take them away from it.

Although Ibn Taymiyya acknowledged Muhammad's intercession, he did not consider it a *condition sine qua non* of human salvation. In his *Wasitian Dogma*, he says that 'God himself in his mercy and kindness takes out huge masses (*aqwāman*) from Hell without intercession'.[106] In his famous treatise *A Significant Rule Regarding Tawassul and Wasila* (*Qaʿida jalila fī al-tawassul wa al-wasila*), Ibn Taymiyya gives a precise definition of the two terms related to intercession (*shafāʿa*) using the example of the early Muslims. He argues that intercession is part of the broader concepts of *tawassul* and *wasīla*, and concludes that seeking Muhammad's intercession after his death in a non-eschatological sense is forbidden. His argument, below, demonstrates that visiting Muhammad's grave to seek intercession is prohibited:

> Therefore *tawassul* has two correct meanings, both accepted by Muslims. It has also a third meaning, which is unattested in Sunna. One of the two correct meanings accepted by Muslims is the fundament of belief and Islam. It is *tawassul* [meaning here seeking proximity] by belief in him and obedience to him [that is, Muhammad]. The latter is his supplication (*duʿāʾ*) and intercession (*shafāʿa*) as was mentioned before. Both are permitted by the agreement of Muslims. Of this sort is the utterance of ʿUmar ibn al-Khattab: 'Oh God, when we suffered from drought we sought mediation with you through our Prophet and we were given rain. We seek mediation with you by the uncle of our Prophet, so give us rain,' that is, by his supplication (*duʿāʾ*) and intercession (*shafāʿa*). Of this sort is also God's utterance: 'Seek the means [*al-wasīla*, see Qurʾan 4:35] to Him,' that is, the nearness to him through obedience to him. Since the obedience of His Messenger is obedience of God. For He said: 'He who obeys the Messenger, has indeed obeyed God' [Q 4:85]. Such *tawassul* is the fundament of religion and no Muslim can deny it. Regarding *tawassul* by his supplication and intercession as in the utterance of ʿUmar, it is *tawassul* by his supplication, not by himself. That is why they turned [in the mentioned hadith] away from *tawassul* through him

towards *tawassul* through his uncle 'Abbas. Had it been *tawassul* through the Messenger himself, it would have been more appropriate than *tawassul* through 'Abbas. Nevertheless, as they turned away from *tawassul* through the Messenger towards *tawassul* through 'Abbas, it is known that what could have been done during Muhammad's lifetime was hardly to be done after his death – to the contrary of *tawassul*, by which is meant belief in him and obedience to him. This is legal constantly. Therefore, the term *tawassul* has three meanings: first, *tawassul* by paying obedience to Muhammad, and this is a duty without which belief cannot exist. Second, *tawassul* through his supplication (*duʿāʾ*) and intercession (*shafāʿa*). This one existed during his lifetime and will be on the day of resurrection, when people will seek his intercession. Third, *tawassul* through him means to swear to God by himself[107] and ask through him. This was not the practice of the Companions.[108]

Ibn Taymiyya argues that for as long as the Prophet's room was separated from the mosque – that is, until the time of al-Walid ibn ʿAbd al-Malik – nobody entered it for ritual prayer, rubbing or invocational prayer; instead, believers performed acts of worship in the mosque.[109] When the early Muslim community, that is, the Companions of the Prophet and the second generation of their followers, greeted the Prophet and wanted to pray *al-duʿāʾ*, they faced the *qibla*, not the grave – because invocational prayer is, according to one hadith, the essence of devotion and as such belongs exclusively to God. Similarly, with regard to standing (*al-wuqūf*) while greeting the Prophet, Ibn Taymiyya quotes Abu Hanifa's opinion, that in this instance too the *qibla* is to be faced, not the grave – although the majority of imams argued that it was the grave that was to be faced in this case.

According to Ibn Taymiyya, nobody had claimed that the *qibla* was to be faced during invocational prayer. This is to protect God's unicity, because treating graves as places of worship is akin to associating things with God. All imams agreed that the grave was not to be rubbed nor kissed. The same pious deeds that are performed in the Prophet's room – praying (*al-ṣalāt*), greetings (*salām ʿalayhi*), praising (*thanāʾ*), paying respect (*ikrām*), and mentioning the Prophet's merits and good qualities (*dhikr maḥāsin wa faḍāʾil*) – can be performed in other mosques, too. The Prophet said: 'Do not turn my abode into a place of visiting, for your prayers reach me wherever you are.'

Two traditions are of primary importance in this context: 'May Allah curse the Jews and Christians who took the graves of their prophets as places of prayer' and 'Verily, those before you took graves as places of prayer, so do not take graves as mosques, as I forbade you that.' Ibn Taymiyya prohibits travel exclusively for the purpose of visiting the Prophet's grave, but not the custom (*sunna*) of visiting it after praying in his mosque, because that was the way of his Companions. This is because the legal intention of invocational prayer is to ask God's mercy for the Prophet, not to ask the Prophet himself for help or intercession (*shafāʿa*); therefore, there should be no need to go to the Prophet's grave because prayer can reach the Prophet from anywhere. Needless to say, popular practice did not adhere to this distinction.

As we can see, Ibn Taymiyya does address the particular question of invocational prayer (*duʿāʾ*) at the Prophet's grave. This is quite important, because from later reformist literature we learn that Sufis often argue that *duʿāʾ* in general is not a kind of worship. Ibn Taymiyya clearly refutes this, since for him *duʿāʾ* is the core of worship (*mukhkh al-ʿibāda*). Just as a Muslim must face in the direction of the Kaʿba when reciting a ritual prayer (*ṣalāt*), the same applies to invocational prayer.

Moreover, his prohibition on visiting graves as places of prayer is based on Muhammad's prohibition, not on the impurity of such places; this is in line with Muhammad's saying that the whole world is a place of worship, except for graveyards and toilets. Besides, according to a common Muslim belief, the corpses of prophets and pious men do not decay – they have a sweet odour. Of course, the true reason for the prohibition was that Muhammad was concerned that people could be tempted to worship the dead (*khawf al-fitna bi-l-qabr*). This was a concern shared by al-Shafiʿi and other early Muslims, who commanded that all graves should be levelled indiscriminately (*taswiyat al-qubūr*) and anything that might arouse such a temptation was to be effaced (*taʿfiya mā yatafattan bihi minhā*).[110] Ibn Taymiyya mentions another means of preventing this temptation, namely, the exhumation and burial of the Prophet Daniel's corpse, whose grave the second caliph ʿUmar had effaced because his governor, Abu Musa al-Ashʿari, had informed him in a letter that people were asking the prophet for rain. ʿUmar reportedly ordered Abu Musa to dig up thirty graves in daylight and then bury the prophet's corpse, unmarked, in one of them at night.[111]

As for the *ziyāra* itself, for Ibn Taymiyya it represented not only a legal, but also a semantic issue. Although he was a fierce critic of *ziyāra*, he makes a distinction between heretical *ziyāra* (*ziyāra bidʿiya*) and legal *ziyāra* (*ziyāra sharʿiya*, *ziyāra mashrūʿa*), and only pronounces the heretical and innovative *ziyāra* illegal. According to him, *ziyāra* is a legal term (*ism sharʿī*), but its original meaning was changed such that it came to denote heretical practices. For that reason, he argues, imam Malik ibn Anas disliked saying 'I visited the Prophet's grave,' because people understood it to refer to the prohibited way. Ibn Taymiyya defines a legal visit in the following way: to greet the dead and petition for them in the manner of the prayer for the dead (*ṣalāt ʿalā al-janāza*), as the Prophet instructed his Companions when they were visiting graves. God recompenses the living for praying on behalf of a dead believer, as long as he is not a hypocrite or an unbeliever.[112]

In this legally permissible act of *ziyāra*, the living do not have any need for the dead, nor do they make any direct request from the dead person (*masʾala*) or seek intercession (*tawassul*) on their own behalf. On the contrary, God has mercy upon the dead as a result of the prayers of the living for the dead and their act of charity towards the dead, and God recompenses the living for their act.[113] The point is that legal visits are useful for the dead on account of the charitable behaviour of the living, and are simultaneously useful for the living, but only because God might reward them. Besides, the merit of such a visit is due to memento mori (*iʿtibār*, *ʿibra*). Accordingly, the Prophet abrogated his first ban regarding grave visiting: 'I was prohibiting you from visiting graves, but now you can visit them, because it will remind you of the Afterworld.'[114] It is also possible to visit the graves of unbelievers – because the Prophet himself visited his mother's grave, crying so much that it made bystanders cry too. The Prophet said: 'I asked my Lord for permission to request forgiveness for her, but He did not allow me that. So I asked him for permission to visit her, and he gave it to me. So visit graves, because they remind you of death.'

To support his arguments, Ibn Taymiyya invokes the aforementioned hadith about setting out for journeys for the purpose of visiting graves. After visiting the Prophet's grave in a legal way it is also desirable to visit the graves of the martyrs of the battle of Uhud and to pray in the al-Qubaʾ Mosque, the first mosque built by the Prophet. Ibn Taymiyya criticises hadiths encouraging visits to the Prophet's grave, pronouncing them all forgeries and lies. According to him, the most famous of this kind are: 'He who performs the pilgrimage and does not visit me, has shunned me'; and 'Whoever visits my grave must ask me for intercession.' Ibn Taymiyya notes that although some of these hadiths are part of Daraqutni's collection, they are not included in the main hadith collections of al-Bukhari, Muslim, Abu Dawud and al-Nasa'i, nor are they part of the *Musnad* of Ibn Hanbal. He observes that with regard to visiting the Prophet's grave, the ulama rely only upon hadiths according to which the Prophet must be greeted (*al-salām wa al-ṣalāt 'alayhi*). Ibn Taymiyya's criticism of such hadiths is based on their contents encouraging visits – simply because they contradict the principle of monotheism of cult.

Al-Dhahabi, a pupil of Ibn Taymiyya who is believed to be a reliable source, describes his master's funeral: 'It was estimated that some sixty thousand people were there, and fifteen thousand women in the street [who] wept and grieved for him all the more. He was buried in the Sufi cemetery beside his brother. People paid visits to his grave, and he was seen in a number of good dreams.'[115] Some authors point to Ibn Taymiyya's burial in the Sufi cemetery as an apparent paradox, although Makdisi notes that some writers, under the delusion that Ibn Taymiyya was a sworn enemy of Sufism, wanted to see this as an ironic twist of fate and that in fact it was nothing of the kind; for there was nothing more natural for Ibn Taymiyya, a Sufi, than that he should be buried among Sufis.[116] The fact that Ibn Taymiyya had his own cenotaph was not criticised even by his disciples, yet this is incongruous not only with his own ideas, but also with the views adopted in a more simplistic way by the current Salafi shaykhs – however humble his grave in Damascus may appear.

Ibn Taymiyya left an uneasy legacy for his colleagues and for subsequent generations of ulama of the Mamluk and later eras.[117] More than two centuries after his death, learned Muslim scholars like al-Suyuti (1445–1505) and al-Sakhawi (1428–97) still found it necessary to refute Ibn Taymiyya's arguments. One of the most eloquent counter-opinions was offered by the Shafi'i chief judge of Damascus, Taqi al-Din al-Subki, in his *Shifa' al-siqam fi ziyārat khayr al-anam* (*The Remedy for the Ill in Visiting the Best of Mankind*), originally to be named *Shann al-ghara' 'ala man ankara safar al-ziyara* (*Launching an Attack on the One Who Denies Travel for the Ziyara*). In this work, al-Subki examines hadiths regarding the institution of *ziyāra* in their abundance (such as 'My mediation is assured for whoever visits my grave' or 'He who performs the pilgrimage and does not visit me, has shunned me') and found clear support for it. Al-Subki also emphasises the fact that visiting Muhammad's grave was a well-established practice from the earliest period and the first generations of Muslims disagreed only over whether one should first visit Mecca and then Medina or the other way around. Muhammad himself visited the graves of the martyrs of the Battle of Uhud in the al-Baqi' cemetery. Al-Subki also mentions examples of Hanbali scholars and jurists who did not oppose the practice either, or who recommended it outright, namely, Abu Bakr al-Ajiri (d. 970), Ibn Batta (d. 997) or Ibn Qudama al-Maqdisi (d. 1223). Based on the textual evidence and a point-by-point refutation of Ibn Taymiyya's opinions, al-Subki concludes that the Prophet's Sunna commands visiting tombs in general, primarily in order to contemplate the inevitability of death.[118]

* * *

The views on graves in Sunni Islam, visiting them and the building of funerary structures over them, have undergone a long and complicated development process. In pre-Islamic times the cult of the dead was probably widespread, as was the practice of visiting the graves of ancestors, which were ascribed a solemn significance. With the emergence of Islam, however, a new trend, discrediting pagan rituals, emerged. Muhammad himself, if we are to believe the Islamic tradition, did not have clear-cut opinions regarding such issues. We are told that he feared that Muslims could emulate other monotheistic religions, especially in venerating the dead, and that graves could become places of idolatry and polytheism. For the latter reason, Muhammad also prohibited the building of funerary monuments. Yet the practice of his immediate successors added another layer to such debates. Muhammad's grave itself became a frequently visited place and the existence of other funerary structures, or the building of new ones, helped to transform Medina with its holy grave landscape into an important site and to promote it as an Islamic holy city. Further development was then characterised by a degree of discordancy between the ideals expressed by a number of purists and everyday reality. While the majority of the ulama did not broadly criticise all grave-related customs and accepted the visiting of shrines as unproblematic, rather focusing – if at all – on appropriate modes of behaviour and modesty, a minority of scholars opined otherwise. The first concerted opposition to these practices emerged among Hanbali scholars, culminating in the pronouncements of Ibn Taymiyya, the foremost and still today the most widely quoted critic of 'heretical' practices in Sunni Islam.

The main concern of this line of thought was that the veneration of saints and associated visits might lead to religious confusion and the distortion of Islamic identity. This is not to say that more radical voices condemning grave visiting were non-existent. Ibn Taymiyya thought of himself rather as representing the moderate position. Moreover, despite a certain degree of controversy associated with his name in religious history, as a Hanbali (both in theology and law, in spite of his claims of absolute *ijtihād*), he was part of orthodox Sunni Islam, even though he did not represent its mainstream thinking. He believed that it would be unsustainable to absolutely forbid grave visiting since it is well attested in the hadith. Moreover, no jurist and theologian possessed the power to eradicate this phenomenon, which had been nurtured by earlier Muslim dynasties. We have no evidence that Ibn Taymiyya confronted the Mamluk sultans regarding their monumental architecture and tombs. On the contrary, he was rather cooperative and loyal, while making an effort to regulate funeral architecture and grave veneration in general in order to defend the identity of Islam in the face of religious syncretism, Judaism and Christianity (the latter was largely dealt with by Ibn Qayyim al-Jawziyya). It seems that Ibn Taymiyya's legal opinions regarding *ziyāra* were to some extent used only as the pretext for his persecution, as he, in fact, challenged the three pillars of Mamluk religious authority: law, Sufism and theology. He questioned the religious authority of the established ulama by criticising the *madhhab* system (claiming *ijtihād*) supported by Mamluks, Sufi leaders and religious practices connected with heretical *ziyāra*, as well as Ash'ari theology.

Nevertheless, such purist ideals were in sharp contrast to the widespread folk religious practices and beliefs and the monumentalism supported by Muslim rulers. Very early on, probably even much earlier than the eleventh century, when constructed tombs and shrines had become common in the larger Middle East region, the building of spectacular funeral and commemorative monuments began to flourish. From the perspective of the state or the ruling dynasties, this provided a significant means of enhancing their personal legitimacy and popularity. Besides, almost all Muslims, including the rulers, ulama and ordinary believers, participated in rituals such as the veneration of saints and visits to their tombs and shrines. In any case, the period between the emergence of Islam and, roughly, the fifteenth century laid the foundations for the subsequent, uneasy debates regarding issues related to grave visiting.

Notes

1. Edward Pococke, *Specimen historiae Arabum* (Oxford, 1649).
2. See, among others, Bergmann, *De religione Arabum anteislamica*; Osiander, 'Studien über die vorislämische Religion der Araber'; Krehl, *Über die Religion der vorislamischen Araber*; or Smith, *Lectures on the Religion of the Semites*; and Smith, *Kinship and Marriage in Early Arabia*.
3. For a detailed description of these works and their later followers, especially as far as idolatry and the cult of ancestors in the pre-Islamic Bedouin society are concerned, see Henninger, 'Pre-Islamic Bedouin Religion', pp. 3–22.
4. In later times on this topic, cf. Tritton, 'Muslim Funeral Customs', pp. 653–61; Grutter, 'Arabische Bestattungsbräuche in frühislamischer Zeit' (1954), pp. 147–73 and (1957), pp. 168–94; or esp. Taylor, *In the Vicinity of the Righteous*. On funeral rituals in early Islam see also Zaman, 'Death, Funeral Processions, and the Articulation of Religious Authority in Early Islam', pp. 27–58.
5. Cf. also Abdesselem, *Le thème de la mort dans la poésie arabe*.
6. Cf. Chelhod, *Le Sacrifice chez les Arabes*; Henninger, 'Menschenopfer bei den Arabern', pp. 721–805; or Wheeler, 'Gift of the Body in Islam', pp. 341–88.
7. Cf. Goldziher, 'Le sacrifice de la chevelure chez les Arabes', pp. 49–52; or Henninger, 'Zur Frage des Haaropfers bei den Semiten', pp. 349–68.
8. Findings from rare archaeological sites have confirmed that the habit of erecting stones at graves was not general and most likely happened only in very particular cases. For example, in the al-Aflaj area of central Arabia, a large number of subterranean tombs were found with structures only slightly elevated above ground level, presumably from the Hellenistic era. See al-Saud, 'Central Arabia during the Early Hellenistic Period', p. 116. Findings from the United Arab Emirates and Oman suggest that the primary concern in the siting of graves was that the dead should not be disturbed, be it by flood flows or by animals. For

this reason, graves were usually sited on raised ground or natural terraces. Some of them had walls, branches or biers to protect them from animals. See Lancaster and Lancaster, 'Observations on Death, Burial, Graves and Graveyards at Various Locations in Ra's al-Khaimah Emirate, UAE, and Musandan *wilayat*, Oman, Using Local Concerns', p. 321. For the shapes of graves and customs related to visiting them in pre-Islamic times, see also Schöller, *The Living and the Dead in Islam*, pp. 171–7. For an interesting comparison from Syria, see Bradbury, 'Presencing the Past', pp. 200–18, or Frank, 'Funeral Practices at Tell Masaikh (Syria)', pp. 93–120. A general overview of mortuary/burial archaeology in Islamic lands is provided in Petersen, 'The Archaeology of Death and Burial in the Islamic World', pp. 241–58, or Insoll, *The Archaeology of Islam*. Cf. also Weeks, *Death and Burial in Arabia and Beyond*.

9. Munt, *The Holy City of Medina*, p. 23.
10. Goldziher, 'On the Veneration of the Dead in Paganism and Islam', p. 211.
11. See Musil, *V posvátném Hedžázu (In the Sacred Hijaz)*, p. 146. The existence of a similar tradition in Yemen is attested by Freya Stark (1893–1993), a British explorer who visited southern Arabia in 1935. She, besides taking rare photographic material, speaks of the habit of keeping a strip of long hair (*gamzūz*) from childhood, and the ancient belief that cutting it is a formal business to be performed by the grave of an ancestor or local saint. Stark, *Seen in the Hadhramaut*, p. 132.
12. Musil, *V posvátném Hedžázu (In the Sacred Hijaz)*, p. 147; Musil, *V zemi královny Zenobie (In the Land of the Queen Zenobia)*, p. 182; or Musil *Mezi Šammary (Among the Shammars)*, pp. 289–90.
13. Musil, *V biblickém ráji: Z mých cest při středním Eufratu a Tigridu (In the Biblical Paradise: From My Travels to the Central Euphrates and Tigris)*, pp. 58–9.
14. See, for instance, Westermarck, *Ritual and Belief in Morocco*, esp. vol. 2, pp. 434–41, 460, 493–5 and 499–501. For further analysis of the specific case of the Maghrib, see esp. Seesemann, 'Ziyara: Funktionen und Bedeutungen in der Tiganiya (Westafrika)', pp. 157–69; Gellner, *Saints of the Atlas*; Eickelman, *Moroccan Islam*; K. L. Brown, *People of Salé*.
15. Cf. Dieste, *Health and Ritual in Morocco*, p. 163.
16. Massignon, 'La Cité des morts au Caire', p. 56.
17. See Peake, *A Commentary on the Bible*, p. 208. Cf. also Jeremiah 9:26, 25:23 and 49:32.

18. Most of these hadiths are considered valid and come from the canonical collections from the chapters 'Kitab al-jana'iz'. On the evolution of some of these hadiths, see Schöller, *The Living and the Dead in Islam*, pp. 13–22.
19. Early Islamic grave-related habits are described by Grütter, 'Arabische Bestattungsbräuche in frühislamischer Zeit' (1954), pp. 147–73 and (1957), pp. 168–94.
20. For an analysis of the end of Muhammad's life in early Islamic memory, as well as the controversy surrounding the circumstances of his burial, see Shoemaker, *The Death of a Prophet*, ch. 2. A controversy also existed regarding the exact arrangement of the graves of the Prophet, Abu Bakr and 'Umar in the enclosure, cf. Munt, *The Holy City of Medina*, p. 110. In later times, the huge mystery around Muhammad's grave and whether he was actually buried in his mosque in Medina even drove some foreigners to look for the answers. A. J. B. Wavell, who visited Islam's holy cities at the beginning of the twentieth century, speaks of a legend he heard in Medina that many years ago two Europeans had entered the city in disguise and attempted to tunnel through from their house into the mausoleum. However, they were discovered in the process and crucified. See Wavell, *A Modern Pilgrim in Mecca*, p. 95.
21. See Schöller, *The Living and the Dead in Islam*, pp. 192–3.
22. al-Samhudi, *Kitab wafa' al-wafa'*, vol. 1, p. 484.
23. Cited from al-Harigi, 'The Relationship between the Prophet's Mosque and its Physical Environment', pp. 37–8.
24. On the reconstruction of Muhammad's burial site and mosque, see Halevi, *Muhammad's Grave*, pp. 191–6. For the general history of the Mosque of the Prophet in Medina, see, for example, Sauvaget, *La mosquée omeyyade de Médine*; or Bisheh, 'The Mosque of the Prophet at Madinah'.
25. Munt, *The Holy City of Medina*, pp. 98, 119, 125.
26. Ibid., p. 137. For a general description of the topography of Medina, with a detailed account of the burial places of the Prophet's wives and children and the al-Baqi' cemetery, see al-Samhudi, *Kitab wafa' al-wafa'*.
27. For a discussion of the transformation of Medina into a pilgrimage site, see mainly Munt, *The Holy City of Medina*, esp. pp. 123–83.
28. For a description of the opposition to tombstones and tombstone inscriptions, see Halevi, *Muhammad's Grave*, pp. 32–42. Cf. also Schöller, *The Living and the*

Dead in Islam, esp. pp. 315–597. If there is a general tendency in the inscription culture, it is that over the centuries religious content has reduced and been replaced primarily with the lineage and titles of the deceased.

29. Cf. Hillenbrand, *Islamic Architecture*, p. 253.
30. Halevi, *Muhammad's Grave*, p. 36.
31. See Meri, *The Cult of Saints*, p. 126; or Leisten, 'Between Orthodoxy and Exegesis', pp. 13–14. For an example of one such prescriptive guideline, *Murshid al-zuwwar ila qubur al-abrar* written by Ibn 'Uthman, and its analysis, see Taylor, *In the Vicinity of the Righteous*, pp. 70–9.
32. Leisten, 'Between Orthodoxy and Exegesis', p. 16.
33. Schöller, *The Living and the Dead in Islam*, pp. 203–5, 219–20.
34. Cf. al-Haytami, *al-Fatawa al-kubra al-fiqhiyya*, vol. 2, 'Kitab al-jana'iz'.
35. Cf. Taylor, *In the Vicinity of the Righteous*, pp. 210–18.
36. Cf. also Schöller, *The Living and the Dead in Islam*, pp. 25–6.
37. This belief was – besides the popularly venerated shrines across the region – also associated with Muhammad's tomb. The earth from around it was used in powdered form, usually for the treatment of eye diseases.
38. Fierro presents the following list of books against innovations: Ibn Waddah, *Kitab al-bidaʿ*; al-Turtushi, *Kitab al-hawadith wa-l-bidaʿ*; Ibn al-Jawzi, *Talbis Iblis*; al-Maqdisi, *Ittibaʿ al-sunan wa-jtinab al-bidaʿ*; Abu Shama, *al-Baʿith ʿala inkar al-bidaʿ wa-l-hawadith*; Ibn Taymiyya, *Kitab iqtidaʾ al-sirat al-mustaqim mukhalafat ashab al-jahim*; Ibn al-Hajj, *Madkhal al-sharʿ al-sharif*; al-Shatibi, *Al-iʿtisam*; al-Turkumani, *al-Lumaʿ fi l-hawadith wa-l-bidaʿ*; Zarruq al-Fasi, *ʿUddat al-murid al-sadiq/al-Bidaʿ wa-l-hawadith*; al-Suyuti, *al-Amr bi-l-ittibaʿ wa-l-nahy ʿan al-ibtidaʿ*; Uthman ibn Fudi, *Ihyaʾ al-sunna wa-ikhmad al-bidʿa*. See Fierro, 'The Treatises Against Innovations', pp. 207–9.
39. Abu Shama, *al-Baʿith ʿala inkar al-bidaʿ wa al-hawadith*, p. 91. The editor of the book, Muhammad Muhibb al-Din Abu Zayd, disagrees with the author on that point. He makes this comment in a footnote: 'Every bidʿa is repugnant (*mustaqbaha*) and aberration (*dalāla*) as in the hadith "Every bidʿa is aberration."' According to him, innovations should not be divided into good (*hasan*) and repugnant (*qabīh*).
40. al-Turtushi, *Kitab al-hawadith wa al-bidaʿ*, pp. 304, 336, 338.
41. Taylor, *In the Vicinity of the Righteous*, p. 191.

42. For the legal debates around women and their visits to graves, see Schöller, *The Living and the Dead in Islam*, pp. 36–8, 39–40. For more on the observance of some women's rituals in modern times in the Gulf, see Doumato, *Getting God's Ear*.
43. See Juynboll, *Muslim Tradition*, pp. 102–8.
44. Later on, a typical diatribe against women visiting the dead was expressed by Ibn al-Hajj (d. 1336), an Egyptian Maliki jurist and a contemporary of Ibn Taymiyya: 'Let us now speak of women and their conduct when visiting the graves! They ride to and fro on donkeys, and the muleteers touch them and lay their arms around them when they mount or get off. He will put his hand on her leg and she will lay her hand on his shoulder, both her hand and wrist being uncovered and unveiled . . . It also happens that the woman gossips with the muleteer and speaks to him as if he were her husband or somebody else of her family. What a wondrous thing, then, that her husband or somebody else in charge of her either witnesses this scene directly or knows that it happens when they are not present! . . . When the women arrive in the cemetery, things become even worse and more disgusting, because their presence leads to numerous scandalous acts, such as women who during their visit walk together with men at night, that is, being hidden from view (by the darkness) and there are many buildings easy to disappear in; the women will uncover their cases and other parts, quite as if they were with their husbands in privacy. Moreover, they will converse with unacquainted men, they will jest and play, they will laugh and sing a lot . . .' Quoted from Schöller, *The Living and the Dead in Islam*, pp. 39–40.
45. For further details about the shaping of Kufan traditions and Kufan attitudes towards women's role in funerary rites, see Halevi, *Muhammad's Grave*, pp. 127–42, 235–8.
46. Quoted from Cuffel, 'From Practice to Polemic', p. 412.
47. Taylor, 'Reevaluating the Shi'i Role in the Development of Monumental Islamic Funerary Architecture', p. 4. See also Y. Raghib, 'Les prémiers monuments funéraires de l'Islam', *Annales Islamologiques*, 9 (1970).
48. Creswell, *The Muslim Architecture of Egypt*, vol. 1, p. 111. It is important to mention, however, that even today the issue of the function of that *qubba* remains uncertain; it is unclear whether the domed building was constructed as a mausoleum for the caliph al-Muntasir or the imams al-'Askari and al-Hadi, or whether it was completely profane.

49. For an interesting debate on this topic, see Leisten, 'Between Orthodoxy and Exegesis', pp. 12–22.
50. See al-Ibrashy, 'Death, Life and the Barzakh in Cairo's Cemeteries'. For the phenomenon of the al-Qarafa cemetery, see Taylor, *In the Vicinity of the Righteous*, pp. 15–61.
51. al-Harithy, 'The Four Madrasahs in the Complex of Sultan Hasan (1356–61)'.
52. Berkey, *The Transmission of Knowledge*, p. 146.
53. Cf. Wheeler, *Mecca and Eden*, pp. 87–9.
54. Lambton, *Continuity and Change in Medieval Persia*, p. 35.
55. Abou El Fadl, *The Search for Beauty in Islam*, pp. 224–5.
56. Peirce, *Morality Tales*, p. 62. See also Scherberger, 'The Confrontation between Sunni and Shiʻi Empires', p. 58; and Şahin, *Empire and Power in the Reign of the Süleyman*, p. 98.
57. al-Bahrani, *al-Kashkul*, vol. 1, p. 274.
58. For Imam al-Shafiʻi and his post-mortal fate, see Kecia, *Imam Shafiʻi*, esp. ch. 6.
59. *Ibn Khallikan's Biographic Dictionary*, trans. by B(aro)N Mac Guckin de Slane (Paris: 1843), vol. 4, p. 45.
60. Ibn al-Jawzi, *Virtues of the Imam Ahmad ibn Hanbal*, vol. 2, pp. 423–32.
61. For the debate about the true location of Ahmad ibn Hanbal's tomb, see, for instance, at: http://www.ahlalhdeeth.com/vb/showthread.php?t=359397, last accessed 9 August 2016.
62. *Rihlat Ibn Jubayr*, p. 173.
63. For a great analysis of the veneration of saints in medieval Islam, see, among others, Meri, *The Cult of Saints*; Grehan, *Twilight of the Saints*; Taylor, *In the Vicinity of the Righteous*; Talmon-Heller, *Islamic Piety in Medieval Syria*; Shoshan, *Popular Culture in Medieval Cairo*; Chiffoleau and Madoeuf, *Les pèlerinages au Maghreb et au Moyen-Orient*; or Fartacek, *Pilgerstätten in der syrischen Peripherie*. Cf. also Goldziher, 'Veneration of Saints in Islam', pp. 255–341.
64. For a more detailed explanation of the shift that occurred in the twelfth century and the construction of various monuments, see Mulder, *The Shrines of the ʻAlids in Medieval Syria*, esp. pp. 251–3. Cf. also Cobb, 'Virtual Sacrality', pp. 35–55; Jalabert, 'Comment Damas est devenue une métropole Islamique', pp. 13–42; or Frenkel, 'Baybars and the Sacred Geography of *Bilad al-Sham*', pp. 153–70.
65. Grehan, *Twilight of the Saints*, pp. 86, 188.
66. Ibid., pp. 56–63. Cf. also Albera and Couroucli, *Religions traversées*.

67. See, for instance, Prager, 'Alawi Ziyāra Tradition and Its Interreligious Dimensions', pp. 41–61.
68. Kressel, Bar-Zvi and Abu-Rabi'a, *The Charm of Graves*, p. 40.
69. As extensively argued by Mulder, *The Shrines of the 'Alids in Medieval Syria*.
70. Grehan, *Twilight of the Saints*, pp. 165, 188.
71. 'Abd al-Rahman al-Dimashqi (d. 1725) puts the total number of prophets buried in southern Syria alone (including Palestine) at around 1,700. Cf. Grehan, *Twilight of the Saints*, p. 87. The village of Awarta even hosted a shrine to 'Forty Prophets'.
72. The reuse of architectural fragments and archaeological remains (for example, from ruined Roman–Byzantine structures) for tombs has been widely recorded. Cf. Bradbury, 'Presencing the Past', pp. 208–15.
73. According, among many others, to Ibn al-Zayyat, *al-Kawakib al-sayyara fi tartib al-ziyara*, p. 30.
74. For a general discussion of pilgrimage, see esp. Turner and Turner, *Image and Pilgrimage in Christian Culture*.
75. For the examination of women's involvement in festivals, see, for example, Cuffel, 'From Practice to Polemic', pp. 401–19.
76. Meri, *The Cult of Saints*, p. 59.
77. Ibid., pp. 262–72. Cf. also Hillenbrand, *Islamic Architecture*; or Leisten, *Architektur für Tote*.
78. For their treatment, see Wheeler, *Mecca and Eden*, pp. 99–122.
79. For a discussion of pilgrimage guides, see al-Harawi, *Guide des lieux de pèlerinage*, pp. xxvi–xlii; or Meri, *The Cult of Saints*, pp. 141–67. For a useful overview of visiting guides to the Maghrib, Egypt, Levant, Persia and the Arabian Peninsula, see Schöller, *The Living and the Dead in Islam*, pp. 295–314. For the specific case of travel itineraries to the Qarafa Cemetery in Cairo, see Taylor, *In the Vicinity of the Righteous*.
80. This is not to say that the advocates of *ziyāra* did not rely on hadith too. They did, but on quite different reports, many of them being gathered in Daraqutni's collection of hadiths.
81. Ibn Taymiyya, *Kitab iqtida' al-sirat al-mustaqim mukhalafat ashab al-jahim*, p. 40.
82. For the early generations of Hanbalis, see Meri, *The Cult of Saints*, pp. 126–30. For Ibn 'Aqil's opinions on visiting graves, see Makdisi, *Ibn Aqil*, pp. 209–13.

83. Quoted from Leisten, 'Between Orthodoxy and Exegesis', p. 14.
84. As aptly noted by Taylor, *In the Vicinity of the Righteous*, p. 168.
85. There are rumours circulating especially among some Kurdish intellectuals that Ibn Taymiyya was of Kurdish origin. Although these are sometimes reflected in academic literature, such as Muhammad Abu Zahra's biography of Ibn Taymiyya, there is hardly any biographical evidence to prove this.
86. For an outstanding study on *ziyāra*, see esp. Taylor, *In the Vicinity of the Righteous*. See also Schöller's second volume of *The Living and the Dead in Islam*. For Ibn Taymiyya's positions specifically, cf. Olesen, *Culte des saints et pèlerinages chez Ibn Taymiyya*; Memon, *Ibn Taymiya's Struggle against Popular Religion*; or Kabbani, *Die Heiligenverehrung im Urteil Ibn Taimīyas und seiner Zeitgenossen*. Laoust's *Essai sur les doctrines sociales et politiques de Taki-d-Din Ahmad b. Taimiya* still remains a useful study on Ibn Taymiyya.
87. In some Western traditions, 'Orthodox' and 'reformer' may be seen to be at odds, but in the eyes of the Salafis the two go hand in hand, as the Arabic word *tajdīd* (renewal) implies a return to Islam as practised and professed by the Prophet, *ṣaḥāba* and other *salaf*. Ibn Taymiyya defines Orthodoxy, the only Saved Sect, as follows: 'Those who adhered to the pure Islam, not contaminated with admixtures, became Sunnis' (*ṣāra al-mutamassikūn bi-l-islām al-maḥḍ al-khāliṣ ʿan al-shawb hum ahl al-sunna wa-l-jamāʿa*), see al-ʿUthaymin, *Sharh al-ʿaqida al-wasitiyya*, p. 675. These admixtures are all innovations (*bidaʿ*) opposed to Sunna, and as such they are regarded as heresy.
88. For Ibn Taymiyya's theological opinions regarding God's attributes and names, see Ibn Taymiyya, *al-Asmaʾ wa al-sifat*. For a good survey of anthropomorphism, see also Swartz, *A Medieval Critique of Anthropomorphism*.
89. Muhammad ibn Abi Bakr was called Ibn Qayyim al-Jawziyya after his father, who was a director (*qayyim*) of the famous Hanbali school in Damascus, al-Jawziyya. The scholar is not to be confused with another Hanbali scholar Ibn al-Jawzi, the eponym of the mentioned school. Ibn Qayyim al-Jawziyya was a jurist, theologian, Qurʾanic exegete, linguist and a scholar of hadith.
90. For a different interpretation, see Krawietz, 'Ibn Qayyim al-Jawziyah: His Life and Works', pp. 19–64.
91. Ibn Rajab, *al-Dhayl ʿala tabaqat al-hanabila*, vol. 5, p. 176.
92. al-Shawkani, *al-Badr al-taliʿ bi-mahasin man baʿda al-qarn al-sabiʿ*, vol. 2, p. 143.

93. See 'Ibn Qayyim al-Djawziyya', *EI2*.
94. 'Ibn Taymiyya', *EI2*.
95. Ibn Taymiyya, *Manasik al-hajj wa al-'umra*, pp. 45–6.
96. al-'Uthaymin, *Sharh al-'Aqida al-wasitiyya*, vol. 2, pp. 297–306.
97. See Ibn Taymiyya, *al-'Aqida al-wasitiyya*, p. 131, fn 2. *Al-Durar al-sunniyya* hosted by the domain dorar.net, an encyclopaedic project led by a Saudi citizen 'Alawi ibn 'Abd al-Qadir al-Saqqaf, is an example of a project that omits this passage from the main text.
98. See Kister, 'You Shall Only Set Out for Three Mosques', pp. 173–96.
99. Ibn Taymiyya, *Majmu' at al-fatawa*, vol. 27, p. 10.
100. Ibid.
101. Ibid., p. 12.
102. Grabar, 'The Umayyad Dome of the Rock in Jerusalem', p. 35. See also Mathews, 'A Muslim Iconoclast (Ibn Taymiyyeh)'.
103. Grabar, 'The Umayyad Dome of the Rock in Jerusalem', p. 44.
104. Ibn Taymiyya, *Majmu' at al-fatawa*, vol. 27, p. 12.
105. See the treatise in Arabic edited by Mathews, 'A Muslim Iconoclast (Ibn Taymiyyeh)', p. 9.
106. 'Uthaymin, *Sharh al-'aqida al-wasitiyya*, vol. 2, pp. 168–79.
107. As is the instance of 'I ask you by virtue of your prophets' (*as'aluka bi-haqq anbiyā'ika*).
108. Ibn Taymiyya, *Qa'ida jalila fi al-tawassul wa al-wasila*, pp. 85–6.
109. Ibn Taymiyya, *Majmu' at al-fatawa*, vol. 27, p. 48.
110. For this argument, see ibid., p. 70.
111. Ibid.
112. Ibid., p. 44.
113. Ibid. In the translation of this passage in the entry 'Ziyara', *EI2*: 'and God the Exalted has mercy upon the living who supplicate for the dead', we see a misreading of Ibn Taymiyya's position.
114. Ibn Taymiyya, *Majmu' at al-fatawa*, vol. 27, p. 69. There are many versions of the hadith.
115. Bori, 'A New Source for the Biography of Ibn Taymiyya', p. 348. See also Ibn 'Abd al-Hadi, *al-'Uqud al-durriyya min manaqib shaykh al-islam Ibn Taymiyya*, p. 387.
116. Makdisi, 'Ibn Taymiyya: A Sufi of the Qadiriya Order', p. 124.

117. For the reception of Ibn Taymiyya's writings, cf. also Schöller, *The Living and the Dead in Islam*, pp. 76–82.
118. For a comprehensive analysis of al-Subki, see Taylor, *In the Vicinity of the Righteous*, pp. 195–210. It is fair to say, however, that even in the eyes of al-Subki the legality of *ziyāra* did not apply to all without reservation, as the question of women visiting graves was a much more complicated issue for him.

2

Early Wahhabism and the Beginnings of Modern Salafism

All inhabitants of Arabia, both sedentary and nomads, believe in one, personal, invisible and omnipresent Allah. Among nomads, and camel keepers in particular, this belief is reminiscent in terms of its rituals of the religion of the Old Testament Patriarchs. They have no holy sites, objects or mediators between man and Allah, neither do they have fixed prayers. They are Muslims only by name; in fact, they pay little attention to Islamic prescriptions. Meanwhile, the sedentary people, who dwell in various settlements, do have their own holy places, such as holy trees, rocks and springs, at which they perform prayers. They venerate the dead as their patrons and build gravestones for them, of varying size. The sedentary people are all reliant on the good will of the Nomads, because only with their permission can they leave their settlements to make trade journeys or other trips from one oasis to another, or to populated regions. No wonder that it seems to many a thoughtful town dweller that the Nomads' one Allah is more powerful than all the sedentary peoples' patrons put together, and that the Nomads' rituals are more effective. This reasoning usually results in an effort to erase the religious extremes thriving in the oasis, and to make religious life simpler and more profound, in the manner of the Nomads. There has hardly been a single century, in which such a tendency did not appear.

Musil, *Mezi Šammary* (*Among the Shammars*), p. 79

The practice of Muhammad ibn Abdul-Wahhaab was truly completely consistent with the teachings of the Prophet Muhammad . . . however averse the people may be to that fact. One can say with certainty that neither the

Prophet ... nor any of his Companions ever built a mosque, mausoleum, tomb or structure over any grave.

> Zarabozo, *The Life, Teachings and Influence of Muhammad ibn Abdul-Wahhaab*, p. 261

From the fifteenth century onwards, Hanbali teachings decreased in importance in the Arab world, mostly due to the lack of political support and funding, the only exception being in the Arabian Peninsula, where it survived. This was mostly due to the influence of Hanbali religious scholars from Baghdad, as well as those travellers who passed through the Najd on their way to Mecca and Medina. While the Mamluks preferred to support the opponents of the Hanbalis, the Ottomans openly encouraged the expansion of the Hanafi–Maturidi 'symbiosis' and made it the official school of their empire. This environment, which prevented any further development of Hanbalism, changed in the middle of the eighteenth century, when it received a new impulse from the very centre of the Arabian Peninsula. By the eighteenth century, Hanbalism in all likelihood had achieved the status of being the leading tradition in the Najd.[1] However, well into the middle of the twentieth century, the ulama of the Hanbali–Wahhabi establishment relied only on a very select list of religious writings.[2]

The Wahhabi movement emerged in eighteenth-century Najd, in the heart of the Arabian Peninsula. It strictly opposed folk practices and rules that 'differed' from tradition and from the Qur'an and the Sunna, and also combated the cult venerating righteous men and ancestors who were believed to intercede on behalf of the living. Ibn Ghannam (d. 1810), one of the two contemporary chroniclers of the early Wahhabi movement, described the religious situation in Arabia at the time of the religious reformer Muhammad ibn 'Abd al-Wahhab (1703–92) in deliberately dark terms. At this time the worship of stones and sacred trees, at least we are told so, had become quite common, along with the veneration of the graves of saints. People would either make requests directly to the saint or seek their intercession with God.[3] His words became a standard description of pre-Wahhabi Arabia and were used in most of the Saudi chronicles which applauded Ibn 'Abd al-Wahhab's goal of reviving the pure religion by returning to the tradition of the pious ancestors and through the Qur'an and hadiths. However, this image painted by the Wahhabis of the idolatrous nature of pre-Wahhabi Arabia, and almost universally taken for granted, does not need to fully reflect the reality.[4]

The movement established by Ibn ʿAbd al-Wahhab in its fight against popular religious habits widely drew upon similar ideas and concepts elaborated upon by Ibn Taymiyya. Ibn ʿAbd al-Wahhab's writings do not stand out for their sophistication; they essentially summarise classical Hanbali teaching. That Ibn ʿAbd al-Wahhab's doctrine contained such a strict opposition to the veneration of shrines comes in contrast to the teaching of other reformers of his time, such as Shah Waliullah (d. 1762) in India, ʿUthman ibn Fudi (d. 1817) in west Africa or others whose reformist zeal was far less concerned with these issues. Yet before the rise of Ibn ʿAbd al-Wahhab's movement, the same principles had caused a short-lived religious riot in October 1711 – known as the 'pre-Wahhabi *fitna* (strife)' – among mostly illiterate Turkic soldiers in Egypt, led by a Turkic student of religion. Fundamentalist fervour, inspired by Ibn Taymiyya's teachings, led them to attack Sufi institutions, rituals and beliefs. Among other things, they opposed the practice of burning candles and oil lamps at the graves of saints and kissing their thresholds, and labelled those pursuing such practices as unbelievers. The movement also drove Muslims to destroy the domes that were built over graves.[5]

The cult of the dead was widespread in the Islamic world, if we are to believe the numbers reported by local witnesses of that time. ʿAli Basha Mubarak (d. 1893), a famous Egyptian politician, informs us that in Cairo itself there were 294 mausoleums. Egyptian traveller ʿAbd al-Rahman al-Sami (d. 1932), who visited Damascus in 1890, counted 194 mausoleums in the city and its suburbs. At a similar time, traveller Muhammad Raʾuf Taha al-Shaykhili visited Baghdad. According to his account, in the fourteenth century of Hijra, only a few of the 150 congregational mosques there were without a mausoleum. In Constantinople, there were 481 mosques, most of which contained a mausoleum. According to Egyptian historian Mahmud Fahmi al-Muhandis (d. 1983/4), the people of Najd destroyed more than eighty domes and mausoleums of *Ahl al-bayt* (members of the prophet's family) after entering Mecca.[6]

The beginnings of modern reformism can be found among an intellectual group in eighteenth-century Medina.[7] Medina had become a natural centre for this movement because of its strategic position as a holy place, usually visited by pilgrims after the *hajj*. Scholars from all around the Islamic world used to stay there for a certain period of time to exchange religious knowledge, especially of hadith. From the mid-seventeenth century onwards, Medina witnessed a considerable revival of hadith scholarship. This revival was connected to the revision of the *madhhab* system. Alongside this tendency, which emerged in the field of Islamic jurisprudence, a critical reconsideration of Ash'ari theology developed. And so it was that an inclination to rehabilitate the ideas of Hanbali–Salafi orthodoxy of Ahmad ibn Hanbal and Ibn Taymiyya appeared. The Medina circle also endeavoured to harmonise the lawyers' normative Islam with Sufism. The latter engendered a lot of controversy mainly due to its popular innovative (heretical) cults of saints and the dead, although the sophisticated teachings of Ibn 'Arabi, very influential chiefly among elites and Sufi orders, were labelled as pantheism. The majority of the circle, who tried to counterbalance these challenges, were members of the Naqshbandiyya Sufi order. Naqshbandiyya, especially in its reformist interpretation of Indian scholar Ahmad Sirhindi (d. 1624), is commonly described in secondary literature as an 'orthodox' Sufi order due to its stress on Shari'ah. This aspect was shared with the Qadiriyya order, popular with Hanbali *madhhab* and of which Ibn Taymiyya was supposedly a member. In other words, criticism of certain Sufi practices did not only exist outside Sufi discourse. It should be emphasised that the sharp Sunni–Sufi dichotomy is of later origin and is mainly expounded upon in the Wahhabi tradition.

Yemeni Traditionalism

The legacies of Ibn Taymiyya and Ibn Qayyim al-Jawziyya were also palpable in Arabia in the eighteenth-century traditionalist movement. In Yemen, the most prominent figures in this movement were Muhammad ibn Isma'il al-San'ani (referred to as al-Amir al-San'ani, d. 1769) and Muhammad al-Shawkani (d. 1839). Lesser known outside Salafi circles is Husayn ibn Mahdi al-Nu'mi (d. 1773/4). Their contemporaries in the Najd were most notably Ibn 'Abd al-Wahhab, along with the less influential Hamad ibn Nasir ibn 'Uthman Al Mu'ammar (d. 1811), referred to as Ibn Mu'ammar.[8] In law, these scholars called to *ijtihād* and renounced *taqlīd*. In doctrinal issues, they strongly defended monotheism and criticised all religious practices they considered to be forms of polytheism (*shirk*). This approach led to disagreement with scholars of major Sunni schools of law, especially because they had different opinions on heretical practices (*bidaʿ*). All these reformers shared the same sentiment, that the Islamic world was in a state of *jāhilīya*, meaning pre-Islamic ignorance, barbarism and polytheism. Accordingly, everyone's duty should be to return Islam to its pristine form.[9]

The call for *ijtihād* thrived in Yemen and the central region of Arabia, while in cosmopolitan Hijaz religious scholars adhered strictly to *taqlīd*. In Yemen, a distinct version of Zaydi Shiʿism was disseminated by the Hasanid imams, who had ruled Yemen since around 900. Due to a Zaydi doctrine of permanent revolution, each imam's imamate began and ended with himself, and this was a source of constant political instability. This situation changed with the formation of a dynasty known as the Qasimis (1598–1851), within which the imamate was transferred from father to son. In order to foster their religious legitimacy, the imams sought to propagate a more pragmatic line of Islam, referred to by some scholars as 'Sunnisation of Zaydism'.[10] During the rule of caliph al-ʿAbbas al-Mahdi li-din Allah (d. 1775), al-Amir al-Sanʿani and his pupil Husayn Ibn Mahdi al-Nuʿmi forbade sacrifices (*dhabh*) and oath-making (*nadhr*) on graves, and ordered the destruction of tombs in certain parts of Yemen.[11] These acts embittered Shafiʿis, who sought support from scholars of Mecca to issue a *fatwā* stating that tomb destruction was reprehensible (*munkar*) and forbidden (*mamnūʿ*). In 1763, which happens to be the year in which Ibn Saʿud began the conquest of his neighbours, al-Nuʿmi wrote a refutation of the Meccan scholars, calling once again for graves to be destroyed.[12] It is noteworthy that one of many arguments the traditionalists (be it al-Shawkani, al-Amir al-Sanʿani or al-Nuʿmi) used against Shafiʿis is a locution of al-Shafiʿi in his *Kitab al-umm* 'I saw the imams (leaders) in Mecca ordering that what had been built was to be destroyed' (*raʾaytu al-aʾimma bi Makka yaʾmurūn bi-hadm ma yubnā*).

Al-Amir al-Sanʿani, while travelling across some parts of the Arabian Peninsula, including Yemen, Tihama and the Hijaz, observed practices that in his opinion contradicted Islam. He was especially concerned with the proliferation of a cult of the dead and with practices of venerating living charlatans who claimed knowledge of occultism and illuminations. To illustrate al-Amir al-Sanʿani's stance towards necrolatry, we present a short translation from his book titled *Purification of the Doctrine from the Filth of Unbelief* (*Tathir al-iʿtiqad ʿan adran al-ilhad*), the most famous on the topic. Central to his treatise is the idea that God does not accept mere belief in creationism[13] without being properly worshipped. This means that it is crucial not to attribute partners to God, not to call God by any other than his beautiful names and not to approach God via mediators (*shufaʿāʾ*).[14]

> From this you have all learned that if someone believes that any of a tree, stone, grave, angel, jinni, the living and the dead, can help or harm, or approach God, or intercede with Him for mundane needs ... they thus associated things to God and believed in what it is not allowed to believe, as polytheists (*mushrikūn*) believe in idols. Not to speak of one who makes a vow upon his property or son to the dead or the living, or demands of them what can be only demanded from the Exalted God. This is indeed exactly the same polytheism (*shirk*) of the idolaters (*ʿubbād al-aṣnām*). Making vows to the dead with property, making sacrifices on graves, seeking help from the dead, and asking favours from them is exactly the same polytheism as in the pre-Islamic period of barbarism (*jāhilīya*). They committed it by what they call an idol (*wathan wa ṣanam*) ... In the same way grave-worshippers (*qubūriyun*) commit it by what they call a patron (*walī*), grave and shrine ... Each person has a man whom they invoke. The people of Iraq and Hind invoke ʿAbd al-Qadir al-Jilani [founder of the al-Qadiriyya order]; the people of Tihama have the deceased in every town and they invoke their names 'Oh, Zaylaʿi, oh Ibn al-ʿUjayl'; and the people of Mecca and Taʾif 'Oh, Ibn ʿAbbas'; the people of Egypt 'Oh, Rifaʿi, oh Badawi [Saints and founders of the Rifaʿiyya and Badawiyya Sufi orders],' and 'Oh, descendants of Abu Bakr [*al-sāda al-bakrīyya*, descendants of the first caliph Abu Bakr al-Siddiq]'; and the people of the Mountains say 'Oh, Abu Tayr' while the people of Yemen 'Oh, Ibn ʿAlwan.' In every village there they pronounce and invoke the names of the deceased, asking them to bring them good and revert evil. This is the same as what the polytheists do with idols, as we said in our verses from Najd (*al-abyāt al-najdīya*).[15]

These last mentioned verses are a reference to al-Amir al-San'ani's famous poem also known by its opening line *Greetings to Najd and Those who Dwell in Najd* (*Salamati 'ala Najd wa man halla fi Najd*). The poem was written around 1749/50[16] to praise Wahhabis for their religious effort: 'He erects pillars of God's law by destroying mausoleums in which people strayed from the right way.'[17] Note that al-Amir al-San'ani uses the Arabic word *hādiman* here, which leaves no room for ambiguity; it means very explicitly 'destroying', not just levelling graves (*taswiyat al-qubūr*).

The poem is a good example of how Wahhabi ideas were reflected by a kindred Yemeni scholar – from original approval to sobering standoffishness. According to Michael Cook, in 1756 al-Amir al-San'ani examined some of Ibn 'Abd al-Wahhab's works, and from this he concluded 'that the Shaykh was an ill-educated man who had not studied with scholars who could have given him guidance; instead he had read some works of Ibn Taymiyya and Ibn Qayyim al-Jawziyya, and adopted their views in a naïve and imperfect fashion'.[18] Besides, al-Amir al-San'ani retracted the poem a year later upon receiving news of systematic Wahhabi excommunication (*takfīr*) of fellow Muslims, including the Zaydis, and the brutality the Wahhabis inflicted during their expansionist attacks.[19] He supposedly wrote a poem denouncing Ibn 'Abd al-Wahhab for shedding the blood of those who venerate the dead in their graves.

From the very beginning, in their effort to seek legitimisation of Ibn 'Abd al-Wahhab's opinions, Wahhabi scholars have referred to al-Amir al-San'ani and al-Shawkani in introductory parts of various Wahhabi texts. They omitted the second part of the story though, and only later on did they embark on an apologetic mission. Sulayman ibn Sahman (d. 1930), a great Wahhabi apologist, argues that to denounce the poem would contradict what al-Amir al-San'ani wrote in *Purification of the Doctrine*.[20] It is true that in this treatise al-Amir al-San'ani permitted jihad to be waged, and legalised the same treatment of those who insisted on polytheism (*shirk*) as the Prophet had given to polytheists. As instances of polytheism he cites making a pledge (*nadhr*) to the dead, making sacrifices (*nahā'ir*) to them and circumambulation of their graves (*tawāf bi-l-qubūr*). It is the leaders' and scholars' duty to inform polytheists about the true Islam, he writes, before proceeding to treat them accordingly.[21]

The controversy over necrolatry is also reflected in the work of Muhammad al-Shawkani. Al-Shawkani was an outstanding scholar of hadith of his time, who made a lasting impression on later Salafi thought in Yemen, India, Iraq and Syria. He was himself influenced by traditionalist Shafi'i scholars of Egypt, such as Jalal al-Din Suyuti (d. 1505) and Ibn Hajar al-'Asqalani (d. 1448),[22] as well as by Hanbali scholars like Ibn Taymiyya and Ibn Qayyim al-Jawziyya. According to Bernard Haykel, al-Shawkani even modelled himself on these Hanbali scholars, seeking to emulate the polymathic nature of their work, and perhaps wanting to be considered like them to be a first-rank scholar and 'renovator'.[23]

Al-Shawkani is often cited in Wahhabi sources in support of the legitimacy of Ibn 'Abd al-Wahhab. Al-Shawkani, in addition to al-Amir al-San'ani, also wrote a panegyric poem praising Ibn 'Abd al-Wahhab. In academic discourse, he is also depicted as his admirer who, contrary to Wahhabi interpretation, ended up changing his mind when Wahhabis raided Yemen and excommunicated and killed Muslims there. However, it is doubtful whether such a straightforward interpretation is plausible. First of all, we must consider the historical context, especially the political aspect of the relations between the Qasimis and Najdis, when it comes to interpreting iconoclasm. An anonymous chronicler informs us that Imam al-Mutawakkil (r. 1809–16), faced with the expanding military power of Ibn Sa'ud, was forced to seek a diplomatic solution. As a result, a group of missionaries (*al-matāwi'a*) arrived in 1811 to address al-Mutawakkil concerning the destruction of mausoleums and domes erected upon the graves of the righteous and of imams. Having taken counsel with ulama and noblemen of the state, he decided to give permission for their destruction on the basis of the example of the caliph 'Ali, who had ordered graves to be levelled.[24] At that time al-Shawkani wrote *Opening of the Hearts by Forbidding Elevation of the Graves* (*Sharh al-sudur fi tahrim raf' al-qubur*), in which he accuses medieval Zaydi religious scholar Yahya ibn Hamza (d. 1346) of being the first to opine that there is nothing the matter (*lā ba's*) with domes and mausoleums on the graves of noble men (*fuḍalā'*) and kings (*mulūk*). He then gives evidence from hadiths that erecting (*raf'*) graves and building upon them is forbidden and that the graves must be levelled (*taswiya*) and what is raised must be destroyed (*hadm mā irtafa'a minhā*). One of the cited hadiths is a locution of the fourth caliph 'Ali ibn

Abi Talib, whose example might be more convincing for Zaydis and Shi'is: 'Should I not prompt you to do what the Messenger of God prompted me to? That you leave no statue without effacing it, or any raised grave without levelling it?'[25] As a result, several mausoleums of Zaydi–Qasimi imams in San'a' and its surroundings were demolished. It is evident that al-Mutawakkil did this for the purpose of expediency. If we are to rely on an anonymous chronicler's account, al-Mutawakkil simultaneously corresponded with the Sublime Porte and accepted gifts from Muhammad 'Ali Pasha and the Ottoman sultan, whose army put an end to Ibn Sa'ud in the same year.[26]

It seems, then, that al-Shawkani sympathised with Ibn 'Abd al-Wahhab, although he was critical of Ibn Sa'ud's military activities, especially his engagement in Tihama and the expulsion of the Sharifs from Mecca. In *Rising Moon* (*al-Badr al-tali'*), al-Shawkani mentions some controversial issues ascribed to Najdis, one of which is that Ibn Sa'ud considered anyone who was not subject to his rule to be a non-Muslim (*khārij 'an al-islām*). He also mentions that certain news reached him, although he is uncertain of its veracity, suggesting among other things that Ibn Sa'ud permitted the killing of those who called for help from anyone other than Allah and their property to be taken. Al-Shawkani fully agrees with this, although he does not agree that Wahhabis are Kharijis. He explains that Ibn Saud and his followers were instructed by Ibn 'Abd al-Wahhab – a Hanbali scholar who studied hadith in Medina, then returned to the Najd to use *ijtihād* in accordance with later Hanbalis such as Ibn Taymiyya and Ibn Qayyim al-Jawziyya; he adds that both these scholars were the harshest critics of belief in the dead (*wa humā min ashadd al-nās 'alā mu'taqidī al-amwāt*). He also mentions that in 1801 two thin volumes (*mujalladān laṭīfān*) were sent by Ibn Sa'ud to the Yemeni imam. One of the books contained Ibn 'Abd al-Wahhab's treatises on the topics of monotheism, *shirk* and necrolatry. Al-Shawkani found that his arguments were based on the Qur'an and Sunna.

As for al-Shawkani's political opinions, he notes that the conquest of Tihama by Wahhabis and the expulsion of the Sharifs from Mecca, especially emir Ghalib, with whom he sympathised, was too much. Al-Shawkani notes that Wahhabi proselytic activities in Yemen after this conquest were more palatable. Many delegations from Ibn Sa'ud (ruled the first Saudi state 1803–14) arrived in San'a' to visit imam al-Mansur and his son al-Mutawakkil, bringing them letters supporting the monotheistic mission and the destruction of elevated graves and domes (*hadm al-qubūr al-mushayyada wa al-qibāb al-murtafiʿa*), as well as some books (*kutub*) to al-Shawkani himself, together with the book for the imams. This resulted in the destruction of domes and elevated graves in Sanʿaʾ and its surroundings, and in Dhammar. After this, al-Shawkani reports, the Egyptian pasha sent his army to conquer Mecca, Medina and al-Ṭaʾif.[27]

It is evident from the *Opening of the Hearts* that al-Shawkani's opinions on necrolatry were consistent. In the book he recommends another of his treatises, in which he goes into greater detail regarding necrolatry. According to Haykel, that treatise, *The Book of Well-Strung Pearls Rendering the Word on God's Unicity Exclusively to Him* (*Kitab al-durr al-nadid fi ikhlas kalimat al-tawhid*), was written in reaction to menacing Wahhabi activity in Tihama, and especially in Mashham, a Sunni town where the veneration of saints and the practice of visiting the graves of righteous people thrived. Al-Shawkani begins his treatise by defining the terms *tawassul, istighātha* and *istiʿāna* using Ibn Taymiyya's legal opinions. He then proceeds to define true monotheism and renounce various forms of polytheism (*shirk*), including asking favours of the dead, using talismans, venerating trees, swearing (*khalf*) by anything other than Allah, building on graves and lighting lights on them, fortune-telling and magic, depiction (*taṣwīr*), making vows (*nadhr*) to the dead and making sacrifices to them (*dhabḥ*), and 'hidden *shirk*', a religious term for hypocrisy. According to Haykel, although al-Shawkani condemns all such practices, he nevertheless concludes his treatise with an important injunction that allows for visits to graves as long as a bad example is not set for the ignorant masses.[28]

In *Opening of the Hearts*, al-Shawkani poetically describes the psychological effect of temptation on the ignorant masses, if a grave is left unlevelled:

> The very reason for belief in the dead is what the devil has embellished by erecting graves, putting curtains on them, plastering, ornamenting and adorning them so much that an ignorant person, if his eyes fall on a grave, will see a dome and will enter it. If he sees splendid curtains and glittering lanterns on the graves, while the smell of a censer spreads around him, there is no doubt that his heart will be filled with the grandiosity of that grave. His

intellect will become faint in figuring out what position the dead has. From such magnificence and dignity Satanic beliefs will creep into his heart, which are Satan's greatest trick on Muslims and the most severe means of leading worshippers astray. It will steadily shake him out of Islam, such that he will ask the buried for that which only Allah has the power to do, and eventually he will become one of the unbelievers.[29]

Based on this, it seems reasonable to argue that the positions of Ibn 'Abd al-Wahhab and al-Shawkani did not differ much.

Ibn 'Abd al-Wahhab's Teachings

The history of the early Saudi state shows us the iconoclastic drive of the Wahhabis. One of Ibn 'Abd al-Wahhab's first acts was thus to demolish graves associated with 'innovative' rituals. The destruction of a grave was one of three acts – the other two being cutting down a sacred tree and stoning an adulteress (stoning to death had been performed only infrequently in Islamic history) – that came to symbolise the nature of the Wahhabi movement. A grave in al-Jubayl in Wadi Hanifa that was destroyed by Ibn 'Abd al-Wahhab himself reputedly belonged to Zayd ibn al-Khattab, brother of the second caliph 'Umar ibn al-Khattab and one of Muhammad's Companions. It was allegedly a famous site of veneration visited by many people who offered prayers to Zayd, and its selection by Ibn 'Abd al-Wahhab was premeditated. We are also informed that the oasis dwellers planned to defend their place of worship, but that when they saw Ibn 'Abd al-Wahhab accompanied by 600 men, they stood aside and observed the destruction of the site.[30]

According to a polemical epistle written by Sulayman ibn Muhammad ibn Suhaym, a religious instructor (*muṭawwiʿ*) of the al-Majmaʿ oasis to the Muslims of Basra and al-Ahsaʾ, Ibn 'Abd al-Wahhab destroyed (*hadama*) the graves of Zayd and his companions and dispersed them (*baʿtharahā*). Sulayman explains that the graves had been elevated because the ground was rocky and it was impossible to dig there, so those who buried them – Khalid ibn al-Walid and his companions – had placed stones upon them to the height of approximately a cubit (*dhirāʿ*) in order to prevent smells and deter beasts. Ibn 'Abd al-Wahhab allegedly also destroyed a mosque for the same reason.[31]

In other words, Sulayman accuses him of destroying an elevated grave that otherwise fulfilled the legal requirements.

Ibn ʿAbd al-Wahhab replied to the letter, stating that veneration of the righteous – such as ʿAbd al-Qadir al-Jilani, Ahmad al-Badawi or ʿAdi ibn Musafir (a descendant of the Umayyad caliph Marwan ibn al-Hakam venerated by the Yazidis) – constitutes major *shirk* (*al-shirk al-akbar*), which implies that it is a reason for excommunication. He also claims that the truth is with him, because the Islamic religion of his day is among the strangest things (*dīn al-islām al-yawm min aghrab al-ashyāʾ*), by which he means that it is difficult to find Islam in its pristine form.[32] He admits that he excommunicates those who make pledges (*nudhūr*) in order to get close to anyone other than Allah, and those who sacrifice to Jinn; however, he refutes the accusations that he would destroy the chamber of the Prophet (*hadm ḥujrat al-nabī*) if he had the capacity to do so, that he wants to replace the gold rain gutters of Kaʿba (*mīzāb al-kaʿba*) with wooden ones, that he forbids visiting one's parents' grave, or that he excommunicates those who swear (*ḥalf*) by anyone other than God.[33] Ibn ʿAbd al-Wahhab does not mention the destruction of Zayd's grave in his reply, but this was far from the only such place that drew visitors that he had destroyed: among other famous graves were those of the Prophet's wives Khadija and Maymuna bint al-Harith, where men mingled freely together with women. In the Najd, people sought intercession with God at the grave of a blind hermit who was believed to be blessed. Near Dirʿiyya there was a cave on a hill that was believed to belong to a young girl with similar spiritual powers.[34]

As the iconoclasm of the Wahhabi movement and its struggle against polytheism was fuelled by the teachings of Ibn ʿAbd al-Wahhab, a closer look at his writings may help to outline his worldview. Although he authored many texts, three of his treatises became the most influential, at least from the perspective of the later development of Wahhabism–Salafism. These are *The Book of Monotheism* (*Kitab al-tawhid*), *Clarification of Doubts* (*Kashf al-shubuhat*) and *The Three Principles* (*Thalathat al-usul*). Committing these three main works by Ibn ʿAbd al-Wahhab to memory is part of institutionalised clerical education in Saudi Arabia even today. These books convey the basic ideas of Ibn ʿAbd al-Wahhab's socio-religious reform. They all share a strong emphasis on the monotheism of cult (*tawḥīd al-ʿibāda*),

Figure 5 The grave, near Mecca, of the last of the nine wives of the Prophet Muhammad, Maymuna, and the surrounding camp of Meccan pilgrims who had travelled there, *c.* 1888.

('Das Grab der Mèjmūnah und die nächste Umgebung'. Photographer: al-Sayyid 'Abd al-Ghaffar, British Library: Visual Arts, X463/10, in Qatar Digital Library, available at: http://www.qdl.qa/en/archive/81055/vdc_100023510750.0x000026.)

while the theology of God's names and attributes that was so important to Ibn Taymiyya and central to Wahhabi–Salafi literature in later periods, is not particularly stressed. Nevertheless, it is evident from his other writings and the writings of his contemporaries that Ibn 'Abd al-Wahhab was familiar with Salafi methodology in theology.[35]

The style of Ibn 'Abd al-Wahhab's treatises is very brief and referential, which makes reading them quite a precarious task without proper knowledge of their historical and religious context. 'Abdullah al-Salih al-'Uthaymin, a current Saudi historiographer (not to be confused with his brother, Muhammad al-Salih al-'Uthaymin, the famous Saudi religious authority), puts this tactfully: 'In general, his style is simple and does not strive for literary effect.'[36] This is not to belittle the treatises as such. It seems plausible that Ibn 'Abd

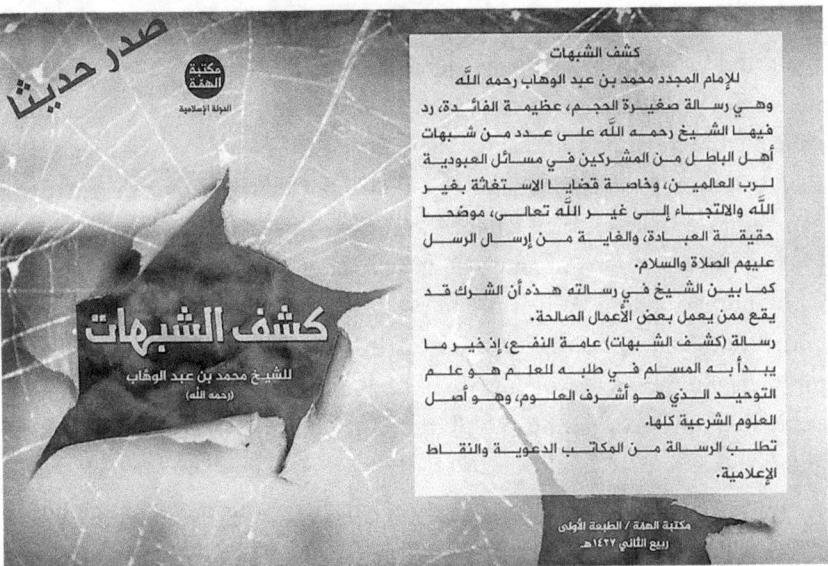

Figure 6 An advertisement by ISIS for Ibn ʿAbd al-Wahhab's book: *The Clarification of Doubts* (*Kashf al-shubuhat*)
(from ISIS's weekly newspaper, *al-Naba*', 14 March 2016, p. 11.)

al-Wahhab conceived his texts – with the exception of his letters – as personal notes for didactical needs and discussion with auditors. In other words, the ideas conveyed in the texts were simplified and clear-cut in order to be intelligible to the ignorant masses. A good example of this simplification can be found in his *Inculcating the Principles of Faith to the Common People* (*Talqin usul al-ʿaqida li-l-ʿamma*), which is itself a simplified version of *The Three Principles*. In order to be intelligible to the masses, Ibn ʿAbd al-Wahhab uses some phrases of vernacular language, such as the colloquial *ēsh* (what) in place of the formal *mādhā*. To the best of our knowledge, this is quite an unusual phenomenon in Muslim religious literature.

The Book of Monotheism is the most famous of Ibn ʿAbd al-Wahhab's writings. In it, he describes polytheistic practices such as occultism, the cult of the righteous, intercession, oaths calling on anyone other than God himself, sacrifices or invocational prayers to anyone other than God, and asking anyone other than God for help. Important features of graves are detailed in a chapter titled 'About the condemnation of one who worships Allah at the grave of a righteous man, and how then of a man who worships the Dead himself.'[37] Ibn 'Abd al-Wahhab begins by quoting a hadith: 'Umm Salama told the messenger of Allah about a church she had seen in Abyssinia in which there were pictures. The Prophet said: "Those people, when a righteous member of their community or a pious slave dies, they build a mosque over his grave and paint images thereon; they are for God wicked people." They combine two kinds of *fitna*: the *fitna* of graves and the *fitna* of images.' He then continues with another hadith: 'When the messenger of Allah was close to death, he said: "May Allah curse the Jews and Christians who make the graves of their prophets into places of worship; do not imitate them."' From this hadith Ibn 'Abd al-Wahhab derives his prohibition for building places of worship over graves, because that would mean glorifying their inhabitants, which would amount to an act of worship to an entity other than Allah. This opinion is in agreement with Ibn Taymiyya's and Ibn Qayyim al-Jawziyya's positions.

The following chapter of *The Book of Monotheism* is titled 'About exaggeration in the graves of the righteous, and how they become idols worshiped beside Allah.' At the end of this chapter, Ibn 'Abd al-Wahhab quotes a hadith about God's curse on women who visit graves. Later, this hadith would serve as the basis for some of today's Salafi ulama completely prohibiting women from *ziyāra*. One of the last chapters, which deals with the question of intercession, is titled 'Allah may not be asked to intercede with his creatures' and is introduced by the following hadith: 'A Bedouin came to the Prophet and said: "Oh, messenger of Allah! The people are exhausted, families are starving, and wealth has perished, so pray to your Lord for rain, and we will seek Allah's intercession upon you and yours upon Allah." The Prophet said: "Allah is exalted! Allah is exalted!" He continued to say so until the effect of it was apparent in the faces of his Companions. Then he said: "Woe to you! Do you not know who Allah is? Allah's nature is far greater than that, and there is no intercession of Allah upon anyone!"'

It is noteworthy here that many of his arguments, presented as locutions from the Qur'an and hadith, are neither innovative nor divergent from traditionalist literature. To give an example, the idea of combining of two kinds of *fitna* – the *fitna* of graves and the *fitna* of images (*tamāthīl*) and identifying images (*ṣuwar*) with statues (*tamāthīl*) – is in all likelihood drawn from Ibn Qayyim al-Jawziyya's *Rescue of the Troubled from the Snares of Satan*

(*Ighathat al-lahfan min masayid al-shaytan*).³⁸ The passage concerned is based on the opinions of the *salaf* and Ibn Taymiyya, that after the death of Prophet Noah the pagan tribes (*qawm Nūḥ*, in the Islamic tradition considered as *mushrikūn*) began to combine two kinds of *fitna*: the *fitna* of graves (*qubūr*) and the *fitna* of images (*tamāthīl*).

In *Clarification of Doubts*, Ibn ʿAbd al-Wahhab outlines his vision of a rotten society, even more ignorant of religious rules than in the pre-Islamic era (*jāhilīya*). Hence, the most criticised aspect of his teachings, namely, the excommunication of those Muslims who are not true monotheists. In the eleventh chapter he states that pre-Islamic polytheism (*shirk al-awwalīn*), which was the reason for the revelation of the Qurʾan and Muhammad's fight with polytheists (*mushrikūn*),³⁹ was not as grave as the polytheism (*shirk*) of his time. We must bear in mind that his criticism and accusation of polytheism was aimed at the majority of Muslims, at least in a nominal sense. According to him, most Muslims of his day were truly unbelievers, and he illustrates this by giving some examples: an unbeliever is one who does not believe in the Qurʾan and Sunna as a whole; who recognises monotheism, but refuses to pray; who recognises monotheism and prayer, but refuses to pay religious taxes; who recognises all this, but refuses to fast or to make the pilgrimage to Mecca. Even one who recognises all this, but denies belief in the resurrection, is an unbeliever in the absolute sense and his blood and property may thus be taken.

To put it simply, Ibn ʿAbd al-Wahhab states that even if someone claims to be a Muslim, he is not a Muslim if he omits even one of his religious duties or does not fully believe in Muslim dogma. This, and the associated practice of excommunicating fellow Muslims and accusing them of being renegades because they commit *shirk*, was a controversial aspect of the Wahhabi teachings and shows how differently Ibn Taymiyya's and Ibn Qayyim al-Jawziyya's opinions could be interpreted. For example, Ibn ʿAbd al-Wahhab frequently refers to caliph ʿAli ibn Abi Talib, who had his companions (who claimed to be Muslims) burnt to death, because they believed in him (*iʿtaqadū fī ʿAlī*). In *An Instructive Work for the One Who is Ready on the Topic of the Unbelief of the Neglector of Monotheism* (*Mufid al-mustafid fi kufr tarik al-tawhid*), which is considered to be an elaboration of sorts on *Clarification of Doubts*, written as a response to criticism from his own brother, Ibn ʿAbd al-Wahhab uses the same argument for excommunication of the Muslims who invoked ʿAli ibn Abi Talib. To support his argument, he cites Ibn Taymiyya from a respected Hanbali jurisprudential compendium *Persuasion of Those Who Seek Usufruct* (*al-Iqnaʿ li-talib al-intifaʿ*) written by Sharaf al-Din al-Hijawi (d. 1560). To give an example of quite the opposite view, Sulayman ibn ʿAbd al-Wahhab, himself a Hanbali judge, accused his older brother Muhammad of being ignorant, of not fulfilling the requirements of the *mujtahid*, and misunderstanding Ibn Taymiyya and Ibn Qayyim al-Jawziyya on the issue of excommunication because of committing *shirk*. Ironically enough, he recommends al-Hijawi's book to him, among others.[40]

In *The Three Principles*, Ibn ʿAbd al-Wahhab outlines his vision of Islamic renewal by emigration (*hijra*) from the world of *jāhilīya*. Crucial to his argument is the Qurʾanic imperative 'and avoid uncleanliness (*wa al-rujz fa-hjur*)' (74:5).[41] The Qurʾanic word *rujz* is usually translated into English as 'uncleanliness'. However, Ibn ʿAbd al-Wahhab interprets the word as traditionalist Qurʾanic exegetes did (for example, Ibn Kathir's exegesis of the Qurʾan, which is highly respected in traditionalist circles), reading *rujz* as 'idols', which fits with his imagery of *jāhilīya* and idolatry. Moreover, he relates this verse to the Qurʾanic imagery of Abraham, who denounced his own family and tribe because they worshipped idols.

Another point is relevant here. The fact that Ibn ʿAbd al-Wahhab places stress on the *jāhilīya* of his day being even worse than that of the pre-Islamic or early Islamic period means that emigration to the world of Islam was not only a duty for the early Muslim community, but, in his view, it also constituted an urgent duty in his own day. His conception is modelled on the example of the Prophet Muhammad and the early Muslim community (*salaf*), logically following the phases of proselytism (*daʿwa*) as a non-violent invitation to Islam, followed by refusal and emigration (*hijra*) to the world of true Islam, then excommunication (*takfīr*) and war (*jihād*) against unbelievers. If we look back at the history of the Wahhabi movement, especially to the so-called first and third Saudi states, we can see this theory acted out in practice.

Elsewhere in *The Three Principles*, Ibn ʿAbd al-Wahhab states that it is every Muslim's duty to learn three issues (*masāʾil*). The first two issues relate essentially to the two aspects of monotheism – belief in God's creation and worshipping none other than him. However, the third issue does not relate to the monotheistic nature of God's names and attributes (*tawḥīd al-asmā' wa al-ṣifāt*), as would be usual in classical theological texts. Instead, Ibn ʿAbd al-Wahhab underlines the socio-religious aspect of monotheism – one who is obedient to God and worships only God must not be on intimate terms with or feel emotional inclination (*muwālāt*) towards one who opposes (*ḥādda*) God and his Messenger, even if that is his closest relative (*aqrab qarīb*).[42] He gives the example of the religion of Abraham (*millat Ibrāhīm*), who denounced polytheism (*shirk*) and the polytheists (*mushrikūn*) in his own family.[43] The treatise concludes with a warning not to believe in *ṭāghūt*, but God. *Ṭāghūt* is a Qur'anic proper name and generic word for an idol, but in traditionalist literature it has a variety of meanings. To define what he means by *ṭāghūt*, Ibn ʿAbd al-Wahhab cites Ibn Qayyim al-Jawziyya: 'It is Satan; everyone who agrees to be worshiped; everyone who demands to be worshipped; everyone who claims a certain knowledge of occultism; everyone who rules by anything other than what Allah revealed (*man ḥakama bi-ghayr mā anzala Allāh*).'[44]

Iconoclasm between Wahhabism and Ahl al-hadith

The Wahhabi scholars made an effort to put Ibn ʿAbd al-Wahhab's legacy into mainstream Sunni Islam by connecting it with traditionalist scholarship. This endeavour was motivated by an anti-Wahhabi religious polemic depicting Wahhabi Islam as heresy in the worst form, and the historical circumstances and practical demands of the Saudi states. These attempts to place Wahhabi teachings in accordance with broader traditionalist scholarship primarily evolved in interaction with Egypt and India. In Egypt, following the Mongol attacks on Central Asia, the shrinking of Muslim rule in Andalusia and the collapse of the great Sunni universities, al-Azhar University became the most renowned Sunni university and the only place of shelter for scholars forced out of their homes.[45] One of those was ʿAbd al-Latif ibn ʿAbd al-Rahman ibn Hasan Al al-Shaykh (d. 1876), a great-great-grandson of Ibn ʿAbd al-Wahhab, who was deported to Egypt together with his father after the destruction of the first Saudi state. His enforced stay in Egypt brought him into closer contact with non-Hanbali religious scholarship. His task in this new milieu was to defend Ibn ʿAbd al-Wahhab's teachings and his harsh rebuttal of grave-worshippers (*qubūriyūn*) in particular. He attempted to put Ibn ʿAbd al-Wahhab's teachings in the context of broader Sunni scholarship across different legal schools, ranking him not only among Hanbalis such as Ibn Taymiyya, Ibn Qayyim al-Jawziyya and Ibn ʿAqil, but also the Hanafi scholar Sunʿallah al-Halabi, the Shafiʿi scholar al-Maqrizi and the traditionalist Yemeni scholars and *mujtahid*s Muhammad ibn Hasan al-Nuʿaymi al-Zubaydi (NB: evidently mistaken for Muhammad ibn Hasan al-Nuʿmi!),[46] al-Amir al-Sanʿani and Muhammad ibn ʿAli al-Shawkani.

Sunʿallah al-Halabi (d. 1708/9) was quite an exception among Hanafis, who otherwise sided with the Ottoman Empire and seemed to be more tolerant of the cult of saints. He authored a book condemning the practice of veneration of dead saints at their graves, titled *God's Sword on Those Who Tell a Lie About God's Friends* (*Sayf Allah ʿala man kadhaba ʿala awliya' Allah*), cited by ʿAbd al-Latif's father, shaykh ʿAbd al-Rahman in *Inspiration of the Glorious, Explanation of the Book of Monotheism* (*Fath al-Majid, sharh kitab al-tawhid*).[47] During his exile in Cairo, shaykh ʿAbd al-Rahman attended lessons at al-Azhar with scholars from the other Sunni legal schools and acquired knowledge from the vast library there. He became one of the most learned figures of his era.[48] It was after his return to Riyadh, during a brief renewal of the Saudi state (1824–91), that he wrote his most respected commentary, based on Ibn Taymiyya and Ibn Qayyim al-Jawziyya.

Both ʿAbd al-Rahman and his son educated a number of Wahhabi scholars, some of whom were descendants of Ibn ʿAbd al-Wahhab (Al al-Shaykh), but the most prominent of whom were from other Najdi families, such as Hamad ibn ʿAtiq (d.1883/4) and Sulayman ibn Sahman (d. 1930). These latter are said to have been students of ʿAbd al-Rahman and ʿAbd al-Latif, respectively. Hamad ibn ʿAtiq is an example of a scholar who studied the works of Ibn Taymiyya and Ibn Qayyim al-Jawziyya in order to support Ibn ʿAbd al-Wahhab's arguments. He copied manuscripts of works of Hanbali scholarship, including some books by Ibn Taymiyya and Ibn Qayyim al-Jawziyya.[49] His own attitudes were influenced by the historical circumstances – the threats of Ottoman soldiers in the Najd. He wrote *Refuge from Befriending Renegades and Polytheists* (*Sabil al-najat wa al-fikak min muwalat al-murtaddin wa ahl al-ishrak*), with frequent references to Ibn Taymiyya. This treatise, which stresses enmity and isolation not only towards polytheism, but to polytheist as well, was very influential on later development of Salafi doctrine of loyalty and disavowal (*al-walā' wa al-barā'*) and Abrahamic religion (*millat Ibrāhīm*).

Hamad ibn 'Atiq was one of the first Wahhabi scholars seriously concerned with the question of God's names and attributes, which had been rather neglected by previous exponents of the same school who had focused primarily on idolatry and necrolatry. He was also keen to be in contact with traditionalist scholars, and respected Siddiq Hasan Khan (1832–90), a famous proponent of the *Ahl al-hadith* movement in Bhopal state, who identified himself with reformist Shah Waliullah, under whose grandson he studied hadith. In a letter Hamad sent to Siddiq Hasan Khan, he praises the latter for his erudition and informs him that he would like to send his son to learn from him. He also praises him for a Salafi commentary on the Qur'an he had published in print in Cairo. He proceeds in the letter by saying that he is sending him a book by Ibn Qayyim al-Jawziyya titled *The Sufficient and Healing on the Vindication of the Saved Sect* (*al-Kafiyya al-shafiyya fi al-intisar li-l-firqa al-najiyya*), and would like his commentary on it, because he has trouble understanding it. Indeed, *al-Kafiyya* is a very long poem with rhyme on 'n' (hence also called *al-Qasida al-nuniyya*), which describes Salafi dogma in all its theological complexity. At the same time, Hamad recommends other books by Ibn Taymiyya and Ibn Qayyim al-Jawziyya to Siddiq as a good tool when fighting heretics. Finally, he politely proposes several amendments (*tahqīq*) to Siddiq's commentary regarding God's attributes and names, especially as concern the question of God's ascension to the throne (*istiwā'*) and proper Salafi methodology as coined by Ibn Taymiyya: 'There is no doubt that this is also your belief, what I want to say is that you have adopted some terms from heretics without thinking out of what they meant by them, so be please alert to such things.'[50] Siddiq Hasan Khan allegedly took his words to heart and embarked on a study of both shaykhs. As for Hamad ibn 'Atiq's son, he did indeed study in India with Siddiq Hasan Khan and many other traditionalist scholars, and so established links with the *Ahl al-hadith* movement there.[51]

Siddiq Hasan Khan was deeply influenced by the writings of al-Shawkani, which is demonstrative of the influence that Yemeni scholars were exerting on Indian scholars at that time.[52] Moreover, as he notes in his *Alphabet of Sciences* (*Abjad al-'ulum*), he read the majority of the books penned by Ibn

Qayyim al-Jawziyya, having acquired 'these very useful books during his journey to Hijaz'. However, he laments that rest of his books were very hard to find at that time, because 'spiders of forgetfulness have spun their webs upon them'.[53] He also mentions that he owns the majority of the books of al-Amir al-San'ani.[54] Siddiq Hasan Khan ranks Ibn Qayyim al-Jawziya and al-Amir al-San'ani among the greatest guardians of Islam (*huffāz al-islām*), together with the Prophet Muhammad, Ibn Taymiyya and Muhammad al-Shawkani. However, he did not rank Ibn 'Abd al-Wahhab among them.[55]

The reason for not including Ibn 'Abd al-Wahhab among these greatest guardians of faith is rather obvious. Siddiq Hasan Khan did not want to be associated with the Wahhabi movement, which at the time many Muslims and also the British considered synonymous with fanaticism and puritanism. In India, rumours began to spread that Siddiq Hasan Khan was a Wahhabi himself, and, when the British began to examine his books critically, they discovered some writings in which the theory of jihad was explained at length. When the British further detected that seventeen scholars from the Najd had come to study in Bhopal, they began to think an international network of anti-British agitators had grown up, reaching from Bhopal to Egypt, Istanbul, and the Mahdist Sudan.[56] In *Tarjuman-i wahhabiyya* (*An Interpreter of Wahhabism*), written in 1884, Siddiq Hasan Khan objected to the Wahhabist label not only because of its anti-British connotations, but because he found it too rooted in geography and culture, a kind of territorialism and closure that he as a universalist did not wish to be stifled in. He cites a hadith attributed to the second caliph 'Umar: Prophet Muhammad was giving his blessing to Yemen and al-Sham (Greater Syria) when someone said that he should also pray for the Najd. He remained silent. When this request was repeated three times he replied that by his silence he expressed his disapproval of the Najdi way of localising Islam. He said that this would only create strife and raise unnecessary issues and would offer an ideal playing field to Satan.[57]

Siddiq Hasan Khan also stresses the fact that there was no communication between the inhabitants of India and those of the Najd and that no work of Ibn 'Abd al-Wahhab was published in India. He states that in India the worshippers of tombs and those who venerate saints have, out of sheer enmity and ill-will, labelled the believers of the true God as Wahhabis, referencing the fact that the latter are connected to Muhammad ibn ʿAbd al-Wahhab of Najd.[58]

In India, Siddiq Hasan Khan was the main protagonist of a movement concerned with the veneration of saints, dead or alive, and more broadly with visits to the Prophet's grave in Medina. From among his numerous writings in Arabic, Persian and Urdu, we examine his vast commentary on the Muslim hadith collection *Glaring Lantern in Revealing Issues of Sahih of Muslim ibn Hajjaj* (*al-Siraj al-wahhaj fi kashf matalib Sahih Muslim ibn Hajjaj*) where he addresses this topic from a legalistic perspective. In a chapter titled 'Command of grave levelling' (*Bab al-amr bi-taswiyat al-qubur*) he deals with the issue of grave levelling from the point of view of a *mujtahid*, who takes into account the varied opinions of different Sunni schools of law. He claims that the scholars agree that graves should be raised by approximately the span of one hand, and that making a small mound (*tasnīm*) of earth or flattening the earth (*tasṭīḥ* or *tarbīʿ*) are both permissible. However, he notes that the scholars have different opinions on which of these two practices is better, as hadiths on the topic differ. Those who inclined to flattening graves thought that making small mounds would lead to some inappropriate elevation (*baʿḍ al-ishrāf*).

Siddiq Hasan Khan then recommends al-Shawkani's *Opening of the Hearts by Forbidding Elevation of the Graves*, part of which he translated into Persian in his own book *Guidance of Who Is Asking* (*Hidayat al-saʾil*). He concluded that building upon graves, a common practice for kings and noblemen should be forbidden, and warns that people should not be fooled by the fact that kings and noblemen have done this. He also bases the chapter 'The reprehensibility of building upon graves and plastering them' (*Bab karahiyat al-bināʾ wa al-tajsis ʿala al-qubur*) of his commentary on al-Shawkani's works. He explains that this practice falls into the category of forbidden things (*ḥarām*), regardless of whether the building is private or public (unlike the view of Shafiʿis on this issue).[59]

The case of the *Ahl al-hadith* movement in India shows that their opinions on necrolatry and idolatry at that time were not modelled on Wahhabi literature, but rather on Yemeni scholarship, most notably al-Shawkani, who in turn followed in the steps of Ibn Taymiyya and Ibn Qayyim al-Jawziyya.

Moreover, due to their knowledge of Persian and Urdu – languages that became yet more important for Indian Muslims in the years that followed – Indian traditionalists were able to influence later opinions on necrolatry and iconoclasm.

It was not only the British who conceived Wahhabis as a threat to their imperial interests. As the Saudi state expanded and came into confrontation with the Ottoman authorities in the Arabian Peninsula, Syria and Iraq, Ottoman statesmen and religious scholars alike began to vilify the Wahhabis. Any identification with Ibn Taymiyya in scholarly circles would frequently result in accusations of Wahhabi attitudes.[60] The Salafi movement was instrumental in reviving Ibn Taymiyya's thought in the Arab metropolises of Baghdad, Damascus and later Cairo. The movement emerged in the late 1870s in Baghdad and spread during the 1880s to Syria, from where it was subsequently taken to Egypt and other parts of the Islamic world. The early Salafis were mostly middle-class men of religion who opposed Abdülhamit II's autocratic regime in general and his encouragement of popular Sufi brotherhoods and conservative ulama in particular. They had firmer roots in the Khalidi (Naqshbandi) tradition than their colleagues in Istanbul, but they also detached themselves more sharply from the then leaders and practices of the brotherhood in favour of the teachings of Ibn Taymiyya. At the centre of this Salafi movement stood the issue of *ijtihād* versus *taqlīd*, which implies revisions of *ziyāra* and the cult of the dead.

Rehabilitation of Ibn Taymiyya and Ibn ʿAbd al-Wahhab

The rise of the modern Salafi trend was heralded by the publication in 1881 of *Clearance of the Eyes in Trying the Two Ahmads* (*Jala' al-ʿaynayn fi muhakamat Ahmadayn*), a lengthy treatise in defence of Ibn Taymiyya penned by the Baghdadi scholar Nuʿman Khayr al-Din al-Alusi (d. 1899). Thanks to financial support from Siddiq Hasan Khan, this book was published in print, which at the time was a very modern medium in the Middle East, and was soon widely circulated amongst Muslim scholars. The work combines a sharp critique of the Sufi practices of saint worship and tomb visiting, with a new rationalist notion of *ijtihād*, and rehabilitates several opinions that had been wrongly ascribed to Ibn Taymiyya. Nuʿman defends Ibn Taymiyya on several fronts: theologically, he denies that Ibn Taymiyya is an anthropomorphist (an accusation tantamount to idolatry), stating that his theological opinions did not deviate from orthodoxy, because they conformed with the opinions of the early Muslim community (*salaf*). Legally, he defends the right to *ijtihād*, however, he does not deny *taqlīd* and the *madhhab* system as such, as, for example, *Ahl al-hadith* does. What interests us the most is his reassessment of Ibn Taymiyya's opinions on visiting graves. He explains that what Ibn Taymiyya objected to was the visiting of a tomb being the premeditated purpose of a pilgrimage, including those to the tomb of the Prophet Muhammad, rather than visiting tombs as such.[61]

In his anti-Sufi diatribes, Khayr al-Din followed in the footsteps of his father Abu al-Thana' al-Alusi (d. 1854), who had imbibed the Wahhabi ideas prevalent in early nineteenth-century Baghdad while also belonging to the circle of shaykh Khalid, the founder of the Khalidiyya form of Naqshbandiyya. Khalidiyya became very popular in Iraq as well as in Mecca and Medina after the inauguration of the Tanzimat reforms in 1839. Many shrines in Iraq were rebuilt so as to better respect the authority of the Ottoman sultan. However, the Khalidiyya order later lost much of its credibility due to its connection with the sultan. Abu al-Thana''s admiration for Khalid had never waned, but his quarrel with the master's successors led him later in life to incline towards a peaceful version of the Wahhabi teachings.[62]

Weismann links both al-Alusis with Wahhabi teachings;[63] however, we must bear in mind that Ibn 'Abd al-Wahhab's name does not figure in Nu'man's list of Salafi scholars for one reason or another. Instead, he ranks his own father among the most important students of Ibn Taymiyya, together with al-Kurani, al-Shawkani, Shah Waliullah and Siddiq Hasan Khan. If Nu'man was in touch with Wahhabi scholars, this was surely due to his correspondence with some Al al-Shaykh, whom he asked for manuscripts of Ibn Taymiyya's works. Without a doubt, Nu'man al-Alusi was instrumental in mediating between Ibn Taymiyya and religious scholars and intellectuals in the Arabic metropolises. It was Mahmud Shukri al-Alusi, another member of the al-Alusi family, who introduced them to Ibn 'Abd al-Wahhab's teachings in the light of the works of Ibn Taymiyya and Ibn Qayyim al-Jawziyya. His initial interest in both scholars led to contacts with Wahhabi ulama, from whom he sought manuscripts that were missing from the Baghdadi collections.[64] In a letter dated 1908 to Salafi rationalist reformist Jamal al-Din al-Qasimi (d. 1914), Mahmud Shukri al-Alusi complains about the difficulties of collecting and publishing their works:

> Regarding the work of the two shaykhs and other Salafis, as you pointed out, the Hanbalis belong to the most incompetent as concerns the care it well deserves. Despite the fact that I am in constant correspondence with the people of Najd, I have yielded throughout mere promises. Still, I managed to get some treatises from abroad through some friends from among the orientalists, who though they could not part with them, provided me with a photocopy. I had great difficulties with the books, the publishing of which in Egypt and India would please Allah.[65]

Mahmud Shukri al-Alusi's affinity with Wahhabi ideas is evident from his works. He completed an unfinished polemic treatise by shaykhs 'Abd al-Latif ibn 'Abd al-Rahman Al al-Shaykh and 'Abdullah ibn 'Abd al-Rahman al-Babutayn against the leader of the Naqshbandi–Khalidi Sufis in Baghdad, Da'ud ibn Jirjis. Ibn Jirjis disagreed with the Wahhabis concerning the excommunication of those who venerate saints and *taqlīd*. Ibn Jirjis challenged the Wahhabi scholars, as is evident from the polemics they devoted to refuting his ideas. He settled in the Najdi oasis of Unayza, where he argued with Wahhabi scholars by citing Ibn Taymiyya's and Ibn Qayyim al-Jawziyya's works.

In a similar vein, Mahmud Shukri al-Alusi elaborated a number of 'drafts' by Ibn 'Abd al-Wahhab, in particular one titled *Questions of the Barbarian Age* (*Masa'il al-jahiliyya*). In the introduction to his commentary, Mahmud Shukri al-Alusi notes that he gets the impression that it looks like the chapter list of a book without the book content itself, that the drafts are extremely brief, so much so that they could almost be considered a kind of quiz.[66] The subjects of the treatise are various errors of *jāhilīya*, each dealt with separately. The most important issue in *Questions of the Barbarian Age* is the invocation of righteous people (*du'ā' al-ṣāliḥīn*) and requesting mediation from them (*shafā'a*), because this was the very reason why the Prophet opposed polytheists and insisted upon monotheism and sincere devotion (*ikhlāṣ*). For the same reason, people were divided into two groups – Muslims and infidels – and enmity sprouted up among them and jihad came to be legalised.[67] In the treatise the question of veneration of the graves of righteous people, visiting them, worshiping the relics of the prophets, and placing lanterns upon graves, places of festivals or sacrifices are dealt with by Ibn ʿAbd al-Wahhab and in Mahmud Shukri al-Alusi's commentary on his text.

Mahmud Shukri al-Alusi's effort to strip 'Wahhabism' of its unorthodox label is further evident in his *History of Najd* (*Tarikh Najd*), a book published in Egypt with a supplement by Wahhabi scholar Sulayman ibn Sahman. Mahmud Shukri al-Alusi refuses the label Wahhabis for Najdis, who are all Muslims and monotheists (*muwaḥḥidūn*). He defines them as Salafis on the basis that their beliefs are modelled on those of the early pious Muslim community (*hum ʿalā ʿaqāʾid al-salaf al-ṣāliḥ*). In theology (*uṣūl al-dīn*), their way is the way of Sunnis (*ahl al-sunna wa al-jamāʿa*), and their methodology is the methodology of the Salaf, 'which is sounder and even more wise', which is a reference to medieval theological dispute over superiority of one of the two approaches: that of *al-salaf* (traditionalist or Hanbali approach) and that of *al-khalaf* (later, more or less rationalist generations). This is because Salafis affirm the literal meaning of God's attributes in the Qur'an and hadith (*yuqirrūn āyāt al-ṣifāt wa al-aḥādīth ʿalā ẓāhirihā*). Here he explicitly mentions the attribute of God's sitting on the throne (*al-istiwāʾ*).[68] Al-Alusi's claim is important because it theologically connects the Salafi movement with Ibn Taymiyya's definition of Salafis. This would come to define the later trend in the Salafi movement of renouncing rationalist approaches to theology (a fine example is Muhammad ʿAbduh's theology, labelled as Muʿtazili), while sharing the Wahhabi aversion to Sufism. In law, Muhammad Shukri al-Alusi defines 'Wahhabis' as Hanbalis who do not refuse *taqlīd*. From this claim it seems reasonable to deduce that Rashid Rida did not attempt to portray Ibn ʿAbd al-Wahhab as an advocate of *ijtihād*.[69] This is perhaps the reason why the theology of God's attributes and names is stressed in order to underline the orthodox character of Wahhabis and connect them with the medieval tradition of Hanbalis as both a legal and a theological school.

Much of the book is devoted to thwarting anti-Wahhabi accusations regarding *ziyāra*, *takfīr* and necrolatry. Mahmud Shukri al-Alusi makes it clear, in accordance with Ibn Taymiyya's opinion, that Wahhabis do not forbid visits to the tomb of the Prophet Muhammad as such. In other words, they do not divert in any way from the Sunni mainstream – neither in theology, nor in their legal opinions.

Moreover, Muhammad Shukri al-Alusi tried to strip 'Wahhabis' of the extremist label (*khawārij*) ascribed to them because of their practices of excommunication and their fight against 'grave-worshippers', both Sufis or Shi'is. He highly appreciated this aspect of the Wahhabi movement, especially mentioning the abundance of necrolatry in Iraq. Muhammad Shukri al-Alusi was perhaps even more uncompromising in his rejection of Sufism than were Rashid Rida and other proponents of Salafism. Al-Alusi himself had been close to the Rifa'iyya Sufi order in his youth, but later turned into a staunch critic of Sufi brotherhoods and even threatened with death anyone who knowingly performed 'unlawful' visits to the dead.[70] Muhammad Shukri al-Alusi can be considered a pioneer of the rapprochement between non-Wahhabi Salafi reformers (many of whom were rationalist) and Wahhabism, which continued later under the influence of Egyptian scholars, most notably Rashid Rida and the movement of Ansar al-sunna al-muhammadiyya, represented by Muhammad Hamid al-Fiqi (d. 1969).

Rashid Rida (1865–1935) evolved as a famous religious reformer. At the beginning of his career he had experience with Sufism. He first joined the Naqshbandiyya order in Tripoli, but he also became a critic of Sufi practices later in his life. While still in Lebanon, he was influenced by reading *Clearance of the Eyes in Trying the Two Ahmads*, which acquainted him with the basic teachings of Ibn Taymiyya.[71] Rida's criticism of Sufi 'heretical' practices intensified after he left Lebanon for Egypt in 1898, where he came under the influence of Muhammad 'Abduh's modernist thought and the works of Ibn Taymiyya and Ibn al-Jawzi (d. 1201, not to be confused with Ibn Qayyim al-Jawziyya) and launched his famous Salafi journal, *al-Manar*.

Rida embraced Salafism as he perceived it to be a better vehicle against the threat of atheism. Along with the superiority of Hanbali theology over Ash'arism, he also accentuated Ibn Taymiyya's strict conception of *tawḥīd*.[72] Later in his life, after the death of Muhammad 'Abduh, Rashid Rida began to propagate Wahhabi ideas in the journal *al-Manar*. He defended the Saudi ruler 'Abd al-'Aziz, who restored the third Saudi state by conquering Riyadh in 1902, and the renewal of the Wahhabi religious movement by Islamisation and the sedentarisation of Bedouins, who left their tribal bonds to become brothers (*ikhwān*) in Islam. With the help of the Ikhwans ʿAbd al-ʿAziz conquered the Najd and Hijaz, and in 1932 he became the king of Saudi Arabia. Rashid Rida was strongly politically engaged in the Saudi case. The reasons for Rashid Rida joining the ranks of ʿAbd al-ʿAziz's supporters in the wider Arab world had to do with his disenchantment with Sharif Husayn's dynastic scheming for the Middle East. This brought Rashid Rida into the anti-Hashemite camp and 'by the time the new ruler of the Hijaz convened a Muslim congress in Mecca in the summer of 1926, Rida was receiving funds from him'.[73]

Rashid Rida was instrumental in disseminating printed Wahhabi texts across the Arab world. Besides India, he also published books by Ibn Taymiyya, Ibn Qayyim al-Jawziyya and many Wahhabi texts in Egypt. In 1923, his al-Manar printing house published 'by order of ʿAbd al-ʿAziz' a collection of Wahhabi religious texts edited by Sulayman ibn Sahman under the title *Sunni/Splendid Gift and Wahhabi Present from Najd to All Our Monotheistic Brothers of the True Islamic Religion and Muhammadan Path* (*al-Hadiyya al-sunniyya/al-saniyya wa al-tuhfa al-wahhabiyya al-najdiyya li-jamiʿ ikhwanina al-muwahiddin min al-milla al-hanifiyya wa al-tariqa al-muhammadiyya*). The book deals almost exclusively with topics related to necrolatry, such as invocational prayer to the living and the dead, asking mediation of the Prophet Muhammad and visiting his grave,[74] making graves places of worship, *tawassul*, the enmity of those who venerate graves towards those who regard their practices as heresy, the exaggerated veneration of saints and prophets, and Ibn ʿAbd al-Wahhab's monotheism. In 1927, Rashid Rida supervised the edition of a 'package' of texts by the most prominent Wahhabi scholars, published at the expense of ʿAbd al-ʿAziz under the title *Monotheistic Collection from Najd* (*Majmuʿat al-tawhid al-najdiyya*). In 1928, just one year later, he also published the *Collection of Treatises and Questions from Najd* (*Majmuʿat al-rasaʾil wa al-masaʾil al-najdiyya*).[75]

The impact of print publication in spreading Salafi ideas during the first half of the twentieth century can be demonstrated by the case of Muhammad Hamid al-Fiqi, a figure familiar to everyone who came across the early editions of Ibn Taymiyya, Ibn Qayyim al-Jawziyya and other Salafi and Wahhabi authors, whose works he edited and published for the first time, until they were replaced by more advanced editions of Saudi provenance. Al-Fiqi founded the first Salafi organisation in Egypt, Ansar al-sunna al-muhammadiyya, which quickly spread to Sudan, where it played a major role in spreading Salafi ideas and challenged the traditional Sufi orders. The members of that movement also played a role in building the Saudi educational system.

Wahhabi Attacks on Funeral Architecture and Travellers' Testimonies

Many of the aforementioned ideological and theological debates laid the foundation for translating theory into practice. The early nineteenth century, as well as the first decades of the twentieth century, thus saw a wave of funerary monument destruction by Wahhabis. European travellers to the Middle East at the time of the Wahhabi conquests of the Hijaz tried to shed light on this 'recent' movement that had emerged in the heart of Arabia. Those who visited the region brought back valuable reports, some of which concerned grave-related habits and Wahhabi attitudes to them. The testimony provided by these European travellers must, of course, be taken with some reservations; in their writings we can sometimes detect a certain level of storytelling and plagiarism. In addition, only a few of these authors had any personal contact with the Wahhabis themselves; most relied on second-hand accounts and interlocutors.[76] Still, these European accounts – together with the information provided by local Arab chroniclers – form the main source of our knowledge of the early evolution of Wahhabism and, in particular, its stance towards necrolatry. Although some of them helped to create a positive picture of Wahhabis as authentic restorers of the pure Islamic faith and reformers within Islam, most of these accounts had the opposite effect. Their reports of the destruction of venerated tombs was intended to ignite popular resentment against the Wahhabis, mobilise opposition against them and justify military interventions.

In 1801, the Wahhabis launched raids on Shi'i targets in Iraq (mainly in Najaf and Karbala, later also Basra), including important Shi'i shrines. On the day of Ghadir Khumm, 21 April, a few thousand Wahhabi warriors led by amir Su'ud ibn 'Abd al-'Aziz attacked Karbala. The Mamluk garrison fled and left the Wahhabis to plunder the town and massacre several thousand people. In accordance with their anti-Shi'i and anti-shrine attitudes, the attackers also desecrated the shrines of al-Husayn and 'Abbas (both sons of 'Ali) and looted their treasures.[77] Chronicler Ibn Bishr estimated the number of victims at around two thousand. He also mentions the destruction of the dome over al-Husayn's mausoleum and the robbery of all valuables from it.[78] Jean-Baptiste Louis Rousseau (1780–1831), an orientalist and diplomat who was consul in Basra, Aleppo and Tripoli, adds to this description that the Wahhabis 'put everything to fire and the sword', and after murdering and plundering, which brought them 'more spoils than they had ever seized' before and which had to be carried away by 'two hundred camels', they destroyed imam al-Husayn's mausoleum and 'turned it into a ditch of filth and blood'.[79]

Both cases of grave destruction of *salaf* – that previously mentioned at the tomb of Zayd in the Arabian Peninsula by Ibn ʿAbd al-Wahhab himself and this at al-Husayn's mausoleum in Karbala by the later generations of his followers – show that the monuments were destroyed regardless their occupants' high status in Islam. The first was one of the Prophet Muhammad's Companions (*ṣaḥāba*), the latter a member of the Prophet's family (*ahl al-bayt*) – his grandson – and venerated by the Imami branch of Shiʿa as their political and spiritual leader. Paradoxically, the Wahhabi attacks indirectly helped to create a semi-autonomous Karbala, which then took an active role in the promotion of Shiʿi identity in the area. The Shiʿi ulama subsequently expanded their proselytisation activities and several of the most important Iraqi tribal confederations were converted to Shiʿa in the eighteenth century.[80] The attacks also enabled the Shiʿis to raise sympathy and donations from India.

The Shiʿis became the target of Wahhabi zeal early on. Some of them attempted to defend themselves against religious attacks denouncing Shiʿi practices, particularly those of visiting graves, and of so-called polytheism. Several Shiʿis wrote religious treatises highlighting the fact that they had always been true Muslims and their grave-related practices were not attempts to deny the unity of God, but a means of reaching God. Acknowledging their military inferiority, they even accompanied these written defences with gifts for the Wahhabis, up until the 1801 raids.[81]

The booty from raids on Shiʿi enclaves in Iraq enabled the Wahhabis to begin their conquest of the western part of the Arabian Peninsula. The Wahhabis first conquered the Hijaz, with Mecca and Medina, in 1803 and then again in 1805, after which followed a period of Egyptian military tutelage until the 1840s. During the very first conquest, the Wahhabis smashed many graves and sacred places and razed centuries-old cemeteries to the ground, not only in Mecca and Medina, but also in Hadramawt and elsewhere. The spiritual head of the Wahhabi movement at that time, ʿAbdullah ibn Muhammad ibn ʿAbd al-Wahhab (d. 1826), issued a *fatwā* in which he systematically laid out the basic doctrinal tenets of the movement. Among the main guidelines he listed that: (1) saintly intercession (*shafāʿa*) with God is an illusion and anyone practising it is automatically excommunicated and liable to capital punishment, even if he believes in divine superiority; (2) Muslim saints are not to be the subject of any form of worship; (3) all religious rites established after the third century of the Hijra are blameworthy innovations (*bidaʿ*) and are categorically condemned; and (4) Ibn Taymiyya and Ibn Qayyim al-Jawziyya are seen as great Sunni authorities, and their works are deeply respected.[82]

The Wahhabis focused their destruction of tombs and shrines on those that were domed, because each domed structure marked the burial place of a saint deemed to have miraculous powers. The commander-in-chief and heir to the Saudi throne who assumed rule in 1803, Suʿud ibn ʿAbd al-ʿAziz, allegedly sent a letter to the Ottoman sultan, Selim III, in which he proclaimed: 'I entered Makkah ... I destroyed all things [tombs] that were idolatrously worshipped.'[83] Suʿud also gathered the local citizens together in the Holy Mosque and preached the tenets of Islam to them, ordering them to participate actively in the destruction of domes on the tombs of revered figures, of mausoleums and of 'idols, so that no one other than God would be worshipped'.[84] That the Wahhabis did so fervently is again attested by Rousseau, among others, who writes of pilgrims to Mecca who found 'all the mosques demolished, pulpits overturned, external manifestations of the cult abolished'.[85]

Johann Ludwig Burckhardt (1784–1817), a Swiss orientalist and traveller who witnessed the first period of Saudi rule over the Hijaz and whose book thus provides an eyewitness account of the Saudi conquest of Mecca, gives us this general description: 'Mohammedan saints are venerated as highly as those of the Catholic church, and are said to perform as many miracles as the latter.' In the eyes of the Wahhabis, Burckhardt notes, all men were equal before God and even the most virtuous could not intercede with him. Consequently, it was 'sinful to invoke departed saints, and to honour their mortal remains more than those of any other persons'.[86] As for the destruction of tombs, he continues:

Wherever the Wahabys carried their arms, they destroyed all the domes and ornamented tombs ... The destruction of cupolas and tombs of saints became the favourite taste of the Wahabys. In Hedjaz, Yemen, Mesopotamia, and Syria, this was always the first result of their victory; and as many domes formed the roofs of mosques, they were charged with destroying these also. At Mekka, not a single cupola was suffered to remain over the tomb of any renowned Arab: even those covering the birth-place of Mohammed, and of his grand-sons, Hasan and Hosseyn, and of his uncle, Abou Táleb, and his wife, Khadydje, were all broken down.[87]

The only tomb that remained intact was the Prophet's tomb in his mosque. Carsten Niebuhr (1733–1815), a German scientist who participated in the famous expedition to Arabia sponsored by Denmark (1761–67), left us probably the most valuable and reliable notes. In his *Travels through Arabia* he writes that Muhammad's tomb is:

> situated in a corner of the great square ... For fear that the people might superstitiously offer worship to the ashes of the Prophet, the tomb is enclosed within iron rails, and is only to be seen by looking through them. It is of plain mason-work, in the form of a chest ... [Muhammad's] tomb is placed between two other tombs, in which rest the ashes of the first Caliphs ... [T]he building that covers it is hung with a piece of silk stuff embroidered with gold, which is renewed every seven years by the Pacha of Damascus. This building is guarded by forty eunuchs, chiefly for the security of the treasure which is said to be kept in it. This treasure consists chiefly of precious stones, the offerings of rich Mussulmans.[88]

The destruction of this particular tomb would probably have been far too outrageous, and might potentially have aroused the anger of the entire Islamic world. Burckhardt states that it 'was destined to share a similar fate'. Its destruction was allegedly ordered by Suʿud, who was motivated by his attempt to discourage an illicit form of the cult of intercession. However, Burckhardt explains, 'its solid structure defied the rude efforts of his soldiers; and after several of them had been killed by falling from the dome, the attempt was given up. This the inhabitants of Medinah declared to have been done through the interposition of Heaven.'[89] That the destruction of the dome over Muhammad's mosque had been prevented only by the death of two Wahhabis in the process was also acknowledged by Rashid Rida on the pages of the *al-Manar* journal.[90] Such claims that those trying to destroy domes over graves had been miraculously killed were repeated many times throughout Islamic history and also have some contemporary repercussions. Ironically, the ulama have always used a similar narrative strategy in order to dispel their opponents. Their disapproval of raised graves was often accompanied by recurring legends of buildings that had been destroyed soon after their completion by the saint whose grave they were to adorn.[91]

As for the supposed sack of Muhammad's tomb in Medina, over time the negative attitudes mobilised by learning about this act induced chroniclers and Wahhabi apologists to avoid mentioning the episode or even to deny that it had ever taken place. Furthermore, others have claimed that the robbing of the tombs in Medina had occurred – at the hands of previous custodians – before the Wahhabis even took control of the city and that Suʿud did not enrich himself but shared the booty with others.[92] A similar line of argument claims that the ulama of eighteenth-century Najd actually promulgated much stricter juridical opinions, sentencing all those guilty of the cult of the dead to death, while Ibn ʿAbd al-Wahhab's position was far more modest, emphasising the need for re-educative missionary activity.[93]

Another account of the Wahhabi conquests and acts comes from Louis Alexandre Olivier de Corancez (1770–1832), a French consul to Aleppo who had previously taken part in Napoleon's campaign in Egypt. De Corancez notes in his *Histoire des Wahabis*, that this new movement destroyed the tombs of the prophets and shaykhs respected by other Muslims and that they despised those who adorned or ornamented their tombs.[94] William George Browne (1768–1813), an Englishman who spent several years in the Middle East, gathered some information about the Wahhabis while travelling through Syria on his way back home in 1797. In his *Travels in Africa, Egypt, and Syria* (1799), openly citing Niebuhr as the most credible authority on these subjects, Browne states that Ibn ʿAbd al-Wahhab 'destroys all the mosques he can seize', and that the Wahhabis believe that 'a prophet, when dead, deserves no homage, and that of course to mention him in a creed, or in prayers, is absurd'.[95]

Domingo Badía y Leblich (aka Ali Bey al-Abassi, 1767–1818), a Spanish explorer and most likely an agent for both Napoleon and the British, also witnessed the Wahhabis' arrival in Mecca. He writes in his *Travels of Ali Bey* that Ibn 'Abd al-Wahhab declared boldly that 'this species of worship rendered to the saints was a very grievous sin in the eyes of the Divinity, because it gave him companions. In consequence of this, his sectaries have destroyed the sepulchres, chapels, and temples elevated to their honour.' Ibn 'Abd al-Wahhab is also said to have 'forbidden his sectaries from visiting the tomb of the Prophet at Medina'.[96] John Malcolm (1769–1833), a Scottish diplomat and soldier who participated in the East India Company's Persian missions, adds another element to the 'peculiar tenets' of the Wahhabis: 'They deem it a species of idolatry to erect magnificent tombs; but to kiss relics and so on is idolatry itself; and they therefore affirm that it is an action acceptable to God to destroy the tombs of Mahomedan saints in Arabia and Persia, and to appropriate their rich ornaments to worldly purposes, and that they say it is wicked to mourn for the dead.'[97]

George Annesley (1770–1844), second Earl of Mountnorris and ninth Viscount Valentia, wrote an account while staying in Mocha in his way to Abyssinia of what he heard about the Wahhabis and their treatment of the tombs after they had conquered the cities of the Hijaz. In his case, too, we observe a heavy reliance on Niebuhr's views. Annesley provides a standard description of the destruction of graves (including the one belonging to Khadija, Muhammad's first wife) and the profanation of Muhammad's tomb in Medina: 'The religious prejudices of the Wahabee were greatly offended by above eighty splendid tombs, which covered the remains of the descendants of Mohammed, and formed the great ornament of Mecca. These were levelled with the ground, as was also the monument of the venerable and respected wife of the prophet, Kadija ... The holy places were plundered of their valuable articles.'[98] A similar fate was met by the city of Medina: 'In 1804 Medina, with its treasure, which had accumulated for ages by the donations of the faithful, became a prey to the Wahabee.' In his account, however, we can see a slight shift regarding the alleged destruction of Muhammad's tomb, as Annesley writes that it 'shared the fate of those of his descendants'.[99]

Similar accounts were then replicated by several others. Maurice Tamisier (1810–75), a French participant in an unsuccessful Egyptian expedition against the Asir region in 1834, denounces the 'vandalism of Ouahabis' and 'the destruction of domes over graves',[100] while Félix Mengin, a French merchant and Napoleonic agent in Cairo, mentions that Ibn 'Abd al-Wahhab's proscriptions included the following: 'not to raise domes and mausoleums and to destroy the existing ones, the pomp promoting idolatry'.[101] What is remarkable in all these and previous European accounts is that they do not mention the connection between Ibn ʿAbd al-Wahhab's ideas and those of Ibn Taymiyya at all. This only came to light much later, beginning with Ignaz Goldziher in 1878.[102]

What is also striking in the accounts provided by some European travellers, besides their descriptions of the level of destruction, is that they clearly show that even the Wahhabis' zeal was not capable of eradicating some of the 'un-Islamic' customs of the time. Those Europeans who were able to visit Mecca and Medina, in particular, left valuable descriptions of the ceremony of visits to the Prophet's grave, from which it is clear that many visitors still continued to prostrate themselves in front of Muhammad's grave, rubbing their cheeks with the dust. Burckhardt, who visited Mecca and Medina in 1814–15, provides an interesting description of some of these ceremonies. Among other things, he mentions that the visitors invoked their own intercession in heaven, and distinctly mentioned the names of all those of their relatives and friends whom they wished to include in their prayers.[103] In a description of visits to Hamza's grave, he also observes that Hamza and his companions were invoked to intercede with God in order to obtain faith, health and wealth for the pilgrim and all of his family, and the utter destruction of all their enemies.[104] Burckhardt also noticed that in Medina – though this was not the case in Mecca – it was thought very indecorous for women to enter the mosque, and that those women who came from foreign parts visited graves during the night, after the last prayers, while local women hardly ever ventured to enter the mosque.[105] He remarks also on how during the time of the Wahhabis nobody dared to visit other holy places in the vicinity of Mecca for fear of exposing themselves to their hostility.[106]

Sir Richard Francis Burton (1821–90), who set off on the *ḥajj* in 1853, reports that when visiting the Prophet's grave, men should not kiss it, touch it with their hand, press their bosom against it or rub their face with dust collected from near the sepulchre. He also writes that those who prostrate themselves before it – as was the habit of many pilgrims, especially from India – are held to be guilty of deadly sin.[107] Burton also mentions the usual prayers recited at the Prophet's grave, citing, among others, the following passage:

'We thy friends, O Prophet of Allah, appear before thee ... longing to ... obtain the blessings of thine intercession, for our sins have broken our backs, and thou intercedest with the Healer ... O Prophet of Allah, intercession! Intercession! Intercession!' Burton concluded how this had to be offensive to the Wahhabis, who consider it blasphemy to assert that a mere man – even Muhammad – can stand between God and a believer.[108]

The difference between the habits of nomads and the settled population was captured by the English traveller and writer Charles Montagu Doughty (1843–1926). In his 1888 book *Travels in Arabia Deserta*, he describes the graveyard in Ha'il, the capital of the Rashidis: 'Poor and rich whose world is ended, lie there alike indigently together in the desert earth which once fostered them, and unless it be for the sites here or there, we see small or no difference of burial.' Doughty then adds that 'the first grave is a little heap whose rude headstone is a wild block from the basalt hill, and the last is like it, and such is every grave', and that 'in the border Semitic countries is a long superstition of the grave; here is but the simple nomad guise, without other last loving care or adornment'.[109]

Wahhabi iconoclasm was also directed against the oldest and most celebrated cemetery in Medina, the Baqi' al-Gharqad ('the field of thorny trees', also known as Jannat al-Baqi' or simply al-Baqi'), whose history dates back to early Islam, if not to pre-Islamic times. Muhammad himself used to visit this cemetery on a regular basis and greet the dead.[110] After the emergence of Islam, the first to be buried in the al-Baqi' cemetery was allegedly 'Uthman ibn Maz'un, Companion of Prophet Muhammad who died in 624 during the Battle of Badr. Muhammad is said to have buried his Companion himself, placing two rocks over the grave to clearly mark it. In the second half of the seventh century, Marwan I, who governed Medina, ordered the elimination of the gravestone marking Ibn Maz'un's burial site. The next person to be buried there was Ibrahim, Muhammad's infant son. After that, al-Baqi' became the place of final rest for many important figures in Islamic history[111] – the third caliph 'Uthman ibn 'Affan[112] and the imam of Medina Malik ibn Anas being the most famous. Many of the Prophet's relatives were also buried there: his grandson al-Hasan, several of his wives, his uncle 'Abd al-Muttalib and aunt Safiyya, and many others. As Burckhardt observes: 'Indeed so rich is Medina in the remains of great saints that they have almost lost their individual importance, while the relics of one of the persons just mentioned would be sufficient to render celebrated any other Moslim town.'[113] The graves of the most famous dead had grand cupolas and domes built over them, some of them even had gold ones (such was the case of the grave of al-Hasan ibn 'Ali). The splendour of the al-Baqi' cemetery in medieval times was documented, for example, by two famous Muslim travellers, Ibn Jubayr (1145–1217) and Ibn Battuta (b. 1304), who described the cemetery with its elevated domes and shrines.

Figure 7 The al-Baqi' cemetery, Medina, the first Islamic cemetery, located immediately to the southeast of the Masjid al-Nabawi. Many of the structures visible in this image were restored in the late nineteenth century by Sultan Abdülhamit II after the destruction and damage to the graveyard caused in 1806 as a result of the Wahabbi conquest.

('Picture of the Paradise Garden of al-Baqi''. Photographer: H. A. Mirza & Sons, British Library: India Office Records and Private Papers, photograph 174/12, in Qatar Digital Library, available at: http://www.qdl.qa/en/archive/81055/vdc_100023483748.0x000023.)

Figure 8 A current image of the al-Baqi' cemetery, Medina
(An image grab taken from a video, 'Inside Jannat Al-Baqi', published 31 August 2014, 'shakeel shahzad', available at: https://www.youtube.com/watch?v=HUZpHLgsoF4.)

In Saudi Arabia the al-Baqi' cemetery has been among the most venerated places, especially by the Shi'is as it was believed that four of the 'Alid imams, al-Hasan b. 'Ali, 'Ali Zayn al-'Abidin, Muhammad al-Baqir and Ja'far al-Sadiq, as well as Muhammad's daughter Fatima were buried there. The cemetery thus served as a recommended Shi'i pilgrimage site, as evidenced by several pilgrimage guides to Medina describing the best routes via al-Baqi', the Quba' Mosque and the graves of the martyrs of Uhud.[114]

In 1806, the Wahhabis entered Medina and, as we are told by Ibn Bishr, 'destroyed all the domes which were over graves and shrines'.[115] The destitution of the place was such that Burckhardt wrote: 'considering the sanctity of the persons whose bodies it contains, [the cemetery] is a very mean place, and perhaps the most dirty and miserable burial-ground in any eastern town of the size of Medina. It does not contain a single good tomb, nor even any large inscribed blocks of stone covering tombs, but instead, mere rude heaps of earth.' It is fair to add that Burckhardt himself acknowledged that although the Wahhabis were accused of having defaced the tombs, they would not have annihilated every modest tomb built there. Instead, he concludes that the cemetery must have been in a miserable state already, and attributes this 'to the niggardly minds of the towns-people, who are little disposed to incur any expense in honouring the remains of their celebrated countrymen'.[116]

Another wave of destruction came after the rise of the third Saudi state. In 1902, the young Saudi emir ʿAbd al-ʿAziz ibn ʿAbd al-Rahman Al Suʿud (1870–1953) conquered the city of Riyadh; he then continued with further conquests and built up tribal unions. Once he had re-established the Saudi position, he set off to the Hijaz to retake Mecca and Medina. His subjugation of the Hijaz was preceded by the conquest of al-Taʾif, during which ʿAbd al-ʿAziz's troops slaughtered hundreds of citizens. When the Wahhabis entered al-Taʾif, they also destroyed the *qubba* of Ibn ʿAbbas and many other pilgrimage sites. Jeddah also surrendered in September 1924 without a fight, after its citizens became afraid of suffering the same fate as those in al-Taʾif. On 5 December 1924, ʿAbd al-ʿAziz entered Mecca; Medina surrendered shortly afterwards, and on 22 September 1932 the Kingdom of Saudi Arabia was officially proclaimed. The arrival of the Wahhabis in Mecca and Medina was once again accompanied by the widespread destruction of funerary architecture.

More than one hundred years since the first Wahhabi conquest of Hijaz, the situation had not changed much. Eldon Rutter (1894–1956?), an English traveller who performed his first *ḥajj* in 1925, had the opportunity to witness the new order imposed under the political auspices of ʿAbd al-ʿAziz, founder of modern Saudi Arabia. Rutter observed that the Wahhabis, together with other puritans, were heavily influenced by the writings of Ibn Taymiyya, and that it was through reading his books that Ibn ʿAbd al-Wahhab had felt impelled to launch his campaign, a detail that Rutter heard on many occasions from various learned shaykhs.[117] Rutter also describes the destruction of the Meccan cemetery of al-Muʿalla, where Muhammad's mother Amina, wife Khadija, grandfather and many famous early Muslims were buried and whose tombs 'were formerly crowned by small but handsome domes'. These were, however, 'demolished, together with most of the tombstones' and their guardians 'no longer dare to spread their handkerchiefs on the ground to receive the pilgrims' alms'.[118] Rutter goes on to mention one of his companions, who addressed 'extravagant salutations and supplications . . . regarded as unholy' by the Wahhabis, and was 'guilty of *bid'a*' because he said while at the Prophet's grave, 'We beg that thou wilt intercede for us.'[119] He also described a raised platform, north of Fatima's enclosure, where several of the eunuchs would usually sit and invite pilgrims of distinction to join them and perform their prayers. The advantage of the platform lay in its unique position: when the worshipper was stationed there and faced Mecca for his prayers, he also faced the Prophet's grave.

Further destruction affected also the al-Baqi' cemetery. Rutter describes a sight resembling a town that had been razed to the ground or demolished by an earthquake. All over the cemetery nothing was to be seen except little indefinite mounds of soil and stones, along with broken brick rubble. All the great white domes that had formerly marked the graves of Muhammad's relatives and successors had been demolished. To complete the scene, there was a group of devastated Indian pilgrims led by an old man with a vacant look and tears pouring from his eyes in a ceaseless stream.[120]

For others, it proved rather difficult to visit some of the tombs and shrines of the holy cities. This was, for instance, the case of Arthur J. B. Wavell (1881–1916), a British explorer whose cousin Archibald served as Viceroy of India, and who achieved fame by being arrested in Yemen, was paraded handcuffed, publicly beaten and eventually imprisoned by the Ottoman authorities there. Wavell tried several times to visit the al-Baqi' cemetery, but was prevented by heavy fighting. When he was eventually able to visit the site, he found the tombs 'tedious'.

> The outstanding feature of them all is the 'shoddy' character of the buildings and state of neglect in which they are allowed to remain. This is indeed surprising when one reflects on the millions that have been spent on religious edifices in other Moslem countries – the magnificent mosques of Cairo and Damascus, the golden spires of Kerbela, and the profuse extravagance that Indian travellers describe. Yet here, in the very birthplace of the religion, the tombs of the Prophet's wives, Ibrahim his infant son, Hassan his grandson, and many others whose names are never mentioned without a blessing, are very inferior in size and beauty, and kept in worse repair than many private vaults in other places. I can offer no explanation of this anomaly.[121]

After the first destruction by the Wahhabis in early nineteenth century, many monuments were restored in splendid aesthetic style by the Ottoman sultans (particularly Abdülhamit II) only to be destroyed, in what some Shi'is call 'the great crime' (*al-jarīma al-kubrā*),[122] once again in 1925–6 by 'Abd al-'Aziz, along with the graves of the holy personalities in Mecca.

Unlike the poorly documented events of the early nineteenth century, we have much better evidence of the later wave of Wahhabi conquests in the 1920s. Apparently, the British were worried by the advances made by 'Abd al-'Aziz and the Wahhabis and what these might mean for the security of pilgrims and for the monuments in the region. In a letter to 'Abd al-'Aziz dated 13 September 1924, the Secretary of State for the Colonies reminds him of the treaty and requests that he ensures 'that British pilgrims and residents in Hedjaz are free from molestation', stating that His Majesty's Government attaches 'the greatest importance to freedom of access to the Holy Places ... and that they are confident that he will neither do nor allow to be done by his followers anything calculated to prejudice that freedom'.[123]

After the seizure of Mecca, and a period of several months during which no reliable information was received about the events in the city, R. W. Bullard, the British consul in Jeddah, wrote in a letter to the Secretary of State for Foreign Affairs, Austen Chamberlain, dated 15 June 1925: 'The accounts previously received of the attitude of the more extreme of the Wahhabis ... were correct. All the tombs of the saints ... have been demolished.' He also nicely encapsulates the ambiguous relationship between the ruler and the religious establishment when mentioning that 'Abd al-'Aziz admitted frankly that 'he did not approve of this interference in harmless religious practices' and that he himself did not believe that Khadija's remains really lay under the tomb which bears her name, nor did he believe in praying at tombs. However, 'he did not wish to interfere with pilgrims who differed from his on these points; only, he must defer for the present to his fighting tribes, who happen to be the most fanatical'.[124]

The American Consulate in Aden proved to be worse at reading the whole situation. In a letter to the Secretary of State in Washington dated 8 July 1925, the consul writes: 'It is recalled that the Wahabi sect, while accepted essentially as Mohammedanism by the Moslem world, is regarded nevertheless as being outside the pale of Islam on account of its objection to tomb worship', and concludes that 'they could never be accepted as the rulers of Mecca, the very holiness of which is founded upon the existence of certain tombs therein.'[125]

After the Wahhabi attack on Medina, Vice-Consul Jordan reported to Austen Chamberlain on 14 September 1925 that during the hostilities the forces of ʿAbd al-ʿAziz had most likely destroyed the tomb of Hamza, the Prophet's uncle and one of the first martyrs of Islam, and also that the dome over the Prophet's tomb had been struck by bullets.[126] While ʿAbd al-ʿAziz vehemently denied touching the *qubba* over the Prophet's tomb, he made no mention in his correspondence of the tomb of Hamza or the other monuments. The allegations were later confirmed in a letter dated 25 May 1926, by an Acting British Agent in Jeddah to the Foreign Office in London: 'From reliable information it is now certain that the tombs of the Prophet's family in Medina have been destroyed including the tomb of Hamza. There are also rumours that the dome of the Prophet's tomb may be removed.'[127]

False reports about the damage of the green dome over the Prophet's tomb, done by ʿAbd al-ʿAziz's artillery, had already in October 1925 brought an Iranian mission of investigation and protest letters from all over the world, especially from India, but also Egypt and Iraq.[128] ʿAbdullah ibn Bulayhid, the chief Wahhabi judge of Hijaz, assembled the local ulama and consulted with them on the legality of raised structures in the al-Baqiʿ cemetery. After two weeks of deliberation, a *fatwā* was issued sanctioning the destruction of the tombs, domes and other structures in the cemetery.[129] Besides the al-Baqiʿ cemetery, ʿAbd al-ʿAziz ordered the demolition of graves and tombs in the al-Muʿalla cemetery in Mecca. Further destruction concerned tombs of the martyrs of the battle of Uhud, burial site of Muhammad's first wife Khadija, and many others.[130]

Another report for the period 1–30 June 1926 mentions the following:

> I have received many complaints from pilgrims ... on account of the destruction of the tombs in and around Mecca. At first pilgrims were not allowed to enter the cemetery where these tombs were situated, but eventually ... the cemetery was opened for several hours daily, but Wahabi police

Figure 9 The al-Muʿalla cemetery, situated northeast of the Masjid al-Haram in Mecca, in which several of the Prophet Muhammad's relatives are buried
('Picture of the Paradise of al-Maʿala'. Photographer: H. A. Mirza & Sons, British Library: India Office Records and Private Papers, photograph 174/11, in Qatar Digital Library, available at: http://www.qdl.qa/en/archive/81055/vdc_100023483748.0x000021.)

were in attendance to prevent any departure from the puritanical Wahabi beliefs. It appears that most of the tombs have been razed to the ground and the component parts of the edifice scattered abroad, except in the case of the tomb of Khadijah, the Prophet's wife, where, although the tomb has been destroyed, the tiles and marbles forming part of the edifice have been preserved and stacked on one side. It is confidently rumoured that a fetva has been issued authorising the destruction or demolition of the dome over the Prophet's tomb in Medina, and that Ibn Saud is awaiting the departure of the pilgrims before he proceeds with this further act of vandalism.[131]

The Wahhabis were also reported to have forbidden all the pilgrims from kissing or touching any shrine and to have punished and fined several of them for not obeying these orders. The wide reporting of these events led to protests by Muslims from various parts of the world. The same report thus informs us of the results of anti-Wahhabi propaganda in India and Persia, which 'seems to have been swallowed wholly by the more ignorant Moslem communities in both those countries. Many telegrams . . . have been addressed to Ibn Saud . . . in the most scurrilous terms,' and further reports that a 'mass meeting consisting of nearly 100,000 Moslems . . . resolved to express its anger, hatred, vehemence and contempt towards Ibn Saud and his wild army . . . and the violation of the sacred objects, and advises those fools to leave imprudent course and save religion.' Similar reactions were also noted among the Guild of Grocers in Tehran and other Muslim communities.[132] Indian pilgrims are traditionally depicted as the most devoted when it came to the Prophet's tomb. Arthur Wavell speaks of 'the extravagant emotion of the Indians, when they actually see with their own eyes this tomb which they have from childhood been taught to regard with superstitious awe . . . Many burst into tears and frantically kiss the railings,' and states that he has seen 'Indians and Afghans fall down apparently unconscious.'[133]

A further confirmation of the extent of the destruction came from Munshi Ihsanullah, an Indian Punjabi merchant and confidant of the British Foreign Service, who reported in May 1926:

> Not only the Wahabis of Nejd but also a number of Indians who have embraced the Wahabi faith are persuading Ibn Saud to forcibly convert all who visit Mecca and to destroy tombs and all religious edifices, which they claim amount to idolatry. I learned that it is intended to demolish the four Makams of the four Imams, as well as the Makam Ibrahim, and also to demolish the minaret of the holy mosque . . . Orders have been issued for the destruction of the Tomb of Eve at Jeddah and also for the demolition of the Dar-el-Khazran (the place where Omar the Great was converted). The birthplace of the prophet 'Moulid-el-Nabi' has been destroyed, and the place is overrun with pie-dogs.[134]

Some Indian Muslims called a conference in Lucknow and debated, first, whether to cancel the *hajj* altogether for as long as the Wahhabi government ruled, and, second, the destruction of the tombs. They also wrote to the ulama of Medina regarding the tombs, and received this response:

> With regard to domes: If walls are built round, or a dome built over, a tomb lying in land dedicated to the burial of Moslem dead, they should be destroyed, for it is sinful to take up more dedicated ground than is (strictly) necessary. The Imam should pull them down. If the land (on which the tomb is built) is private property, it is wrongful to erect a tomb ... When Sultan Abdul Aziz Al Saud wanted to demolish the domes, he consulted the Ulema of Medina and they gave their fetwa to the effect that such action was allowable. He therefore acted according to the fetwa of the Ulema, and not according to his own conviction alone. Signed by eighteen persons from among the Ulema of the four Sects at Medina.[135]

When the frustrated Indian Muslims' efforts did not yield any results, they approached the British, whom they held responsible for the Wahhabis' destructive acts. The British, however, considered this to be an internal religious affair and were not particularly interested in intervening in the Hijaz. At that point, they were far more occupied with the need to determine the boundaries between their claimed territories in Iraq and the Persian Gulf emirates and the emerging Wahhabi state.[136]

A report dated 30 January 1937 written by the British Legation in Jeddah to the Foreign Secretary Anthony Eden demonstrates that the Wahhabi observance of the strict funerary rules did not relax even after several years. The report confirms that the visiting of graves was still forbidden. Whenever visits to a shrine, which were discontinued after the Wahabi conquest of the Hijaz, were resumed, the authorities removed the remains to a general cemetery and destroyed every trace of the building under which they had lain. According to the report, 'it is not even permitted to visit the graves of relatives and friends'.[137]

* * *

The negative opinions against grave visiting formulated by mostly Hanbali scholars were significantly enhanced in the eighteenth-century Arabian Peninsula. This was due, primarily, to the revival of hadith scholarship, accompanied by a critical reconsideration of the prevalent juristic system and Ashʿari theology. Traditionalist movements mostly flourished in Medina and Yemen. In relation to doctrinal issues, the main emphasis was given to the defence of monotheism and a criticism of all practices considered to be polytheistic, including the potential for graves to tempt the ignorant masses and lead them into eventual unbelief. These trends culminated in the middle of the eighteenth century with the emergence of Muhammad ibn ʿAbd al-Wahhab. His iconoclastic teaching strictly opposed folk practices and combated the cult of venerating saints and ancestors. In so doing, Ibn ʿAbd al-Wahhab drew upon the ideas and concepts popularised by Ibn Taymiyya and Ibn Qayyim al-Jawziyya more then four centuries earlier. Ibn ʿAbd al-Wahhab mostly summarised the existing classical Hanbali teaching, without adding much new material or ideas. His contribution, however, lay in connecting theory with practice or, in other words in gaining political and military support, with himself and his followers actually destroying the graves of saints and ancestors. Ibn ʿAbd al-Wahhab's foremost legacy consists in formulating the basic vision of a rotten society, ignorant of 'proper' religious rules, allowing the excommunication of those Muslims who were not true believers and monotheists, and demolishing anything with an idolatrous potential. As regards excommunication or the labelling of someone as a *kāfir* (unbeliever), it is noteworthy that the theological and doctrinal differences that existed between Ashʿaris/Maturidis and Salafis (alternatively referred to as Atharis or Hanbalis), in particular concerning God's names and attributes, had been debated theoretically in Ibn Taymiyya's era, but began to involve more visible consequences during Muhammad ibn ʿAbd al-Wahhab's time. According to Salafi theology, any consideration of one's beliefs or unbelief should take into account three issues: language, heart and hand, that is, one's profession of faith (the aspect of *islām*, or *iqrār*), one's inner beliefs (the aspect of *īmān*, or *taṣdīq*) and one's deeds and acts (*ʿamal*). Conversely, Ashʿaris/Maturidis do not view deeds and actions as theological foundations, thus being more tolerant. It was therefore the question of *takfir* that brought Wahhabis more generally into conflict with other Muslims.

The ideas of Muhammad ibn 'Abd al-Wahhab were disseminated in the form of printed Wahhabi texts, appearing in other parts of the Muslim world, most notably in Egypt in the west and, in the east, as far as India, thus generating the subsequent growth of a trend later to be described as Salafi Islam. The growing Salafi movement, of which Wahhabism was only one part, was in turn responsible for the revival and spread of Ibn Taymiyya's teachings. Subsequently, there was a wider rehabilitation of both him and Ibn 'Abd al-Wahhab and the further dissemination of iconoclastic ideas. This was accomplished at a time when many thinkers considered Salafism to be the proper antidote to competing religious and other trends (including Sufism and atheism) and were in the process of building their religious beliefs on the strict concept of *tawḥīd*. During this period, the use of the term Salafi becomes somewhat confusing. It does not mean a school of theology opposed to Ash'arism, especially when it comes, for example, to the so-called enlightened Salafism of Muhammad 'Abduh, but it does include the ideas of those who selectively reflected some aspects of Ibn Taymiyya's reformist thought. This is why we see Muhammad 'Abduh criticising *taqlid*, while at the same time expounding a theology considered to be too rationalist. This 'enlightened' trend in Salafism was, however, rather ephemeral. It was 'Abduh's pupil Rashid Rida, himself a critic of heretical Sufi practices, whose al-Manar (Lighthouse) printing house, financed by the Saudis, disseminated Wahhabi texts in Egypt and elsewhere, thus supporting the establishment of more traditionalist (hadith-oriented rather that rationalist) Salafis, such as Ansar al-sunna al-muhammadiyya.

Significantly, as in the case of Ibn 'Abd al-Wahhab's original movement, these trends and the dissemination of associated ideas led to an ever-growing number of physical attacks on funeral architecture, best exemplified by the Wahhabi conquest of the Hijaz in the early nineteenth century, followed by similar events in the first decades of the twentieth century. This trend, as will be shown in the following chapter, was further solidified in the second half of the twentieth century with the growth of pan-Islamism, propagated mostly by Saudi Arabia and its religious establishment.

Notes

1. Mouline, *The Clerics of Islam*, pp. 41–2.
2. Cf. Steinberg, 'Ecology, Knowledge and Trade in Central Arabia (Najd) during the 19th and Early 20th Centuries', pp. 77–120. See also Mouline, *The Clerics of Islam*, p. 45.
3. Three editions of Ibn Ghannam's *History of Najd* are known to us. The most popular one, released by Dar al-Shuruq, is rather a simplified paraphrase of Ibn Ghannam's text. We find the Riyadh edition of Sulayman al-Khurashi (2010), which is a revision of the 1948 Riyadh release, more reliable.
4. As succinctly noted by Al-Rasheed, *Contesting the Saudi State*, pp. 22–4, who explains the Wahhabi demonisation of past Arabian society as a means by which to gain legitimacy.
5. On this subject, see Peters, 'The Battered Dervishes of Bab Zuwayla', pp. 93–115; and Flemming, 'Die Vorwahhabitische Fitna im osmanischen Kairo 1711', pp. 55–65.
6. Based on the introductory study in Ibn Ghannam, *Tarikh Ibn Ghannam*, vol. 1, pp. 101–2.
7. See Voll, 'Muḥammad Ḥayyā Al-Sindī', pp. 32–9; and Voll, 'Hadith Scholars and Tariqas', pp. 3–4.
8. He is worth mentioning because of his book on necrolatry: Hamad ibn Nasir ibn 'Uthman al-Mu'ammar, *Al-nubdha al-sharifa al-nafisa fi al-radd 'ala al-quburiyyin*, ed. 'Abd al-Salam ibn Burjis ibn Nasir Al 'Abd al-Karim (Riyadh: Dar al-'asima, wizarat al-shu'un al-islamiyya wa al-awqaf wa al-da'wa wa al-irshad, 1998/9). The book was included in *Majmu'at al-rasa'il wa al-masa'il al-najdiyya* and *al-Durar al-saniyya fi al-ajwiba al-najdiyya*. It was also separately published by Rashid Rida's al-Manar publishing house under the title *Haqiqat al-tawhid wa al-'ibada, al-farq bayn du'a' al-'ibada wa al-'ada*.
9. See, for example, a work by a nineteenth-century chronicler: Ibn Bishr, *'Unwan al-majd*, vol. 1, pp. 27–34.
10. Cook, *Commanding Right*, p. 247.
11. al-Mutayri, 'Masa'il al-i'tiqad', p. 18.
12. See al-Nu'mi, *Ma'arij al-albab*.
13. See al-San'ani, *Tathir al-i'tiqad*.

14. al-Amir al-San'ani focused primarily on the first two aspects of monotheism. He calls them *tawḥīd al-rubūbīya*, or *al-rāziqīya*, and *tawḥīd al-'ibāda*. See al-San'ani, *Tathir al-i'tiqad*, pp. 32, 35.
15. Ibid., pp. 52, 55–60. It seems, however, that this kind of criticism is not always based on a personal experience, as a very similar passage can be found in al-Shawkani, see Haykel, *Revival and Reform in Islam*, p. 132.
16. 1163 AH according to al-San'ani, *Tathir al-i'tiqad*, p. 60.
17. '*Ya'mur arkāṇ al-sharī'a hādiman mashāhid ḍāll al-nās fīhā 'an al-rushd.*' This particular verse is not cited in the book, since the poem is very long.
18. Cook, 'On the Origins of Wahhābism', pp. 200–2. With reference to Siddiq Hasan Khan's *Abjad al-'ulum*.
19. Haykel, *Revival and Reform in Islam*, p. 129.
20. Ibn Sahman, *Tabri'at al-shaykhayn*, p. 3. As regards the authenticity of the poem, it is strange that it begins with swearing by one's life instead of Allah himself, '*wa hādha la-'amrī ghayr mā anta fīhi min tajāribika fī qatl li-man kāna fī Najd*'. See also 'Abd al-Rahman Al al-Shaykh, *Fath al-Majid*, pp. 4–5. However, the general question of whether *la-'amrī* is a kind of oath by other than God (which would be tantamount to *shirk*) or not, has been debated even by Salafis themselves. See, for instance, a treatise *al-I'lan bi-anna la-'amri laysat min al-iman*, pp. 111–19, in Abu 'Abd al-Latif Hammad ibn Muhammad al-Ansari, *Rasa'il fi al-'aqida* (Maktabat al-furqan, n.d.).
21. al-San'ani, *Tathir al-i'tiqad*, p. 69.
22. Ibn Hajar al-'Asqalani's book *Attainment of the Objective* (*Bulugh al-maram*), which is a commentary on traditions of legal relevance (*aḥādīth al-aḥkām*) drawn from numerous hadith collections, such as Bukhari, Muslim, Abu Dawud, al-Tirmidhi, al-Nasa'i, Ibn Maja and Ahmad ibn Hanbal, was highly influential in traditionalist circles. This is evident from the fact that it was abbreviated and commented on by al-Amir al-San'ani, and once again by hadith scholar Nasir al-Din al-Albani. The book is of interest here because it also contains hadiths relevant to the issue of *ziyāra* and necrolatry: while the first is recommended even for women, the latter is rebutted. See 'Kitab al-jana'iz', especially 'al-Bina' 'ala al-qubur wa tajsisuha', 'Ziyarat al-nisa' al-maqabir' and 'Ma yuqal wa yuf'al 'inda ziyarat al-qubur' in Muhammad ibn Isma'il al-San'ani, *Subul al-salam, sharh bulugh al-maram li-Ibn Hajar al-'Asqalani*, with commentary by Muhammad Nasir al-Din al-Albani (Riyadh: Maktabat al-ma'arif, 2006), vol. 2.

23. Haykel, *Revival and Reform in Islam*, p. 86.
24. al-Habashi, *Hawaliyat yamaniyya*, p. 22.
25. al-San'ani, *Majmu' at al-rasa'il*, pp. 8, 11, 14.
26. al-Habashi, *Hawaliyat yamaniyya*, pp. 23–4.
27. al-Shawkani, *al-Badr al-tali'*, see biographical entries 'Ghalib ibn Musa'id' (pp. 355–8) and 'Sharif Mecca and Su'ud ibn 'Abd al-'Aziz' (pp. 182–6).
28. Haykel, *Revival and Reform in Islam*, p. 133.
29. al-San'ani, *Majmu' at al-rasa'il*, pp. 17–18.
30. For a description of the act, see Ibn Bishr, *'Unwan al-majd*, vol. 1, p. 39.
31. 'al-Risala al-sab'a', in *Tarikh Najd*, p. 271.
32. Another image of a handful of true believers, besides *jāhilīya*, is that of a sentiment of strangeness (*ghurba*). It occurs quite often in Sunni reformist literature, because it gives the impression of a rotten society in need of socio-religious reform. This image is based on a hadith (mentioned in Muslim's *Sahih*) that 'Islam began as something strange [alt. a stranger] and will revert to being something strange, so blessed are the strangers' (*bada'a al-islām gharīban wa saya'ūdu gharīban kamā bada' fatūbā li-l-ghurabā'*). According to another version, the believers asked the Prophet who these strangers were. Muhammad is reported to have responded that they were 'those who remedy what people spoiled from my Sunna', 'emigrants (*al-nuzzā'*) from tribes' and 'pious people as a minority in the world of evil'. Cf. the explanation given by Ibn Baz, the former Grand Mufti of Saudi Arabia, available at: www.binbaz.org.sa/fatawa/4716, last accessed 9 September 2016.
33. *Mu'allafat al-shaykh imam Muhammad ibn 'Abd al-Wahhab*, vol. 5, pp. 11–12.
34. Other tombs are mentioned in Wahba, 'Wahhabism in Arabia', pp. 460–1.
35. al-'Uthaymin, *Muhammad ibn 'Abd al-Wahhab*, p. 97, states that this particular topic is dealt with in *The Fundamentals of Belief* (*Usul al-iman*). Ibn 'Abd al-Wahhab did not consider God's attributes and names as a part of *tawḥīd*, rather he viewed it in the broader context of doctrines (*'aqā'id*) and theology (*uṣūl al-dīn*), see Ibn Ghannam, *Tarikh Ibn Ghannam*, vol. 1, pp. 321–3. For early apologetics, see Al Mu'ammar, *al-Tuhfa al-madaniyya fi al-'aqida al-salafiyya*.
36. al-'Uthaymin, *Muhammad ibn 'Abd al-Wahhab*, p. 97.
37. All of the quotations that follow are extracted from Muhammad ibn 'Abd al-Wahhab, 'Kitab al-tawhid', pp. 7–97. Because there are numerous editions of this work, we prefer to quote from it based on chapter names rather than page numbers.

38. Ibn Qayyim al-Jawziyya, *Ighathat al-lahfan*, vol. 1, pp. 332–3. Compare the same argument at the very beginning of Ibn ʿAbd al-Wahhab, 'Kitab al-tawhid'.
39. The term 'polytheists' is a rather inaccurate translation of the Arabic *mushrikūn*, that is, those who associate something else (be it gods or things) to God. In Muslim historical narrative, this term designates the polytheism of the Quraysh in pagan Mecca. However, recent studies both on early Muslim history and on the use of the term in the Qurʾan have led to the hypothesis that Islam originated in a Judeo-Christian milieu and that the term *shirk* was not literal polytheism, but a failure (in the eyes of their opponents) to maintain a full and proper form of monotheism. The opposite of *shirk* is not simply monotheism (*tawḥīd*), but the pure and intense type of monotheism indicated by *ikhlāṣ*. For more, see especially Hawting, *The Idea of Idolatry*, p. 61.
40. Sulayman ibn ʿAbd al-Wahhab, *al-Sawāʿiq al-ilahiyya*, p. 52.
41. al-ʿUthaymin, *Sharh thalathat al-usul*, p. 124.
42. Ibid., p. 34. In these treatises a lot of questions are posed. Because it might be confusing, we must clarify here that Ibn ʿAbd al-Wahhab understands the three principles to be knowledge of God, religion and his Messenger, not these questions (*masāʾil*).
43. See ibid., pp. 37, 69, 72.
44. Ibid., p. 153.
45. Patel, *The Arab Nahda*, p. 76.
46. ʿAbd al-Latif Al al-Shaykh, *Misbah al-zulam*, p. 22. It is strange that his name was corrupted. Mahmud Shukri al-Alusi also mistakenly spells Nuʿaymi (Hasan ibn Muhammad al-Nuʿaymi al-Yamani), see his *Tarikh najd*, p. 78.
47. According to Salih ibn Fawzan Al Fawzan, author of the foreword in Sunʿallah, *Sayf Allah*, p. 17.
48. Commins, *The Wahhabi Mission*, p. 45.
49. Ibn ʿAtiq, *Hidayat al-tariq*, p. 12.
50. Ibid., p. 125.
51. The *Ahl al-hadith* movement had close personal ties with Wahhabi scholars who were willing to study with great scholars in India. Some members of the *Ahl al-hadith* movement, such as Muhammad Bashir Sahsawani (d. 1874), undoubtedly openly sympathised with Wahhabis. Sahsawani lived in Bhopal under the auspices of Siddiq Hasan Khan. He became known to a wider public after entering a debate with ʿAbd al-Hayy Lakhnawi Farangi Mahalli (d. 1887)

on the subjects of visiting the Prophet's grave and monotheism. His controversial religious outlook and style of preaching led to various public debates with almost all the other religious movements of the time. He also wrote a refutation titled *Preventing the People from the Devilish Insinuations of Shaykh Dahlan* (*Siyanat al-insan 'an waswasat shaykh Dahlan*), arguing against his contemporary Ahmad Zayni Dahlan (d. 1886). Shaykh Dahlan was a Shafiʿi mufti of Mecca, who gained some prominence by accusing Wahhabism of extremism. In his refutation, Mahalli frequently cites Ibn Taymiyya to support his argument, but without indicating specific works. It might be assumed, as Preckel suggests, that Muhammad Bashir used Ibn Taymiyya's *Book of the Greater and Smaller Pilgrimage to Mecca* (*Kitab al-hajj wa al-ʿumra*), which was available to him in Siddiq Hasan Khan's private library, see Preckel, 'Screening Siddiq Hasan Khan's Library', p. 217.

52. Brown, *Rethinking Tradition*, pp. 27–8.
53. Siddiq Hasan Khan, *Abjad al-ʿulum*, vol. 3, pp. 142–3.
54. al-Mutayri, 'Masa'il al-iʿtiqad', p. 32.
55. Siddiq Hasan Khan, *Abjad al-ʿulum*, vol. 3, p. 143.
56. Preckel, 'Wahhabi or National Hero'.
57. See Alavi, 'Siddiq Hasan Khan', p. 9.
58. Siddiq Hasan Khan, *An Interpreter of Wahabiism*, p. 30.
59. Siddiq Hasan Khan, *Al-siraj al-wahhaj*, vol. 3, pp. 377–86.
60. See Nafi, 'Salafism Revived', pp. 49–97.
61. Ibid.
62. Weismann, *The Naqshbandiyya*, p. 142.
63. Ibid., pp. 142–3.
64. Commins, *The Wahhabi Mission*, p. 132.
65. al-ʿAjami, *al-Rasa'il al-mutabadala*, p. 47.
66. Mahmud Shukri al-Alusi, *Masa'il al-jahiliyya*, p. 17.
67. Ibid., p. 20.
68. Mahmud Shukri al-Alusi, *Tarikh Najd*, p. 48.
69. In Wahhabi religious literature and Wahhabi historiography, Ibn ʿAbd al-Wahhab is sometimes referred to as a *mujtahid* and *mujaddid*. In Sunni religious literature the term *tajdīd*, meaning renewal, is usually related to one of the two ideas – reformism connected with millennialism and Mahdism (such as Sanusiyya, Ahmadiyya or Mahdists of Sudan) and reformism is connected with the concept

of *ijtihād* and hadith scholarship and fight against innovations (such as of Ibn Taymiyya, Shah Waliullah, al-Shawkani and al-San'ani).

70. Lauzière, *The Making of Salafism*, p. 49.
71. Hourani, *Reason and Tradition*, p. 238.
72. Lauzière, *The Making of Salafism*, pp. 46–7.
73. Commins, *Wahhabi Mission*, p. 132. For the rationale behind Rashid Rida's pro-Saudi inclination, see also Lauzière, *The Making of Salafism*, pp. 60–94.
74. It is interesting that the traditions related to visiting Muhammad's grave, as narrated by Daraqutni, are denounced as fabricated and false. Without doubt this is a reference to Taqi al-Din al-Subki (d. 1355), a great Shafi'i judge of Damascus, who wrote a renunciation of Ibn Taymiyya's legal opinions on *ziyāra*. Al-Subki draw mainly on Daraqutni's collection of hadiths, which conveys narrations of the Prophet suggesting that visiting the Prophet's grave is a duty, such as 'He who performs the pilgrimage and does not visit me, has shunned me' (*man ḥajja wa lam yazurnī faqad jafānī*).
75. It is worth mentioning that this collection, as far as we know, contains one of the first occurrences in a Salafi context of the term loyalty and disavowal (*al-walā' wa al-barā'*) as one of the three principles along side *rubūbīya* and *ulūhīya*.
76. As observed by Bonacina, who provides an insightful analysis of the Europeans' early attempts to interpret the new movement. Bonacina, *The Wahhabis Seen through European Eyes (1772–1830)*, p. 9.
77. Litvak, *Shi'i Scholars of Nineteenth-Century Iraq*, p. 121. Colourful description of the looting in Najaf and Karbala is also to be found in Euting, *Tagbuch einer Reise in Inner-Arabien*, pp. 159–60.
78. Ibn Bishr, *'Unwan al-majd*, vol. 1, p. 257.
79. Rousseau, *Description du Pachalik de Bagdad*, pp. 73–4.
80. See Nakash, *The Shi'is of Iraq*, pp. 27–8.
81. For one instance of such a defensive tract, see *Manhaj al-rashad li-man arada al-sadad* (*The Path of Guidance to Whoever Wants the Right Course*) written in 1795 by the prominent Najafi *mujtahid*, Ja'far Kashif al-Ghita' (d. 1812). For its analysis, see Litvak, 'Encounters between Shi'i and Sunni 'Ulama' in Ottoman Iraq', pp. 74–7.
82. Quoted from Mouline, *The Clerics of Islam*, pp. 72–4.

83. For the text of the letter, see Hughes, *A Dictionary of Islam*, p. 660. Another version of the letter, contained in Annesley, *Voyages and Travels*, vol. 2, p. 390, has 'I destroyed all the tombs' instead of 'things'. For the debate about the true provenance of the letter, see Traboulsi, '"I Entered Mecca . . ."', pp. 197–217.
84. Traboulsi, '"I Entered Mecca . . ."', pp. 205–6.
85. Rousseau, *Description du Pachalik de Bagdad*, p. 171.
86. Burckhardt, *Notes*, vol. 2, p. 108.
87. Ibid., pp. 108–9. This is also reported by Ibn Bishr, *'Unwan al-majd*, vol. 1, p. 263.
88. Niebuhr, *Travels through Arabia*, vol. 2, pp. 40–1.
89. Burckhardt, *Notes*, vol. 2, pp. 109–10.
90. Cf. Lauzière, *The Making of Salafism*, p. 66.
91. That was, among others, the fate of the mausoleum of Ahmad ibn Hanbal in Baghdad. Goldziher, 'On the Veneration of the Dead in Paganism and Islam', p. 233.
92. As noted by Bonacina, *The Wahhabis Seen through European Eyes (1772–1830)*, p. 174, fn. 96.
93. Cf. DeLong-Bas, *Wahhabi Islam*, pp. 66–9.
94. Corancez, *Histoire des Wahabis*, pp. 19–20.
95. Browne, *Travels in Africa, Egypt, and Syria*, p. 389. The destruction of mosques in this case refers to the destruction of domes and tombs built for saints, which were often situated at or inside a mosque.
96. Ali Bey, *Travels of Ali Bey*, vol. 2, p. 148.
97. Malcolm, *History of Persia*, vol. 2, pp. 263–4 fn.
98. Annesley, *Voyages and Travels*, vol. 2, p. 389.
99. Ibid., p. 391.
100. Tamisier, *Voyage en Arabie*, pp. 277, 279.
101. Mengin, *Histoire de l'Égypte sous le gouvernement de Mohammed-Aly*, vol. 2, p. 452.
102. As duly noted by Bonacina, *The Wahhabis Seen through European Eyes (1772–1830)*, p. 131, fn. 34.
103. Burckhardt, *Travels in Arabia*, vol. 2, p. 179.
104. Ibid., pp. 228–9.
105. Ibid., pp. 195–6.

106. Ibid., vol. 1, p. 312.
107. Burton, *Personal Narrative of a Pilgrimage to El Medinah and Meccah*, p. 293.
108. Ibid., p. 305.
109. Doughty, *Travels in Arabia Deserta*, vol. 1, p. 618
110. al-Samhudi, *Kitab wafa' al-wafa'*, vol. 2, pp. 78–9. For its history, see, for example, Ibn Battuta, *Travels of Ibn Battuta*, vol. 1, pp. 178–80; Ibn Jubayr, *The Travels of Ibn Jubayr*, pp. 195–7; Burckhardt, *Travels in Arabia*, vol. 2, pp. 222–6; and Rutter, *The Holy Cities of Arabia*, pp. 256–8.
111. For the long list of significant figures buried in the al-Baqi' cemetery, see al-Hajiri, *Al-Baqi'*, pp. 45–64, the list of imams pp. 48–53.
112. Although his body was first buried at the Jewish cemetery in Medina and only later, during the reign of Mu'awiya ibn Abi Sufyan, was it transferred to the al-Baqi' cemetery.
113. Burckhardt, *Travels in Arabia*, vol. 2, p. 225.
114. Munt, *The Holy City of Medina*, p. 126.
115. Ibn Bishr, *'Unwan al-majd*, vol. 1, p. 288. Cf. also al-Hajiri, *Al-Baqi'*, pp. 82–5.
116. Burckhardt, *Travels in Arabia*, vol. 2, pp. 222–3.
117. Rutter, *The Holy Cities of Arabia*, p. 502.
118. Ibid., p. 274.
119. Ibid., pp. 501, 503.
120. Ibid., pp. 256–8.
121. Wavell, *A Modern Pilgrim in Mecca*, pp. 97, 113–14.
122. al-Hajiri, *Al-Baqi'*, p. 26.
123. *Records of the Hajj*, vol. 5, 'The Hashemite period (1916–1925)', p. 607.
124. Ibid., p. 640.
125. Ibid., p. 736.
126. Ibid., p. 743.
127. Ibid., vol. 6, 'The Saudi period (1926–1935)', p. 9.
128. For the description or transcript of some of these protest letters, especially from India and Iran, see al-Hajiri, *Al-Baqi'*, pp. 147–81. Some of the official answers can be found in ibid., pp. 203–8.
129. Ibid., pp. 113–43.
130. For more about some of these destructions, see, for example, Valentine, *Force and Fanaticism*, pp. 182–9.

131. *Records of the Hajj*, vol. 6, 'The Saudi period (1926–1935)', p. 72.
132. Ibid., vol. 5, p. 746.
133. Wavell, *A Modern Pilgrim in Mecca*, p. 93.
134. *Records of the Hajj*, vol. 6, 'The Saudi period (1926–1935)', p. 10.
135. Ibid., p. 78.
136. Others offered a more sober account of the events at hand. The Deputy Secretary to the Government of Bengal wrote a letter, dated 4 October 1932, to the Foreign Secretary to the Government of India: 'To the personal knowledge of the Hon'ble Member in charge, the alleged desecration of tombs and shrines is false and the alleged "inhuman and dastardly actions of the Nejdis" exist only in the imagination of the memorialists. As regards the demolition of tombs there are no tombs that have been demolished in the literal sense of the term. Over certain tombs in Mecca and Medina there existed gorgeous mausoleums to which ignorant pilgrims unaware of the exact teachings of Islam used to resort and indulge in idolatrous and un-Islamic practices. In order to stop such evil practices the mausoleums have, in some cases, been demolished and they have been replaced by simple puritanic tombs. There was a certain spot in Mecca over which one thousand years after the death of the Holy Prophet a grand structure was built, and it was alleged that this was the spot where the Prophet was born. Soon after the conquest of the Hedjaz by King Ibn Saud, a careful enquiry was held as to the birth place of the Prophet. It was reported that he was born in a certain quarter of the town of Mecca but that there was no authentic proof to show that the place in which the beautiful domed structure was erected was the actual spot. Hence in the absence of an authentic proof this particular building was demolished and its rich materials in the shape of marbles etc. used to construct the Central Hospital in Mecca, an action which has had the approval of all enlightened Moslems.' *Records of the Hajj*, vol. 6, 'The Saudi period (1926–1935)', p. 431.
137. Ibid., 'The Saudi period', vol. 7, p. 183.

3

Saudi Arabia between pan-Islamism, Iconoclasm and Political Legitimacy

Praise be to Allah, we seek His help and His forgiveness. We seek refuge with Allah from the evil of our own souls and from our bad deeds. Whomsoever Allah guides will never be led astray, and whomsoever Allah leads astray, no one can guide. I bear witness that there is no god but Allah, the One, having no partner. And I bear witness that Muhammad is His slave and Messenger.

An opening formula, referred to as the *khuṭbat al-ḥāja*, the sermon of necessity, and used at an early stage by Ibn Taymiyya. After reciting this, the supplicant may ask for something from Allah. The formula has become popular in modern Salafi discourse and Wahhabi–Salafi writings can often be discerned by its presence.

As the threat posed by the Islamic State (IS) grows greater and more sinister, Saudi Arabia stands at the front line of the battle against the extremists. Saudi Arabia is adamant that it has the unique knowledge, expertise, and legitimacy to effectively lead the effort to defeat IS. The country's guardianship of the two holy mosques in Mecca and Medina underpins Saudi credibility in pushing back against the misguided interpretation of the Islamic faith that IS is now propagating in the heart of the Arab world . . . Saudi Arabia believes that policy should be guided by the idea that Sunni empowerment is the key ingredient needed to defeat Sunni extremism.

Obaid and al-Sarhan, 'A Saudi View on the Islamic State', p. 79

Shaykh Ibn Baz, all the Islamic world is filled with his knowledge.[1]

Nasir al-Din al-Albani

In a collection of *fatāwā* (religious opinions), issued by a group of prominent Saudi ulama, we find the following question: 'I live in a neighbourhood that has a graveyard, and every day I walk along a path that passes beside it . . . What is obligatory upon me in this situation? Should I always give the greetings of peace to the deceased, or what should I do? Please give me some direction.'[2] It must be stressed that questions of this sort are very common. The answer of Ibn Baz, once the highest mufti of Saudi Arabia and a revered Islamic scholar, may not be surprising given that the Prophet Muhammad himself is said to have greeted the dead when passing by their graves, and that this practice is encouraged even by fierce critics of grave visits. But the answer is not what matters in this context. Rather, it is the question itself, which encapsulates the ambiguity with respect to graves and related customs in certain parts of today's Islamic world and the consequent uncertainty regarding proper conduct on the part of ordinary believers. It also shows how the influence of some clerics permeates the everyday lives of Muslims, who feel compelled to ask for guidance in every sphere of daily life.[3]

The purpose of this chapter is twofold. Our aim is, first, to describe the structures of the official Saudi religious establishment and how it became institutionalised, and, second, to shed some light on how Wahhabi teachings have interacted with other currents, Salafi and non-Salafi, in modern times, and how *ziyāra* and various related issues have been perceived. It focuses especially on Salafi scholars, such as Muhammad ibn Ibrahim Al al-Shaykh, Ibn Baz and Nasir al-Din al-Albani, since they are regarded as the most influential iconoclasts of pro-Saudi orientation, and also considers various mutations that have arisen through interaction with the ideology of the Muslim Brotherhood. Arguably, in the past, although doctrinal issues were relatively fixed, other aspects related to the realisation of political goals and the relationship with the Saudi regime were prone to turbulent change. During the first two Saudi states (1744–1818 and 1821–91), Wahhabism was perceived by other Muslims as an interpretation of Islam, confined, along with Saudi politics, within the borders of the Saudi state, especially in its homeland of the Najd. The ideology of the Wahhabi movement drew a strict division between the world of true Islam, as represented by their followers, and the outer worlds of polytheism. In the beginning, those regarded as polytheists were fellow Muslims who were committing the sin of *shirk* – in particular because of their veneration of graves and the dead. Enemies of the state were those who refused to be 'Islamised', that is, to become subject to the Saudi authorities. With the emergence of the third Saudi state, and especially after the Kingdom of Saudi Arabia was created in 1932 and was able to secure the enormous revenues provided by the discovery of oil, the country's political and cultural isolation was reduced, with it opening up, albeit only in a limited way, to the outside world. Since the enemies of the Wahhabi ideology were not only traditional polytheists, such as 'grave-worshipping' Shi'is and Sufis, but other groups as well, the notion of *shirk* was intentionally reformulated in order to denounce aspects of the new political reality – in addition to the *shirk* of idols and graves, the new *shirk*s of worshipping democracy and worshipping a tyrannical ruler (*tāghūt*) found their way into religious discourse.

Religion between Zealotry and Loyalty

The Saudi case is rather unique. First, Saudi Arabia is a particularly opaque society, its politics are not institutionalised but rather highly personal in nature. In addition, in the Saudi case, it is the state that is essentially 'Islamist', seeking to enhance the Islamic cause and supporting Islamic institutions, both locally and abroad. The kingdom has a basic set of laws, but most importantly it claims that the Qur'an is its constitution. Since its creation in 1932, the Saudi kingdom has had problems in recognising the nation-state structure.[4] Instead of creating a centralised bureaucracy, the Saudi regime decided to opt for a reliance on the moral authority of the religious establishment. Only gradually did Saudi Arabia take steps to conform to the notion of a modern state. The process, leading to the emergence of a hybrid Shari'ah/nation-state, consisted of creating government bodies and ministries and also of bureaucratising the religious structures. Most of the process was completed by the early 1970s, with some protracted evolutionary developments still currently taking place. Even today, however, we can witness the efforts of the Saudi ulama to present themselves as the only possessors of religious truth and salvation and acting collectively as the sole holder of ideological authority.[5]

As Zaman has noted, the ulama 'in the Muslim world are a crucial part of the changes sweeping through these societies in increasingly significant, often unprecedented ways'.[6] This is perhaps best applicable in relation to Saudi religious circles, even though the official Saudi ulama have been incorporated into the state's administrative apparatus and, in general, have been rather modest in their opinions and have not sought to question the king's authority. In Saudi Arabia, the ulama are traditionally in charge of justice and education. Other than that, their opinions on major developments (regarding, among other areas, domestic and foreign policy) have been rejected. However, they still belong to the political elite and the influence of their collective bodies and individual members is usually heightened in times of crisis, when they manage to increase their power and extend their control (this happened, for instance, after the 1979 occupation of the Grand Mosque in Mecca, after the Gulf War and, more recently, after the Arab uprisings).

Even the first two Saudi states were based on a mixture of the doctrine of Wahhabism, as transmitted by Ibn 'Abd al-Wahhab's descendants and successors, Al al-Shaykh, and the chieftaincy system. The ruler was required to consult the ulama and abide by their ruling. This was fully in line with Ibn Taymiyya, who envisioned the division of power in a way that the rulers (*umarā'*) should be in charge of maintaining security and internal order, and the ulama were to be responsible for teaching and upholding the values of Wahhabi morality.[7] Consequently, the main interest of Wahhabism was in attaining an ideal society rather than in elaborating on the proper execution of political affairs and the division of power. Even when Wahhabi influence was at its strongest in the eighteenth century, it did not bring about a transformation of the political habits of the region. As for the beginnings of the third Saudi state, the position of the ulama was further weakened. 'Abd al-'Aziz (aka Ibn Sa'ud, 1876–1953) himself appointed ulama to their posts and transferred them from one department to another. The ulama held certain moral leverage, but they had neither the policy-making authority nor the organisational infrastructure at their disposal to implement their rulings.[8] The use of the term 'Wahhabism' was becoming more normalised by the beginning of the twentieth century. However, King 'Abd al-'Aziz prohibited its use in 1929, opting instead for the term 'Salafism'. As Mouline puts it, the main purpose of this movement, like its predecessors that had appeared in the form of politico-religious movements since medieval Islamic times, was to legitimise a political and/or religious approach and provide it with a salvational depth.[9]

With the revival of the last Saudi state, a new wave of extremism and iconoclasm afflicted the Najd, Hijaz and the surrounding regions. In the period of the re-conquest of the lost domains, between 1902 and 1932, the Saudi ruler, ʿAbd al-ʿAziz, revived the Wahhabi teachings of *tawḥīd* in support of the unification of Saudi Arabia. In doing so, he instigated the emergence of the Ikhwan movement. The Ikhwan formed a military religious brotherhood of Bedouin warriors, who were to become the driving force behind the Saudi conquest of much of the Arabian Peninsula under ʿAbd al-ʿAziz's leadership. They were supposed to be brothers in Islam, a motif found in a Qurʾanic sura (3:103): 'And hold firmly to the rope of Allah all together and do not become divided. And remember the favour of Allah upon you – when you were enemies and He brought your hearts together and you became, by His favour, brothers. And you were on the edge of a pit of the Fire and He saved you from it.'[10] After the halt of the expansionist movement as a result of new political circumstances, mostly due to the delimitation of borders with Iraq in the zone under British influence, the Ikhwans began to complain and question ʿAbd al-ʿAziz's authority. ʿAbd al-ʿAziz's efforts to subdue them, sedentarise them and tax them resulted in an open conflict between ʿAbd al-ʿAziz and part of the Ikhwan movement. In addition, much of the friction with the Ikhwan must be ascribed to their religious zeal and fanaticism, especially when it came to their wish to 'purify' the newly conquered Hijaz with its holy shrines. In order to curb the cult of the dead, as mentioned in the previous chapter, the Ikhwan had already destroyed the shrines of Masjid al-mawlid (the Prophet's birthplace), Bayt Khadija (the house of the Prophet's first wife), Bayt Abu Bakr (the house of the first caliph, Abu Bakr al-Siddiq) and many other pilgrimage sites. Moreover, in December 1924, grave-worship was declared illegal.

The Ikhwan also continued to exert pressure on the authorities to destroy the dome of the Prophet's tomb in Medina. Motivated by pragmatism, as well as by his commitment to calming growing international Muslim pressure and to surviving in the international arena, ʿAbd al-ʿAziz decided to moderate Ikhwan zealotry. In his declaration to the Islamic world in 1925, he announced that no damage would be done to the holy shrines in the Hijaz.[11] The conflict between some rebellious Ikhwan and ʿAbd al-ʿAziz over leadership and authority finally led to their military elimination with the blessing of the Najdi ulama and the assistance of the British Air Force. The fact that during ʿAbd al-ʿAziz's clashes with the Ikhwan, the ulama, perhaps fearing their actions might encourage anarchy, eventually opted for obedience and rejected the option of being disloyal to the imam as their leader and rebelling against him, presaged their significant future role. At the same time, they paid tribute to him as the king of the Najd and Hijaz and the surrounding areas.

Judging by the subsequent evolution of Wahhabism, this represented an important watershed as ʿAbd al-ʿAziz began to act as a secular ruler and not as the religious leader of the Wahhabi movement. His authority was projected into the sphere of political rule and his legitimacy started to be based on the religious establishment. Essentially, the crushing of the Ikhwan movement in the late 1920s led to the establishment of the centralised Saudi state run by ʿAbd al-ʿAziz, which was marked by a commitment to modernisation. To illustrate the uneasy double role played by the Saudi ulama, as both employees of the king and religious supervisors of the puritan Wahhabi teachings, one can point out the paradoxical way in which Muhammad ibn Salih al-ʿUthaymin, a prominent Saudi scholar, dealt with heretical innovations used in the language. In one of his short booklets, aimed at distinguishing between *sunna* and *bidʿa* in the language, he criticised many of the reprehensible locutions people often used without being aware that they were committing *shirk*. For example, one should not say 'sunflowers', because, when translated into Arabic, their name means 'sun worshippers' (*ʿibād al-shams*). However, it is allowed to say 'followers of the Sun' instead. In a similar vein, he used religious argument to erase the phraseme 'freedom of thought' (*ḥurriyat al-fikr*) from the vocabulary of Islamic books. However, he saw nothing wrong with using titles such as 'majesty' (*jalāla*), 'possessor of majesty' (*ṣāḥib al-jalāla*) and 'highness' (*ṣāḥib al-sumū*), although in Muslim theology 'majestic' (*al-jalīl*) and 'possessor of majesty and generosity' (*dhū al-jalāl wa al-ikrām*) belong among the beautiful names of God.[12] This is in sharp contrast to the Ikhwan's opposition to the use of the title king (*malik*) after ʿAbd al-ʿAziz's conquest of the Hijaz as it is also one of God's names, but in Islamic history the term 'kingship' (*mulk*), promoted by the Umayyads, has the connotation of tyranny.

The Saudi regime subsequently based its authority on an institutionalised religious system in which Al al-Shaykh assumed important positions in the government and state institutions. However, the role of the descendants of Muhammad ibn ʿAbd al-Wahhab in the third Saudi state, perhaps with the exception of the first mufti, was not comparable to the positions they held during the first and second Saudi states, for they had never fully recovered from the wounds inflicted as part of the Egyptian campaign. Since 1929, the clergy have been de facto officers within the state bureaucracy, and their independence has become open to question. This process was further accelerated with the death of the Grand Mufti, Muhammad ibn Ibrahim ibn ʿAbd al-Latif Al al-Shaykh, the man who contributed most to the establishment of a global and centralised clerical organisation. The office of the Grand Mufti was created in 1953. The mufti had the capacity to issue recommendations and opinions to administrative offices, to the ruling family and also to Saudi citizens. Muhammad ibn Ibrahim became the first holder of the office of Grand Mufti.

The Guardians of Ibn ʿAbd al-Wahhab's Legacy

Muhammad ibn Ibrahim ibn ʿAbd al-Latif Al al-Shaykh (1893–1969) was a scholar whose opinions did not diverge from the positions established in early Wahhabism.[13] He, for instance, acknowledged the *takfir* of an individual (*takfir al-muʿayyan*) and rejected secular laws (*qawānīn*). He, in fighting against the import of 'western fallacies', recommended the deletion from the educational curriculum of the teachings of heliocentrism, the roundness of the Earth and the lunar phases, because 'it is useless and it could obscure the religious conviction, especially in the case of youth'.[14] Muhammad ibn Ibrahim's office was also in charge of the censorship of printed materials, books and journals in public libraries, and making sure that they did not contain any photographs. The office also regulated religious writings, especially if they contravened the Salafi doctrine in the sphere of theology (as was the case with Ashʿarism). Muhammad ibn Ibrahim's opinions regarding graves were to a large degree based on those of Ibn Taymiyya and Ibn Qayyim al-Jawziyya. He repeated, for instance, their call for the destruction of buildings or structures built over graves. In a public speech made in 1964, the Saudi prince, Mishʿal ibn ʿAbd al-ʿAziz, governor of the province of Mecca, announced the launch of a project by the municipal council of Mecca (*amānat al-ʿāṣima*) to reconstruct the al-Muʿalla cemetery close to Mecca, where a large number of the figures of early Islam were buried, such as Khadija and Muhammad's son ʿAbdullah. The reasons behind the reconstruction were not religious, but functional – to provide the cemetery with a fence, security, maintenance and pathways among the graves. While he did not object to these changes in particular, Muhammad ibn Ibrahim was concerned about the doctrinal aspects. He forbade the use of marble and the planting of trees there, as well as the creation of cisterns to water them, because he believed such developments would resemble Christian practices, which made their cemeteries similar to parks. He also forbade the illumination of the cemetery, fearing that it could lead to the lighting of lanterns on graves (*isrāj al-qubūr*). He warned that 'It is possible that the one who recommends the illumination of the cemetery and the planting of trees is one of those who has something to do with visiting graves and superstition.'[15] On several occasions, he urged that such innovations should be removed. In a letter from 1965, for example, he thanks the director of the Committee for the Promotion of Virtue and the Prevention of Vice in the western province for sending him a copy of a letter addressed to the Riyadh municipal council and asks him whether the buildings over the graves of Khadija and other surrounding graves have already been removed (*uzīla*) or not.[16]

Figure 10 Khadija's shrine at the al-Muʿalla cemetery
(Available at: https://commons.wikimedia.org/wiki/File:Khadija_tomb.jpg.)

It must also be noted that although Muhammad ibn Ibrahim was very strict about the need to keep the graves simple and levelled, he by no means meant to desecrate them. He deemed it reprehensible that people polluted cemeteries with garbage, dirt, cardboard and waste water, and ordered their removal (as in the case of the Shilliqa cemetery).[17] It is interesting that in these cases, which have no connection with *tawḥīd* and *shirk*, he forbids the transformation of cemeteries into parking zones, playgrounds or sections of highway. In the latter case, he argues that the exhumation of bodies during the construction of a highway is forbidden because the dead have their dignity and, according to one hadith, 'breaking a Muslim's bones when he is dead is tantamount to breaking them when he is alive'.[18] He even warns the municipality of Khaybar not to level the cemetery (*taswiya*) as part of the construction of a highway. The same reasoning is evident in the case of a historical cemetery in the proximity of the mosque of Dihlawiyya in the centre of al-Hafayir, approximately 120 km northeast of al-Ta'if. The position of the cemetery is no excuse for humiliating the dead, whose dignity is more important than the dignity of the living and must therefore be protected.[19] He also forbade the extension of streets at the expense of graves.[20]

It is evident from the above that Muhammad ibn Ibrahim did not allow changes to be made to graves in order to make way for railways, playgrounds or streets. This is in sharp contrast to the attitude adopted by the Saudi authorities in relation to other places which could possibly become places of worship. For example, the site where the Prophet Muhammad's first wife, Khadija, lived and where the Prophet received his first revelations about the Qur'an, was turned into a public toilet. Another good example is Muhammad's supposed birthplace (*mawlid an-nabī*) in Mecca. Saudi authorities built a small public library (*Maktabat Makka al-mukarrama*) on the site. However, this did not deter some Muslims from worshipping there, despite the warnings placed directly at the entrance: 'Dear visitor: it is not permitted to visit this library as a place of worship, because there is no evidence to support this', and 'Dear brothers in Islam: There is no proof that the Prophet Muhammad (peace be upon him) was born in this place. Therefore, it is forbidden to use this place as a specific site for prayer supplications or requests for blessings.'[21]

After Muhammad ibn Ibrahim's death in 1969, the office of Grand Mufti was discontinued and the structure of the ulama experienced profound institutional changes. King Faysal transferred the competencies of the Grand

Mufti to the newly created Ministry of Justice. In September 1970, the king appointed the first Saudi Minister of Justice, Shaykh Muhammad Al-Harakan. Unlike the institution of Grand Mufti, which did not have to report to anyone and whose decisions were final, the new Ministry of Justice needed to report to a higher authority. The creation of the ministry thus further undermined the political strength of an independent religious authority.[22] Only in 1992 was the office of the Grand Mufti renewed, as evidenced by the installation of Ibn Baz. After his death in 1999, Ibn Baz was replaced by a student of his, 'Abd al-'Aziz ibn 'Abdullah ibn Muhammad ibn 'Abd al-Latif Al al-Shaykh, another member of the Al al-Shaykh family, who, again, held similar views to those of Ibn Baz and his predecessors.

'Abd al-'Aziz Ibn Baz (1910–99) belonged to the influential generation of senior ulama, many of whom have passed away in the past twenty years, who were considered to be the real holders of religious knowledge. Besides Ibn Baz, the list included, in particular, 'Abdullah ibn Jibrin (1933–2009), Muhammad Nasir al-Din al-Albani, Muhammad ibn Salih al-'Uthaymin and Salih ibn Fawzan al-Fawzan (b. 1933). Before Ibn Baz became the Grand Mufti, that is, a religious leader with ministerial rank in the government, he held several other influential positions, which made him the most powerful *'ālim* in the contemporary history of Saudi Arabia. He was the head of the General Presidency, member of the Board of Senior Ulama and member of the Permanent Committee. Ibn Baz's prominence among Saudi ulama was in all likelihood due to the fact that he was a student of Muhammad ibn Ibrahim, with whom he differed only on a few issues.[23] It was Muhammad ibn Ibrahim who recommended Ibn Baz for his first job as a judge in al-Kharj in 1938. He became a teacher at the religious institute in Riyadh in 1952 and an Islamic law lecturer at Riyadh University in 1953. In 1963, he was appointed head of the board of Islamic scholars and by 1975 he was vice chancellor of the Islamic University of Medina. From 1978 until his death, he was chair of the prestigious Permanent Committee, which carries ministerial status in the Saudi Arabian government. Ibn Baz also chaired a Constituent Council of the Muslim World League, which called for the rigorous application of the Shari'ah in all spheres of life, as well as underlining the responsibility of Muslims to defend Islamic interests throughout the world. Ibn Baz also contributed by supervising an office charged with dispatching Saudi-sponsored proselytisers to combat Sufism and other religious 'innovations'.[24] As for the worldview of Ibn Baz, he was also very conservative and maintained the same line as his predecessor, as indicated in many of the writings and legal opinions he issued. In 1976, for instance, Ibn Baz ruled that the Earth was flat and that it was a great blasphemy to suggest otherwise.[25]

Another Saudi religious authority, Muhammad ibn Salih al-'Uthaymin (1925–2001), held more or less the same positions as Ibn Baz. In the sphere of grave rituals, he prohibited women from intentionally (*qaṣdan*) visiting graves. However, he argued that if the visit were unintentional, such as when passing a grave on the way home, there was nothing wrong (*lā ba's*) in greeting the deceased.[26] The reason for the prohibition was that if a woman were allowed to visit a graveyard, she would be exposed to wicked and sinful people who might attend such an empty place, and something detestable might happen to her.

Al-Albani: Re-evaluation of Hadith and Iconoclasm

However, it was Muhammad Nasir al-Din al-Albani (1914–99), the 'iconoclast extraordinaire',[27] as Jonathan Brown aptly dubbed him, who belonged among the most prominent and also the most controversial figures of twentieth-century (not only Salafi) Islamic intellectual history. Al-Albani's influence on global Salafi discourse was so eminent that it is worth pausing for a moment to discuss his opinions in greater detail. As his name partially suggests, he was born in Albania to a family of Hanafi scholars. His family left for Syria in search of political asylum during the oppressive rule of Ahmet Zogolli (Zogu). When in Syria, he followed in the footsteps of his ancestors and studied Hanafi jurisprudence. He started down the path of reformist thinking when he read the influential reformist magazine *al-Manar*, which he came across in a bookstore at the Umayyad mosque. He was also attracted by Rashid Rida's criticism of the great Sufi Abu Hamid al-Ghazali.[28] When critically studying al-Ghazali, he found a book by a hadith scholar Zayn al-Din al-'Iraqi (1325–1404), which detailed the weak hadiths used by al-Ghazali in his *Revival of the Religious Sciences* (*Ihya' 'ulum al-din*), widely regarded as the greatest work of Muslim spirituality. These works, al-Albani recollects, sowed the seeds of mistrust in his heart in relation to Sufism and weak hadiths. When he discovered that the Umayyad mosque had formerly been the Church of St. John, built over his tomb, he refused to pray there. Paradoxically, al-Albani was in this respect more critical than his idol, Ibn Taymiyya, who delivered

Figure 11 Shrine of John the Baptist in the Umayyad Mosque, Damascus. Undated; turn of the nineteenth/twentieth century

(From Alois Musil's (1868–1944) collection of photographs held by the Institute of Near Eastern and African Studies, Charles University, Prague.)

sermons there and, in all likelihood, prayed there too, despite the fact that the mosque holds a shrine that is said to contain the head of John the Baptist.[29]

Al-Albani's opinions regarding grave veneration resulted in a conflict with his father, who stopped supporting him financially. In retrospective recollections, al-Albani presents himself as one who, from early on, was trying to purify the doctrine of those around him. Thus, al-Albani said about his father: 'He used to go to the mosques in which were graves, as did a majority of the shaykhs, and I used to say to him: "My father, this is not allowed."'[30] Al-Albani was very committed and persevered with his mission. When he was young, he used to visit the grave of Ibn 'Arabi in the company of a certain shaykh and would pray there. When al-Albani realised it was forbidden, he discussed the issue with the shaykh until he found the right path, feeling grateful that he had been enlightened.[31]

Studying as an autodidact in the Zahiri library of Damascus, the first Syrian public library founded by Tahir al-Jaza'iri, turned al-Albani into a controversial as well as a nonconformist figure. He recollects that he had formerly gone from his work to the library by bicycle, wearing a white turban – therein following an erroneous custom, based on weak hadiths and *madhhab* tradition – and thus attracting strange looks from the people of Damascus when they saw a shaykh riding a bicycle. Soon he recognised that wearing a long traditional garment, a *jubba*, was not Islamic, so he started wearing normal clothes, as did other people. By borrowing books from private libraries, he soon discovered that the careful study of hadith had long been abandoned. No one missed the books on this topic that he borrowed, even though he held on to them for two years.[32] After he had established himself, he came to be viewed by some as the most respected scholar of hadith in modern times. Others, however, questioned his credentials due to his unconventional approach to Islam. However, according to some accounts, he was given permission (*ijāza*) to transfer religious knowledge by a Halabi hadith scholar, Raghib al-Tabbakh.[33] In Syria he was imprisoned twice, persecuted and abused.[34] Al-Albani recollects that for him prison provided the necessary solitude needed for reflection and study, as had been the case with Ibn Taymiyya before him. He had even managed to improve the bad lighting conditions, which allowed him to study. It was also while in prison that he worked on an abridged version of Muslim's *Sahih*.[35] In the Damascene Citadel, the same prison where Ibn Taymiyya had died, he preached the Qur'an and Sunna and established collective Friday prayers. When the Islamic University of Medina was founded, he was already so famous that he was invited by Muhammad ibn Ibrahim Al al-Shaykh to teach hadith there, even though he had had no appropriate formal education.[36] During his affiliation with the university between 1961 and 1964, he established the foundations of hadith studies worldwide.

As a hadith scholar, he thought that the science of hadith was still alive and that Prophetic traditions must therefore be critically re-evaluated, which was a method (*al-jarḥ wa al-taʿdīl*) used by medieval hadith scholars. Accordingly, he subjected all respected collections of Sunni hadiths to critical scrutiny. Hadith collections were viewed by many Muslims as 'canonical' books, which they considered to be untouchable. This belief applied, in particular, to the collections of al-Bukhari and Muslim, the most venerated collections.

Al-Albani published shortened editions of their collections, removing what he considered to be the weak hadiths. He also published his own monumental collections of both sound (*ṣaḥīḥ*) and weak (*ḍaʿīf*) hadiths, as well as a number of minor works of weak hadiths produced by Abu Dawud, al-Tirmidhi, al-Nasa'i and Ibn Maja. When engaging in hadith criticism, he followed the medieval or later scholars of hadith, among whom Ibn Taymiyya, Ibn Qayyim al-Jawziyya, al-Sanʿani and al-Shawkani were the leading lights. Ibn Taymiyya asserted that al-Bukhari and Muslim did not agree on a hadith unless it is undeniably authentic. This enabled him to criticise hadiths found in only one of the two. For Ibn Taymiyya, the canon proved to be very useful, since the collections of the two shaykhs, as he called al-Bukhari and Muslim, provided the centrepiece for his efforts to shift the ultimate authority for determining the Prophet's true legacy towards hadith scholars as opposed to the later substantive laws of the jurists. This was the same method he utilised against Ashʿaris in the field of theology.[37]

A huge controversy was instigated by al-Albani's book *Warning to the Praying One Not to Take Graves as Places of Worship* (*Tahdhir al-sajid min ittikhadh al-qubur masajid*), published in 1957. It was plainly interpreted as a call to demolish the Prophet Muhammad's tomb. In the book, al-Albani mentions that he was motivated by what he had witnessed in Syria, where prominent Muslims and benefactors had been buried in mosques bearing their names and, what is more, even in the direction of *qibla*. In Islam, al-Albani states, mosques and graves should not be combined, which is the ruling based directly on the work of Ibn Taymiyya.[38] Al-Albani begins his treatise with a hadith of ʿA'isha, who narrates the words uttered by the Prophet Muhammad shortly before his death: 'God cursed Jews and Christians, who took graves of their prophets as places of worship' (*laʿana Allāh al-yahūd wa al-naṣārā ittakhadhū qubūr anbiyā'ihim masājid*). This hadith, according to al-Sanʿani and al-Shafiʿi, suggests three prohibitions: ritual prayer conducted at graves and praying rituals or invocational prayers centring on them; the building of mosques upon them; and seeking them out as places where prayer requests can be made.[39]

Al-Albani is also known as a harsh advocate of the prohibition of imagery in all its forms – be it statues, pictures or photographs. Al-Albani argues against pictures by reference to hadith narrated by ʿA'isha: 'Umm Habiba and Umm Salama made mention before the Messenger of Allah of a church which they had seen in Abyssinia, which had pictures in it. The Messenger of God said: "When a pious person amongst them dies they build a place of worship on his grave, and then decorate it with such images. They would be the worst of creatures before God.'" According to al-Albani, creating pictures was a form of idolatry (*wa huwa min jins ʿibādat al-awthān*).[40]

Despite the fact that al-Albani, as a *mujtahid*, was a critic of the *madhhab* system, he offered evidence across the four Sunni schools of law, aimed at demonstrating the prohibition of building on graves and praying at the sites. It is well known that Shafiʿis and Hanafis used to denounce these practices as abhorrent (*karāha*). In order to address this problem, al-Albani adopted Ibn Taymiyya's and Ibn Qayyim al-Jawziyya's semantic method, according to which one must seek the meaning of the words in their historical context. Therefore, he notes that in al-Shafiʿi's idiolect, the expression 'I dislike', such as in 'I dislike a mosque being built upon a grave' (*akrah ʿan yubnā ʿalā al-qabr masjid*), actually provides an explicit prohibition, based on an assertion that al-Shafiʿi was highly influenced by the language of the Qurʾan, where *karāha* is tantamount to a prohibition (49:7). As for Hanafi *madhhab*, the word 'dislike' also usually means a prohibition, especially when it is used unrestrictedly.[41] Al-Albani cites Muhammad al-Shaybani, a pupil of Abu Hanifa, who believed that nothing should be added that stands out from the grave. In addition, he disliked the practice of plastering or daubing the grave or building a mosque close to it (*lā narā an yuzād ʿalā mā kharaja min al-qabr, wa nakrahu an yujaṣṣaṣa aw yuṭayyana aw yujʿal ʿindahu masjidan*). Hanbalis, for their part, also prohibited it. Al-Albani cites Ibn Qayyim al-Jawziyya's book *Provisions for the Hereafter* (*Zad al-maʿad*), in which the latter provides an example of the Prophet, who destroyed and burnt down places of disobedience, for example, the mosque of al-Darar. Al-Albani cites a legal opinion of Ibn Taymiyya regarding mosques with graves: 'It is not allowed to bury the dead in a mosque. If the mosque existed before the burial, let it be changed, be it by levelling the grave (*taswiyat al-qabr*) or by exhumation if the grave is new. If the mosque was built after the grave, so either the mosque or the shape/form of the grave (*sūrat al-qabr*) should be removed (*yuzāl*).'[42]

It is noteworthy that the above-mentioned legal opinion of Ibn Taymiyya was used in 1940 by the Egyptian Dar al-iftaʾ (*Dar al-iftāʾ al-misriyya*), a fact which al-Albani points out.[43] It was issued by the mufti ʿAbd al-Majid Salim. To our knowledge, he was the first Egyptian mufti in modern Egyptian history who based his argument on Ibn Taymiyya's *fatwā*. In a collection of *fatāwā* issued by a traditionalist group of Egyptian scholars in 2007, in support of their fight against necrolatry, an earlier *fatwā* issued by the 'rationalist Salafi' Muhammad ʿAbduh, who happened to be the first Egyptian mufti of the Egyptian Dar al-ifta', was published. It supports the view that a dome built over a grave should be destroyed. However, the rationale behind this legal opinion does not appear to be doctrinal, but, rather, pragmatic. ʿAbduh was asked whether it was possible to destroy a historical dome (*qubba*) and to transfer the tomb (*ḍarīḥ*) to a nearby mosque bearing the name of the dead. The reason was that the dome was situated in a frequently used street, exposed to urine and filth. ʿAbduh, himself a Hanafi, replied with an opinion based on the work of Abu Hanifa, that building a dome upon a grave was a reprehensible thing (*makrūh*), so there was nothing wrong with destroying the dome (*lā baʾs bi-hadm al-qubba*), maybe it was even more appropriate in this case due to its exposure to filth. As for the tomb, he opined, it should be made level with the street, because if there were a corpse, it would already have disintegrated.[44] These opinions, however, are only illustrative and of minor importance. They also appear to contradict the position expressed in one of the most popular and highly influential compendiums of law, titled *Fiqh al-sunna*, which has been used by many jurists and translated into many languages. It was published in the mid-1940s by a sympathiser of the Muslim Brotherhood, al-Sayyid Sabiq. Sabiq's approach is characterised by its lack of adherence to any particular school (reprehensibly referred to as *taʿaṣṣub*), although it is not a traditional systematic work of *ikhtilāf*, which would provide opinions from each of the four schools. In this regard, it reflects the Salafi *ijtihād*. It relies on the works of Ibn Qudama al-Maqdisi, Ibn Qayyim al-Jawziyya, al-Shawkani and al-Sanʿani. Al-Albani later offered 'friendly corrections' to al-Sayyid Sabiq's work in his book *Perfection of Kindness in the Commentary on Fiqh al-sunna* (*Tamam al-minna fi al-taʿliq ʿala fiqh al-sunna*). It seems that al-Albani found inspiration in the *Fiqh al-sunna* for his opinions on the *ziyāra* of women. *Fiqh al-sunna* was also widely received among both Muslim scholar and student circles worldwide.

The issue of the legality of women visiting graves, as well as different opinions on the role of women and their rights, became an object of disagreement between al-Albani and the Wahhabi ulama. Al-Albani held very conservative positions with regard to social issues. However, his opinions regarding women did not agree with those of the Wahhabi scholars, whose beliefs seem to have been rooted more specifically in Najdi society rather than in the broader Hanbali tradition. Moreover, al-Albani also disagreed with regard to the legality of women driving cars. Finally, in his book *Veiling of a Muslim Woman and Her Dress at Prayer* (*Hijab al-mar'a al-muslima wa libasuha fi al-salat*), al-Albani rejects the Wahhabi position that a Muslim woman must cover her face, arguing through reference to a hadith that, according to him, proved that it was not common practice in the early Muslim community of *salaf*. This is said to be the reason[45] behind his expulsion from Saudi Arabia in 1963; his contract at the University of Medina not being extended. Only in 1975 was he rehabilitated and named as a member of the university council.

As for the issue of women, in his book *Funeral Rules and Their Innovations* (*Ahkam al-jana'iz wa bida'uha*), which can be considered the most comprehensive manual to be written in modern times on the topic, al-Albani argues that visiting graves is legal because it is a good example of *memento mori*. However, during the visit one should not anger Allah, for example, by invoking the spirit of the deceased and asking him for help rather than by calling on Allah. Al-Albani argues through reference to two groups of hadith. The first group, according to him, absolutely permits grave visits by both genders. The most important hadith from this set is narrated by Burayda ibn al-Hasib and incorporated within the collections of Muslim, Abu Dawud, Bayhaqi, al-Nasa'i and Ahmad ibn Hanbal. The hadith says: 'I was prohibiting you from visiting graves, but now you can visit them' (*innī kuntu nahaytukum 'an ziyārat al-qubūr, fa-zūrūhā*). The core of the hadith is the same, followed by various additions, such as 'because it will remind you of the Afterworld' (*fa-innahā tudhakkirūkum al-ākhira*), 'Indeed, the visiting of them enhances good' (*wa la-tazidkum ziyāratuhā khayran*) and 'Whoever wants to visit – visit, but do not talk inappropriately/idly' (*fa-man arāda an yazūra fal-yazur, wa lā taqūlū hujran*).[46]

The second group of hadiths underlines the focus on *memento mori*. This is the case with a hadith narrated by Sa'id al-Khudri: 'I forbade you to visit graves, but visit them, because in it is *memento mori*; and do not say what infuriates Allah' (*innī nahaytukum 'an ziyārat al-qubūr fa-zūrūhā, fa inna fīha 'ibra; wa lā taqūlū mā tuskhiṭu al-rabb*). It also concerns the hadith narrated by Anas ibn Malik: 'I used to forbid you to visit graves, but visit them indeed, because they soften the heart, make an eye cry and remember the hereafter. But do not talk inappropriately' (*kuntu nahaytukum 'an ziyārat al-qubūr, alā fa-zūrūhā fa-innahā turiqqu al-qalb, tudmi'u al-'ayn, wa tudhakkiru al-ākhira, wa lā taqūlū hujran*). Moreover, al-Albani supported his argument by reference to two relevant hadiths narrated by the Prophet's wife, 'A'isha. The first one is from 'Abdullah ibn Abi Mulayka. According to him, one day 'A'isha was coming from the cemetery, so he asked her: 'Oh mother of the believers, where are you coming from?' She replied: 'From the grave of 'Abd al-Rahman ibn Abi Bakr.' So he asked her: 'Did not the Messenger of God forbid grave visiting?' She replied: 'Yes, but then he ordered them to be visited.' Ibn 'Abd al-Birr, in his *Tamhid*, writes that Ahmad ibn Hanbal adduces this report as proof that women are permitted to visit graves, as Abu Bakr al-Athram said: 'I heard Ahmad ibn Hanbal being asked about a woman who visited a grave. He replied: "I hope, if God wills, there is no harm (*lā ba's*) in that – 'A'isha visited the grave of her brother."'[47]

Most significant is al-Albani's understanding of a hadith used by the Saudi ulama, who forbid women from visiting graves. According to him, the hadith, 'God/the Messenger of God cursed those who frequently visit graves' (*la 'ana Allāh/rasūl Allāh zawwārāt al-qubūr*) only means that it is forbidden to visit graves frequently because it can lead women to do things that contradict the law, such as speaking in a loud voice, displaying their charms, making graves the resting places for trips, and wasting time in idle chatter.[48] Al-Albani argues that only the word *zawwārāt*, implying frequent visits, is correct, not *zā'irāt*. From the legal terminology standpoint, this hadith fits into the category dealing with specifics (*khāṣṣ*); therefore, it cannot be used as a tool for challenging those hadiths that permit visits to graves in general (*'āmm*). This is the reason why the specific details of individual hadith cannot be used to abrogate (*naskh*) those that carry a general meaning; it is better to combine them (*jam'*). Therefore, visits to graves are legal, even for women; however, they are not permitted to make frequent visits. This was the approach of al-Qurtubi and al-Shawkani, who stated in *Nayl al-awtar*: 'This speech is what should be relied upon when combining hadiths with contradictory meanings.' According to al-Albani, al-San'ani came to the same conclusion; however, he argued in favour of the legality of women visiting graves by theorising (*naẓar*). It is likely that al-Albani was influenced in this opinion by al-Sayyid Sabiq's *Fiqh al-sunna*, as this is the same argument, and nearly the same formulation, as used by Sabiq on the legalisation of grave visits by women.[49]

As for al-Albani's opinions regarding the prohibition on erecting buildings over graves, they were in accordance with those of the Wahhabi shaykhs. However, it seems that in their legal reasoning the latter were more afraid of *fitna*, in one of its two basic meanings – temptation or seduction, and a riot or civil strife. If we consider al-Albani's opinion concerning the converting back of Muhammad's burial site to its original state (a euphemism for destruction) and the Saudi reluctance to do so, we find that the decision was based on the fear of dissent and civil strife. This can be illustrated by a *fatwā* of Ibn Baz. When he was asked for a formal legal opinion regarding building domes over graves and why Muhammad ibn 'Abd al-Wahhab did not destroy the dome of the Prophet Muhammad, he acknowledged that the domes are innovations and forbidden things (*munkar*). However, he argued that this particular dome had not been destroyed by Ibn 'Abd al-Wahhab and that the reason it still existed in the Saudi state was because of the fear of the strife (*fitna*) that its destruction might provoke.[50]

Moreover, Wahhabi scholars went further than al-Albani in the application of *fitna* as they sought to support their position on the prohibition of women visiting graves. Ibn Baz, for instance, in his *fatwā* on this issue relies only on the single hadith about the Prophet's curse on females visiting graves (*zāʾirāt al-qubūr*). His opinion is more based on his general reasoning that women are in most cases impatient and their impatience causes wailing (*niyāḥa*). In doing so, women provoke the temptation (*fitna*) of men during funerals or grave visits. As the purpose of God's law (*sharīʿa*) is to prevent all activities that lead to corruption and temptation, it forbids women from showing their charms (*tabarruj*) and seducing men by their words, as well from being alone and travelling without a *maḥram*, that is, a legal male companion. However, for men it is recommended (*mustaḥabb*) that they should visit graves, be it the grave of the Prophet himself or other graves, such as those in Baqiʿ al-gharqad, Shuhadaʾ or the Qubaʾ Mosque. However, one must not travel with the sole purpose of visiting graves.[51]

If we look at Hanbali scholarship, even that of the Najdi region, we find evidence that the prohibition of women visiting graves is not equivocal. To offer just one example, we can look into a Hanbali legal manual *Hidayat al-raghib li-sharh 'umdat al-talib*, written around the year 1689 by 'Uthman Ahmad al-Najdi, a Hanbali scholar from al-'Uyayna (the birthplace of Muhammad ibn 'Abd al-Wahhab), who died in Egypt. The manual says that the visits to graves by women is reprehensible (not forbidden), with the exception of the grave of the Prophet Muhammad and his two Companions. Here, it does not state explicitly whether the exception in the case of the Prophet's grave means prohibition or permission.[52]

To conclude, Al-Albani and Ibn Baz differ in their interpretation. What is even more important, however, is that they hold the same opinion when it comes to the *fitna* of graves, the very reason for their destruction.

Salafi Melting Pot: Politics and Puritanism

Having considered the position of both scholars in relation to issues connected with *ziyāra* and funeral architecture, let us turn now to another crucial role of al-Albani in influencing the Salafi discourse: his diatribes against the Muslim Brotherhood and other non-Salafis. Wahhabi scholars, be they from Al al-Shaykh or not, such as Ibn Baz, Ibn Jibrin and al-Fawzan, three of the most prominent, were unable to offer advice when it came to polemics and the refutation of various Islamic trends, movements and organisations that began gaining influence in Saudi Arabia as the result of the Saudi pan-Islamic call for solidarity. New currents of political Islam began to infiltrate the Kingdom from the 1970s when Faysal opened the door to foreign workers – labourers, specialists and academics. Many of them were associated with the Muslim Brotherhood, be they quietist organisations, activism-orientated Bannawis (followers of Hasan al-Banna) or radical Qutbis (followers of Sayyid Qutb) from Egypt or Syria (most notably, Muhammad Surur). The former, due to their organisational skills, helped to build up a network of educational, charitable and other organisations. In 1972, the Muslim Brothers helped to create the World Assembly of Muslim Youth (*al-Nadwa al-'alamiyya li-l-shabab al-islami*), one of the most active propagandist institutions, which was successful in disseminating a great number of religious texts worldwide. While the organisation was formally ruled over by Salih Al al-Shaykh, the

Muslim Brothers published a number of magazines and worked as teachers in all phases of education, from elementary schools to universities. This was one of the most important activities as the majority (approximately 85 per cent) of the Saudi population was illiterate at that time.

However, those 'exogenous' Muslims posed a challenge both to the Saudi authorities and traditional religious elites. It was evident that religious pluralism had no place in a uniform and totalitarian milieu, where all forms of political activity were forbidden. Although the majority of those immigrants who were active in aspects of religious education did not engage in the field of theology (*uṣūl al-dīn*) and doctrine (*'aqīda*), some of them eventually became influential even in these areas. This was regarded as a threat to the traditional domain of the Wahhabis. The most dangerous was the ideology of Qutbism, that is, the teachings of the Egyptian radical ideologue Sayyid Qutb (executed in 1966). In the beginning, Qutbism was welcomed by Wahhabi scholars, partly due to the similarities that existed between some of Qutb's writings and the teaching of Ibn 'Abd al-Wahhab, and partly due to his martyrdom. Qutbism established itself in Saudi Arabia due to the activities of Muhammad Qutb, the younger brother of Sayyid, who sought political asylum in Saudi Arabia in the early 1970s. Muhammad Qutb paraphrased some of the ideas of his brother, for example, in his famous book *Jahiliyyat al-qarn al-'ishrin* (*Jahiliyya of the Twentieth Century*). This book is inventive in the sense that it does not use the rigid language of Wahhabi scholars, confined as it is to the world of *tawḥīd* and *shirk*. Muhammad Qutb's enemies are not polytheists (*mushrikūn*), but infidels (*kuffār*) and Crusaders (*ṣalībīyūn*), rhetoric closer to that of Bin Ladin rather than to Ibn Baz and al-Albani. Muhammad Qutb therefore offers a telling example of the challenge posed to Wahhabi exclusivism. He became a professor of doctrine at Umm al-Qura University (known under this name since 1981). He taught modern Islamic schools of thought (*Madhāhib fikrīya mu'āṣira*), material he later used in his book. Based on Islamic principles, Muhammad Qutb refuted secularism, communism and democracy, that is, categories and notions that Wahhabi scholars found difficulty in dealing with through the use of traditional language. However, this influx of ideas into the Wahhabi pool of thought was frowned upon by the latter as being too rationalist. It was argued that the approach was unnecessary since pure doctrine (*'aqīda*) was already available. These new ideas, however, became part of the propagandist literature published by Saudi organisations and school texts. Such was the case in relation to *Milestones* (*Ma'alim fi al-tariq*) by Sayyid Qutb, which was approved as an official school text. Traditional Wahhabi texts and Qutbi literature influenced the Sahwa (Awakening) movement that challenged the Saudi regime on a political level.⁵³

The nature of Muhammad Qutb's pedagogic activities can be seen through reference to the themes of the theses he supervised, for example, the master's thesis of Muhammad ibn Sa'id al-Qahtani concerning the doctrine of *al-walā' wa al-barā'* (loyalty and disavowal), which was published in Arabic (later in French and English) with a foreword by 'Abd al-Razzaq 'Afifi. The work was influenced by both the teachings of Sayyid Qutb and the Wahhabi notion of the mutual friendship of believers and enmity towards polytheists and polytheism (*al-muwālāt wa al-mu'ādāt*). The notion in this form was unknown to Wahhabi discourse, and neither was it used within the Hanbali medieval tradition.⁵⁴ Al-Qahtani, however, attributes it to Ibn Taymiyya and Ibn 'Abd al-Wahhab. Another student of Muhammad Qutb was Safar al-Hawali, spiritual father of the Sahwa movement. In his doctoral thesis on theology, devoted to the phenomenon of *al-irjā'* (*The Concept of Irjā' in Islamic Thought – Zahirat al-irjā' fi al-fikr al-islami*), he follows in the steps of Ibn Taymiyya's criticism of Ash'arism and Murji'a. Murji'a was given this name because it postponed (*irjā'*) the decision as to whether one is unbeliever or not. This theological approach was adopted by the Umayyads, known for their transgressions of Islamic law. However, al-Hawali's criticism was not aimed at the Umayyads, but rather at the Saudi regime and its religious establishment, regarded as being apolitical and reluctant to use *takfīr*.⁵⁵ In *Zahirat al-irjā'*, al-Albani is mentioned several times. Al-Albani was a harsh critic of political activism and partisanship (*ḥizbīya*), because he believed that plurality always leads to the fragmentation (*furqa*) of Muslim society. Al-Albani admonished extremists and followers of *takfīr*, labelling them as modern-day Kharijis (*khawārij al-'aṣr*). He refused *takfīr* and jihad as premature and ineffective ways of establishing the Shari'ah. Instead, he urged believers to build the foundations (*al-qā'ida*) upon which a future Muslim government (*al-ḥukūma al-muslima*) would stand, and to achieve this by following the Sunna of the Messenger of God, through which he educated (*rabbā*) his Companions.⁵⁶ Al-Hawali also took the idea of God's sovereignty (*ḥakimīya*) from Muhammad Qutb, which meant that the adoration of a leader who does not rule in accordance with the Shari'ah law is tantamount to worshipping *ṭāghūt* and *shirk*. The idea of *irjā'* gained in importance in the aftermath of the Afghan conflict and also during the Second Gulf War.

Al-Albani called for the purification (*tasfiya*) of doctrine. He believed that the real cause of all the problems experienced by the Islamic world lay in doctrinal impurity. However, he believed that purification alone would not be sufficient and that one would also have to educate (*tarbiya*) young people in terms of correct dogma. He criticised those Islamic groups – some of which had existed for nearly a century – which only made a show of their willingness to establish an Islamic government, without actually fulfilling this goal and shedding the blood of innocents. 'I conclude by what a preacher said and I was hoping his followers would persevere in it and realise it: "Build the Islamic state in your hearts, it will be built for you on earth." For Muslims, as long as their doctrine (*'aqīda*) is correctly based on the Book and Sunna, there is no doubt that their worship, morals and manners will also be corrected.'[57] This journey into al-Albani's thought is relevant for many reasons. Most importantly, the idea that impure doctrine is the reason behind the rottenness of the world has been the prevalent belief of those who struggle to rectify the situation according to Wahhabi or Salafi principles – encapsulated in the absolute *tawḥīd* (the non-accreditation of things to God), with necrolatry being the actual cause of *shirk*. Al-Albani himself praised Ibn 'Abd al-Wahhab for disseminating the correct doctrine, although he deemed Ibn 'Abd al-Wahhab and some of his followers (especially the Ikhwan) to be somewhat extreme in their views.

Another famous scholar of hadith was Muqbil ibn Hadi al-Wadi'i (1933–2001), known by his admirers as the Shaykh from the Arabian Peninsula (*shaykh al-jazīra*), or simply Shaykh Muqbil. Al-Wadi'i is a good example of a religious scholar who received his education in Saudi Arabia and who was to spread his beliefs beyond its borders, especially in Yemen. Yet he was also influential in locations as varied as Bahrain, Indonesia and Somalia, as well as in Birmingham. Al-Wadi'i was born in northern Yemen into a Zaydi tribe. He wanted to study at a Zaydi school, but was refused on elitist grounds, for he was not a descendant of the Prophet. So he travelled to Saudi Arabia, where he converted to Sunni Islam in its Wahhabi–Salafi form, one which proclaimed the equality of all Muslims, regardless of their origin, nationality or genealogy. Furthermore, its fight against the cult of ancestors (*aslāf*), the dead, saints and graves was attractive to people like al-Wadiʿi. He studied in Mecca and then at the Faculty of the Shariʿah of the Islamic University of Medina, where he was one of the many students of Ibn Baz. He also respected al-Albani, whose lectures he attended while in Medina at the time when the latter was not officially employed at the university. Among other scholars, he looked up to al-ʿUthaymin, Salih ibn Fawzan, ʿAbd al-Muhsin al-ʿAbbad and Rabiʿ ibn Hadi al-Madkhali, whom he praised as being 'one of God's signs in the knowledge of the supporters of *ḥizbīya*'.[58]

Al-Wadiʿi's opinions were in accordance with the *Ahl al-hadith* movement and those of al-Albani. He allowed women to visit graves under the same conditions as al-Albani ruled. In a similar vein, he was a harsh critic of funeral architecture, being accused by his adversaries of being paid by the Wahhabis, who openly called for the elimination of the Prophet's dome (*izālat al-qubba*) in order to return his grave to its previous state.[59] While at the Islamic University of Medina, al-Wadiʿi wrote a thesis titled *Ruling about the Dome Built over the Prophet's Grave* (*Hukm al-qubba al-mabniya ʿala qabr al-rasul*), in which he demanded that the Prophet's grave should be brought out of his mosque and the dome destroyed. He claimed that the presence of the holy grave and the noble dome constituted major innovations.[60] Al-Wadiʿi states that his interest in this topic arose when he encountered a *fatwā* answering the following question: 'Is it permitted to build domes over graves?' The answer was positive, on the basis that 'the community of believers already accepted the dome built over the Prophet's grave'. Al-Wadiʿi disapproved of this position and in his treatise he reiterates the basic concepts connected with this issue, drawing on the collections of hadith and frequently quoting Ibn Taymiyya and Muhammad al-Shawkani, among others. He blames the Ummayad caliph al-Walid ibn ʿAbd al-Malik (668–715) for incorporating the Prophet's grave into the mosque, and the Mamluk sultan of Egypt, al-Mansur Qalawun al-Salihi (1222–90), for building the dome above the grave.

Al-Wadiʿi concludes that such constructions are illegal and represent an act of infidelity (*kufr*). Therefore, it is the duty of Muslims to return the mosque and the grave to their original condition at the time of the Prophet – meaning that the mosque should be moved westward so it does not encompass the grave, and also that the dome should be destroyed.⁶¹ Finally, he exhorts the ulama to teach Muslim society about the harm caused by building over graves in general, and to remind rulers that it is their duty to destroy such structures.⁶² In another book, titled *Khomeinian Heresy in Saudi Arabia* (*al-Ilhad al-khumayni fi ard al-haramayn*), al-Wadi'i condemns the heretical practices of Shi'i Islam. It is noteworthy that al-Wadi'i personally visited many such prohibited places in Iran. He twice visited the grave of the 'Imam of the heresy', Khomeini, and also the graves of Imam Zade Salih, Imam Shah 'Abd al-'Azim and Imam 'Abdullah.

Juhayman al-'Utaybi: Traditionalism Simplified and Militarised

In 1979, al-Wadi'i was expelled from Saudi Arabia after being accused of involvement in the Juhayman al-'Utaybi's group. The al-'Utaybi's revolt – the armed seizure of the Grand Mosque with its Ka'ba sanctuary – presented the most serious challenge to Saudi legitimacy since the Ikhwan rebellion that had been suppressed in the 1920s. In his book of memories, titled *What I Saw in Saudi Arabia* (*Mushahadati fi al-mamlaka al-'arabiyya al-su'udiyya*), al-Wadi'i recollects his expulsion with feelings of resentment. Although he posed a security threat for Saudi authorities, he did not cease to be on friendly terms with Ibn Baz and al-'Uthaymin. Through the intervention of Ibn Baz, his relations with the Saudi regime were eventually reconciled as al-Wadi'i was later invited to seek medical treatment in Saudi Arabia, which he remembers with great gratitude.

The unintended effect of al-Wadi'i's expulsion was that he became a propagator of Salafi thought in Yemen, attracting many students from abroad, especially from those regions that were traditionally in close contact with Yemen, such as Indonesia. As he became disgruntled by the proliferation of the Muslim Brotherhood in Yemeni schools, he decided in the early 1980s to open his own religious school (Hadith institute – Dar al-hadith) in Dammaj, in the Sa'da governorate, in order to propagate a puritanical Salafi interpretation of Islam and confront the Shi'i movement. He also launched an open onslaught against Zaydi tombs, declaring his intention to destroy the tombs of the Zaydi imams and their domes in Sa'da. His zealous followers carried out his ideas and destroyed many of the gravestones in the cemeteries just beyond Sa'da's city wall.⁶³

The emergence of the al-'Utaybi movement in the 1970s coincided with the arrival of new ideological influences on the Medinan religious scene and the rise of the *Ahl al-hadith* movement. The ideals of puritanical teachings propagated both by Wahhabism and the *Ahl al-hadith* movement were in sharp contrast to the changing reality of Saudi society, brought about by the sudden and vast influx of oil revenues and the ensuing technological changes. Such developments challenged and accelerated the country's exposure to what was considered to be an undesirable alien influence.[64] In 1965, a small group of *Ahl al-hadith* followers attacked a store displaying female mannequins, an incident referred to as 'the breaking of images' (*taksīr al-ṣuwar*),[65] and were arrested for the destruction of private property. Among the arrested were students of the Islamic University of Medina, most notably 'Abd al-Rahman 'Abd al-Khaliq, who was later to found a political Salafi movement in Kuwait, and 'Umar al-Ashqar, a prominent ideologue of the Salafi wing of the Jordanian Muslim Brotherhood.[66] Although the followers of hadith involved in the incident in Medina were mostly poor foreign students, they were not the only ones to vehemently oppose the modernisation of the country. The technological developments were even challenged by members of the Saudi royal family. In September 1965, for example, another group, led by Prince Khalid ibn Mus'ad ibn 'Abd al-'Aziz, attacked the newly erected television studios in Riyadh.

In 1966, shortly after the 'breaking of images', the 'Salafi group for *ḥisba*' (*al-Jama'a al-salafiyya al-muḥtasiba*) was founded, with Ibn Baz as its official spiritual guide (*murshid*). Besides Ibn Baz, the meetings of the group were attended by Abu Bakr al-Jaza'iri as his deputy, and also by the shaykh of hadith, 'Ali al-Mazru'i from the Dar al-hadith Institute. *Ḥisba* is a term related to the Islamic principle of 'commanding good and forbidding wrong' (*al-amr bi al-ma'rūf wa al-nahy 'an al-munkar*), and is also related to the name of the Wahhabi 'religious police' force (*muṭawwa'a*), which was institutionalised in 1940 as the Office for Commanding Good and Wrong (*Hay'at al-amr bi al-ma'ruf wa al-nahy 'an al-munkar*) in order to enforce the Shari'ah law. The group wanted to distinguish itself from Jama'at al-tabligh, one of the most active proselytic organisations of that time, because it was connected with Sufism. Members of the group referred to themselves simply as brothers (*ikhwān*) and they met in the House of Brothers (*Bayt al-ikhwān*).[67]

In the early 1970s, the Salafi group experienced rapid growth and spread to nearly all major cities in Saudi Arabia. The members of the group, which had its headquarters in the ultraconservative, lower-class suburbs of Medina, were in close contact with various other Salafi groupings and scholars from abroad. The group was also influenced by al-Albani's new approach to religion, especially as one of the founders, Sulayman ibn al-Shutaywi, had studied under al-Albani at the Islamic University of Medina. As al-Huzaymi, one of the former members of the Salafi group recollects, he was strongly influenced by the writing and lectures of al-Albani, whose simple approach, based on the Qur'an and Sunna, suited those brothers who were uneducated in religious sciences. He was also influenced by the *Kitab al-tawhid* of Ibn 'Abd al-Wahhab and, finally, by a chapter from Sayyid Sabiq's *Fiqh al-sunna*. As for the personal library of Juhayman al-'Utaybi, leader of the group, we are informed that it contained most of al-Albani's books, the six collections of hadiths and their commentaries. In addition, it contained the Qur'anic exegesis written by Ibn Sa'di and Ibn Kathir, and *Ithaf al-jama'a bi-ma ja'a fi al-fitan wa al-malahim wa 'ashrat al-sa'a* by Hamud al-Tuwayjiri, a genre of apocalyptic literature that influenced al-'Utaybi's apocalyptic imagery. Al-Shawkani's book *Nayl al-awtar*, Ibn al-Amir al-San'ani's *Subul al-salam*, *Majmu'at al-tawhid*[68] and the books of Ibn Taymiyya and Ibn Qayyim al-Jawziyya, as well as the commentary of *al-'Aqida al-tahawiyya*, were also included.[69]

The opinions of Juhayman al-'Utaybi are presented in his short treatise, known as *Rasa'il Juhayman al-'Utaybi*, which was to become a jihadi literature 'bestseller'. The treatise has influenced later generations of jihadis, such as Abu Muhammad al-Maqdisi, and, arguably, also impacted the ideology of ISIS. Both al-Maqdisi and ISIS strongly accentuate what they consider to be correct doctrine and iconoclasm, on the one hand, while also denouncing the Saudi regime because of its unwillingness to put its doctrines into practice, on the other.

In a short treatise, *Khilafa Based on the Methodology of Prophethood and Tyrannical Kingship* (*al-Khilafa allati 'ala minhaj al-nubuwa wa al-mulk al-jabri*), al-'Utaybi criticises the Saudi authorities as a tyrannical monarchy. Among the religious arguments he uses are the hadiths in which the Prophet Muhammad predicted the forms of rule that would follow his death. These were, in sequence, the caliphate on Prophetic methodology, oppressive monarchy (*mulk 'ādd*), tyrannical monarchy (*mulk jabrī*), and, again, a caliphate which would be based on Prophetic methodology.⁷⁰ The reason why al-'Utaybi deemed governments of his day to be examples of tyrannical rule lies in the fact that the caliph is not chosen by Muslims themselves. Moreover, the caliph is not from the Quraysh, a condition that must be fulfilled according to certain hadiths. Al-'Utaybi strongly accentuates the principles of loyalty and disavowal (*al-walā' wa al-barā'*) and, accordingly, he criticises today's rulers for cooperating with infidel Christians, Jews, communists and Shi'is.⁷¹ One is also required to isolate (*i'tizāl*) oneself from false rulers. It is relevant to note that al-'Utaybi does not derive the term *i'tizāl* from Sayyid Qutb, as anyone familiar with Qutb's writings might suppose, but it is taken directly from Qur'anic imagery of the prototype of the true monotheist, the Prophet Abraham, who says: 'I dissociate myself from you [*a'tazilukum* in the original] and whatever you invoke besides Allah. I will supplicate my Lord. Hopefully, I will not be disappointed in supplicating my Lord' (19:48). Also highly relevant is the following Qur'anic verse (60:4):

> There has already been for you an excellent pattern in Abraham and those with him, when they said to their people, 'Indeed, we are disassociated from you and from whatever you worship other than Allah. We have denied you, and there has appeared between us and you animosity and hatred forever until you believe in Allah alone', except for Abraham's saying to his father, 'I will surely ask forgiveness for you, but I have not [power to do] for you anything against Allah. Our Lord, upon You we have relied, and to You we have returned, and to You is the destination.'

In *Unveiling the Confusions* (*Raf' al-iltibas*), al-'Utaybi applies the ideal of Abraham's religion to the present day. Accordingly, worship belongs only to God, while at the same time it is necessary to disavow the *shirk* and polytheists, to whom one must show enmity. Al-'Utaybi criticises three groups of missionaries who fail to meet this principle in their proselytising activities. The first group claims that the basis of religion is to fight grave-worshippers (*muhārabat al-qubūriyīn*), whom they warn and to whom they show enmity. They also fight against Sufis and Shi'is. By this group, al-'Utaybi means the Ansar al-sunna al-muhammadiyya, whose members mostly hail from Egypt and Sudan, while being active in Saudi Arabia. The second group is similar to the first, except that they are the leaders in the campaign against a blind adherence to the *madhhab* system and are mostly concerned with purification and hadith studies. This is a reference to al-Albani's followers in Syria and Kuwait. Huzaymi, a former companion of al-ʿUtaybi, mentions that although he has been in contact with a Salafi group in Kuwait, the one in Medina was far more serious, as he does not, for example, recollect whether or not they would go out for *kunāfa* (cheese pastry) or ice-cream. Al-ʿUtaybi and his followers, who implemented the idea of abandoning society and living in seclusion (*iʿtizāl*), even settled in the desert near Medina in order to live in absolute austerity and simplicity, even willing to suffer from head lice. The third group was obsessed with anti-communist polemics, as well as the necessity of proving God's existence, and was engaged in politics in order to seize power, an evident reference to the Muslim Brotherhood. Al-ʿUtaybi appreciated the first two groups for being concerned with hadith studies and doctrinal issues, particularly in relation to denouncing necrolatry; however, he criticised them for lacking the power to implement such ideas.[72]

Leaving his criticism of various Islamic groups and returning to his criticism of the Saudi regime, al-ʿUtaybi concludes that a rebellion (*al-khurūj ʿalā*) against a tyrannical ruler is legitimate, while refuting accusations that his attitude reflects the position of the extremist Kharijis.[73] Although, to our knowledge, the reasons behind his unwillingness to pronounce *takfīr* are uncertain, one may argue that it is because he does not wish to be associated with Sayyid Qutb and Qutbism. However, in the aftermath of the seizure of the Grand Mosque, both the Saudi authorities and the pro-regime Saudi ulama attributed the extremism of the movement to it having been influenced by Qutbism. Al-ʿUtaybi's feelings of resentment, furthermore, were influenced by the fact that he was a descendant of a personal friend of Sultan ibn Bijad, one of the three leaders of the rebellious Ikhwan. One of his arguments in support of a rebellion against Saudi rule is that in the 1930s ʿAbd al-ʿAziz forbade the waging of jihad against Shiʿi grave-worshippers in Iraq and even waged war against the Ikhwan, who were actually engaged in fighting them. Instead, the Saudi state began to cooperate with Christians, Jews and Shiʿis and laid the foundations for the worship of the riyal.[74]

Both in theory and in practice, it is evident that for al-ʿUtaybi, the concept of the Prophetic caliphate meant an apocalyptic, millennialist vision, inspired by al-Tuwayjiri's books and the apocalyptic traditions of the Sunni collections of hadiths, with no connection to the similar ideas behind the Iranian revolution of 1979. As evidence of his apocalyptic vision, he interpreted various current struggles and temptations (*fitna*), usually limited by his personal experience in the milieu of Saudi society, but in accordance with the apocalyptic imagery associated with the portents of the hour (*ashrāṭ al-sāʿa*). In 1978, al-ʿUtaybi declared that it had been confirmed to him in a dream that his companion, Muhammad al-Qahtani, was the Mahdi, the prophesied redeemer of Islam, which led to a split as some of his followers were not convinced by this apocalyptic direction of the movement.[75] It is noteworthy that the Saudi regime after the insurrection started to support various Saudi clerics such as al-ʿArifi, who tried to weaken millennialist tendencies by providing an accurate interpretation of the portents of the hour. However, as is evident from the ideology of ISIS, the apocalyptic imagery still presents a powerful vehicle through which Saudi legitimacy can be challenged.

The ideas of Juhayman al-ʿUtaybi had a strong influence on Abu Muhammad al-Maqdisi (b. 1959), the most famous ideologue of jihadism and a prominent critic of the Saudi regime, who himself influenced later generations of Salafi jihadis. At the beginning of his career, al-Maqdisi was influenced by the Syrian ideologue Muhammad Surur (b. 1938), who, while maintaining the political discourse of the Muslim Brotherhood, used some of the books of Ibn ʿAbd al-Wahhab to criticise Saudi rulers. Al-Maqdisi also admired Sayyid Qutb's idea of the *takfir* of secular governments, albeit that he was fully aware of Qutb's mistakes and excessive rationalism. He believed that many Salafis had discarded Qutb's ideas simply because he was not a Salafi. In his writings, however, he came to the same conclusion as Qutb, that is, rulers are infidels and their laws are un-Islamic. He also became acquainted with the teachings of al-Albani and Ibn Baz. Al-Maqdisi considered his sojourn in Saudi Arabia to be the most important period of his life, and it was there that he became a real Salafi.[76] While it was not officially acknowledged that he held the status of student, he had the permission of Ibn Baz to use the facilities of the Islamic University of Medina. In the library of the Prophet's Mosque he came across *Resplendent Pearls in Answers from Najd* (*al-Durar al-saniyya fī al-ajwiba al-najdiyya*), a voluminous collection of Wahhabi literature, starting with Ibn ʿAbd al-Wahhab. Among many works included in this collection, a radical treatise by Hamad ibn ʿAtiq inspired him in particular to write his most famous book, *Abraham's Religion* (*Millat Ibrahim*), published in 1984. Al-Maqdisi wrote it in Peshawar for a group of Algerian fighters during the Afghan War.

The book's title refers to the Qurʾanic depiction of the Prophet Abraham as a true monotheist and iconoclast, a person who disavowed *shirk* and even his own family for worshipping idols. As such, it is in line with early Wahhabi literature, be it Ibn ʿAbd al-Wahhab's *Kashf al-shubuhat* or Hamad ibn ʿAtiq's treatise. Al-Maqdisi marks the point of departure for his book by referencing the well-known saying of Ibn ʿAbd al-Wahhab, that the foundation (*aṣl*) of religion and its basis (*qāʿida*) lies in two matters. The first is the imperative to worship God alone and not the partners associated with Him, as well as the encouragement to do so through allegiance (*al-muwālāt*) based upon this requirement and a declaration of disbelief (*takfīr*) for whoever rejects it. The second is a warning against *shirk* in the worship of God and a requirement to be firm about this and show enmity towards those who commit *shirk* and declare them unbelievers (*takfīr*).[77] Al-Maqdisi also criticises the division of monotheism into doctrinal and practical segments (*tawḥīd iʿtiqādī* and *ʿamalī*), which was known to be the strategy used by al-Albani to denounce *takfīr*. The same argument is used as a means of criticising the Saudi regime:

> Indeed, we witness this clearly in the so-called state of Saudi Arabia, which deceives the people by its encouragement of monotheism and the books of monotheism, as well as by permitting, or even encouraging scholars to wage war against necrolatry and Sufism (*muḥārabat al-qubūr wa al-ṣūfiya*) and the *shirk* of amulets, *ṭawla* (magic used by women to attract men), trees and stones and other than that from what it [Saudi Arabia] does not fear and is not threatened by. Nor does it have any effect upon its foreign or domestic policies.[78]

Saudi Ulama, the Issuance of *Fatāwā* and Global Outreach

Saudi Arabia uses a plethora of methods to disseminate various religious stances, which include its *fatwā* institutions and several proselytic organisations. The term *fatwā* (pl. *fatāwā*) means a non-binding advisory opinion to an individual questioner (*mustaftī*). It is a special domain of the jurisconsult (*muftī*). The work of the muftis rests on the high degree of authority associated with their opinions. As such, the institute of *fatwā* perhaps represents the closest Islamic equivalent to the Anglo-American legal mechanism of case-law precedent.[79] This institute has a substantial history in Islam. However, in modern times it has experienced a significant organisational development in the form of the appearance of specialised committees charged with the collective issuance of *fatāwā* (*iftā'*).[80] *Iftā'* is an important source for the definition of norms, especially if it is supported by the state. By stating the virtues of a good Muslim, the ulama have been able to position themselves as a legitimising force within the government.

The main public agency charged with *fatwā* issuance in Saudi Arabia is the Board of Senior Ulama.[81] Other important bodies charged with the supervision and expansion of the religious sphere are the Council of Higher Judges (*Majlis al-qudat al-'ali*), the Committee for the Promotion of Virtue and the Prevention of Vice (*Hay'at al-amr bi al-ma'rūf wa-l-nahy 'an al-munkar*), officially set up in 1926 and charged with the enforcement of a strict observance of the principles of Islam, and the Saudi Muslim World League (*Rabitat al-'alam al-islami*), established in 1962 and charged with the task of exporting Wahhabism abroad.

In 1971, King Faysal announced the establishment of the Board of Senior Ulama (*Hay'at kibar al-'ulama'*), headed by Ibn Baz. The Board became the highest religious body in Saudi Arabia. Members of the Board were recruited from the older generation of pro-regime clerics, such as al-'Uthaymin, Ibn Jibrin and Salih ibn Fawzan. Traditionally, although the committee seeks to give an illusion of openness and to represent all regions, the vast majority of the committee members come from the Najd.[82] The members, appointed by the king and usually varying in number between fifteen and twenty-five, are the only clergy who can exercise substantive political influence on the ruling family.[83] However, the members of the Board are still employees of the state and receive their salaries in accordance with public servant categories. As such, the Board clearly reflects the state's interests and the Saudi regime has regularly used it *ex post* to approve its decisions and the acts it has already implemented. On the rare occasions when the Board's views differ from those of the state, such disagreements are typically conveyed through its silence.⁸⁴ According to Faysal's decree, the Board is required to express its opinions in matters of the Shari'ah; to advise the king on political questions; to provide religious leadership for Muslims in the areas of belief, prayers, and secular affairs; and to confirm the successor to the throne. In essence, an organisation has been created which, by means of its edicts on Islamic law, books and recordings of sermons, has the capacity to serve kings whenever they need religious sanction for their policies. Its establishment marked the completion of a centralisation process that has made religion in Saudi Arabia dependent on the authority of the state. It also resulted in a serious disruption of earlier developments, as the creation of the Board marked the end of the Al al-Shaykh era in Saudi history. In addition, as Bligh points out, 'for the first time a permanent forum was brought into being to serve the King in his future need for religious authorisation and approval'.⁸⁵

The part of the Board responsible for the preparation of *fatāwā* is formed by the Permanent Committee for Scholarly Research and Fatwas (*al-Lajna al-da'ima li-l-buhuth al-'ilmiyya wa al-ifta'*). The Committee was founded by royal decree No. 137/1, on 29 August 1971. The Committee falls administratively under a larger autonomous government agency, the General Presidency (*al-Ri'asa al-amma li-idarat al-buhuth al-'ilmiyya wa al-ifta' wa al-da'wa wa al-irshad*), which, besides having a responsibility for *fatwā* issuance is also charged with religious research, the propagation of Islam and public instruction in religion.⁸⁶ According to the decree, the Committee is tasked with issuing legal opinions on Islamic jurisprudence in areas of creed (*'aqīda*), worship (*'ibāda*) and social issues, and with the preparation of research papers for the Board of Senior Scholars. At the time of its creation, the Committee had various sub-committees and was formed as a result of the efforts of a close-knit network of loyal ulama, who were simultaneously active in many other institutions and were members of university boards or holders of other positions. The *fatāwā* issued by the Board are based on research studies conducted by its members, especially those from the Committee, and as such are the outcome of the combined *ijtihād* of many of the most respected ulama. According to Vogel, 'the board's decisions seem to have a near-legislative effect on judicial decisions' and many judges (*qāḍī*) accept their holdings axiomatically, especially when they are often reinforced by the order of the king to implement them.⁸⁷

The interference of the rulers in the composition and inner workings of the Board has been clearly demonstrated in connection with the issuance of a Memorandum of Advice in 1992, which heavily criticised the regime. The Saudi rulers, however, convinced Ibn Baz to condemn the signatories of the memorandum. Subsequently, six of the eighteen members of the Board refused to sign the *fatwā* denouncing the memorandum. Shortly afterwards, the king nominated new members, thus replacing those who had not complied. In 1993, Ibn Baz, who proved to be a loyal defender of the regime, was declared Grand Mufti in an attempt to underscore the central place of the official ulama as the highest authority in religious matters.

To complete the full institutionalisation of the *iftā'* institution, the late Saudi king, 'Abdullah, issued a royal edict in August 2010, according to which the authority to publish official *fatāwā* was endowed only with the members of the Board of Senior Scholars and members of the Permanent Committee.[88] In addition, a new sub-committee of the Permanent Committee, headed by Salih ibn Muhammad al-Luhaydan, was created to supervise the issuance of *fatāwā* and to prevent the involvement of unauthorised scholars. The sub-committee, which opened offices throughout Saudi Arabia, was also charged with the responsibility for appointing approved scholars to evaluate the legitimacy of *fatāwā*. In his edict, King 'Abdullah stated that it to be a violation of Islamic law when unqualified individuals issue *fatāwā*, and that such actions undermine the official state institutions and stray into the arena of state jurisdiction. This royal decree exemplified how the Saudi state is working to impose its primacy in religious matters and its control of the religious establishment. The restriction was also a part of an attempt to reform the religious establishment, a trend that had been evident in Saudi Arabia since 2003. Since the edict, several unauthorised *fatwā* webpages and TV and radio call-in shows have been terminated.[89] Unsurprisingly, a number of senior scholars voiced their strong support for the king's edict.

Traditionally, the rulings of these bodies have been concerned, among other things, with issues such as veiling, the status of women and relations with non-believers. It was also the Committee that prepared the groundwork for statements regarding issues associated with graves, tombs and shrines. The Committee made a clear declaration regarding this issue: 'Building over graves is a disagreeable heresy (*bid'a*) . . . and leads to polytheism (*shirk*). It is therefore incumbent upon the ruler of Muslims or his deputy to remove what is over graves and level them to the ground.'[90] Ibn Baz and other senior ulama also imposed an absolute (*mutlaq*) prohibition against women visiting graves. The reason is, according to Ibn Baz, that women are 'impatient', and their visits to graves or attendance at funerals might pose a temptation (*fitna*) for men. Therefore, Ibn Baz concludes, it was out of God's mercy that He prohibited women from *ziyāra*.[91] For men, on the other hand, it is recommended (*mustahabb*), according to Ibn Baz, that they visit the graves of the Prophet and his Companions – but it is not permitted to touch or kiss these graves or to perform circumambulation around them. However, Ibn Baz, against popularly accepted belief, asserts that visiting the Prophet's grave is not obligatory (*wājib*) for Muslims and is by no means a legal and necessary part of the *hajj*.[92]

The prohibition of mixed-gender groups (*al-ikhtilāt*) also clearly belongs among the main concerns of both the Saudi ulama and religious police (the field agents of the Committee for the Promotion of Virtue and the Prevention of Vice). Such gender mixing is viewed by many of the religious establishment as a permanent danger, leading to *fitna* and eternal damnation. In their own words, the clerics were 'astounded' by their realisation of 'how far the so-called modern Muslim woman falls short of the noble level which Allah wants for her'.[93] In order to attain that, several manuals of proper behaviour for women were published in Arabic, translated into many languages and distributed worldwide. One of these states:

> The Muslim woman who knows the teachings of her religion has insight and is balanced and self-controlled. When she is stricken by the death of one of those whom she loves, she does not let grief make her lose her senses, as is the case with shallow, ignorant women who fall apart with grief . . . She never wails over the deceased, because wailing is not an Islamic deed; it is the practice of the *kuffaar*, and one of the customs of *jaahiliyah*. The Prophet was very explicit in his emphatic prohibition of wailing, to the extent that it was regarded as *kufr*: 'There are two qualities in people that are indicative of *kufr*: casting doubts on a person's lineage, and wailing over the dead' (Muslim). The Prophet effectively excluded from the Muslim community those men and women who wail and eulogise the dead when he said: 'He is not one of us who strikes his cheeks, or tears his garment, or speaks the words of *jaahiliyah*.'[94]

As for attending funerals,

> the Muslim woman who truly understands the teachings of Islam does not attend [them], in obedience to the command of the Prophet ... In this case, women's position is the opposite of men's position. Islam encourages men to attend funerals and to accompany the body until it is buried, but it dislikes women to do so, because their presence could result in inappropriate situations that would compromise the dignity of death and the funeral rites.[95]

Both the Board and the Committee are part of the bureaucratic apparatus and are responsible for the spreading of the Wahhabi doctrine. The dispersion of knowledge is based on the network of acknowledged scholars and institutions and a process by which correct teachings are transmitted. Individual scholars study with the prominent senior ulama and, after completing their education, graduate and receive *shahāda* (a diploma confirming their formal religious training and credentials in an established institution), and *ijāza* (a certificate by which the teacher acknowledges the transmission of his knowledge to the pupil and authorises him to spread it further). As Meijer points out, the Saudi religious establishment is based on three principles: (1) regarding doctrine, Salafism is considered the only true Islam, all other forms and interpretations are deviations and innovations; (2) only the Salafi movement is a movement of the ulama who have the correct knowledge of the texts. On this basis, the Saudi ulama have a monopoly of the truth; (3) there is a hierarchy among the Saudi ulama, with the mufti at its head and the Permanent Committee as the supreme consultative body.[96]

In the 1980s, Saudi Arabia began to support Islamic communities in non-Islamic countries. Various Saudi religious or charitable organisations dedicated to the Salafi mission started to print millions of translated Qur'ans and, more importantly, other religious texts (including hadith literature) and distribute them worldwide. Everywhere they went they also established contacts with similarly minded ultraconservative Islamic groupings and financed their education in the Salafi doctrine. This effort was boosted after 1979 – not only because the Iranian Revolution posed a threat of activating Shi'i communities in the Islamic world, but also in response to the threat that came with the Afghan jihad against the USSR.

An important educational institute is the Islamic University of Medina. It was established in 1961 as a result of the backing provided by Muhammad ibn Ibrahim, who became its first president with Ibn Baz as co-president. The university's objectives were stated in its charter: 'The University was created to revive Islamic dogma. Muslims throughout the world conveyed at Medina to learn the doctrine of true Islam and to return to their countries to propagate it.'[97] An important aspect of the Islamic University thus consists in the fact that it allocates the absolute majority of its places to Muslims from outside Saudi Arabia. The Islamic University was supposed to become a counterbalance to the renowned Sunni university of al-Azhar in Cairo as both countries, Saudi Arabia and Egypt, competed for influence in the 1960s. In practice, the reform of al-Azhar in 1961 imposed a high degree of state control. In addition, the prestige of al-Azhar was no match for the oil resources of Saudi Arabia. Another religious university, Imam Muhammad ibn Saud Islamic University, was opened in Saudi Arabia in 1974 in Riyadh as a counterbalance to the oldest university in Saudi Arabia, King Saud University in Riyadh, which also offered non-religious study programmes. In 1981, the Umm al-Qura University in Mecca was established. Due to the general modernisation of the education system, the gates have been opened to accommodate an influx of both foreign teachers and students.

Many similarly oriented religious institutes, especially in South Asia – such as Nadwatul Ulama, the education enterprises of the Ahl-i hadith of India and Pakistan, and the Deobandi madrasas – have traditionally sought to attract Saudi assistance. These institutes, as with other purification movements, have since striven to eradicate such practices as *ziyāra* to the shrines of saints and other popular religious customs. Saudi financial support was also crucial in the establishment of numerous madrasas for Afghan refugees in Pakistan, which later helped to produce the Taliban. It is worth mentioning that 'Saudi patronage' originates not only from the state, but also from international associations (such as the Muslim World League), various charitable organisations and from wealthy private individuals. This patronage network helps to directly promote certain Saudi national interests.[98]

The *Ahl al-hadith* movement was established in Saudi Arabia in the 1960s, together with other Muslim movements such as the Muslim Brotherhood, Tabligh, Hizb al-tahrir and Ansar al-sunna al-muhammadiyya, to give just a few examples. In the 1960s and 1970s, Prince Faysal, the prime minister and, after 1964, the king of Saudi Arabia, propagated the idea of pan-Islamism as a counterweight to al-Nasir's secular nationalism. It also served a domestic purpose, that is, to boost the Saudi regime's religious credentials.[99] Faysal, whose father ʿAbd al-ʿAziz was criticised by the Ikhwan for sending his son to Great Britain on a diplomatic mission, became the mastermind behind the highest level of financial and political support for non-secular Sunni Islam in the history of Saudi Arabia. He was respected by both the Hijazis as a pro-Westerner and the Najdis for his religiosity. It was he who revived the idea of pan-Islamism, which seemed to be a mere utopian dream after the abolition of the Ottoman Empire. Pan-Islamism came hand in hand with the idea of 'Muslim solidarity' (*al-taḍāmun al-islāmī*), which brought together various Muslim organisations and individuals of non-Wahhabi backgrounds and offered them Wahhabi teachings. At the beginning of the 1960s, Faysal helped to establish the Islamic University of Medina and the Muslim World League in Mecca. The former propagated pan-Islamism through international education, the latter on a political and diplomatic level.

Since the creation of most of the organisations and institutions described above, they have sought to serve Muslims far beyond Saudi Arabia and have helped to establish or influence contemporary networks of religious scholars all across the Islamic world. Their impact on the global nature of Islamic proselytisation can thus be demonstrated through reference to dozens of examples. Customs related to graves, for instance, form an important part of the works produced by Muhammad ibn Jamil Zinu (1925–2010). Zinu was an Islamic scholar, originally from Syria, who ended up teaching at the Grand Mosque in Saudi Arabia and also in Dar al-hadith al-khayriyya. His colourful publications, many of them produced by the thousand and spread for free worldwide by Saudi Arabia, gained wide popularity in the Islamic world, especially in certain circles (such as prisons).[100] His books were also translated into a number of languages, in particular because of their easy style and introductory character. They usually have a common purpose, that is, to depict correct Islamic doctrine through the presentation of hadith.

Zinu emphasises the principle not to venerate the saints and righteous persons in all their forms, be it idols, statues or images, as they are tantamount to *ṭāghūt*. He criticises both the eastern and western countries, including those

Islamic countries that imitate them. Erecting statues of George Washington, Napoleon or Stalin leads to their veneration, according to Zinu, exactly as was the case of the people of Noah who venerated statues, thus committing *shirk*. The same prohibition of imagery applies to the pictures of seductive women (*al-nisā' al-fātināt*) omnipresent in the streets, homes, shops or media, which corrupt the youth. Zinu calls for the destruction of all kinds of these idols, based on the famous hadith 'Do not leave any statue without destroying it nor any raised grave without levelling it.' Zinu elaborates on this idea by using another version of this hadith mentioned in Ahmad ibn Hanbal, which is only rarely used and which adds 'nor any picture without ruining it (*wa lā ṣūra illā laṭakhtahā*)'.[101]

In his widely circulated booklet, *Methodology of the Saved Sect* (*Minhaj al-firqa al-najiyya wa al-ta'ifa al-mansura*), Zinu uses the same hadith for confirming the basic Salafi views regarding graves (do not build over graves; do not place flowers upon graves, among other things). He begins one of the chapters by saying: 'The shrines that we see in Islamic countries, such as Syria, Iraq, Egypt and other countries are against the teachings of Islam.' He then concludes by quoting the hadith mentioned above and claims that Islam forbids the construction of buildings over graves and that these must be destroyed and levelled with the ground (*lā tatruk qabran murtafi'an illā kasartahu wa ja'altahu qarīban min al-arḍ*).[102]

Another example of the spread of this line of thought, which is also replicated in many other European countries, can be found in Germany. The Salafi webpages at www.selefiyyah.de, which often quote the *fatāwā* of Saudi religious scholars, list, within their doctrinal section, a brochure provided by Abd ul-Aziiz S. Al-Shumar, called *Wichtige Lektionen für jeden Muslim* (*Important Lessons for Every Muslim*).[103] Lesson 13, which is called 'Die verurteilung dessen, der Allah an den Gräbern rechtschaffener Menschen anbetet und wie dies zur Anbetung des Menschen führen kann' ('The condemnation of those who worship Allah at the graves of righteous people and how this can lead to the worship of men'), emphasises, among other things, the following points: the warnings made by the Prophet against the building of mosques close to graves and the earlier injunction of the Prophet that his grave should not lie in a mosque.

* * *

Over the course of its history, Saudi Arabia has emerged as a hybrid Shariʿah/nation-state, built on a mixture of Wahhabism (gradually rebranded as Salafism) and the chieftaincy system. In the 1960s, Saudi Arabia established religious international institutions in order to export, orchestrate and control the character of Salafism worldwide. By the 1970s, the Saudi regime had almost entirely institutionalised, bureaucratised and, in the process, instrumentalised its religious structures. It was intended that Salafism should be spread worldwide as part of a Saudi pan-Islamic policy, promulgated in particular by King Faysal. This change was significant, since until then Wahhabism, with its iconoclastic teachings had only had substantial influence in the local arena. Now it was to have an impact across the Islamic world in relation to both non-Salafi and Salafi streams of what had originally been a non-Wahhabi movement.

One of the main purposes of the institutionalised Salafi ulama and teachings, besides presenting the image of an ideal society, has been the legitimisation of the Saudi regime. The opinions of most of the official Saudi ulama were still based mostly on the work of Ibn Taymiyya, Ibn Qayyim al-Jawziyya and Ibn ʿAbd al-Wahhab and his followers. These opinions were to gain the status of a proper doctrinal position and, as such, have since been disseminated worldwide. This has been achieved through a plethora of methods at the disposal of the Saudi state, mainly thanks to their oil revenues, and has involved the provision of support for religious universities, *fatwā* institutions and proselytic organisations, as well as the abundant printing of religious materials and their free distribution.

In particular, a further boost to iconoclastic ideas has been provided by the *Ahl al-hadith* movement, especially the work of Muhammad Nasir al-Din al-Albani, who – through his critical re-evaluation of hadith, the strict prohibition of imagery in all its forms and his call for the purification of doctrine – has more than anybody else influenced global Salafi discourse in relation to iconoclastic issues. Many of the subsequent movements or ideologues took inspiration from these theological and legal stances, oftentimes in highly simplified and sometimes even militarised forms. Often, the degree of simplification seems to coincide with the multiplicity of competing ideological (or even political or military) influences, as will be clearly demonstrated in the following chapter.

Notes

1. Cited from al-Barik, *al-Ijaz*, p. 28.
2. Ibn Baz, *al-Fatawa al-muhimma*, p. 473.
3. Or, as Abou El Fadl aptly put it, when questioning the right of a monopoly of jurists to speak in God's name, 'Are Muslims going to need a jurist to go to the toilet?' See Abou El Fadl, *And God Knows the Soldiers*, p. 105.
4. This is also why some authors call Saudi Arabia an 'ante-state', cf. Hammond, *The Islamic Utopia*, p. 6.
5. For a deeply researched history of the formation of the Saudi religious establishment, or 'the corporation' as he puts it, see Mouline, *The Clerics of Islam*.
6. Zaman, *The Ulama in Contemporary Islam*, p. 2.
7. According to Michael Cook, to his knowledge, Ibn 'Abd al-Wahhab does not refer to Ibn Taymiyya's work *al-Siyasa al-shar'iyya*, even though he knows the corresponding work of Ibn Qayym al-Jawziyya, *al-Turuq al-hukmiyya fi al-siyasa al-shar'iyya*. However, he mentions that according to Ibn Bishr, Ibn Taymiyya's *al-Siyasa al-shar'iya* was one of the texts that used to be read at gatherings in the home of Turki during his reign. See Cook, *Commanding Right*, p. 178, fn. 92.
8. Kostiner, *The Making of Saudi Arabia*, pp. 4–6, 73, 106.
9. Mouline, *The Clerics of Islam*, p. 9.
10. See Wahba, *Jazirat al-'arab*, p. 311.
11. Kostiner, *The Making of Saudi Arabia*, p. 103.
12. al-'Uthaymin, *al-Sunan wa al-bida'*, pp. 8, 39, 41. Al-'Uthaymin, Ibn Baz and al-Albani were not always in agreement as regards restrictions in using some words; see al-Barik, *al-Ijaz*, pp. 69–78.
13. As for the creed, he had been educated in the Wahhabi tradition by his father and uncle. He also knew some works by Ibn 'Abd al-Wahhab, Sulayman ibn 'Abdullah Al al-Shaykh and Ibn Taymiyya, and he studied hadith with Sa'd ibn 'Atiq. See Ibn Qasim, *Fatawa wa rasa'il*, vol. 1, p. 10.
14. Ibid., vol. 12, pp. 108–10.
15. Ibid., vol. 3, pp. 200–1. One should note the paradox embodied in Muhammad ibn Ibrahim's prohibition of the planting of trees at cemeteries, as it is in contrast to the toponyms and ethymology of the cemeteries themselves. For example, two of the greatest cemeteries in Saudi Arabia, Baqi' al-Gharqad in Mecca and al-'Ud in Riyadh, are named after plants. Gharqad means boxthorn in Arabic, while 'Ud designates sandalwood, from which one of the

most popular perfumes in the Muslim world is made. Both cemeteries have also been called 'garden' or 'paradise' (*janna*), which might suggest that they used to be planted with trees, such as Jannat al-Muʿalla (or al-Hajun, named after the mound on which it is situated). Another word for a tomb in Arabic is *rawḍa*, which also means garden. 'Prophetic garden' (*al-rawḍa al-nabawīya*) is a term for the place in between Muhammad's grave and his *minbar*. For some examples of the combination of gardens and graves, see Ruggles, *Islamic Gardens and Landscapes*, pp. 103–16.

16. Ibn Qasim, *Fatawa wa rasaʾil*, vol. 1, p. 136.
17. Ibid., vol. 3, p. 202.
18. Ibid., p. 205.
19. Ibid., vol. 3, p. 211.
20. Ibid., pp. 211–15.
21. Available at: https://www.youtube.com/watch?v=VIxDLpEK0a8, video dated 9 April 2012, last accessed 5 September 2016.
22. Bligh, 'The Saudi Religious Elite', p. 43.
23. Both Ibn Baz and Muhammad ibn Ibrahim were influenced to some extent by the *Ahl al-hadith* movement through Saʿd ibn ʿAtiq. Al-ʿUthaymin, overshadowed by Ibn Baz, was a student of ʿAbd al-Rahman ibn Nasir al-Saʿdi (d. 1956), who was himself a student of the highly respected Shaykh al-Shinqiti (d. 1973), while Ibn Jibrin's authority stemmed from the fact that he studied with Ibn Baz and ʿAbd al-Razzaq ʿAfifi. Al-Fawzan's authority, in turn, came from him being a student of al-Saʿdi, Ibn Baz, al-Shinqiti and ʿAfifi. Al-Albani, the most learned and original scholar among them, was himself an autodidact who, as such, faced accusations from his adversaries that he had no *ijāza*, that is, authority to transmit religious knowledge.
24. Commins, *The Wahhabi Mission*, p. 112.
25. For the opinions of Ibn Baz on heliocentrism, see, for example, at: www.ibnbaz.org.sa/mat/9141, last accessed 5 September 2016.
26. al-ʿUthaymin, *al-Jamiʿ li-ahkam fiqh al-sunna*, p. 50.
27. Brown, *The Canonization of al-Bukhari and Muslim*, p. 324.
28. See ibid., p. 321.
29. Although Ibn Taymiyya does not mention John the Baptist's head by name, he is of the opinion that the graves of all prophets are unknown, with the exception of the Prophet Muhammad and, probably, Ibrahim. See Ibn Taymiyya, *Majmuʿat al-fatawa*, vol. 27/445, pp. 235–6.

30. al-Sahadan, *al-Imam al-Albani*, p. 95.
31. Ibid., p. 95.
32. Ibid., pp. 19–20.
33. Ibid., p. 14.
34. Ibid., pp. 40–54.
35. Ibid., p. 50.
36. Ibid., p. 22.
37. Brown, *The Canonization of al-Bukhari and Muslim*, p. 313.
38. al-Albani, *Tahdhir al-sajid*, p. 28.
39. Ibid., pp. 21, 31.
40. See ibid., pp. 12–13.
41. Ibid., p. 41.
42. Ibid., p. 45.
43. Ibid., p. 45. He refers to *Majallat al-Azhar*, vol. 11, pp. 502–3. The *fatwā* prohibits a request made by the administrator (*ra'is khidam al-masjid*) of Izz al-Din Aybak mosque, who wants to be buried in one of the two existing graves because his grandfather was buried there. The *fatwā* is based on various opinions, but primarily on those of Ibn Taymiyya and of Ibn Qayyim al-Jawziyya in *Zad al-ma'ad*, who opine that if a dead person is buried in a mosque, the body must be exhumed. It should be noted that this *fatwā* is not obligatory, cf. at: http://www.ansaralsonna.com/web/play-1926.html, last accessed 5 September 2016.
44. See *Fatawa kibar al-'ulama' al-azhar al-sharif*, pp. 18–19, 48–9. The treatise was written in 2007 by a group of scholars, among them 'Abdullah Shakir al-Junaydi, a professor of Islamic theology and leader of Ansar al-sunna al-muhammadiyya in Egypt.
45. See, for example, al-Huzaymi, *Ayyam ma'a Juhayman*, p. 20, who states that the book was a 'black stain' on al-Albani's academic career in Saudi Arabia.
46. al-Albani, *Ahkam al-jana'iz*, p. 227.
47. Ibid., p. 230 and fn. 1.
48. Ibid., p. 235.
49. Sabiq, *Fiqh al-sunna*, vol. 1, pp. 394–5. With an introduction of Hasan al-Banna.
50. See at: http://www.binbaz.org.sa/noor/1367, last accessed 5 September 2016.
51. Ibn Qasim, *Fatawa wa rasa'il*, vol. 3, pp. 205–11, the same *fatwā* is included in *Fatawa 'ulama' al-balad al-haram*, pp. 664–7, a collection composed of the *fatāwā* of Ibn Baz, al-'Uthaymin, Ibn Jibrin, al-Fawzan and al-Shinqiti.

52. The book was edited by Hasanayn Muhammad Makhluf, with a foreword by Shaykh ʿAbd al-Malik ibn Ibrahim Al al-Shaykh. The fact that a Hanafi scholar and mufti edited Hanbali legal work illustrates his affinity with Wahhabism. See ʿUthman, *Hidayat al-raghib*, p. 338.
53. For more details about the Sahwa movement, see Lacroix, *Awakening Islam*.
54. In his *al-ʿAqida al-wasitiyya*, Ibn Taymiyya mentions only *al-tawallī wa al-tabarrī*, which means to refrain from the extremes of *nawāṣib* (those who hate the Prophet's family *ahl al-bayt*) and *rawāfiḍ* (Shiʿis, who refute the legitimacy of the righteous caliphs, Abu Bakr, ʿUmar and ʿUthman), fully in accordance with his concept of the middle way, as based on the Qurʾanic *ahl al-wasaṭ*, people of the centre.
55. For more details, see Lav, *Radical Islam*, pp. 86–119.
56. al-Albani, *Fitnat al-takfir*, pp. 35–6.
57. Ibid., pp. 43–4.
58. al-Wadiʿi, *Tuhfat al-mujib*, p. 160.
59. al-Wadiʿi, *Riyadh al-janna*, p. 7.
60. For his opinions, based on his thesis, on the issue of building structures over the Prophet's grave, see al-Baydani, *Majmuʿ fatawa al-Wadiʿi*, vol. 1, pp. 157–232.
61. Ibid., pp. 205, 217.
62. Ibid., p. 208.
63. Haykel, 'A Zaydi Revival?', pp. 20–1. See also Johnsen, 'Profile of Sheikh Abd al-Majid al-Zindani', pp. 3–7 and, for a broader context, Johnsen, *Last Refuge*.
64. Nevo, 'Religion and National Identity in Saudi Arabia', p. 39.
65. Note that 'images' can refer to imagery or idolatry, regardless of its form.
66. Lacroix, *Awakening Islam*, p. 90.
67. See Hegghammer and Lacroix, 'Rejectionist Islamism', pp. 103–22. Ibn Baz is mentioned in an interview with al-Huzaymi (audio source with transcription), a former member of the al-Jamaʿa al-salafiyya al-muhtasiba, available at: http://www.kingkhalid.org.sa/Gallery/Text/ViewBooks.aspx?View=Page&PageID=85&BookID=5.
68. In all likelihood, *Majmuʿat al-tawhid al-najdiyya*, a collection of Wahhabi literature published by Rashid Rida.
69. al-Huzaymi, *Ayyam maʿa Juhayman*, p. 27.
70. Rifʿat, *Rasaʾil Juhayman*, p. 64. This hadith in many variations is cited elsewhere by al-ʿUtaybi, and it is common in the ideology of Hizb al-tahrir and ISIS. See, for example, *Dabiq*, No. 1, p. 33.

71. Rif'at, *Rasa'il Juhayman*, pp. 66, 68.
72. al-Huzaymi, *Ayyam ma' Juhayman*, p. 106.
73. Rif'at, *Rasa'il Juhayman*, p. 68. Of course, it is clear from reference to the etymology used in traditional heresiographic literature, such as al-Shahrastani's *Kitab al-milal wa al-nihal*, that the idea of rebellion (*khurūj 'alā*) is traditionally ascribed to the early Kharijis as being one of the three plausible etymologies of their name; the others being leaving (*khurūj min*) the camp of 'Ali during the battle of Siffin, and an allusion to the Qur'anic terms regarding passivity (*qu'ūd*) or activity (*khurūj*) in one's willingness to wage jihad.
74. Ibid., p. 82.
75. Hegghammer and Lacroix, 'Rejectionist Islamism', p. 112.
76. Wagemakers, *A Quietist Jihadist*, p. 35.
77. Cited from al-Maqdisi, *Millat Ibrahim*, pp. 12–13.
78. Cited from al-Maqdisi, *Millat Ibrahim*, p. 16.
79. M. K. Masud, B. Messick and D. S. Powers, 'Muftis, Fatwas, and Islamic Legal Interpretation', pp. 3–4.
80. Ibid., pp. 27–8.
81. For a description of the procedure of *fatāwā* issuance, see Mouline, *The Clerics of Islam*, pp. 158–61.
82. Cf. ibid., pp. 181–2.
83. An important aspect of the Royal Decree announcing the establishment of the Board is that membership is not restricted only to Saudi scholars but can also be granted to non-Saudi specialists.
84. Boucek, 'Saudi Fatwa Restrictions and the State–Clerical Relationship'.
85. Bligh, 'The Saudi Religious Elite', p. 3. For an argument supporting the claim that Saudi *fatwā* mechanisms enable a mutually beneficial partnership between the religious establishment and the government, see Al-Atawneh, *Wahhabi Islam Facing the Challenges of Modernity*, p. 149 and elsewhere. Those who study the Saudi ulama usually confirm their subservient position towards the government. See, for example, Layish, 'Ulama and Politics in Saudi Arabia'; Al-Yassini, *Religion and State in the Kingdom of Saudi Arabia*; Bligh, 'The Saudi Religious Elite'; or Salamé, 'Political Power and the Saudi State'. For a nuanced view, see A. G. Marines, 'The Relationship Between the Ulama and the Government in the Contemporary Saudi Arabian Kingdom: An Interdependent Relationship?', unpublished PhD thesis, Durham University, available at: http://etheses.dur.ac.uk/3989, last accessed 15 May 2015.

86. Vogel, 'The Complementarity of *Ifta'* and *Qada*", p. 263.
87. Vogel, *Islamic Law and Legal System*, pp. 115–16.
88. For the text of the edict, see at: http://www.alwatan.com.sa/Local/News_Detail.aspx?ArticleID=16807&CategoryID=5, last accessed 5 September 2016.
89. Cf. Boucek, 'Saudi Fatwa Restrictions and the State–Clerical Relationship'.
90. Ibn Baz et al., *al-Bida' wa-l-muhdathat*, p. 294.
91. Ibn Baz, *al-Fatawa al-muhimma*, p. 112.
92. Ibn Baz, *al-Tahqiq wa al-idah li-kathir min masa'il al-hajj wa al-'umra wa al-ziyara*, p. 82.
93. al-Hashimi, *The Ideal Muslimah*, p. 23.
94. Ibid., pp. 514–15.
95. Ibid., pp. 520–1.
96. Meijer, 'Politicising *al-jarh wa-l-ta'dil*', pp. 378–9.
97. Schulze, 'La *da'wa* saoudienne en Afrique de l'ouest', p. 25.
98. Zaman, *The Ulama in Contemporary Islam*, pp. 175–6.
99. Hegghammer, *Jihad in Saudi Arabia*, p. 17.
100. Cf. 'Saudi Publications on Hate Ideology Invade American Mosques' (Washington, DC: Center for Religious Freedom, Freedom House, 2005), p. 22.
101. Zinu, *Majmu'at rasa'il al-tawjihat al-islamiyya li-islah al-fard wa al-mujtama'*, pp. 65–7.
102. Ibid., p. 200.
103. Available at: www.selefiyyah.de/aqidah-tauhid, last accessed 5 September 2016.

4

Following Current Paths of Destruction: ISIS and Beyond

> I fall sleep in the midst of battle before sirens and tanks
> owned by enemy ranks
> Hit cloud nine
> with the smell of turpentine,
> nations wiped clean of filthy shrines
>
> Excerpt from a poem, titled 'Take Me to the Lands Where the Eyes are Cooled', by a female ISIS convert, Asia Siddiqui, who was arrested in New York and accused of conspiring to prepare an explosive device to be detonated in the United States. The poem even made it into the al-Qaeda magazine, *Inspire*.[1]

In recent years, iconoclastic incidents have taken place in various parts of the Islamic world and the discourse that has influenced these acts is also current in various Islamic communities in the West. In this chapter, we look at some of these events within both their local context and wider settings, focusing first at ISIS, and, in order to ensure comparative depth, we also take a look at iconoclastic incidents in the Arabian Peninsula, the Levant, North, West and East Africa, and parts of Asia.

Before we do so, it is only right and proper that we should emphasise that not all iconoclastic stances over the last century have been influenced by Wahhabism–Salafism. This was, for instance, certainly the case in the Soviet Union, where Sufi orders were considered to be primary enemies of the Communist state. The Soviet authorities quite rightly identified the Sufi orders as keepers of traditional religious order and as obstacles in the way of the full integration of their regions into the Soviet realm. A similar pattern was to be observed in the newly established republic of Turkey, where all Sufi orders were dissolved and visits to shrines – among other practices – were prohibited. Many of the shrines (*ziyaret*) of the numerous saints (*evliya*) were destroyed in the zealous secular republicanism of the 1930s and 1940s. Extreme anti-Sufism to some extent declined after the ending of the Republican People's Party rule in 1945. Several years later, tombs were reopened for pilgrimage purposes. Even then, however, Turkish Islam continued to devalue the role of the saints and to become increasingly mosque-centred. Due to modernist ideas, many Muslims started to scorn shrine visits and view faith in the power of saints as being inappropriate.[2]

However, most of the acts of destruction linked to religious sites that have occurred in the Islamic world, particularly since the final quarter of the twentieth century, may well be connected to the increase in activity of various Saudi religious bodies and institutions, as discussed in the previous chapter. Another thread can be traced back to the increasing number of pilgrims visiting Mecca and Medina, as well as the more forceful proselytisation efforts of Saudi institutions targeting pilgrims from abroad. This is not, of course, a new phenomenon as the *hajj* has served as an important means of spreading a variety of thoughts and ideologies over many centuries. In modern times, for example, clearly anti-Shiʿa stances were carried all the way to China by the famous Chinese Muslim reformer Ma Wanfu (aka Guoyuan Hajji, 1849–1934) of Gansu. Ma Wanfu visited Mecca in 1888 at a time when it was controlled by the Ottomans. However, he spent four years studying in a garrison town set up for the Saudi Ikhwans. After his return to China, he even called his newly established movement *Yihewani*, a phonetic rendering of the Ikhwan, which criticised 'non-Islamic' customs, such as the veneration of saints, their tombs and their shrines. Ma Wanfu also set up a mosque and declared his ten points, one of them specifically requiring that there should be 'no visit to tombs'. In the 1930s, the Yihewani movement served as the breeding ground for the creation of the Chinese Salafiyya movement, which has been responsible for keeping Ma Wanfu's traditions alive until today.[3]

If we move away from China, the broader attractiveness of grave-related issues is attested by the fact that even one of the perpetrators of 9/11, Muhammad Atta, gained inspiration from them. This can be deduced from his last will and testament, written in 1996 while he was living in Germany.

In relation to the period after his death, Atta wrote, 'I don't want anyone to weep and cry or to rip their clothes or slap their face because this is an ignorant thing to do.' He also added, 'I don't want any women to go to my grave at all during my funeral or on any occasion thereafter.'[4]

ISIS

In July 2012, a suicide bomber was responsible for an explosion at the shrine of Sayyida Zaynab on the outskirts of Damascus. In July 2013, the site was attacked again with mortar shells. Several other shrines were also desecrated, including that of Hujr ibn 'Adi in 'Adra, whose remains were exhumed and removed. Of course, it is problematic to interpret all such attacks against shrines as intentional attempts at their destruction. Some of these attacks did not target the site itself, but military or civilian facilities in the surrounding neighbourhood. In any case, all this was only a prelude to what was to come later. After the beginning of the civil war in Syria, the destruction and desecration of Sufi and Shi'i shrines, in itself quite a new type of terrorism, became entirely common. In the case of Iraq, the destruction of religious sites had also started there long before the creation of ISIS. Shi'i shrines and mosque complexes were attacked by Sunni extremists as early as 2003. One of the most spectacular attacks, on the golden-domed Imam 'Abbas Mosque in Karbala, occurred in 2007. The destruction of shrines was also part of the repertoire of other small 'Islamic emirates', such as the Ansar al-islam organisation that was active in northern Iraq between 2001 and 2003 and controlled a number of villages outside Halabja, close to the Iranian border. In addition to establishing training camps and Shari'ah courts, the members of the organisation also destroyed Sufi shrines.[5] In Iraq, the escalation of violence was instigated, to a large extent, by the Sunni bombing of the Shi'i shrine in Samarra in February 2006. The shrine housed the tomb of Hasan al-'Askari, the eleventh imam of Twelver Shi'i Islam, who was buried there in 874. This was followed by an increase in anti-Sunni terrorism by Shi'i militias.

All this was completely superseded by the brutal assault on historical monuments that was to be conducted by ISIS, particularly in the case of Mosul. The organisation conquered Mosul on 10 June 2014. The city had been outside government control long before and its conquest proved to be an easy task for ISIS, which capitalised on the general Sunni fear of and hostility towards the Shi'i government headed by Nuri al-Maliki (in office 2006–14). Admittedly, the ideological backgrounds and motivations of individual ISIS members differ significantly. However, at least some of the acts and statements originating from the organisation can clearly be placed in the category usually termed Wahhabism–Salafism or, more precisely, Salafi jihadism. The former leader of ISIS, Abu 'Umar al-Baghdadi (d. 2010) in one of his speeches appealed 'to all Sunnis, and to the young men of Jihadi-Salafism (*al-salafīya al-jihādīya*) in particular, across the entire world.'[6] To this trend belong networks of religious scholars, proselytisers and activists all over the world, oftentimes supported by Saudi Arabia. This radical trend has recently been able to enforce itself as the real guardian of the Salafi tradition and skilfully manipulates and appropriates key texts and their interpretation.

The relationship between ISIS and Saudi Arabia is not easy to deconstruct.[7] Over the course of 2015 and 2016 the virtual space has been flooded by satirical articles and cartoons comparing ISIS with Saudi Arabia. The content of these pieces was usually similar: besides the same features of both entities – such as 'authoritarianism', 'fundamentalism', 'suppression of the rights of women and minorities', 'application of the death penalty', 'regular torture of people', 'regular beheadings' – there stands only one difference: while the first is an enemy of the United States, the latter has been its crucial regional ally for many decades.[8] Saudi Arabia reacted to this campaign in its specific way: it threatened to sue anybody who compared the kingdom to ISIS. Yet the Twittersphere responded promptly by posting hundreds of contributions under the hashtag #SueMeSaudi further comparing the two Islamic entities.

The same or similar features of Saudi Arabia and ISIS aside, it is more important to highlight the analogical ideological roots of the two. The ambivalent relation of Saudi Arabia towards ISIS is visible from the fact that the open letter sent to the ISIS's leader, Abu Bakr al-Baghdadi, which was signed by more then 120 Islamic scholars from all over the world, was supported by only a single Saudi cleric, a prominent Sufi shaykh from the Hijaz.[9] The case of iconoclasm might be further instructive in showing the similarities between Saudi Arabia and ISIS. Both commit vast destruction of the cultural landscape. When we compare the destroyed monuments, one striking element is notable: many sites contained a grave or a tomb on its premises. As shown in previous chapters, it is this strict view on visiting graves and building structures above graves that might serve as a simple distinguishing sign of Salafi movements.

Officially, both Saudi Arabia and ISIS declare the other to be an enemy. However, in the ranks of ISIS there are thousands of Saudis. Besides, it is also estimated that Saudi private channels stand behind parts of ISIS financing arrangements (although these are hard to quantify and most likely do not form a significant portion of the entire ISIS budget). Many voices from Saudi Arabia, both civilian and members of the armed forces, have praised the advances made by ISIS, although Saudi Arabia reacted to the departure of some of its citizens to join ISIS by banning their participation in foreign conflicts through a royal decree.[10] This was also supported by the highest mufti, 'Abd al-'Aziz Al al-Shaykh, who declared in August 2014 that: 'The ideas of extremism, radicalism, and terrorism do not belong to Islam in any way, but are the first enemy of Islam, and Muslims are their first victims, as seen in the crimes of the so-called Islamic State and al-Qaeda.'[11]

In ISIS rhetoric, Saudi Arabia stands as one of its prime targets for criticism. On the pages of *Dabiq*, its propagandist magazine, ISIS predicts that it will soon be flying its black flag in Mecca and Medina.[12] It also addresses its rival in its propaganda through recourse to derisive names, such as 'Saudi' Arabia (with the intentional use of inverted commas).[13] Elsewhere, it avoids using the name altogether and opts for various other description, such as the 'Arabian Peninsula', referring to the Saudi ruling family as 'Al Salul' (instead of Al Sa'ud), and comparing it to *ṭāghūt* (the idol): 'Indeed it is an idol of the Peninsula, the best place on earth and cradle of revelation, which is ruled by this idol, despicable lackey of Jews and Christians.'[14] It even goes so far as to label members of the ruling family as 'apostate rulers'.[15] At the most fundamental level, ISIS questions the legitimacy of Saudi Arabia and its claim to adhere to the teachings of Ibn 'Abd al-Wahhab. For this reason, ISIS makes references to early Wahhabi literature, as well as borrowing some of the concepts of the religious opposition in relation to the Saudi regime (al-'Utaybi, al-Maqdisi). Moreover, ISIS propaganda has further developed and been combined with the idea of *millat Ibrāhīm* and the caliphate, based on the Prophet's methodology. In ISIS ideology, Abraham represents the ideal of *al-walā' wa al-barā'*, meaning the disavowal of polytheism, polytheists and even tyrannical rulers. On this basis, ISIS also justifies its war against those who worship graves (be it Shi'is, non-Salafi Sunnis, Yazidis or Christians), regarding them as its enemies. In the same way, ISIS seeks legitimacy for its war against the Saudi regime through reference to *ṭāghūt*.

In response to the criticism it receives from some official Saudi religious scholars, ISIS scornfully responds that the Saudi regime, as is the case with other frightened Gulf rulers, orders its 'palace clerics' and the media to intensify their attacks against it.[16] The main criticism against Saudi Arabia consists of the claim that the kingdom is not governed according to God's rule; it consorts with the West against other Muslims and tolerates the Shi'i minority living in its lands. Abu Bakr al-Baghdadi, in one of his speeches, identified his fight against the Saudi regime as one of the top priorities, describing the kingdom as the 'head of the snake and epicentre of contagion'. Furthermore, he exhorted his followers to: 'Unsheathe your swords! Your first obligation is to go after the Shi'is wherever you find them, then after Al Salul and their soldiers, before the crusaders and their bases! . . . Tear them to pieces!'[17] The translation of his words into deeds did not take long and ISIS has launched several attacks on Saudi soil, directed primarily against Shi'i targets and the Saudi security services.

We have already dealt with the spread of Wahhabism–Salafism and its influence on the ideology of many organisations and individuals. There is, however, a difference between the extremism of early Wahhabism and the political reality of contemporary Saudi Arabia. The religious authorities, on which the regime bases its power, take inspiration from the same roots as many jihadi movements, including ISIS. Nevertheless, these same authorities are themselves criticised by the jihadists and other opponents of the regime for their servility and co-optation. These jihadists do not question the validity of the early Wahhabi ideals, quite the contrary. They blame the regime and its religio-legal establishment for betraying these ideals. This line of argumentation is typical of the jihadists and some of the religious authorities on which ISIS ideology – directly or indirectly – rests.

Although the fanaticism and belligerence of the early Wahhabis was moderated by the Saudi authorities, with Wahhabism being gradually institutionalised into a state religion, the original Wahhabi, as well as subsequent, radical texts and thoughts are still being disseminated by various Saudi institutions and other official, semi-official or charitable organisations based in the Gulf region. This explains the similarity between the ideology of the contemporary interpretation of Islam in Saudi Arabia and the ideology of ISIS. In other words, we can perceive the extreme ideology of ISIS, on the one hand, as well as the current Saudi regime with its ideology, on the other, as being simultaneously close and interrelated in relation to their origins, genesis and argumentation, and entirely antagonistic in terms of their tactics and the question of legitimacy. This is not to say that there is a direct link between Wahhabi and Saudi propaganda and the emergence of ISIS, that would be a harsh oversimplification of a profoundly more complex and multifaceted phenomenon, and would show disregard for other important – for example, socio-political, tribal, economic – factors. It must also be added that ISIS does not refer merely to the Salafi jihadi trend, which was supported by Saudi Arabia, both financially and ideologically, in the 1980s and 1990s. This discourse, however, is the most accented one and ISIS often relies on various Salafi concepts and terms in its attempt to create a coherent, unifying and legitimate ideology.

ISIS frequently uses, quotes, refers to, paraphrases or re-publishes both older Wahhabi–Salafi texts and its own productions. As for the former, this includes texts that have nothing in common with the organisation itself, such as 'classical' medieval literature (Ibn Taymiyya, Ibn Qayyim al-Jawziyya, collections of hadiths and their exegesis) or the Wahhabi texts that are mostly related to the so-called imams of the Najdi call, especially Ibn ʿAbd al-Wahhab (for example, his *Kitab al-tawhid*, *Kashf al-shubuhat* or *Nawaqid al-islam*) and his descendants until Muhammad ibn Ibrahim Al al-Shaykh. References are also quite often made to Muhammad al-Shawkani. To the same group we can also add the Salafi texts that are not in line with the official Saudi Salafi interpretation, such as various popular jihadi texts produced by al-Qaeda, the thoughts and texts of those who have opposed the Saudi regime (Sayyid Qutb, the Saudi Sahwa movement, Juhayman al-ʿUtaybi or those belonging to the 'Shuʿaybi School'[18]). As for its own productions, the ISIS output includes texts and other multimedia documents stemming from ISIS propaganda. In these, one can easily note the vast difference between the relatively high professional quality of English sources and the austere, both in content and form, texts that appear in Arabic, which are usually also very simplistic. One can thus argue that ISIS propaganda mostly targets foreigners (as a matter of fact, the term for foreigners, *ghurabā'*, is often used in its religious discourse).

ISIS also draws on the work of its own religious authorities, usually from the younger generations. Allegedly, several ISIS judges come from Saudi Arabia.[19] The chief ISIS judge in 2007, for example, was a Saudi scholar, Abu Sulayman al-'Utaybi, who, however, defected shortly afterwards.[20] In recent years, as far as we can judge from the open sources, the prominent position belonged to Turki ibn Mubarak al-Bin'ali (born in 1984 in Bahrain).[21] Al-Bin'ali, after receiving some religious instruction from Abu Muhammad al-Maqdisi, also studied under several Saudi scholars, for example, the high-ranking radical cleric 'Abdullah ibn Jibrin. It was allegedly he who wrote a recommendation to the Islamic University in Medina for al-Bin'ali that was full of praise.[22] Al-Bin'ali authored, among other items, the essential textbook of Islam, referred to as *Muqarrar fi al-tawhid* (*Course in Monotheism*), which was used in ISIS training camps. The text, amounting to some sixty pages, is a typical example of Wahhabi–Salafi writing, frequently quoting Ibn Taymiyya, Ibn Qayyim al-Jawziyya and Ibn 'Abd al-Wahhab.[23]

As for the large-scale destruction of architectural monuments by ISIS, this started shortly after the organisation seized control of Mosul.[24] Only ten days later, the first monument, the tomb of the famous Mosul historian Ibn al-Athir, was bulldozed. Later in the same month, the Mosque of Shaykh Fathi met with the same fate. The most widely reported case was the destruction of the Prophet Jonah (Yunus) mosque/tomb complex in Mosul, but there are many other similar incidents. The destruction has not been limited to Mosul and has occurred in other places, mostly in and around al-Raqqa, Nineveh and Dabiq (where, for instance, the tomb of the seventh Umayyad caliph, Sulayman ibn 'Abd al-Malik, was destroyed).[25] The morality police of ISIS have allegedly forced prisoners to level cemeteries, gravestones and tombs as a punishment, such cases appearing in the city of Mosul and its vicinity. ISIS members also ordered the local people to bury their dead in 'the proper Islamic way', that is, to put a headstone on the grave and keep the earth on the grave levelled.[26] The ISIS fighters also openly called for the demolition of Muhammad's mosque in Medina and the destruction of Muhammad's grave.

Given the often contradictory media reports, it is difficult to assess the exact dates of the destruction of the monuments. Based on the example of Mosul and the time frame of 2014/15, we can deduce that destruction happened in several waves: June–July 2014 (eleven monuments destroyed); September 2014 (four monuments); the turn of 2014/15 (three monuments); February 2015 (three monuments); March 2015 (four monuments). Other destructive episodes that have been detected by satellite imagery were either not reported in the media at all or cannot be linked to any reported destruction with any degree of certainty (roughly, a dozen monuments). In summary, by the end of August 2015, when the last satellite image was analysed, the total number of destroyed monuments in the city of Mosul had reached forty-one.[27]

Based on the case of Mosul, the destroyed monuments can be divided into six typological groups: mosques of the prophets; mosques and shrines of the family of the Prophet Muhammad; mosques of significant, often venerated people native to, or associated with, the town; the separate tombs of Mosul residents; Christian monuments; and cemeteries (both Islamic and Christian). In other areas, ISIS seems to have specifically and systematically targeted aspects of Shiʻi cultural heritage, with Sufi (for instance, the Sufi shrine and tombs near Membij in Abu Qalqal/Abu Abr in September 2014) and Yazidi sites also being included.

The destructive behaviour of ISIS towards historical monuments is often considered to be a highly effective method of producing powerful visual imagery, with the intention of disseminating it, in a 'relentless production of images' and as part of a 'propaganda machine', through recourse to visual media and social networks in order to shock the audience. This line of argument is even expanded so that cultural heritage is, in fact, being destroyed for the express purpose of producing such visual imagery. In this respect, iconoclasm loses its true meaning and exists 'only as a historical reference, a rhetoric' and a well-choreographed and atavistic performance made by 'a super-modern phenomenon, incorporating the most powerful tools of hyper-reality in disseminating their violent acts'.[28] Harmanşah's stance might be very well-founded, but is applicable only in relation to a limited segment of the destroyed heritage. It aptly captures the theatrically staged destructions of, for example, the Assyrian artefacts in Mosul Museum, the reliefs in the

Ashurnasirpal II's Palace in Nimrud, and the Christian symbols found on Mosul's Christian architecture. It cannot, however, fully explain the rationale behind the destruction of a whole range of modest, rather insignificant monuments, for which ISIS has never publicly claimed responsibility in their propaganda material, and which have not even been reported by local people.

As for the ideological aspect, the obligation to destroy funerary sites has already been stressed by Abu 'Umar al-Baghdadi. He stated, when articulating the fundamentals of the Islamic State, 'the necessity to destroy and eradicate all manifestations of idolatry (*shirk*) and prohibit the means leading to it'. He particularised his statement by reference to the Prophetic hadith quoted in the *Sahih* of Imam Muslim on the authority of Abu al-Hayyaj al-Asadi, which states: 'Do not leave a statue without destroying it, or a raised grave without levelling it.'[29] With regard to Mosul, the hadith was quoted immediately after the seizure of the town and can be found in the thirteenth article of the document named 'Wathiqat al-Madina' (Charter of the City), published by ISIS in June 2014. In the document, it is used as the sole explanation of ISIS' stance in relation to idolatrous shrines and tombs.[30]

In its propaganda, ISIS often uses apocalyptic references. A frequently mentioned prophecy connected with apocalyptic times speaks of the worshipping of idols. These can entail not only real idols, but anything that a man worships besides Allah. The first steps taken towards idolatry were made by those Muslims in olden times who started to venerate graves and worship the saints.[31] In ISIS discourse, those who adhere to different interpretations of Islam are not merely 'bad Muslims', but are downright heretics or apostates (this is massively emphasised in relation to Shi'is and Sufis in general). In justifying this position, in its propaganda ISIS has made reference to direct quotations from Muhammad ibn 'Abd al-Latif Al al-Shaykh and Ibn Taymiyya about the need to level graves and fight the 'abominable extremism' of the Shi'a.[32]

Judging by written ISIS-produced propaganda material, it is conceivable that ISIS felt obliged, at least to a certain extent, to explain the motivation behind the destruction to the local people.[33] This can be deduced from the content of widely circulated treatises, designed as e-leaflets, which explain the necessity for the destruction of the graves. The treatises were written in simple language and in a comprehensible style, obviously with the intention of being easily absorbed by common people. At least one of them was intended to be distributed 'shortly before or during the destruction of tombs'. It consisted of an abbreviated version of one of the most authoritative writings on the prohibition of building over graves, composed by Muhammad al-Shawkani. In the treatise, al-Shawkani claims that 'erecting graves, building domes over them and praying near them constitute a major innovation'.[34] Another, though anonymous leaflet, was explicitly intended for the people of Mosul, since it advocated the necessity of destroying the tombs of the four Mosul prophets (Yunus, Shith, Daniyal and Jirjis, whose prophethood is contested), making reference to the opinions of several medieval authorities, as well as the Sunna of the Prophet. In the leaflet, the destruction is advocated within the broader intention of 'annihilating the sources of *shirk* . . . and removing them from the hearts of people', and ISIS claimed that 'if given the opportunity . . . [it will] destroy the domes and buildings on graves and shrines'.[35] The destructions in Mosul were allegedly also approved by a *fatwā* issued by one of ISIS' religious leaders, Husam Naji al-Lami, who based his arguments on the Prophetic tradition.[36]

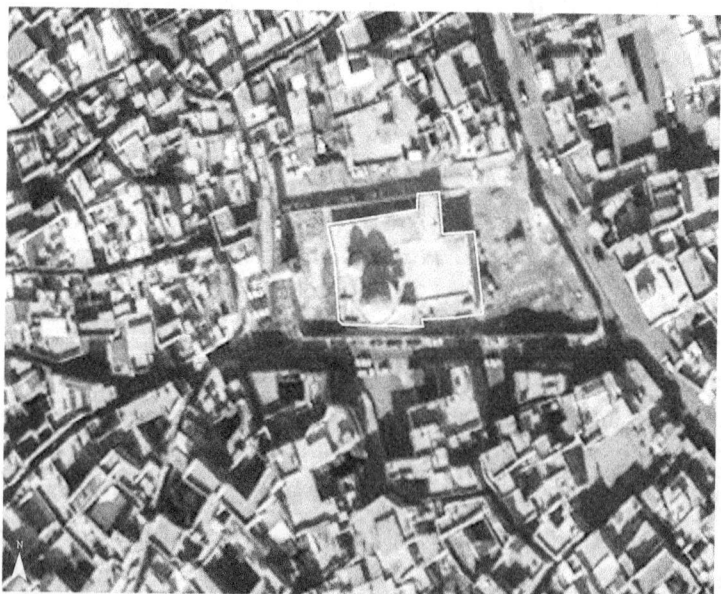

Figure 12a The mosque and shrine of Jirjis: before its destruction, 15 November 2013 (*Source*: Satellite images WorldView-2 and WorldView 3C 2015 DigitalGlobe, Inc., distributed by European Space Imaging GmbH/ARCDATA PRAHA, processed by Lenka Starková.)

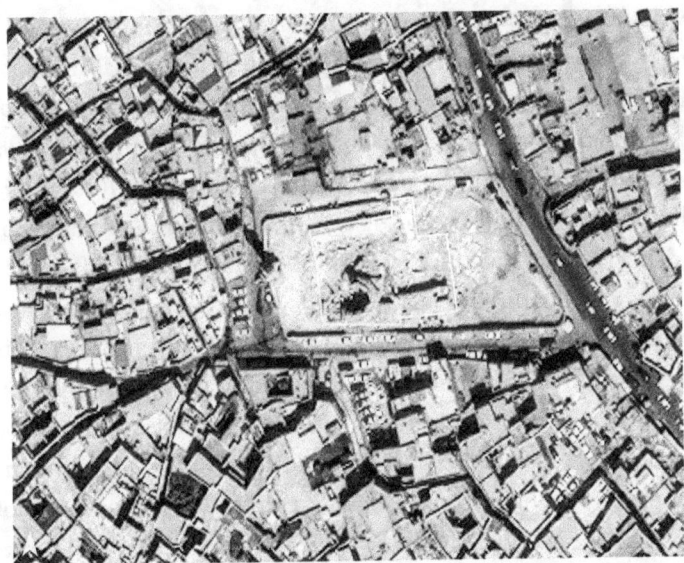

Figure 12b The mosque and shrine of Jirjis: after its destruction, 21 August 2014
(*Source*: Satellite images WorldView-2 and WorldView 3C 2015 DigitalGlobe, Inc., distributed by European Space Imaging GmbH/ARCDATA PRAHA, processed by Lenka Starková.)

Figure 12c The mosque and shrine of Jirjis: approximately one year after its destruction, 29 November 2015 (note that the emptied space serves as a parking lot)
(*Source*: Satellite images WorldView-2 and WorldView 3C 2015 DigitalGlobe, Inc., distributed by European Space Imaging GmbH/ARCDATA PRAHA, processed by Lenka Starková.)

The destruction of architectural heritage monuments was bountifully reported in the world's media, as well as on different social networks. This applied mainly to the destructions of June and July 2014. Some of them were filmed and short clips showing the destruction found their way into news headlines throughout the world.[37] The destruction of June and July was also followed by the publication of two picture reports produced by ISIS, summarising the scale of the destruction (among other items, nine Mosul monuments were reported).[38] The reports were disseminated on a mass scale through news servers and the printed media. The presentation of the June and July wave can certainly be considered to be a part of ISIS' performative visualisations, intended to disseminate the image of violence among both the inhabitants of the occupied city and the outside world. This, however, by no means applied to all detected acts of destruction. With a few exceptions (the destruction of the Mosque of Imam Muhsin and the suspected destruction of the Mosque of al-Abariqi,[39] as well as the staged devastation of Mosul Museum and Christian symbols on church architecture), the other destructive acts in Mosul were not utilised in ISIS' visual propaganda (picture series, videos) at all. To the best of our knowledge, this applies to approximately three-quarters of the destroyed monuments. The information was mainly reported by local people, who contacted the media operating in non-occupied parts of Iraq. Nine of the destructive acts were discovered only by reference to satellite imagery analysis and not to the media (neither English nor Arabic).[40] Such acts can certainly be considered as representing a strategy employed by ISIS as a means of intimidating the local people. Here, however, it should be recalled that in many less publicised cases, the destruction affected rather modest, less significant buildings, all of which contained a tomb.

This is not to say that ISIS was not motivated by other factors. The organisation was fully aware of the importance of controlling the public space through its symbols. That is why, after conquering a new territory, ISIS carefully cleared away all the visual representations of its rivals (be it in the form of public inscriptions, figurative images of Shi'i imams, Christian symbols, monuments from pre-Islamic times or, in our case, shrines of Muslim saints and local righteous figures).

In terms of ideology and doctrine, not all the Salafi preachers condoned ISIS' destruction of graves and tombs. In a *fatwā* issued in July 2014, Abu

Figure 13 The destruction by ISIS of Qabr al-bint (The Grave of a Girl), Mosul, 2014 ('Taqrir 'an hadm al-adriha wa al-awthan fi wilayat Ninawa', available at: http://justpaste.it/atrah, last accessed 9 August 2014.)

Basir al-Tartusi ('Abd al-Mun'im Mustafa Halima), a Syrian cleric, opponent of the al-Asad regime and a theoretician of jihad, criticised ISIS (whose members he called 'Kharijis') and said that destroying mosques in which there were tombs was not allowed and was illegal.[41] ISIS' activities were generally denounced by more then 120 legal and theological Islamic scholars in the form of an open letter to al-Baghdadi. Sunni authorities in this letter criticise, point by point and based on the Qur'an and other religious texts, various aspects of ISIS' ideology and acts. In Article 20, while acknowledging that scholars disagree on the subject of graves, the authors state that 'it is forbidden in Islam to destroy the graves and shrines of Prophets and Companions and disinter their remains, just as it is not permissible to burn grapes under the pretext that some people use them to make wine'. The text, however, is quite unclear about the permissibility of shrines in general, speaking only about the graves of the Prophets or the Companions, 'as the Companions were in consensus regarding burying the Prophet and his two Companions, Abu Bakr and Omar, in a building that was contiguous to the Prophet's Mosque'.[42]

Figure 14 The destruction by ISIS of Imam al-Muhsin shrine in Mosul
(An image grab taken from a video, 'Izalat mazahir al-shirk', released by ISIS, February 2015, available at: https://www.youtube.com/watch?v=EEhWzVBqX-c.)

The Arabian Peninsula

After the destruction of religious sites in the Hijaz in the 1920s, the Saudis continued to carry out similar acts. In 1989, Saudi authorities allegedly removed the remains of ʿAbdullah, Muhammad's father, and moved them to the al-Baqiʿ cemetery. In 1998, despite the vocal protests and fierce criticism from all around the world, the grave of the Prophet's mother, Amina bint Wahb, was demolished in al-Abwaʾ village north of Jeddah. The structure marking her grave was bulldozed and then doused in gasoline and burnt. A similar fate befell the grave of Eve in Jeddah (Hawa, in Islamic tradition), the wife of Adam and mother of humankind. As she was believed to be a giant, her grave was allegedly about 35 metres long. The grave, together with many others, was destroyed in the 1920s and repeatedly thereafter, that is, as soon as it proved to still serve as a popular location for visits, for example, in 1975. The mosque and tomb of Imam Jaʿfar al-Sadiq in the neighbourhood of the Prophet's Mosque (*al-masjid al-nabawī*) in Medina was destroyed by dynamite and flattened on 13 August 2002. The Hijazis similarly lament the destruction of the grave of Khadija, the Prophet's first wife.[43] Of course, the destructions have not taken place in the name of religion, but have usually been justified through reference to 'urbanisation' and 'modernisation' arguments, or by the 'need' to expand Mecca's Grand Mosque and expand the accommodation and service facilities assigned for pilgrims.[44] Many of the destroyed sites meet the criteria associated with the anti-*ziyāra* policy, and many are targeted specifically because of their Shi'i heritage associations. The Saudi Ministry of Islamic Affairs also called for the demolition of the dome over the Prophet's Mosque and for the levelling of the graves of Muhammad, Abu Bakr and 'Umar.

Another occurrence of large-scale grave destruction in the twentieth-century Arabian Peninsula took place in Yemen. In September 1994, approximately two thousand men, armed with rocket-propelled grenades, explosives and shovels,

Figure 15 The grave of Eve, Jeddah
(S. M. Zwemer, *Arabia: The Cradle of Islam*, New York: Fleming H. Revell, 1900, p. 17.)

demolished the cemetery built around the shrine of a local saint in Aden. Not only was his sanctuary destroyed, along with some elaborate wooden decor, but many graves were exhumed and their remains burnt. This event was not the result of an unplanned rampage; it was a well-prepared and systematic event. A bulldozer had even been brought along to level the graves, a feat that was later to be regularly repeated in Libya, Iraq and elsewhere. The violent attack, clearly inspired by the practice of *ziyāra* and rooted in a disagreement over basic issues connected with grave culture, instigated further incidents of grave destruction in other parts of Yemen.[45]

Many individuals and organisations in Saudi Arabia, as well as the governments of Abu Dhabi, Kuwait and Oman, condemned the attack and offered to finance the rebuilding of the complex. On the other hand, the attack on the Aden cemetery was supported in some sermons delivered in Saudi Arabia. In Yemen, Muqbil ibn Hadi al-Wadi'i, one of the leading figures of Salafi Islam in Yemen at that time, had voiced his support for the destruction of graves on widely circulated cassette tapes.[46]

The destruction that occurred in Yemen in 1994 was definitely not the last one. In early 2016, for instance, members of the Yemeni branch of al-Qaeda demolished a number of domed structures and tombs in the al-Shihr district

Figure 16 The destruction of graves in Yemen in 2016
(An image taken from Wikalat al-Athir, http://web.archive.org/web/20160205034621/https:/twitter.com/wkalh22501/status/693336673330032640, last accessed 14 August 2016.)

of Hadramawt province in eastern Yemen. The movement justified its activity by claiming that it was part of the process of eradicating 'manifestations of polytheism' (*maẓāhir al-shirk*). Similar incidents also occurred in the city of al-Mukalla.[47]

Recently in Bahrain, several Shi'i religious sites, including tombs, have been demolished in the aftermath of the wave of popular uprisings in the Arab world. The Al Khalifa royal family managed to suppress the pro-democracy protests by the Shi'i population in 2011, with the military crackdown being assisted by the Gulf Cooperation Council (Saudi Arabia). One of the first acts of the security apparatus (security forces and civil defence personnel) was allegedly to demolish, partially damage or vandalise more than forty mosques, shrines of Shi'i holy men and graveyards. The argument was that these structures had not received proper building permits.[48] It represented, however, another demonstration of the successful campaign applied by Bahrain's more powerful neighbour, Saudi Arabia, against 'improper' religious sites, even though on this occasion it was not as much inspired by theological concepts as by a political strategy aimed at weakening the Shi'i opposition by targeting its symbols and venues. The attacks were not confined to the post-demonstration period in 2011, but continued to take place over the ensuing years. A regular target of the assaults has been, for instance, the shrine of Shaykh Maytham al-Bahrani (d. *c.* 1280), a leading thirteenth-century Twelver Shi'a Islamic theologian, which was vandalised in 2013.

However, there are still places in the Arabian Peninsula where one can encounter domed shrines, especially in Hadramawt, with sites such as Qabr Hud in Yemen,[49] and in Dhofar, where several dozen shrines with distinctive features still exist, some of them originating from as early as the twelfth century and historically attracting pilgrims from South Asia.[50]

North Africa

Wahhabi–Salafi-inspired organisations have mushroomed in recent decades in many parts of Africa. Saudi Arabia has been a very generous supporter of Islamic centres and mosques, which quite often operate outside the purview of the state. And, as elsewhere, Sufi Islam or various forms of folk rituals in Africa are one of the prime targets of the new-found religious zeal. Also here, many of the destructive acts occurred during the chaotic times connected with the wave of popular uprisings against long-established regimes.

Although North Africa has a history of Islamist activity, the presence of radical, iconoclastic, Wahhabi–Salafi ideas is a rather recent phenomenon, hindered by the existence of various well-established Sufi orders. All the countries of the region, that is, Algeria, Egypt, Libya, Mauritania, Morocco and Tunisia, have experienced significant political turmoil during the past few decades. This has been accompanied by social and political unrest and challenges against the state, resulting from the actions of Islamist movements and their philosophy.[51] In most cases, it is the state that has claimed hegemonic power in both the political and religious fields. The harsh response of the state to the ascent of political Islam has had the unintended consequence of creating a power vacuum, which has been filled by an alternative radical culture. Simultaneously, the excessive secularism in the past has led to a significant impoverishment in the religious field. Eventually, the politics of North African regimes brought about the rise of opposition movements based on a variety of discourses, including one derived from Salafi jihadism. In spite of many differences, the region shares one common thread: the influence of Saudi religious discourse and the ability of some Saudi clerics to persuade at least some in the region of the lack of local ulama, thus being able to enforce their religious interpretation over local traditions, with religious texts playing the dominant role. Salafism is thus increasing its presence and popularity, being able to change the local vocabulary, as well as the rites, norms and codes (including, among other things, the dress code). In parallel with this process, we can observe the rise of religiously motivated violence. We can also argue that this is mostly an urban phenomenon, associated with young males.[52]

The coincidence of regime collapse and an increase in destructive activities has clearly been present in Egypt. Visiting shrines, even though frowned upon by some local orthodoxy, has always been an important part of Egyptian Islam.[53] The tombs of holy men are usually located in a side room of a mosque. The *baraka* imbued in these places is also inherent in objects purchased at the shrine. The rituals involve praying, circumambulating the tomb, touching its grillwork and making requests (mostly seeking revenge, redressing grievances or requesting cures from diseases or sterility), often accompanied by leaving letters and money at the shrine. As for shrines near the cemeteries on the periphery of municipal areas, these are usually the object of a full day's outing, connected with get-togethers for families and friends. During the

Arab uprisings, the devastation of Sufi shrines occurred in Alexandria (which is also an important Salafi hotbed in Egypt) and other places. In the period 2011–13, all the shrines associated with Shaykh Zuwayd and Sidi ʿAbd al-Rahman in Qalyoub and Shaykh Hamid Abu Jarir in central Sinai, as well as many others, were destroyed. In many of these cases, the motivation driving the perpetrators of such acts might also be seen as part of an attempt to construct their identity and define their position in a society engulfed by a volatile political environment. On occasions, the Salafi groupings met large-scale resistance from the local population, who gathered to protect the shrines. In doing so, they were supported by the Mufti of Egypt, ʿAli Jumʿa, who after being asked about his opinion on the prohibition on praying in mosques containing shrines, answered: 'Praying in mosques containing shrines of the friends of Allah is not only valid and permissible, but reaches the status of recommendation as confirmed by primary evidence from the Qurʾan and Sunna.'[54]

Following the uprisings of 2011, the destruction of graves, as a new phenomenon, was also witnessed in Libya. Given the general unpopularity of Salafism in Libya, the high public profile activities of the armed Salafi groups might be viewed, as in the Egyptian case, as an attempt to raise awareness about their ideology. Dozens of mosques and shrines were bulldozed or vandalised all around the country, especially in Tripoli, Benghazi, Misurata, Derna and Zlitan. One of the first events occurred in October 2011, when a mosque in the town of Sidi Masri was vandalised. In addition, the remains of two local Muslim scholars were removed. The Salafi zeal was also aimed at cemeteries – such as the Sidi ʿUbayd graveyard in Benghazi, which was wrecked and where tens of corpses were stolen in January 2012. Armed groups also removed the body of Sidi Muhammad al-Mahdi al-Sanusi, a supreme religious leader (1859–1902) of the Sanusiyya Sufi order, from his mausoleum in El Tag, close to the Kufra oasis. Similar events then peaked in August 2012, when, among other activities, in the middle of the night armed groups removed the remains of Ahmad Zarruq (1442–93), a famous Sufi scholar, from his tomb in Misurata and bulldozed the mosque. The perpetrators of these acts were mostly associated with the Libyan Salafi group Ansar al-sharia, which sometimes even hired contractors to undertake such tasks.[55] The speaker of the group, Muhammad ʿAli al-Zahawi, admitted in the first ever interview with the international media that they had indeed carried out the destruction as 'it is a religious duty to remove these shrines because people worship the deceased and this is prohibited. It is not me who says so but rather our religion.'[56]

The Libyan Salafis claimed to be following the guidance of Shaykh Muhammad al-Luhaydan, a prominent Saudi cleric, a member of the Board of Senior Ulama and a former President of the Supreme Judicial Council with the rank of minister. Their acts were opposed by a large section of the Libyan population. Although the Grand Mufti, Sadiq al-Gharyani, initially issued a *fatwā* favouring the destruction of Sufi graves,[57] eventually he delivered sermons legitimising the presence of tombs in mosques as well. Another leading Libyan cleric and member of the League of the Libyan Ulama, 'Umar Mawlud 'Abd al-Hamid, delivered a more scathing degree of criticism, calling the perpetrators 'renegades' and adding that 'assaulting a tomb and exhuming its inhabitant is a grave sin in Islam'. He concluded his statement by calling on the state 'to pressure the government of Saudi Arabia to restrain its clerics who meddle in our affairs . . . [by] promoting millions of free books and tapes in Libya which attack our moderate religious traditions'.[58] What is also telling is that the government's security forces have largely failed to prevent these attacks and – allegedly with the endorsement of the Ministry of the Interior – have sometimes even stood by without intervening while the attackers have destroyed the sites with explosives, bulldozers and heavy drills. Another symptomatic feature of these events lies in the fact that the destruction has not been carried out by local residents but by outsiders.[59]

Another telling example of the influence of Saudi institutions can be found in Tunisia, where dozens of shrines have been destroyed in the recent past, including the shrines of Sidi Bou Sa'id and Sidi Baghdadi in Monastir and Sidi 'Abd al-Jabbar in Jammal. Some members of Tunisian organisations, such as Ansar al-shari'a, who publish their CVs online, claim, for instance, that they 'studied under Ibn Baz'. In their writings, they also use the formalised *khuṭba* or quote from Muhammad ibn 'Abd al-Wahhab's *Kitab al-tawhid*. An example of this can be found in Shaykh al-Khatib al-Idrisi, one of the most respected Salafi religious scholars not only in Tunisia, but across North Africa.[60]

Despite occasional criticism levelled at those who would exaggerate in venerating sacred objects and charlatans posing as saints, Morocco's ulama generally considered the veneration ritual to be an integral part of Islam, often visiting tombs themselves in order to seek and obtain *baraka*. Munson points out that anthropologists usually neglect Moroccan historiography and thus impose their reading of the twentieth-century dynamic within Islam upon the whole of Moroccan history. However, the relationship between popular and orthodox Islam is more complex. By reference to the example of Abu 'Ali al-Hasan al-Yusi (1631–91), one of the greatest Moroccan scholars and Sufis of the seventeenth century, Munson shows how an *'ālim* could condemn the veneration of ostensibly sacred objects, while at the same time continuing to personally visit the tombs of saints regularly during his lifetime. The major distinction lies in the fact that for al-Yusi, seeking to obtain *baraka* from a saint's tomb was in full accordance with religious teaching, as long as one understood its correct role within Islam.[61]

The forerunner of later reformism, Sultan Sidi Muhammad bin 'Abdullah (reigned 1757–90) and his son Mulay Sulayman (1792–1822), banned Sufi festivals in honour of saints because of the involvement of dancing and the mixing of the sexes. On the other hand, Mulay Sulayman insisted that visiting the shrines of saints and seeking *baraka* was recommended by Islamic law under the condition that people clearly understood that it was not the saints themselves who were capable of fulfilling their requests – they could merely ask God to do so. This, in his eyes, was the logic behind the Wahhabi demand to restrict access to the tombs of saints as ordinary Muslims were poorly educated and unable to distinguish between the saint and the one who granted their request. Needless to say, both Mulay Sulayman and his father belonged to the Sufi order of Nasiriyya. In addition, another famous Moroccan scholar and theologian, Sidi Muhammad bin Ja'far al-Kattani (1858–1927) gave his support to traditional acts and events. In his book *Salwat al-anfas wa muhadathat al-akyas bi-man uqbira min al-'ulama' wa-l-sulaha' bi-Fas* (*The Solace of the Souls and Discourses of the Fine Ulama and Saints Buried in Fez*), published in 1898, al-Kattani, when speaking of the saints, declares: 'Without them, the sky would not give forth rain, the earth would not produce plants, and misfortune would pour down upon the people of the world.'[62]

The outright condemnation of *ziyāra* was extremely rare in Morocco until the 1920s. After that, voices calling for the strict application of Shariʿah and the elimination of heretical innovations, influenced by the puritanical revivalism of the Wahhabis, started to appear. One of the most prominent Salafi reformists was Taqi al-Din al-Hilali (1894–1987), himself a former Sufi of the Tijaniyya order. In 1927, al-Hilali published a series of articles denouncing Shiʿi Islam. The articles were produced in response to the claim that it was lawful to visit shrines, particularly those of the Shiʿi imams, as long as such buildings did not become the object of cultic worship. Al-Hilali rejected this line of argument and stressed that the Sunni prohibition against raising structures over graves did not allow for any loose interpretation. Al-Hilali later collated these articles, re-producing them in the form of an anti-Shiʿi pamphlet, thus gaining himself the appreciation of the Saudi king, ʿAbd al-ʿAziz, who ordered his chief *qāḍī* to have the text printed in a thousand copies and then distributed.[63] Yet, until the 1960s, Salafism had only a marginal presence in Morocco. Geertz, in his book *Islam Observed*, speaks of Salafi reformism as an ideologised form of Islam aiming at 'the transformation of religious symbols from imagistic revelations of the divine, evidences of God, to ideological assertions of the divine's importance'.[64] He also notes the role of European colonialism in bringing about this development: 'In a curiously ironical way, intense involvement with the West moved religious faith closer to the center of our peoples' self-definition than it had been before. Before, men had been Muslims as a matter of circumstance; now they were, increasingly, Muslims as a matter of policy. They were *oppositional* Muslims.'[65]

Salafism, and especially Wahhabism, was officially supported by the Moroccan king, Hasan II, partly as a counterweight to both the leftist movements and revolutionary Nasirism, which Arab monarchies perceived as a threat, partly as a counterweight to the Islamic revolution in Iran. Being an ally of the Saudi kings, and depending on Saudi financial support, Hasan II approved the arrival of Saudi preachers in northern Morocco. Salafis were viewed as a conservative power, one that respected established political structures and was apolitical, influenced by Shaykh al-Albani.[66] In 1964, a religious institution, Dar al-hadith al-hasaniyya, was established to support hadith studies, and this can be interpreted as a trend that was congruent with Salafi hadith studies in the 1960s. Moroccans were also influenced by

Salafi thoughts while abroad. They became acquainted with al-Albani's teachings when they were given the chance to study at the Islamic University of Medina, along with many other nationalities. However, this apolitical aspect changed during the Gulf War, when criticism of the apolitical *manhaj* arose with the advance of Salafi jihadism. This switch was also reflected in respect of the Moroccan Salafis. After the 2003 Casablanca bombings, ascribed to Salafi jihadis, the policy against Salafis was radically changed by the current king, Muhammad VI, who began to support traditional Moroccan forms of Islam in order to fight religious extremism, and also revived traditional Sufi orders.[67]

West and East Africa

Attacks against shrines were not limited to North Africa. After the coup in Mali in March 2012, Islamists from the Ansar Dine (Ansar al-din, Supporters of the Religion), a Tuareg rebel organisation, destroyed several Sufi tombs that had been listed since 1988 as UNESCO World Heritage sites, such as Sidi Mahmoud Ben Amar, Cheikh Sidi El Mokhtar Ben Sidi Mohammed and Alfa Moya Lamtouni. The attackers were said to have torn down windows and wooden gates at the grave site and burnt them.[68] The Ansar Dine organisation, led by Iyad Ag Ghaly (aka Abu al-Fadl), is an armed group allegedly linked to al-Qaeda in the Islamic Maghrib (AQIM), which is headed by Iyad's cousin, Hamada Ag Hama. Between late 2007 and early 2010, Iyad Ag Ghaly served as a Malian diplomat in Saudi Arabia, where he was introduced to the Salafi interpretation of Islam. He is said to have been forced out of Saudi Arabia as a persona non grata because of his links with terrorist organisations such as al-Qaeda.[69] The Ansar Dine organisation, at times controlling much of Azawad, a territory in northern Mali, is known for its emphasis on strict Shariʿah rules, including the stoning of adulterers, the veiling of women and the banning of smoking and music. Another official of Ansar Dine, Abou Dardar, has clearly stated the goals of the organisation, including: 'Not a single mausoleum will remain in Timbuktu, Allah doesn't like it. We are in the process of smashing all the hidden mausoleums in the area.'[70] The religious positions of the organisation have further been made clear by its spokesperson, Sheykh Sanda Ould Bouamama. According to him, the organisation 'aspires to reform society' in all aspects of life, including 'belief, worship and morality'. It aims to do so in accordance with the 'methodology of the pious *salaf*' and 'based on *tawḥīd*', as understood from a specific reading of the revelations of texts, as well as by adhering to the Prophetic traditions. This includes the prohibition of the '*kufr* of *ṭāghūt*' in all its forms and hostility towards the 'supporters of *shirk*'. Besides applying the Shariʻah rules in areas under its control, the organisation has also 'preserved *tawḥīd* by the demolition of mausoleums and tombs that go beyond the limits of Shariʻah'.[71] However, the fact that local traditions are not that easy to eradicate has become increasingly apparent. The reconstruction of the shrines, which began in March 2014, was completed in mid-2015.

As seen in the case of Mali, strong opposition towards locally rooted versions of Islam, including Sufi orders, has also emerged in recent decades in many non-Arab parts of Africa. In the case of West Africa, Wahhabism–Salafism spread there only gradually and although its influence was already present during the colonial period, its real impact started following the Second World War.[72] It was mostly due to the increase in numbers of worshippers returning from the pilgrimage to Mecca, which the French colonial administration started to view more favourably after 1935. Thus, ʻAbdullahi Ag Mahmud, for instance, began preaching Salafism in the Niger bend region in the late 1930s, after he had returned from his sojourn in the Middle East. A large number of the West African Salafis were recruited from among the merchant class. In addition to the direct links with Arabia through the mediation of pilgrims, Salafi ideas were also instigated by returning graduates of al-Azhar University in Cairo, bringing with them their reformist ambitions, mostly anti-colonial and anti-traditionalist. Their main objective was to purify Islam, as well as to use it as the basis of an anti-colonial discourse. Besides the merchants, the movement has also been able to recruit members from the large number of underprivileged urban youth.[73]

In his study, O. Kobo demonstrates that one of the key factors enabling the growth of Wahhabism–Salafism in West Africa has been the alliance between secularly educated Muslim elites and Islamic scholars, which has promoted a self-consciously modern religiosity modelled on the example provided by the Prophet Muhammad. Colonial education nurtured new elites, who learned to share the colonial officers' negative attitudes towards African traditions and localised Islamic practices and began to believe that Islam was not a reactionary system. Consequently, it was partly – and unwittingly – colonial education that prepared the minds of some Muslims so that they were more receptive to the radical Salafi message. Furthermore, the Salafi movement would not have been able to flourish if it had not received the support of those public functionaries who saw Salafi ideas as a modern version of Islam.[74]

The direct influence of Saudi Arabia helped to further accelerate the process. Since the 1960s, Africa has witnessed an increase in the number of Saudi-backed institutions and a rise in their influence over the local religious landscape. Among other activities, the Saudis have financed the construction of mosques and Islamic centres. Such activities initially met with strong opposition from local religious leaders. The confrontation between Saudi-financed or -inspired movements and other Muslims in the region stemmed both from their growing influence, hence, their more aggressive stance, and doctrinal disputes. The clashes were particularly palpable in terms of anti-Sufi criticism. However, while the 1960s saw the rise of Salafism as a local phenomenon, the dramatic events of the 1970s transformed the local Salafi movements into part of a global network of Islamic revival and reform groupings.[75] One of the typical priorities for West African Salafi organisations was the purification of Islam by getting rid of all corrupt practices and influences, particularly Sufism and its cult of saints.

In Burkina Faso, two scholars returning from Mecca in the early 1960s were particularly responsible for the spread of Salafi ideas, namely, Muhammad Malick Sana and Sayouba Ouédraogo. These scholars and their movement (originally named Mouvement Sunnite de Haute Volta, but renamed the Mouvement Sunnite du Burkina Faso in 1984) challenged local Tijaniyya practices, including the observance of funeral ceremonies. Wahhabi ideas also experienced rapid success in Ghana. This was largely due to Hajj ʿUmar Ibrahim (b. 1932), the first Ghanaian student to graduate from the Islamic University of Medina. During his studies, he was instructed by leading Saudi clerics, such as Ibn Baz and Nasir al-Din al-Albani. Hajj ʿUmar also became the first Saudi-trained scholar to preach Wahhabi–Salafi ideas in Ghana.[76]

In Nigeria, it was largely the Yan Izala movement (*Jamāʿat izālat al-bidʿa wa iqāmat al-sunna*), established in 1978 by Abubakar Gumi, that stressed the rejection of all innovations and the purification of Nigerian Islam from

Sufi practices, which were viewed as un-Islamic. Among such practices, the visiting of the dead and their role in intercession, as well as pilgrimages to the saints' tombs, were particularly frowned upon. The connection with Saudi Wahhabism was made even clearer by the fact that the Yan Izala received financial support from both the Saudi organisation Muslim World League, as well as Saudi nationals.[77] A similarly harsh stance towards Sufism and other forms of local Islam was replicated later by the insurgent Islamist movement Boko Haram, which was founded in the late 1990s and early 2000s. This movement even opened the Ibn Taymiyya Mosque in Maiduguri, from where it began to expand into the states of Bauchi, Yobe and Niger. It is specifically around Ibn Taymiyya's teachings that the founder and former leader of Boko Haram, Mohamed Yusuf (1970–2009), modelled his doctrine and preaching.[78] The Nigerian religio-political landscape has thus seen, especially in the post-colonial period, the repeated emergence of extreme religiously motivated movements with which the government has been unable to deal. Neither has the government been able to respond effectively to the grievances that have inspired such developments.

It can also be argued that the collusion between the ideas of Islamic reformists and local officials occurred in eastern Africa. In Ethiopia, veneration of saints has long been established and forms a central element in both religious and communal life. Traditionally, pilgrimage plays an important role in almost every community in Ethiopia, with many pilgrimage sites scattered across the country and commanding a high degree of spiritual magnetism. The contemporary discourse regarding the legitimacy of these practices is directly connected to the politics of identity in the region.[79] The fact that the post-1991 era has seen an increasing level of reformist opposition to the practice of veneration of saints is connected to liberalisation within the Ethiopian religious sphere, which in turn has led to the insertion of Ethiopian Islam into global Islam.[80]

In Somalia, al-Shabab fighters were among those who sought to stop 'grave-worshipping' and engaged in the destruction of the tombs of prominent clerics or Sufis, such as those in Kismayo, Somalia's third largest city, as well as in the other parts of southern Somalia which were to fall under al-Shabab control in mid-2008.[81] Similar incidents also occurred in the capital, Mogadishu, where al-Shabab destroyed the shrine of Shaykh Mohammed

Bimalo, the leader of the Qadiriyya order at the beginning of the twentieth century, as well as the shrine of Shaykh Hassan Muʿalim Moʾmin, the founder of the Idrisiyya order in Somalia.

Central, South and Southeast Asia

In recent times, the destruction in March 2001 of the Bamiyan Buddhas, probably at least 1,500 years old, in Afghanistan became one of the most notorious iconoclastic events.[82] Furthermore, the situation has been impacted by the rise of ISIS. Its 'Khorasan' branch, which emerged in Afghanistan in mid-2014, mostly in northern Afghanistan, challenged the Taliban and started conducting attacks.[83] Besides executing the local elders, its tactics also involved the destruction of shrines.

Sacred places (in this region referred to by several terms: *mazār*, *ziyāratgāh*, *maqbara*, among others) have traditionally played an important role in the religious landscapes of Central Asia. There might be as many as 10,000 sacred places in Central Asia. Practically every settlement has traditionally contained such a pilgrimage site. The cult of the dead was part of previous religious traditions and was incorporated into the Islamic framework.[84] Due to extreme remoteness, many regions in Central Asia and eastern Turkestan have developed a tradition of places they refer to as 'second Meccas', or 'second Kaʿbas', which have been viewed as being equivalent in status and function to the sanctuaries of the two holy cities in Arabia.[85]

Many sacred sites were destroyed during the anti-religious campaigns of the 1920s and 1930s, when Soviet propaganda described shrine worship as a form of superstition.[86] Along with many other sites, this was the fate of the *mazārs* dedicated to ʿAli, the son-in-law of the Prophet Muhammad (although ʿAli had, of course, never visited Central Asia). The communists also criticised these practices because they allowed people to gather and perform non-communist rites, and the regime attempted to replace the holy sites with 'red teahouses' and clubs. By the 1930s, most of the *mazārs* (or mosques in general) had been handed over to kolkhoz administrations, which turned some of them into storage buildings or used their bricks for construction projects. In addition, party organisations were ordered to launch fierce propaganda campaigns against various religious traditions, including the visits to saints. The press was required to satirise those who still performed such pilgrimages.[87] The intent was to show the nature of superstitious 'paganistic' rituals and the components that had been incorporated into Islam, as well as the ignorance of religious scholars who were not able to detect these deviations. As a consequence, the changes that took place in the pattern of grave visiting and the worship of saints in Central Asia during Soviet rule were significant.

Officially established clerics, co-opted by the Soviet regime, denounced the veneration of holy sites in their *fatāwā*. Thus, for example, Haji Kurbanov, mufti of the North Caucasus and Daghestan, issued the following *fatwā* in the 1960s:

Question: Does Sharia law permit meeting at a *mazār* to pray?
Answer: No, it does not. Our Prophet said that those people are sinners. He also said that during the pre-Islamic era of ignorance, when a man died, great honours were bestowed on him, a temple was built and people would pray at his image. This is paganism and those who practice it will have to answer on the Day of Judgment. The Prophet also said: 'When I die, do not meet at my grave.'[88]

In particular, two official governing bodies established by the Soviets were charged with administering and controlling Islamic religious activities: the Council for the Affairs of Religious Cults (*Sovet po delam religioznykh kultov*), established in 1944, and the Spiritual Administration of the Muslims of Central Asia (*Sredneaziatskoye dukhovnoye upravleniye musulman*, abbreviated as SADUM), established in 1943. Several SADUM *fatāwā*, deriving their authority from Ibn Taymiyya, also condemned the visiting of shrines and seeking the intercession of the dead as un-Islamic practices.[89] However, the regime's bodies charged with the supervision of religious activities were quite ambiguous in carrying out tasks and their behaviour changed according to the circumstances and local dynamics.[90] They did, however, contain ulama with links to Saudi Arabia's Wahhabism. The normative views on Islam were spread later, particularly by the Mujaddidiyya (those who call for the renewal),[91] a group of Islamic scholars who, together with *mulla-bachas* (young *mullahs*), claimed that praying at graves was a form of polytheism.[92] Another movement, very conservative in its outlook and uncompromisingly basing its pronouncements on hadith as the foundation for regulating all aspects of religious life, was the *Ahl al-hadith* movement, which, in the 1920s, started to be active in Tashkent.[93] That the Soviet assault on traditional society was not without its repercussions can be demonstrated by the following incident. An old Jadid, a wholehearted supporter of the cultural revolution, Hamza Hakimzoda Niyoziy, together with a number of activists, decided to close a shrine attributed to ʿAli, located in Shohi Mardon near Kokand, and turn it into a museum. He and several others were beaten to death by an angry mob.[94]

Overall, of course, the consequences of the attack on Islam, especially the dispersal of Islamic education networks and the almost complete destruction of the status and prestige of the ulama as a social class, was devastating. The measures taken by the Soviet regime, however, did not eliminate the practice of *ziyāra* altogether. Instead, it led to the creation of new local dynamics and patterns in relation to the veneration of saints, which continued during the Soviet era, especially in the countryside. Even during this era, the shrines drew hundreds of thousands of pilgrims during some of the major festivals.[95] In addition, not all religious leaders listened to the state's official policy and many of them continued to support the underground popularisation of holy sites, inviting believers to visit shrines. This was certainly the case in both Central Asia and the Caucasus. Furthermore, although some pilgrimage sites were eradicated, new ones, originating in the Soviet period, were to emerge. In practice, every cemetery contained a holy place that local believers visited.

Islam was, in many senses, reborn after the demise of the Soviet Union. The same goes for a variety of other popular religious practices. New tombs of the Naqshbandi and Qadiri members killed in the anti-Russian or the later anti-Soviet guerrilla fighting were to emerge. Following Gorbachev's Perestroika initiative, many shrines were reopened and rebuilt and their veneration increased, probably most notably in the hectic changes that took place in Tajikistan.[96] Elsewhere, Muslims had managed to retain the unique local Islamic traditions that predated the Soviet period and its anti-religious campaigns.[97] Such traditional forms of Islam, practiced, for example, in the Caucasus, have recently become the propaganda target of Russian-speaking members of ISIS. In addition to the political system, they are keen to criticise the pro-regime Sufi scholars, whom they refer to as 'grave-worshippers' (*mogilopoklonniki*).⁹⁸ In addition, various manuals disseminated by the Islamists describe how to be a proper Muslim. According to this type of literature, Muslims, for example, should not worship graves. Such pamphlets state in very simple terms that building tombs and visiting them are *shirk* and *bid'a*. These sentiments are sometimes expressed in the form of poetry:

> Here's the miserable people damned by Allah,
> awash with blind ignorance,
> here they worship the dead,
> striving for the earthly affluence.
> You, who care about religion,
> who have the power of the righteous,
> Destroy all the idols of mausoleums
> and level all the idols of graves!⁹⁹

A similar tendency of Wahhabism–Salafism of supporting the growth of strong anti-Sufi traditions took place in South Asia. A strong trend aimed at the renewal and reform of popular religious practices, including the condemnation of the cult of saints, has been present there for a long time and continues to the present day. Many of these ideas are often ascribed to Shah Waliullah (1703–62), a contemporary of Ibn 'Abd al-Wahhab, who was perhaps the most influential thinker from early generations of Indian Muslim reformers. Shah Waliullah strove for a return to the assumed original purity of Islam, with a strong emphasis being placed on addressing social problems. In his early works, Shah Waliullah raised no objections to the well-established practice of visiting the shrines of saints. Gradually, however, he came to realise the potential abuses connected with the veneration of saints. This became apparent after his lengthy stays in the holy cities of Arabia in 1731–2. He also became acquainted with the writings of Ibn Taymiyya, whom he regarded as being among 'the most faithful servants of God'.¹⁰⁰ His position towards these issues culminated in the criticism of those who visited the shrine of a saint in order to have an urgent desire granted. According to Shah Waliullah, someone who acts in this way 'commits a sin graver than murder or adultery', and he also stated that 'what people have devised in the matter of shrines . . . belongs to the worst heresies'.¹⁰¹

Nevertheless, Shah Waliullah's position was relatively moderate and more radical ideas were to arrive in South Asia via other channels. A radical pamphlet attacking the cult of saints and visits to their tombs, titled *al-Balagh al-mubin* (*The Clear Communication*), was also ascribed to him. However, the text adopts quite a radical stance, unknown in India before 1818. It condemns the worship of tombs (*gōr-parastī*) and 'saint worshippers' (*pīr-parast*) and denounces all forms of the cult of the dead. It is mostly a fragmentary patchwork of supporting items, be they from the Qur'an, quotations from hadith or borrowings from Ibn Taymiyya and Ibn Qayyim al-Jawziyya, whose writings had probably reached India in the first decades of the nineteenth century as a result of pilgrims returning from the *ḥajj*. The text was most likely written by someone from the Barelvi's reform movement (*Tariqa-i muhammadiyya*) in the mid-nineteenth century. This movement was established by Syed Ahmad Barelvi (1786–1831), who made a career as both a soldier and mystic. Barelvi left behind two books in Persian, *Sirat al-mustaqim* (adopting the same title as Ibn Taymiyya's book was no coincidence) and *Radd al-ishrak*. Both books violently attack all forms of saint worship. Barelvi and his followers also urged people in the countryside to reform their religious practices and destroy shrines. Barelvi undertook a pilgrimage to Mecca in 1822–3, where he also met al-Shawkani, who inspired him in relation to the development of his ideology. It was probably some of his followers who actually produced the text of the *al-Balagh al-mubin*, which was later edited and more widely circulated by members of the Ahl-i hadith movement of Siddiq Hasan Khan, who were keen to add the label 'Salafi' to their names.[102]

In the South Asia region, the term *qabr* (Ar. grave) is rarely used to refer to saintly tombs, and the more honorific terms *dārgāh*, *mazār* or *rawḍa* (Ar. 'saintly grave, shrine') for buildings erected on and around saints' tombs are preferred. A saintly grave differs from the usual Islamic graves by typically being elevated about a metre above the ground. The terms *mazār* and *rawḍa* refer to both the grave itself and the surrounding building. The deceased saint is believed to be present in the tomb in a very real sense and the dead must be revered adequately and greeted as if they are still alive. It is often justified on Qur'anic terms (2:154: 'And do not say about those who are killed in the way of Allah, "They are dead." Rather, they are alive, but you perceive it not.'). This is perhaps why the famous French orientalist, Garcin de Tassy

(1794–1878), noted in 1831: 'What strikes me most about the religious ceremonies of Indian Muslims is the innovations which make them appear as local phenomena . . . Muslims make pilgrimages to the tombs of saints, some of whom are actually non-Muslim, and perform there semi-pagan rites.'[103]

In India, the destruction of Sufi *dargāh*s, shrines marking the burial sites of revered religious figures, has been a repeated occurrence in the Kashmir valley and northern areas. In Pakistan, the shrine of Bari Imam in Islamabad was consecrated in the name of a seventeenth-century miracle-worker, Syed 'Abdul Latif Shah. In May 2005, a suicide bomber detonated himself inside the shrine, killing nineteen and wounding almost seventy. A similar attack took place at the Sufi shrine of Hazrat Data Ganj Baksh 'Ali Hujweri in Lahore in July 2010. The two explosions killed at least forty-two people and injured close to 200.[104] The attackers have often been connected with a network of hard-line Pakistani madrasas.

As for Bangladesh, shrine and *pīr* veneration forms an important aspect of local Islamic traditions. At the same time, it has been one of the targets of various reformist trends that have classed these practices as clearly derived from Hindu influences. The local landscape is dotted with hundreds of shrines devoted to *pīr*s. Every year, on the anniversary of their death, a festival (*urus*) is held, which involves singing well into the night, drumming and ecstatic dancing. The *pīr* cult in Bangladesh also undergoes constant, sometimes radical, changes. Internally, the rituals connected with shrines are being reinvented in line with new notions of popular religiosity. The Faraizi reformists held that *pīrism* was un-Islamic. They were headed by their founder, Haji Shariatullah (1781–1840), who happens to have made a pilgrimage to Mecca at the time when the Wahhabi movement was building its momentum. He resided in Arabia for almost twenty years while studying with the ulama of the Najdi call (under the guidance of a Wahhabi scholar, Shaykh Tahir al-Sumbal al-Makki). In a similar vein, Munshi Samiruddin, another Bengali reformer, wrote: 'There is none other to ask help from but God. Those who put explicit trust in *pīr*s instead of God not only waste their own means, but turn infidels.'[105] Elsewhere he stated: 'Do not worship any false grave, ye Muslims. He who will so do, will die the death of a *Shaitan*. Do not worship [any such shrine] even if it is a genuine one. Worshipping of shrines is idolatrous.'[106] As elsewhere in the Islamic world, the veneration practices, together with *pīr*s and their *dārgāh*s, proved to be hard to eradicate, and even several of the formal reformists later adopted these beliefs. Such was the fate of Haji Shariatullah's son, Dudu Miyan (1819–62), who allowed himself to be referred to as *pīr*.

In contemporary times, reformist ideas have usually been imported into Bangladesh by migrant labourers. Migration to Europe and the Gulf states has generated notions that Katy Gardner refers to as 'global Islam', that is, a scripture-based religious practice, which accepts only Mecca and a few other places as holy sites to the detriment of local shrines. The families of those migrants constitute the dominant classes and thus 'have the power of putting their notion of proper Islam in practice. In consequence, local *pīr*s and *mazār*s lose vital parts of their traditional constituencies; they are being relegated to the lower classes of society and seem to be gradually perishing.' Another consequence of this process has been that the 'shrine cult is integrated into the globalised orthodox notions of this class'.[107] The status of those who spend time in gaining Islamic knowledge, learning a few words of Arabic, acquiring Arabic manners and, most importantly, performing the *ḥajj* in Saudi Arabia are treated with extreme deference. Their claimed knowledge of the religious truth is unchallengeable. It is also these same returned migrants who are most likely to assert traditionalism, often clad in rigid religious doctrinal positions. Gardner also describes the increasing influence of *bidesh* (foreign countries) on the local spiritual centres. Purists, coming either from the West or from Saudi Arabia, condemn the *pīr* cult as being a sign of the ignorance on the part of women, poor men and those influenced by Hinduism. Instead, they attempt to spread the 'correct' form of Islam to rural areas. In so doing, Islamic purism is inherently modernising, without being Westernising, as it promotes the notion of progression towards the ideal of Islamic social order.[108] Reformism in this process has the capacity to redefine some of the popular practices and to reduce levels of shrine and *pīr* veneration.[109]

In southeast Asia, Indonesia has had a long history of clashes between Sufis and various anti-Sufi movements. The debates became radicalised particularly in the 1920s, following the successful campaigns of Al Saʿud in Arabia. Since then, it has also become common for anti-modernist voices to brand the modernists as puritanical or fanatical Wahhabis. The year 1926 witnessed the establishment of the Nahdlatul Ulama, the most influential movement in defending traditionalist Islam in Indonesia, emphasising the importance of visiting holy graves, along with the validity of Sufi ritual. One appropriately titled journal, *Salafy* (1995–2000), recently became a particularly important platform for denouncing various Sufi practices, with its subtitle claiming that its aim was 'to emulate the steps of the generation of the Pious Forebears (*upaya miniti jejak generasi salafus shalih*)'. The journal was published by an institution called Ihya'us Sunna (The Revival of Sunna), led by Ja'far Umar Thalib (b. 1961). Thalib was a former student of the Yemeni scholar Muqbil ibn Hadi al-Wadi'i. Thalib and his cohort gained national prominence following their involvement in the fratricide in the Moluccas in 2000–2. Much of the content of the journal, and its ideas, were taken directly from the teachings of Saudi ulama. For example, issue No. 12 (1996), extensively citing al-Albani, was devoted to condemning the common Sufi practice of building structures over tombs and making a journey with the aim of visiting a grave.[110]

The destruction of shrines has also occurred in the Muslim Malay world, where *keramat* shrines (in the form of graves, trees, anthills and waterfalls) have been venerated for centuries. Malaysia recently started to socially marginalise and penalise, in the name of ideological engineering and faith control (*kawalan akidah*), the worship of any person, place or object. Those violating this prohibition face the possibility of imprisonment and being forced to undergo religious 'counselling'. In parts of Malaysia, religious authorities, particularly Majlis Agama Islam Melaka (MAIM), have even demolished a number of shrines. In Brunei, one can still find some remaining shrines; however, visiting them is illegal (due to the provision of 'better Islamic education since the 1990s').[111]

* * *

If we look back at the history of the twentieth and early twenty-first centuries, it was usually the state that was seen to function as the major actor in the promulgation of anti-Sufi or anti-popular Islam attitudes. Naturally, one should not forget that the iconoclastic incidents that have taken place in various parts of the Islamic world in recent years and decades occurred under very different social and political circumstances.

In the colonial and post-colonial history of Africa, for example, many movements inspired by charismatic leaders set out – in the name of monotheism and religious puritanism – to destroy objects attached to 'polytheistic' practices. They did so because these iconic objects materialised invisible forces that upheld strong levels of popularity and prevented social control. In particular, many of the Muslim movements from these times were iconoclastic towards non-Muslim shrines and objects. Quite often, however, religious iconoclasm only paved the way for its political equivalent, which became crucial in the making of the modern state. While state support for iconoclastic movements was also a feature in other countries, such as Sierra Leone and Liberia, it was the president of the independent Republic of Guinea, Sekou Touré, who, after 1958, supported the campaign for the destruction of 'cultic objects' as a means of eliminating obscurantism. By the end of French rule, a charismatic iconoclastic jihadist figure, witch-finder and fetish destroyer, Asekou Sayon, had already brought a destructive element to the Baga communities in Guinea, and was to use his religious and political ambitions as a vehicle for completely transforming the religious and social landscape. Many members of these communities, particularly the youth, welcomed him and assisted him in his efforts. This was partly due to their anger at the corruption of the contemporaneous chiefs and elders, as despotic chieftaincy was clearly identified with animist practices. That his teaching was not fully in line with Salafism can be deduced from his appearance when he arrived in Bukor in September 1956, where he was required to clear the sacred bush and destroy whatever iconic objects were present. His body was then adorned with medicines and amulets.[112]

What is also telling, and has parallels with current ISIS practice, is that some of the destruction associated with cultic objects was probably staged, with items being sold on at a later stage by Sayon to Western art collectors.[113] Another similarity is in the circulation of stories that many of those who helped Sayon in his campaign to destroy sacred objects were later to die in mysterious circumstances. This case is also instructive in providing us with information about all those who had previously suffered massive levels of intrusion into their ritual traditions. Today, the Baga live in a 'ruptured landscape', and many of their previous traditions appear to have been eradicated.

However, the local population still remembers that a mosque used to be a place where masquerades took place and that many post-1957 mosques were built on the sites associated with pre-iconoclastic religious cultures. In addition, other Guinean communities, such as the Loma, did not permanently abandon their rituals and took them up again once Guinea had opened itself to the concept of religious pluralism, especially in the 1990s, thus proving the point that cultural destruction does not always have an irreversible impact.[114]

Finally, it is an ironic part of the whole story that in an effort to eradicate some forms of folk Islam, its opponents themselves do not hesitate to resort to the realms of the supernatural. Thus, we encounter a frequently recurring legend that, soon after completion, those buildings erected over graves are liable to suffer destruction at the hands of the buried saint. A similar legendary destruction was supposedly the fate, for example, of the mausoleum of Ahmad ibn Hanbal in Baghdad and the dome of the Algerian saint Ahmad al-Kabir, which became a ruin overnight.[115] It is noteworthy that those who support the other side in the debate, that is, the followers of the saints, are not usually completely helpless, as they seek to prove that their traditions are at least as equally deeply rooted as the counterarguments and cannot be ignored. For instance, after the destructive events in Yemen in 1994, as described above, the followers of the saint whose sanctuary had been destroyed claimed that although the attackers had tried to use explosives to destroy the shrine, the explosives had mysteriously failed to detonate. Other popular stories include claims that those who participated in the exhumation of bodies were to die in a subsequent gunfight with government troops, and that the mother of one of the vandals, who was injured and paralysed, personally visited the saint, seeking intercession on behalf of her son.[116]

Notes

1. For more details, see at: http://www.dailymail.co.uk/news/article-3023944/I-taste-Truth-fists-slit-throats-Revealed-blood-thirsty-poem-written-wannabe-bad-b-NYC-terrorist-published-al-Qaeda-magazine-knew-editor.html#ixzz4H7iQTY3S, last accessed 4 September 2016.
2. Tapper, '*Ziyaret*: Gender, Movements, and Exchange in a Turkish Community', p. 237. Cf. also Tapper and Tapper, '"Thank God We're Secular!"', pp. 51–78.

3. For more about Ma Wanfu, see Stewart, *Chinese Muslims and the Global Ummah*, esp. ch. 2. Cf. Also Gladney, *Muslim Chinese*, pp. 55–6.
4. Available at: http://www.abc.net.au/4corners/atta/resources/documents/will1.htm, last accessed 20 August 2016. One cannot but think of the last will and testament ascribed to 'Amr ibn al-'As (c. 585–664), the famous military commander of the early Islamic conquest and a Companion of the Prophet Muhammad: 'When I die, do not weep for me and let no panegyrist (*mādiḥ*) or wailer (*nāʾiḥ*) follow my bier; only put dust on my grave, since my right side deserves the dust no more than my left. Put neither wooden nor stone sign upon my grave. When you have buried me, sit on the grave for the time that the slaughter of a camel and distribution of its meat would take, so that I may enjoy your company for that time.' Quoted from Goldziher, 'On the Veneration of the Dead in Paganism and Islam', p. 232.
5. Cf. Lia, 'Understanding Jihadi Proto-States', p. 35.
6. Quoted from Bunzel, 'From Paper State to Caliphate', p. 7.
7. For the best attempts, see Bunzel, 'The Kingdom and the Caliphate'. Cf. also Al-Rasheed, 'The Shared History of Saudi Arabia and ISIS'; Kirkpatrick, 'ISIS' Harsh Brand of Islam is Rooted in Austere Saudi Creed'; Crooke, 'You Can't Understand ISIS if You Don't Know the History of Wahhabism in Saudi Arabia'; or Daoud, 'Saudi Arabia, an ISIS That Has Made It'.
8. See, for example, Atkinson and Donaghy, 'Crime and Punishment'.
9. See at: http://www.lettertobaghdadi.com.
10. 'Royal Order: Participants in Hostilities Outside the Kingdom Receive 3–20 Years in Prison', 4 February 2014, available at: http://www.alriyadh.com/en/article/907177/royal-order-participants-in-hostilities-outside-the-kingdom-receive-3-20-years-in-prison, last accessed 1 September, 2016.
11. Quoted from Obaid and al-Sarhan, 'A Saudi View on the Islamic State', pp. 82–3.
12. *Dabiq*, No. 5 (October/November 2014), p. 3.
13. *Dabiq*, No. 9 (May/June 2015), p. 18 and elsewhere.
14. 'Akhriju al-rafida al-mushrikin min jazirat Muhammad', 29 May 2015, available at: http://justpaste.it/bttar-tf-rafdh, last accessed 5 September 2016.
15. Cf. *Dabiq*, No. 5 (October/November 2014), p. 27 and elsewhere; *Dabiq*, No. 6 (January 2015), p. 40. 'Salul' is a reference to a figure from early Islamic history,

'Abdullah ibn Ubay ibn Salul, who, because of his behaviour, is described in Islamic tradition as the leader of the hypocrites (*munāfiq*).

16. *Dabiq*, No. 5 (October/November 2014), p. 27. Perhaps the most comprehensive criticism of Saudi Arabia and its religious establishment can be found in *Dabiq*, No. 13 (January/February 2016), pp. 7–8.
17. Cf. the audio-recording of his speech 'Kalima sawtiyya li-mawlana amir al-mu'minin Abi Bakr al-Baghdadi bi-'unwan "Wa law kariha al-kafirun"', 13 November 2014, available at: https://soundcloud.com/ahmed-mahmoud-336/qkqugjmohbnu, last accessed 1 September 2016.
18. In addition to Humud al-'Uqla' al-Shu'aybi, a former professor at universities in Riyadh and al-Qasim, it was mostly Nasir al-Fahd, professor of Islamic theology at the Islamic University of Imam Muhammad ibn Sa'ud in Riyadh, and 'Ali al-Khudayr, who used to teach Islamic theology and law at al-Qasim University. In 2003, these scholars, together with several others, were arrested by Saudi security services and indicted for supporting al-Qaeda in the Arabian Peninsula. Many of these scholars also continued to support ISIS from prison and some – including Nasir al-Fahd – also pledged loyalty to its leader, Abu Bakr al-Baghdadi. See Bunzel, 'The Kingdom and the Caliphate', pp. 15–16. Some of them were executed on 2 January 2016, together with those blamed for terrorism.
19. Cf., for example, Speckhard and Yayla, 'Eyewitness Accounts from Recent Defectors from Islamic State', p. 108. Furthermore, there are suggestions that ISIS has been using – so far probably because of the lack of its own resources – Saudi textbooks when instructing children in the territories it governs. Cf., at: https://mobile.twitter.com/GulfInstitute/status/387596457596837890, last accessed 3 September 2016.
20. For more details, see, for instance, Fishman, 'The First Defector'. Cf. also McCants, *The ISIS Apocalypse*, pp. 39–42.
21. Bunzel, 'From Paper State to Caliphate', p. 11. For more details about Bin'ali, see, for instance, his biography, Abu Usama al-Gharib, 'Minnat al-'Ali bi-thabat shaykhina Turki al-Bin'ali', 2013, available at: https://archive.org/download/minato.alali001/minato.alali001.pdf, last accessed 3 September 2016.
22. Bunzel, 'The Kingdom and the Caliphate', p. 8.
23. For the text in its English translation, see at: www.aymennjawad.org/17633/islamic-state-training-camp-textbook-course-in, last accessed 5 September 2016.

24. Much of the information in the following section comes from the research project 'Monuments of Mosul in Danger' conducted by the Oriental Institute of the Czech Academy of Sciences. The project aims to document and research Mosul monuments that have been destroyed by ISIS since June 2014, based on the analysis of all available reports and satellite imagery. See 'Monuments of Mosul in Danger', at: http://monumentsofmosul.com, last accessed 25 September 2016. We would like to thank our colleagues, Miroslav Melčák, Karel Nováček and Lenka Starková, for allowing us to use the findings of the research team. Some of the following data has also been published in Melčák and Beránek, 'ISIS's Destruction of Mosul's Historical Monuments'.

25. Cf. at: http://www.asor-syrianheritage.org/wp-content/uploads/2015/03/ASOR_CHI_Weekly_Report_01r.pdf, last accessed 5 September 2016. For more about ISIS's destruction of various sites in Syria, see, among other sources, the weekly reports of the Syrian Heritage Initiative at: www.asor-syrianheritage.org/summaries, last accessed 3 September 2016. Cf. also J. Croitoru, 'ISIS' Cultural Vandalism: A Trail of Destruction', 10 July 2014, available at: en.qantara.de.

26. 'The War against Idolatry: Extremists in Mosul Force Their Prisoners to Vandalise Graves', 17 December 2015, available at: http://www.niqash.org/en/articles/security/5180/Extremists-in-Mosul-Force-Their-Prisoners-To-Vandalise-Graves.htm, last accessed 14 September 2016.

27. Of these, the researchers of the 'Monuments of Mosul in Danger' project have been able to identify thirty-four monuments. The identity of the seven other monuments remains unknown. Of the seven unidentified monuments, two are, with a high degree of probability, the Mosque of al-Ridwani and the Mosque of al-Abariqi. The complete list of destroyed monuments in Mosul, created on the basis of the analysis of satellite imagery, is available on the website 'Monuments of Mosul in Danger', at: http://monumentsofmosul.com, last accessed 14 October 2016. The website contains an interactive map and shows images of the monuments before and after their destruction.

28. Harmanşah, 'ISIS, Heritage, and the Spectacles of Destruction in the Global Media', pp. 173, 174–6. For another critical take on ISIS's iconoclasm, see Colla, 'On the Iconoclasm of ISIS', available at: http://www.elliottcolla.com/blog/2015/3/5/on-the-iconoclasm-of-isis, last accessed 15 September 2016; and Colla, 'Preservation and Destruction', available at: http://www.elliottcolla.com/blog/2015/3/27/pm0t4j35d00plvir68mkffl6fyquh0, last accessed 15 September

2016; or Hardy, 'Pornographic Iconoclasm in Terrorist Propaganda'. For a plastic overview of the issue, see also Flood, 'Idol-Breaking as Image-Making in the "Islamic State"', pp. 116–38.

29. Abu 'Umar al-Baghdadi, 'Qul inni 'ala bayyina min rabbi', in *Majmu' tafrighat kalimat al-qadat bi-Dawlat al-'Iraq al-islamiyya'*.

30. 'Wathiqat al-madina', available at: https://azelin.files.wordpress.com/2014/06/islamic-state-of-iraq-and-al-shc481m-charter-of-the-city.pdf, last accessed 5 September 2016. In the updated version of the document, from early 2016, the article, now referenced under number 10, says the same, see at: https://azelin.files.wordpress.com/2016/01/the-islamic-state-22charter-of-the-city-second-edition22.pdf, last accessed 5 September 2016.

31. For more about the apocalyptic dimension of ISIS, see esp. McCants, *The ISIS Apocalypse*.

32. Islamic State of Iraq and al-Sham, 'Clanging of the Swords, Part 4', available at: https://videopress.com/v/ix3vGg7v, last accessed 31 March 2015.

33. While in the case of ISIS, the destruction was sometimes accompanied by looting (as was, for instance, seen in a video available at: https://www.youtube.com/watch?v=9H3ezvFlSQw&feature=youtu.be, last accessed 27 February 2016 – the video has been deleted in the meantime), this does not seem to have been the main objective.

34. 'Namudhaj min al-matwiyat al-da'wiyya allati wuzzi'at fi wilayat Naynawa qubayla wa athna'a hadm al-adriha – Sharh al-sudur bi-tahrim al-bina' 'ala al-qubur', available at: http://justpaste.it/sh_sodor, last accessed 9 August 2014.

35. 'Al-Qawl al-fasil fi mashru'iyat hadm al-qubur al-maz'uma li-anbiya' Allah', Maktabat al-himma, al-Dawla al-islamiyya, 2013, available at: https://azelin.files.wordpress.com/2015/07/the-islamic-state-22the-final-say-on-the-legality-of-the-demolition-of-gravestombs22.pdf, last accessed 9 August 2016.

36. 'Mufti Da'ish al-shar'i: Hadamna maraqid al-Mawsil istinadan li-hadith nabawi', *al-Ghad*, 17 November 2014, available at: http//:www.alghad.com/articles/836900, last accessed 13 May 2016.

37. Selected cases of the destruction also appeared in ISIS's English language journal, *Dabiq*. Cf. issue No. 2, 'On the Destruction of Shirk in Wilayat Ninawa', pp. 14–17; No. 3, 'Da'wah and Hisbah in the Islamic State', pp. 16–17 (which positions the destruction of shrines into their broader proselytisation efforts).

In No. 13, p. 36, *Dabiq* mentions as one of the reasons for pronouncing *takfir* against the Sh'ia that 'they are the sect most famous for grave-worship amongst all deviant sects. Much of the grave-worship that entered into the practice of "Ahlus-Sunnah" [the Sunnis] originated from Rafd and the Rafidah [the Shi'is].' For issues of *Dabiq*, see at: www.clarionproject.org/news/islamic-state-isis-isil-propaganda-magazine-dabiq.

38. 'Taqrir 'an hadm al-adriha wa al-awthan fi wilayat Naynawa', available at: http://justpaste.it/atrah, last accessed 9 August 2016; 'Mulhaq taqrir hadm al-adriha fi madinat al-Mawsil', available at: http://justpaste.it/Adrah, last accessed 9 August 2016.

39. See ISIS' propaganda video (published in rabi' al-thani 1436/January–February 2015) on the legal validity of the destruction of tombs, titled 'Izalat mazahir al-shirk – hadm al-adriha al-shirkiyya', available at: https://www.youtube.com/watch?v=EEhWzVBqX-c, last accessed 8 April 2016.

40. Conversely, there have been false media reports regarding the destruction of monuments, with satellite imagery confirming that they are still standing.

41. 'al-Khawarij al-dawa'ish wa masajid al-muslimin wa quburuhum', available at: https://azelin.files.wordpress.com/2014/07/shaykh-abc5ab-basc4abr-al-e1b9adare1b9adc5absc4ab-22the-khawc481rij-al-dawc481ish-and-the-mosques-of-the-muslims-and-their-graves22.pdf, last accessed 9 September 2016.

42. See at: http://www.lettertobaghdadi.com, last accessed 9 September 2016.

43. See, for example, an article by one of the most vocal opponents of the destruction of historical sites, al-Alawi, 'The Destruction of Holy Sites in Mecca and Medina'.

44. For a description of some of the latest development projects and the related destruction of cultural heritage, see, for example, at: http://www.adhrb.org/wp-content/uploads/2015/10/2015.09.30_MSS-Ch.-7_Dest.-of-Rel.-Sites.pdf, last accessed 9 September 2016. The authors of the report argue that the destruction of historical and spiritual heritage sites serves the combined interests of the Saudi financial and religious elites.

45. For more details about the destruction, see Ho, *The Graves of Tarim*, pp. 5–7.

46. Ibid., p. 12.

47. 'al-Qaʿida yudammir qubaban athariyan fi al-Shihr bi-Hadramawt', 14 February 2016, available at: http://www.khabaragency.net/news51541.html, last accessed 9 August 2016.

48. For more details, see, for example, Michael Sells, 'Shrine Destruction in Bahrain', 9 June 2011, available at: http://divinity.uchicago.edu/sightings/shrine-destruction-bahrain-michael-sells, last accessed 9 August 2016. A report about the destruction, accompanied by photo-documentation, was issued by the Centre for Academic Shiʿa Studies, see Payam Tamiz, 'The Destruction of Places of Worship in Bahrain', September 2014, available at: http://bahrainrights.org/sites/default/files/The%20Destruction%20of%20Places%20of%20Worship%20in%20Bahrain_2.pdf, last accessed 9 August 2016. For a broader socio-political context, see Louër, 'The State and Sectarian Identities in the Persian Gulf Monarchies', pp. 117–42.

49. For a study of Qabr Hud, see Hundhammer, *Prophetenverehrung im Hadramaut*. Cf. also Ho, *The Graves of Tarim*.

50. Cf. Newton, 'Shrines in Dhofar', pp. 329–40.

51. For a good introduction to the topic, see Joffé, *Islamist Radicalisation in North Africa*; Shahin, *Political Ascent*; or Burgat, *L'islamisme au Maghreb*.

52. Cf. Mabrouk, 'The Radicalisation of Religious Policy', pp. 48–70.

53. See, among many others, Gillsenan, *Saint and Sufi in Modern Egypt*; De Jong, 'Cairene Ziyāra-Days'; or a description in Early, *Baladi Women of Cairo*, esp. pp. 122–30.

54. See at: https://islamictext.wordpress.com/building-domes-and-shrines-over-the-deceased-fata-by-the-mufti-of-egypt-ali-jumua, last accessed 9 September 2016.

55. Safia Aoude, 'The Destruction of Mosques and Holy Shrines by Salafi Extremists in Libya', available at: http://aoude.dk/destructionofmosques.pdf. Cf. also Sharron Ward, 'The Battle of the Shrines', *Foreign Policy*, 12 September 2012, available at: http://brown-moses.blogspot.cz/2012/08/images-of-shrines-and-mosques-destroyed.html.

56. Ahmed Maher, 'Meeting Mohammed Ali al-Zahawi of Libyan Ansar al-Sharia', *BBC*, 18 September 2012, available at: http://www.bbc.com/news/world-africa-19638582, last accessed 9 September 2016.

57. His religious ideas, at times, seem very much in line with those of the Salafis, and in his religious edicts, al-Gharyani often bases his opinions on Ibn Taymiyya.

Cf. 'Fatwa al-Shaykh Sadiq al-Gharyani bi-hadm al-adriha fi Libya', available at: https://www.youtube.com/watch?v=-8OzvlDvCkI, last accessed 9 September 2016, or his *fatāwā* at: http://www.tanasuh.com, last accessed 9 September 2016. Another criticism of the Salafi destruction of shrines in Libya was offered by an American mufti, Shaykh Musa Furber, 'Libyan Grave', 29 August 2012, available at: http://seekershub.org/blog/2012/08/libyan-graves-shaykh-musa-furber, last accessed 27 February 2016. Musa Furber supports his criticism by an obvious and straightforward argument: 'If these buildings pose such a risk to the masses, why did the previous generations of Muslims allow these shrines to remain in Libya and elsewhere?'

58. See at: http://shanfaraa.com/2012/08/statement-from-libyan-ulama-on-the-salafi-destruction-of-mosques-and-tombs, last accessed 9 September 2016.
59. The external origins of the perpetrators, as well as their need to rent bulldozers and buy explosives, neither of them particularly cheap, begs the question as to the source of funding and their local networks of support.
60. According to his own credentials, al-Idrisi had studied in Saudi Arabia under Ibn Baz. See his Arabic biography, 'Tarjamat al-shaykh Abi Usama al-Khatib al-Idrisi', available at: www.ahlalhdeeth.com, last accessed 9 September 2016. Cf. also A. Y. Zelin, 'Meeting Tunisia's Ansar al-Sharia', *Foreign Policy*, 8 March 2013, available at: http://mideastafrica.foreignpolicy.com/posts/2013/03/08/meeting_tunisias_ansar_al_sharia, last accessed 9 September 2016.
61. Munson, *Religion and Power in Morocco*, p. 83.
62. Quoted from ibid., p. 87.
63. Lauzière, *The Making of Salafism*, pp. 85–6.
64. Geertz, *Islam Observed*, pp. 61–2.
65. Ibid., p. 65.
66. Belhaj, *La dimension islamique dans la politique étrangère du Maroc*, p. 217.
67. For further reading, see Idrissi, 'The Political Participation of Sufi and Salafi Movements in Modern Morocco ', pp. 91–104.
68. 'Rebels Burn Timbuktu Tomb Listed as U.N. World Heritage Site', *CNN*, 7 May 2012, available at: http://edition.cnn.com/2012/05/05/world/africa/mali-heritage-sites, last accessed 9 September 2016.
69. Steve Metcalf, 'Iyad Ag Ghaly – Mali's Islamist Leader', *BBC Monitoring*, 17 July 2012, available at: www.bbc.com/news/world-africa-18814291, last accessed 9 September 2016.

70. Quoted from https://storify.com/scherzler/not-a-single-mausoleum-will-remain-in-timbuktu-th, last accessed 9 September 2016.
71. See 'Interview exclusive avec le porte-parole de la Jamaat Ansar al-Din, Sheikh Sanda Ould Bouamama', available at: https://archive.org/stream/SheikhSandaOuldBouamama/ansarfr_djvu.txt, last accessed 9 September 2016.
72. For more about the spread of Wahhabi–Salafi Islam to Africa, see, esp. Kobo, 'Wahhabi Reforms in Ghana and Burkina Faso, 1960–1990'; Hunwick, 'Sub-Saharan Africa and the Wider World of Islam'; Kaba, *The Wahhabiyya: Islamic Reform and Politics in French West Africa*; Loimeier, 'Islamic Reform and Political Change'; Amsell, 'A Case of Fundamentalism in West Africa'; Niezen, 'The "Community of Helpers of the Sunna"'; Kane, *Muslim Modernity in Postcolonial Nigeria*.
73. See Amsell, 'Le Wahabisme à Bamako (1945–1985)', pp. 345–57. For the significance of Ibn Taymiyya's legacy, see Hamès, 'Deux aspects du fondamentalisme islamique', pp. 177–90.
74. Kobo, *Unveiling Modernity in Twentieth-Century West African Islamic Reforms*, pp. 14, 19.
75. Ibid., p. 209. Kobo focuses on the growth of Wahhabi–Salafi-oriented movements in two case studies, Ghana and Burkina Faso.
76. For more details about Hajj 'Umar and his influence, see ibid., pp. 211–35. Cf. also Dumbe, 'The Salafi Praxis of Constructing Religious Identity in Africa', pp. 101–4.
77. Cf. Loimeier, 'Islamic Reform and Political Change', p. 292; Commins, *The Wahhabi Mission*, p. 153.
78. Comolli, *Boko Haram*, pp. 45–8; Higazi, 'Mobilisation Into and Against Boko Haram in North-East Nigeria', pp. 305–58. See also the recent study by Thurston, *Salafism in Nigeria*.
79. As argued by Woldeselassie, '*Wali* Venerating Practices', pp. 139–61.
80. For more, see Abbink, 'Religion in Public Spaces: Emerging Muslim–Christian Polemics in Ethiopia', pp. 253–74.
81. 'Somali Fighters Destroying Shrines', *Al-Jazeera*, 20 December 2008, available at: http://www.aljazeera.com/news/africa/2008/12/2008122055527212230.html, last accessed 9 August 2016.
82. For a discussion of this event, see Flood, 'Between Cult and Culture', pp. 641–59; Elias, '(Un)Making Idolatry', pp. 12–29.

83. Johnson, Karokhail and Amiri, 'The Islamic State in Afghanistan'.
84. For a general overview, see, esp., Shinmen, Minoru and Waite, *Muslim Saints and Mausoleums in Central Asia and Xinjiang*. For various aspects of shrine visiting in Central Asia, see Jun and Dawut, *Mazar: Studies on Islamic Sacred Sites in Central Eurasia*.
85. See Zarcone, 'Pilgrimage to the "Second Meccas" and "Ka'bas" of Central Asia', pp. 251–77.
86. For Islamic religious practices under the Soviet Union, see Subtelny, 'The Cult of Holy Places', pp. 593–604.
87. Exnerová, 'The Veneration and Visitation of the Graves of Saints in Soviet Central Asia', pp. 508–14.
88. Quoted from Sirriyeh, *Sufis and Anti-Sufis*, p. 155.
89. Khalid, *Islam after Communism*, p. 111. For more about these *fatāwā*, see Babadzhanov, 'O fetvakh SADUM protiv "neislamskikh obychaev"', pp. 170–84. Cf. also Boboxonov, *Shayx Ziyovuddinxon ibn Eshon Boboxon*.
90. Exnerová, 'The Veneration and Visitation of the Graves of Saints in Soviet Central Asia', pp. 517–18.
91. The Mujaddidiyya scholars specifically sought to 're-Islamise' Muslim society in Central Asia and establish an Islamic state there. For more, see Frank and Mamatov, *Uzbek Islamic Debates*, pp. xi–xii.
92. Exnerová, 'The Veneration and Visitation of the Graves of Saints in Soviet Central Asia', pp. 521–2. See also Dudoignon, *Allah's Kolkhozes*. That the claims of links to Wahhabism were substantiated may be demonstrated by reference to Ziyauddin Babakhan (1908–82) – the son of Eshon Babakhan, the first mufti of SADUM – who studied in Saudi Arabia in the late 1940s and, thereafter, began to rely on the Salafi interpretation of Islam and criticise Sufism. His stance towards pilgrimage and Sufism was much stricter than his father's, and many Hanafi scholars in Uzbekistan today consider him the first official Wahhabi. See Frank and Mamatov, *Uzbek Islamic Debates*, pp. viii–ix. Cf. also Olcott, 'Roots of Radical Islam in Central Asia', p. 11.
93. Cf. Muminov, 'Fundamentalist Challenges to Local Islamic Traditions in Soviet and Post-Soviet Central Asia', pp. 255–8.
94. Khalid, *Islam after Communism*, p. 80.
95. The dynamism of the practice is described in Ro'i, *Islam in the Soviet Union*, esp. pp. 94–7, 370–84.

96. Khalid, *Islam after Communism*, p. 120.
97. In Central Asian countries, among the Kazakhs, Kyrgyz, Turkmen and Uzbeks, a specific form of dedicatory offering consists, for example, of the tying of rags on sacred sites. Cf. Lymer, 'Rags and Rock Art', pp. 158–72.
98. See, for example, the propaganda video produced by the ISIS's media centre al-Hayat, available at Videopress: 'Kavkaz: Bolezn' i isceleniye', https://videopress.com/v/HogjzZlo, last accessed 5 October 2016.
99. Cf. Kavkazcenter, 'Svyato myesto pusto ne byvayet', available at: http://www.kavkazcenter.com/russ/content/2007/09/12/52923/svyato-mesto-pusto-ne-byvaet.shtml, last accessed 5 October 2016; or 'Ziyaraty', available at: http://www.kavkazcenter.com/russ/content/2012/03/23/89585/ziyaraty.shtml, last accessed 5 October 2016.
100. Baljon, 'Shah Waliullah and the Dargah', p. 196, fn. 32. Cf. also Sirriyeh, *Sufis and Anti-Sufis*, pp. 4–8.
101. Baljon, 'Shah Waliullah and the Dargah', pp. 193, 195.
102. See Gaborieau, 'A Nineteenth-Century Indian "Wahhabi" Tract', pp. 198–239. Gaborieau also adds that Syed Ahmad Barelvi's alleged tomb at Balakot has been venerated, similarly to Ibn Taymiyya's in Damascus, until the present day, ibid., p. 207.
103. De Tassy, *Muslim Festivals in India and Other Essays*, p. 32.
104. S. Sengupta and S. Masood, 'Blast Kills 19 at Pakistani Shrine During Muslim Festival', *The New York Times*, 28 May 2005; Declan Walsh, 'Suicide Bombers Kill Dozens at Pakistan Shrine', *The Guardian*, 2 July 2010.
105. Quoted from Ahmad, *The Bengali Muslims 1871–1906*, p. 60.
106. Ibid., p. 61.
107. Cited from Harder, *Sufism and Saint Veneration in Contemporary Bangladesh*, p. 319.
108. Gardner, *Global Migrants, Local Lives*, p. 235.
109. However, this is not universally valid, as there are areas where the contrary is true and new shrines are booming. Those advocating their veneration have managed to align themselves with modern reformist trends. Cf. the case of several areas in Bangladesh in Harder, *Sufism and Saint Veneration in Contemporary Bangladesh*.
110. Laffan, 'National Crisis and the Representation of Traditional Sufism in Indonesia', pp. 149–62.

111. Müller, 'Sharia Law and the Politics of "Faith Control" in Brunei Darussalam', pp. 313–45. For the destruction of shrines in Malaysia, see '"Makam keramat" Pulau Besar diruntuhkan', 14 May 2001, available at: http://www.malaysiakini.com/news/2971, last accessed 1 September 2016.
112. Cf. an anthropological study of an iconoclastic religious movement in West Africa and the relationship between iconoclasm and political transformation, Sarró, *The Politics of Religious Change on the Upper Guinea Coast*, pp. 2–6, 109.
113. Ibid., pp. 134–5.
114. Ibid., pp. 148–9.
115. Goldziher, 'On the Veneration of the Dead in Paganism and Islam', p. 233.
116. Ho, *The Graves of Tarim*, p. 11.

Conclusion

> Protect your Islam by removing yourself from any involvement in any Salafi group. The worst threat that the Muslim *umma* is faced with today is the Salafis . . . causing *fitna*, disunity, problems, conflicts in *masjids* [mosques].
>
> Shaykh Faisal Abdul Razak, President of the Islamic Forum of Canada[1]

Over the course of Islamic history, there have been many unsuccessful attempts by various religious authorities and scholars to eradicate all traces of a possible cult of the dead from Islamic rites. The main goal of these attempts to change funerary practices was to prevent the temptation presented by graves (*fitnat al-qubūr*), because it was seen as possibly leading to polytheism, as well as to clearly differentiate Islamic rituals from those of other religions, most notably Christianity and Judaism. It is important to note that such attempts – if we are to believe in the authenticity of the Sunni tradition – were already being made in the early days of Islam. Muhammad himself feared that Muslims might imitate Christians and Jews in venerating the dead. As a result of traditionalist opposition to any religious practices that were not distinctly established by Muhammad, a wide gap soon arose between the traditionalists' high ideals of 'pure' morality and faith unaffected by other religious traditions, on the one hand, and everyday popular practices, on the other.

The majority of ulama tried to adjust to the widespread popularity of grave visiting and condoned it, but a vocal minority of scholars has always claimed that such practices constitute an unlawful religious innovation (*bid'a*), contradicting the principles of Sunna, the true Muslim path one must follow. What is more, these practices could also constitute *shirk*, threatening the pivotal pillar of Islamic identity as the only true monotheistic religion. These ulama came to the conclusion that some behaviours related to funerals resembled non-Muslim practice far too closely, and that a distinct funerary style could help to distinguish the identity of their religious community, while deepening the existing (and, they believed, desirable) boundaries between men and women. Nevertheless, despite these efforts, to this day many Muslims still flock on a regular basis to saints' graves, asking for blessings or intercession and making vows and sacrifices. The cult of saints is a widespread phenomenon throughout the Islamic world, despite many regulations, and the practice of visiting graves has developed over time into a firmly established form of pilgrimage.

There is much historical evidence that in medieval times rulers had shrines constructed to commemorate venerated figures. For these rulers, building shrines and structures upon graves, including their own, provided an effective opportunity to establish their legacy and prestige in the eyes of the common people. This sort of funerary architecture became part of the Sunni identity and legitimacy at the time of the emergence of institutional Sunnism in the eleventh century.[2] Hadiths regulating *ziyāra* and funeral rites were part of that identity, and collections of the hadiths of al-Bukhari and Muslim were adopted by the Seljuqs. At the same time, they supported the Sunni schools of law against Shi'i influence. Since then, various dynasties have followed more or less the same path. The Seljuqs, Ayyubids, Mamluks and Ottomans competed to leave a greater imprint of their legitimacy and power in local funerary architecture. Hand in hand with this, of course, went acts of destruction, which occurred primarily at significant historical milestones, such as dynastic changes, especially when the ideologies were incongruent, such as between the Ottomans and Safavids. Old monuments and mausoleums were destroyed, and new ones were built to consecrate the new religious legitimacy. In the case of the Sunni dynasties, there was less destruction per se, and one can rather observe an ongoing process of monumental building and rebuilding at holy sites in order to seek political legitimacy and demonstrate the rulers' power.

For common people, the practice of visiting shrines traditionally served multiple purposes. For some, shrines provided a location where they could reach spiritual fulfilment, achieve a state of religious observance and participate in communal Islamic life, especially if they could not afford to go on the *hajj*. For others, visiting shrines was a way of socialising or engaging in commercial activities. The existence of shrines and the habit of visiting them was not at all a peripheral phenomenon. As Meri argues,[3] shrines were fully incorporated into daily life despite the absence of any clear religious hierarchy or centralised control.

Historically, the most critical voices opposing the construction of funerary architecture and unregulated practice of *ziyāra* came from traditionalists, who emphasised the importance of emulating the practices and beliefs of the early Muslim community (*salaf*), and re-evaluated the role of *taqlīd* and *ijtihād*. These critical voices were especially common among Hanbalis, who adhered the most to hadith, both in law and theology. The most influential critic of funerary architecture and necrolatry was Ibn Taymiyya, although he thought of himself as a rather moderate critic of these practices, because he did not forbid *ziyāra* as such. Ibn Taymiyya was mainly concerned by the possibility that the monotheistic religions might converge if such veneration of graves or visits to them too closely imitated the habits of the other religions.[4] However, Ibn Taymiyya lived at a time when the Mamluks ruled in Syria and Egypt and when Sunni Islam seemed to be fully institutionalised. The Mamluks established an equal system of four legal schools based on *taqlīd*, of which the Ash'ari theological school was the most prominent; they also supported Sufi religiosity and built domes and mausoleums. Ibn Taymiyya's opposition to funerary practices of the time must therefore be viewed in the context of his broader effort to undermine the established Sunni system and to return to hadith and the Qur'an as the basis for legal reasoning, orthodoxy and orthopraxy. Hence, it is understandable that he criticised *taqlīd* with its tolerance of funerary architecture and 'heretical' forms of *ziyāra*, and the *madhhab* system, and called for *ijtihād*. His *ijtihād*, applied to various legal issues, enabled him to criticise necrolatry. Besides, he fought against Ash'ari theology and 'heretical' forms of Sufism, which were also central to the *madhhab* system. Ibn Taymiyya did not refute the eponyms of the four legal schools, since they all belonged to the *salaf*, nor did he refute Sufism if it was in agreement with the Shari'ah, or indeed al-Ash'ari himself, whose theology was at certain period of his intellectual development in accordance with the theology of Ahmad ibn Hanbal and the *salaf*. Even so, Ibn Taymiyya's argumentation and activism, based on respected collections of hadith, including the *Sahih* of al-Bukhari and Muslim, resulted in confrontations with the establishment and its ulama. He was accused of and imprisoned for challenging the established *taqlīd* system and for dishonouring the Prophet with his criticism of 'heretical' practices connected with *ziyāra* at the Prophet's grave.

After Ibn Taymiyya's death, Sunni criticism of necrolatry and heretical *ziyāra* practices further evolved with Muslim reformers who tried to re-evaluate the *madhhab* system and the role of hadith and *ijtihād*, mainly following Ibn Taymiyya's example. Among the most influential of these scholars who shaped later Salafism was the Yemeni scholar Muhammad al-Shawkani. Ibn ʿAbd al-Wahhab also left a strong imprint in the shaping of later iconoclasm and anti-Shiʿi hatred. In his attack on *ziyāra* practices, Ibn ʿAbd al-Wahhab incorporated many of Ibn Taymiyya's characteristic ideas, and set an example for future Wahhabi grave destruction. The zeal with which his followers attacked *ziyāra* seems to have far exceeded Ibn Taymiyya's original criticism, and expressed a far more simplistic view of the issues involved.

Ibn ʿAbd al-Wahhab's followers in the three Saudi states monopolised the interpretation of history, suppressing any ideas or writings that deviated from their own views. On a more ambitious level, Wahhabi ulama, who perceived themselves as being part of the broader Salafi trend, strived to shape collective memory and construct an all-embracing and Islamised ideology. By destroying the graves of legendary ancestors and saints or monuments attesting to local religious, cultural and popular history in general, the Salafis attempted to establish their own authority through a monopolised network of new institutionalised mosques and Islamic institutes. Their doctrinal views, firmly rooted in the textual traditions of Prophetic Sunna and the way of the *salaf*, collided with the non-dogmatic rituals and beliefs of popular localised versions of Islam, including the veneration of ancestors. This tendency can also be observed in other parts of the Islamic world under the growing Salafi influence.

During the past century, the Saudi state has been engaged in an intense process of bureaucratising and institutionalising state control over the religious establishment. The Saudi state has usurped most, if not all, of the political influence of its religious scholars, particularly since 1969 when Muhammad ibn Ibrahim Al al-Shaykh, the last quasi-independent mufti of the country, died. As Wagemakers rightly notes, 'this left the *ulama* with little else than issues of personal piety to rule upon', and 'this is probably why they place such extreme emphasis on the pious conduct of individuals since this is the only area the state allows them to have any real influence'.[5] Most studies of the ulama in contemporary Saudi Arabia have pointed out their subservient position vis-à-vis the government, especially since the beginning of the third Saudi state. On the other hand, the ulama's role as the main upholders of religious principles, overseers of public morality, administrators of justice, educators and leaders of various religious organisations with global outreach is still paramount. Even without independent political power, the ulama have remained resilient in the face of the government's ambitions to control religion. The Saudi state has, moreover, depended heavily on the legitimation it derives from the leading ulama. Yet this way of legitimising its rule also continually exposes it to calls for the greater implementation of the Shari'ah and, in what constitutes the other side of the same coin, to allegations that it has fallen short in its professed religious aspirations. The state's response to such attacks has been to reaffirm and extend its dependence on the ulama, while also striving to curb more radical dissidents.[6] Consequently, the ulama share the state's goal of maintaining the status quo.

The Saudi state's claim to rule does not rest on a genealogy going back to the Prophet Muhammad, as is the case of the Hashimis, neither it is based on traditional tribal genealogy, as was the case of the Rashidis. Instead, the Saudi state supports Wahhabi teachings, even though these might seem to clash with the country's material development and modernisation over the last eight decades. The Saudi state and the Salafi ideology it helped to create both put an emphasis on proper doctrine, both as regards a proper understanding of God's attributes and names and in terms of iconoclastic fervour. Contemporary Salafi clerics have particularly emphasised the doctrinal aspect of visiting and constructing graves, on the basis of their exclusionary teaching of *shirk*. Furthermore, they have attempted to create a system that would make them indispensable to the society as religious experts. The outlawing of *ziyāra* and associated customs relating to graves probably represents the most central and unchanging doctrinal opinion of the official Saudi ulama. While the ulama have modified many of their traditional views – regarding education, contact with foreigners, women and other issues – iconoclasm seems to be one of the last strongholds of the Wahhabi–Salafi movement, which continues to place strong emphasis on a literal understanding of hadith and the Qur'an. Perhaps it is worth pointing out that recent years have seen an excessive production of hadith collections, the majority of which have been published in Saudi Arabia, precisely because many of the Salafis' doctrinal teachings are based on the Prophetic tradition rather than on the text of the Qur'an. The influx of oil revenues, in combination with regional ideological conflicts in the second half of the twentieth century, have led to Saudi efforts to spread its pan-Islamist vision. Their financial and ideological support have created a melting pot in which various movements and groups, however different their political agenda might be, have joined in sharing the same view on Islamic purity and on their duty to fight the cult of the dead.

It would, of course, be misguided to jump to simplistic conclusions and attribute the violent destruction of graves across the Islamic world to direct Saudi support. The Wahhabi ulama have traditionally been very careful not to call directly for violence. The problem has arisen, rather, from the often uncontrolled dissemination of their opinions. Many people have studied in Saudi Arabia and, after returning to their homelands, have attempted to destroy local traditions and supersede them with the Wahhabi worldview. This process sometimes backfires and these attempts at Wahhabi–Salafi religious indoctrination help to build criticism of the Saudi state and its religious views (al-Maqdisi, Juhayman al-'Utaybi, ISIS). The critics, however, are usually semi-clerics or even laymen who have not studied at the proper religious institutions in Saudi Arabia. They might have attended some scholarly lectures, but they lack a formal religious education. Based on official religious texts published by Saudi Arabia and their own literal understanding, these groups often arrive at quite radical conclusions – the latest example of this can be found in the form of ISIS and their publications.

Migration (be it for educational, religious or work-related purposes) also has a significant impact on the interpretation of Islam, its belief systems and practices. It has been suggested that migrants from the Islamic world have moved from an Islam based around highly localised cults and a specific religious environment to foreign countries where Muslim newcomers of various nationalities and backgrounds have formed an international version of

Islam. In this version of their faith the holy texts take the most central role, and their literal meaning or very selective reading is sometimes prevalent. Similarly, this international Islam sees Mecca as the only universally accepted place of pilgrimage, and the spiritual core of the Islamic world. Travel and moving into a foreign culture may also result in a heightened sense of 'being a Muslim'.[7] This does not affect all migrants, but can prompt many of them to create a universalist Islam, and to define their new-found piety not so much by what it stands for, but more by what it denounces. This is one of the reasons why opposition towards popular practices is a common feature of Islamic revivalism.

Meanwhile, one of the main reasons behind the harsh approach towards cultural heritage we have observed in the recent past is the fact that it has proved to be a very powerful instrument in the fight against Sufis, Shiʿis and various forms of popular Islam (which is why sometimes even the 'Salafi' graves, the graves of the $ṣaḥāba$, the Companions of Muhammad, are destroyed). Destructive violence has also served as a way of controlling local Muslim communities all around the world, since it removes the communities' previous cultural identity and memory. Naturally, such destructive behaviour can also have very practical goals: to cause sectarian strife, terrorise the local population, allure sympathisers and patrons, humiliate local communities while annihilating their sense of heritage and offend the humanitarian West.[8] As Colla puts it quite simply, 'destroying the arts of the defeated is what triumphalists have always done'.[9] We would therefore argue that the strategic objective of iconoclastic acts, perceived as a religious duty, is to destroy the culture, background and pride of local people and their intellectual bedrock (power centres, shrines, cemeteries, among others) and then build new ones (mosques and institutes) in the 'Salafi' style. We are nowadays witnessing a process of the monopolisation of Islam through Salafi scripturalism, which as we have seen in this book, undermines the basis of a centuries-old cult of the saints and replaces beliefs and practices associated with mysticism with formalised purism, while at the same time colourful reinventions of these practices are taking place. It is important to remember through all this that the interpretation of faith provided by Wahhabism–Salafism, however widely it is reported in the media, does not represent the overall Sunni tradition.

Notes

1. Available at: https://www.youtube.com/watch?v=b_MWVwDfmUc, last accessed 5 September 2016.
2. See Brown, *The Canonization of Bukhari and Muslim*, pp. 372–4.
3. Meri, *The Cult of Saints*, p. 256.
4. It is important to note that this fear was not unknown in the other monotheistic religions. Traditional Judaism, for example, did not encourage the excessive visiting of graves either. The rabbis were well aware of the possibility that frequent visits to cemeteries could easily become a way of life rather than fostering closure, and that graves might be transformed to a sort of idol at which the visitor would pray to the dead rather than to God. And this would violate one of the cardinal principles of Judaism: that God is One, and that there are no intermediaries between a believer and his God. Lamm, *The Jewish Way in Death and Mourning*, p. 193.
5. Wagemakers, 'Framing the "Threat to Islam"', p. 5. Cf. also al-Rasheed, who notes that it was only under the latest generation of official Saudi religious establishment that 'Wahhabiyya ceased to be a religious revivalist Salafi movement and became an apologetic institutionalised religious discourse intimately tied to political authority,' al-Rasheed, *Contesting the Saudi State*, p. 32.
6. Zaman, *The Ulama in Contemporary Islam*, p. 154.
7. Gardner, *Global Migrants*, pp. 242–3. Cf. Eickelman and Piscatori, *Muslim Travellers*, p. 16.
8. Harmanşah, 'ISIS, Heritage, and the Spectacles of Destruction in the Global Media', p. 175.
9. Colla, 'Preservation and Destruction'.

Bibliography

Primary Sources

Abu Shama, Shihab al-din 'Abd al-Rahman Isma'il ibn Ibrahim al-Maqdisi, *al-Ba'ith 'ala inkar al-bida' wa al-hawadith* (Cairo: Maktabat majd al-islam, 2007).

al-'Ajami, Muhammad ibn Nasir (ed.), *al-Rasa'il al-mutabadala bayna Jamal al-Din al-Qasimi wa Mahmud Shukri al-Alusi* (Beirut: Dar al-basha'ir al-islamiyya, 2001).

Al Mu'ammar, Muhammad ibn Nasir ibn 'Uthman, *al-Tuhfa al-madaniyya fi al-'aqida al-salafiyya*, ed. 'Abd al-Salam ibn Burjas ibn Nasir Al 'Abd al-Karim (Riyadh: Dar al-'asima, 1992/3).

Al al-Shaykh, 'Abd al-Latif ibn 'Abd al-Rahman ibn Hasan, *Misbah al-zulam fi al-radd 'ala man kadhaba 'ala al-shaykh al-imam*, ed. Isma'il ibn Sa'd al-'Atiq (Riyadh: Dar al-hidaya, n.d.).

Al al-Shaykh, 'Abd al-Rahman ibn Hasan, *Fath al-Majid sharh kitab al-tawhid* (Cairo: Dar Misr li-l-tiba'a, n.d.).

al-Albani, Muhammad Nasir al-Din, *Tahdhir al-sajid min ittikhadh al-qubur masajid* (Beirut: al-Maktab al-islami, 1983).

al-Albani, Muhammad Nasir al-Din, *Fitnat al-takfir* (Riyadh: Dar Ibn Khuzayma, 1997).

al-Albani, Muhammad Nasir al-Din, *Ahkam al-jana'iz wa bida'uha* (Riyadh: Maktabat al-ma'arif, 2009/10).

al-Albani, Muhammad Nasir al-Din, *Tamam al-minna fi al-ta'liq 'ala fiqh al-sunna* (Dar al-Raya, n.d.).

Ali Bey, *Travels of Ali Bey* (Philadelphia, PA: John Conrad, 1816).

al-Alusi, Mahmud Shukri, *Tarikh Najd* (Cairo: al-Matba'a al-salafiyya, 1928/9).

al-Alusi, Mahmud Shukri, *Masa'il al-jahiliyya allati khalafa fiha rasul Allah salla Allah 'alayhi wa sallam ahl al-jahiliyya* (Cairo: al-Matba'a al-salafiyya, 1928/9).

Annesley, George, *Voyages and Travels to India, Ceylon, the Red Sea, Abyssinia, and Egypt* (London: printed for William Miller, 1809).

al-Ansari, Abu 'Abd al-Latif Hammad ibn Muhammad, *Rasa'il fi al-'aqida* (Maktabat al-furqan, n.d.).

al-Bahrani, Yusuf, *al-Kashkul* (Beirut: al-Hilal, 1998).

al-Barik, Saʻd ibn ʻAbdullah (ed.), *al-Ijaz fi baʻd ma ikhtalafa fihi al-Albani wa Ibn ʻUthaymin wa Ibn Baz* (n.p., 2009).

al-Baydani, Sadiq ibn Muhammad (ed.), *Majmuʻ fatawa al-Wadiʻi* (n.p., 2003).

Bogary, Hamza, *The Sheltered Quarter: A Tale of a Boyhood in Mecca* (Austin, TX: Center for Middle Eastern Studies, University of Texas, 1991).

Burckhardt, Johann Ludwig, *Travels in Arabia: Comprehending an Account of Those Territories in Hedjaz which the Mohammedans Regard as Sacred* (London: Henry Colburn, 1829).

Burckhardt, Johann Ludwig, *Notes on the Bedouins and Wahabys* (London: Henry Colburn & Richard Bentley, 1831).

Browne, William George, *Travels in Africa, Egypt, and Syria* (London: printed for T. Cadell and W. Davies, 1799).

Burton, Richard F., *Personal Narrative of a Pilgrimage to El Medinah and Meccah* (London: Longman, Brown, Green, Longmans & Roberts, 1857).

Corancez, Louis Alexandre Olivier de, *Histoire des Wahabis* (Paris: Crapart, 1810).

Dabiq, magazine published by ISIS, all issues are available at: http://www.clarionproject.org/news/islamic-state-isis-isil-propaganda-magazine-dabiq#, last accessed 15 September 2016.

Doughty, Charles Montagu, *Travels in Arabia Deserta* (London: P. L. Warner, 1921).

Euting, Julius, *Tagbuch einer Reise in Inner-Arabien* (Leiden: Brill, 1896).

Fatawa kibar al-ʻulamaʼ al-azhar al-sharif hawla al-adriha wa al-qubur wa al-mawalid wa al-nudhur (Cairo: Dar al-yusr, 2010).

Fatawa ʻulamaʼ al-balad al-haram (Cairo: Dar al-haytham, 2003).

al-Habashi, ʻAbdullah Muhammad (ed.), *Hawaliyat yamaniyya* (Sanʻaʼ: Dar al-hikma al-yamaniyya, 1991).

al-Harawi, *Guide des lieux de pèlerinage*, trans. Janine Sourdel-Thomine (Damascus: Institut français de Damas, 1957).

al-Haytami, Ibn Hajar, *al-Fatawa al-kubra al-fiqhiyya* (al-Qahira: Maktabat wa matbaʻat al-mashhad al-husayni, 1972).

al-Huzaymi, Nasir, *Ayyam maʻa Juhayman, kuntu maʻa al-jamaʻa al-salafiyya al-muhtasiba* (Beirut: al-Shabaka al-ʻarabiyya li-l-abhath wa al-nashr – Arab Network for Research and Publishing, 2012).

Ibn ʻAbd al-Hadi, *al-ʻUqud al-durriyya min manaqib shaykh al-islam Ibn Taymiyya* (Beirut: Dar al-katib al-ʻarabi, n.d.).

Ibn 'Abd al-Wahhab, Muhammad, 'Kitab al-tawhid', in Muhammad ibn Riyad al-Ahmad (ed.), *Al-Muntaqa min rasa'il a'immat al-da'wa* (Sayda: al-Maktaba al-'asriyya, 2006).

Ibn 'Abd al-Wahhab, Muhammad, *Mufid al-mustafid fi kufr tarik al-tawhid*, ed. with commentary Hamad ibn Ahmad al-Aslani (Jeddah: Maktabat al-Rushd, 2011).

Ibn 'Abd al-Wahhab, Sulayman, *al-Sawa'iq al-ilahiyya fi al-radd 'ala al-wahhabiyya* (Beirut: Dar dhu al-faqar, 1997).

Ibn al-'Atiq, Isma'il ibn Sa'd, *Hidayat al-tariq min rasa'il wa fatawa al-shaykh Hamad al-'Atiq*, 4th edn (Riyadh: Dar al-hidaya, n.d.).

Ibn Battuta, *Travels of Ibn Battuta, A.D. 1325–54*, trans. H. A. R. Gibb (Cambridge: Cambridge University Press, published for the Hakluyt Society, 1958).

Ibn Baz, 'Abd al-'Aziz, *al-Tahqiq wa al-idah li-kathir min masa'il al-hajj wa al-'umra wa al-ziyara 'ala daw' al-kitab wa al-sunna* (Mecca: Mu'assasat Makka li-l-tiba'a wa al-i'lam, 1974).

Ibn Baz, 'Abd al-'Aziz et al., *Al-Bida' wa-l-muhdathat wa ma la asla lahu* (Riyadh: Dar Ibn Jurayma, 1998).

Ibn Baz, 'Abd al-'Aziz, *al-Fatawa al-muhimma* (Cairo: Dar al-ghadd al-jadid, 2006).

Ibn Bishr, 'Uthman ibn 'Abdullah, *'Unwan al-majd fi tarikh Najd* (Riyadh: Darat al-malik 'Abd al-'Aziz, 1982).

Ibn Ghannam, Husayn ibn Abi Bakr, *Tarikh Najd*, ed. Nasir al-Din al-Asad (Cairo: Dar al-Shuruq, 1994).

Ibn Ghannam, Husayn ibn Abi Bakr, *Tarikh Ibn Ghannam*, ed. Sulayman ibn Salih al-Khurashi (Riyadh: Dar al-thuluthiyya, 2010).

Ibn al-Jawzi, *Virtues of the Imam Ahmad ibn Hanbal*, ed. and trans. Michael Cooperson (New York: New York University Press, 2015).

Ibn Jubayr, *The Travels of Ibn Jubayr*, ed. William Wright (Leiden: Brill, 1907).

Ibn Qasim, 'Abd al-Rahman ibn Muhammad, *al-Durar al-saniyya fi al-ajwiba al-najdiyya: Majmu'at rasa'il 'ulama' najd al-a'lam min 'asr al-shaykh Muhammad ibn 'Abd al-Wahhab ila 'asrina hadha* (Riyadh, 1996).

Ibn Qasim, Muhammad ibn 'Abd al-Rahman (ed.), *Fatawa wa rasa'il samahat al-shaykh Muhammad ibn Ibrahim Al al-Shaykh* (Mecca: Matba'at al-hukuma, 1978).

Ibn Qayyim al-Jawziyya, *Ighafat al-lahfan fi masajid al-shaytan*, fin. by Mu'assasat Sulayman ibn 'Abd al-'Aziz al-Rajihi al-khayriyya, ed. Muhammad 'Uzayr Shams (Jeddah: Dar 'alam al-fawa'id, n.d.).

Ibn Rajab, *al-Dhayl 'ala tabaqat al-hanabila* (Riyadh: Maktabat al-'Ubaykan, 2005).

Ibn Sahman, Sulayman, *Tabri'at al-shaykhayn al-imamayn min tazwir ahl al-kadhib wa al-mayn*, printed on the request of King Sa'ud ibn 'Abd al-'Aziz Al Sa'ud (Riyadh, 1957/8).

Ibn Taymiyya, *Kitab iqtida' al-sirat al-mustaqim mukhalafat ashab al-jahim* (al-Qahira: Matba'at al-sunna al-muhammadiyya, 1979).

Ibn Taymiyya, *Dar' ta'arud al-'aql wa al-naql*, ed. Rashad Salim (al-Riyadh, 1991).

Ibn Taymiyya, *Manasik al-hajj wa al-'umra*, ed. Husayn ibn Muhammad ibn 'Abdullah Al al-Shaykh (Saudi Arabia, 1994/5).

Ibn Taymiyya, *Qa'ida jalila fi al-tawassul wa al-wasila*, ed. 'Abd al-Qadir Arna'ut (Riyadh: Tahta ishraf ri'asat idarat al-buhuth al-'ilmiyya wa al-ifta', 1999).

Ibn Taymiyya, *al-Asma' wa al-sifat*, ed. Muhammad Sayyid (al-Qahira: Dar al-da'wa al-islamiyya, 2001).

Ibn Taymiyya, *Majmu'at al-fatawa* (Mansura: Dar al-Wafa, 2005).

Ibn Taymiyya, *al-'Aqida al-wasitiyya*, ed. 'Alawi ibn 'Abd al-Qadir al-Saqqaf (al-Durar al-sunniyya, 2011/12).

Ibn al-Zayyat, Shams al-Din, *al-Kawakib al-sayyara fi tartib al-ziyara* (Misr: al-Matba'a al-amiriyya, 1907).

Malcolm, John, *History of Persia, from the Most Early Period to the Present Time* (London: John Murray, 1829).

Majallat al-Azhar (Matba'at al-azhar, 1940).

Majmu' tafrighat kalimat al-qadat bi-Dawlat al-'Iraq al-islamiyya (Nukhbat al-i'lam al-jihadi, 2010), 14, available at: https://archive.org/download/Dwla_Nokhba/mjdawl.doc, last accessed 15 May 2016.

al-Maqdisi, Abu Muhammad, *Millat Ibrahim* (Manbar al-tawhid wa al-jihad, 2009/10).

Mengin, Félix, *Histoire de l'Égypte sous le gouvernement de Mohammed-Aly* (Paris: A. Bertrand, 1823).

Mu'allafat al-shaykh imam Muhammad ibn 'Abd al-Wahhab, ed. 'Abd al-'Aziz ibn Zayd al-Rumi, Muhammad Baltaji, Sayyid Hijab (Riyadh, 1981).

al-Mutayri, 'Abdullah Muhammad, *Masa'il al-i'tiqad 'inda al-amir al-San'ani Muhammad ibn Isma'il*', diploma thesis, Jami'at al-Qahira, Kulliyat Dar al-'ulum, qism al-falsafa al-islamiyya, 2001.

Niebuhr, M., *Travels through Arabia and Other Countries in the East* (Edinburgh, 1792).

al-Nu'mi, Husayn ibn Mahdi, *Ma'arij al-albab fi manahij al-haqq wa al-sawab*, ed. Muhammad Hamid al-Fiqi (Matabi' al-Riyadh, 1973).

Records of the Hajj: A Documentary History of the Pilgrimage to Mecca (London: Archive Editions, 1993).

Rif'at, Sayyid Ahmad, *Rasa'il Juhayman al-'Utaybi qa'id al-muqtahimin li-l-masjid al-haram bi-Makka* (Cairo: Madbuli, 2004).

Rihlat Ibn Jubayr (Beirut: Dar Sadir, n.d.).

Rousseau, Jean-Baptiste Louis Jacques, *Description du Pachalik de Bagdad* (Paris: Treuttel et Würtz, 1809).

Rutter, Eldon, *The Holy Cities of Arabia* (London: G. P. Putnam, 1930).

Sabiq, al-Sayyid, *Fiqh al-sunna* (Cairo: al-Fath li-l-i'lam al-'arabi, n.d.).

al-Sahadan, 'Abd al-'Aziz ibn Sulayman (ed.), *al-Imam al-Albani, durus wa mawaqif wa 'ibar* (Riyadh: Dar al-tawhid, 2008).

al-Samhudi, 'Ali ibn 'Abdullah, *Kitab wafa' al-wafa' bi-akhbar dar al mustufa* (Misr: Matba'at al-adab, 1908/9).

al-San'ani, ibn al-Amir, *Tathir al-i'tiqad 'an adran al-ilhad*, ed. Abu al-'Abbas al-Shihri (Sa'da': Maktabat al-imam Muqbil al-Wadi'i, 2009).

al-San'ani, Muhammad ibn Isma'il, *Majmu'at al-rasa'il* (al-Jami'a al-islamiyya bi-al-Madina al-munawwara, 1989/90).

Siddiq Hasan Khan, *An Interpreter of Wahabiism*, trans. and ed. Sayyad Akbar 'Alam (Calcutta, 1884).

Siddiq Hasan Khan, *Abjad al-'ulum*, ed. 'Abd al-Jabbar Zakar (Beirut: Dar al-kutub al-'ilmiyya, 1978).

Siddiq Hasan Khan, *Al-Siraj al-wahhaj fi kashf matalib Sahih Muslim ibn Hajjaj*, ed. 'Abdullah ibn Ibrahim al-Ansari (Published at the expense of Qatar, 1997).

al-Shawkani, Muhammad ibn 'Ali, *al-Badr al-tali' bi mahasin man ba'da al-qarn al-sabi'*, ed. Muhammad ibn Muhammad ibn Yahya Zibara (Beirut: Dar al-kutub al-'ilmiyya, 1998).

Sun'allah, ibn Sun'allah al-Halabi al-Makki al-Hanafi, *Sayf Allah 'ala man kadhaba 'ala awliya' Allah* (Cairo: Dar al-kitab wa al-sunna, 2007).

Tamisier, Maurice, *Voyage en Arabie* (Paris: L. Desessart, 1840).

al-Turtushi, *Kitab al-hawadith wa al-bida'*, ed. 'Abd al-Majid Turki (Beirut: Dar al-gharb al-islami, 1990).

al-'Uthaymin, Muhammad ibn Salih, *Sharh thalathat al-usul*, ed. Fahd ibn Nasir ibn Ibrahim al-Sulayman (Riyadh: Dar al-thuraya, 2000).

al-'Uthaymin, Muhammad Salih, *Sharh al-'aqida al-wasitiyya* (Dammam: Dar Ibn al-Jawzi, 2000/1).

al-'Uthaymin, Muhammad ibn Salih, *al-Sunan wa al-bida' al-muta'alliqa bi-l-alfaz wa al-mafahim al-khati'a* (Dar al-imam al-mujaddid, 2005).

al-'Uthaymin, Muhammad ibn Salih, *al-Jami' li-ahkam fiqh al-sunna* (Cairo: Dar al-ghad al-jadid, 2007).

al-'Uthaymin, 'Abd Allah Salih, *Muhammad ibn 'Abd al-Wahhab* (London: I. B. Tauris, 2009).

'Uthman Ahmad al-Najdi al-Hanbali, *Hidayat al-raghib li-sharh 'umdat al-talib*, ed. Hasanayn Muhammad Makhluf (Ta'if: Dar Muhammad, 1996).

al-Wadi'i, Muqbil ibn Hadi, *Majmu' fatawa al-Wadi'i* (Riyadh: S. M. al-Baydani, 2005).

al-Wadi'i, Abu 'Abd al-Rahman Muqbil ibn Hadi, *Tuhfat al-mujib 'ala as'ilat al-hadir wa al-gharib* (San'a': Dar al-athar, 2000).

al-Wadi'i, Abu 'Abd al-Rahman Muqbil ibn Hadi, *Riyadh al-janna fi al-radd 'ala a'da' al-sunna wa ma'ahu al-tali'a fi-l-radd 'ala ghulat al-shi'a [wa] hukm al-qubba al-mabniya 'ala qabr al-rasul* (Maktabat San'a', 2003).

Wahba, Hafiz, *Jazirat al-'arab fi al-qarn al-'ishrin* (Matba'at lajnat al-ta'alif wa al-tarjama wa al-nashr, 1935).

Wavell, Arthur J. B., *A Modern Pilgrim in Mecca* (London: Constable, 1918).

Zinu, Muhammad ibn Jamil, *Majmu'at rasa'il al-tawjihat al-islamiyya li-islah al-fard wa al-mujtama'* (Riyadh: Dar al-Sumay'i, 1997).

Secondary Sources

Abbink, Jon, 'Religion in Public Spaces: Emerging Muslim–Christian Polemics in Ethiopia', *African Affairs*, 110(439) (2011): 253–74.

Abdesselem, Mohamed, *Le thème de la mort dans la poésie arabe: des origines à la fin du IIIe–IXe siècle* (Tunis: Université de Tunis, 1977).

Abou El Fadl, Khaled, *And God Knows the Soldiers: The Authoritative and Authoritarian in Islamic Discourse* (Lanham, MD: University Press of America, 2001).

Abou El Fadl, Khaled, *The Search for Beauty in Islam: A Conference of the Book* (Lanham, MD: Rowman & Littlefield, 2006).

Aghaie, Kamran S., *The Martyrs of Karbala: Shi'i Symbols and Rituals in Modern Iran* (Seattle, WA: University of Washington Press, 2004).

Ahmad, Rafiuddin, *The Bengali Muslims 1871–1906: A Quest for Identity* (Delhi: Oxford University Press, 1981).

Alavi, Seema, 'Siddiq Hasan Khan (1832–90) and the Creation of a Muslim Cosmopolitanism in the 19th Century', *Journal of the Economic and Social History of the Orient* 54(1) (2011): 1–38.

al-Alawi, Irfan, 'The Destruction of Holy Sites in Mecca and Medina', *Islamica Magazine*, 15 (2006).

Albera, Dionigi and Maria Couroucli (eds), *Religions traversées: lieux saints partagés entre chrétiens, musulmans et juifs en Méditerranée* (Arles: Actes sud, 2009).

Amselle, Jean-Loup, 'Le Wahabisme à Bamako (1945–1985)', *Canadian Journal of African Studies / Revue Canadienne des Études Africaines* 19(2) (1985): 345–57.

Amselle, Jean-Loup, 'A Case of Fundamentalism in West Africa: Wahabism in Bamako', in Lionel Caplan (ed.), *Studies in Religious Fundamentalism* (Basingstoke: Macmillan, 1987), pp. 79–94.

al-Atawneh, Muhammad K., *Wahhabi Islam Facing the Challenges of Modernity: Dar al-Ifta in the Modern Saudi State* (Leiden: Brill, 2010).

Atkinson, Mary and Rori Donaghy, 'Crime and Punishment: Islamic State vs Saudi Arabia', *Middle East Eye*, 20 January 2015, available at: www.middleeasteye.net/news/crime-and-punishment--islamic-state-vs-saudi-arabia-1588245666, last accessed 4 September 2016.

Babadzhanov, Bakhtiiar, 'O fetvakh SADUM protiv "neislamskikh obychaev"', in Martha B. Olcott and Aleksei Malashenko (eds), *Islam na postsovetskom prostranstve: vzgliad iznutri* (Moscow, 2001), pp. 170–84.

Baljon, J. M. S., 'Shah Waliullah and the Dargah', in Christian W. Troll (ed.), *Muslim Shrines in India: Their Character, History and Significance* (Delhi: Oxford University Press, 1992), pp. 189–93.

Belhaj, Abdessamad, *La dimension islamique dans la politique étrangère du Maroc: Déterminants, acteurs, orientations* (Louvain: Presses universitaires de Louvain, 2009).

Beranek, Ondrej, 'The Sword and the Book: Implications of the Intertwining of the Saudi Ruling Family and the Religious Establishment', *Crown Center Middle East Brief* 28 (April 2008).

Beranek, Ondrej and Pavel Tupek, 'From Visiting Graves to their Destruction: The Question of Ziyara through the Eyes of Salafis', *Crown Paper* 2, Brandeis University, July 2009.

Bergmann, Frédéric-Guillaume, *De religione Arabum anteislamica: dissertatio historico-theologica* (Argentorati: F. G. Levrault, 1834).

Berkey, Jonathan Porter, *The Transmission of Knowledge in Medieval Cairo: A Social History of Islamic Education* (Princeton, NJ: Princeton University Press, 1992).

Bevan, Robert, *The Destruction of Memory: Architecture at War* (London: Reaktion, 2006).

Bisheh, Ghazi Izzeddin, 'The Mosque of the Prophet at Madinah Throughout the First-Century A.H. with Special Emphasis on the Umayyad Mosque', unpublished PhD dissertation, University of Michigan, 1979.

Bligh, Alexander, 'The Saudi Religious Elite (Ulama) as Participant in the Political System of the Kingdom', *International Journal of Middle East Studies* 17(1) (1985): 37–50.

Boboxonov, Shamsuddinxon, *Shayx Ziyovuddinxon ibn Eshon Boboxon* (Tashkent, 2001).

Bonacina, Giovanni, *The Wahhabis Seen through European Eyes (1772–1830): Deists and Puritans of Islam* (Leiden: Brill, 2015).

Bori, Caterina, 'A New Source for the Biography of Ibn Taymiyya', *Bulletin of SOAS* 67(3) (2004): 321–48.

Boucek, Christopher, 'Saudi Fatwa Restrictions and the State–Clerical Relationship', 27 October 2010, available at: http://carnegieendowment.org/2010/10/27/saudi-fatwa-restrictions-and-state-clerical-relationship/6b81, last accessed 7 September 2016.

Bradbury, Jennie N., '"Presencing the Past": A Case Study of Islamic Rural Burial Practices from the Homs Region, Syria', in Stephen McPhillips and Paul D. Wordsworth (eds), *Landscapes of the Islamic World: Archeology, History, and Ethnography* (Philadelphia, PA: University of Pennsylvania Press, 2016), pp. 200–18.

Brown, Jonathan, *The Canonization of al-Bukhari and Muslim: The Formation and Function of the Sunni Hadith Canon* (Leiden: Brill, 2007).

Brown, Daniel W., *Rethinking Tradition in Modern Islamic Thought* (Cambridge: Cambridge University Press, 1996).

Brown, Kenneth L., *People of Salé: Tradition and Change in a Moroccan City, 1830–1930* (Cambridge, MA: Harvard University Press, 1976).

Bunzel, Cole, 'From Paper State to Caliphate: The Ideology of the Islamic State', Analysis Paper 19, Brookings Project on U.S. Relations with the Islamic World, March 2015, available at: www.brookings.edu/~/media/research/files/papers/2015/03/ideology-of-islamic-state-bunzel/the-ideology-of-the-islamic-state.pdf, last accessed 4 September 2016.

Bunzel, Cole, 'The Kingdom and the Caliphate: Duel of the Islamic States'. Carnegie Endowment for International Peace, Brief, February 2016, available at: http://carnegieendowment.org/files/Brief-Bunzel-Duel_of_The_Islamic_States.pdf, last accessed 4 September 2016.

Burgat, François, *L'islamisme au Maghreb: Tunisie, Algérie, Libye, Maroc* (Paris: Payot, 1995).

Chelhod, Joseph, *Le Sacrifice chez les Arabes* (Paris: Presses universitaires de France, 1955).

Chiffoleau, Sylvia and Anna Madoeuf (eds), *Les pèlerinages au Maghreb et au Moyen-Orient: espaces publics, espaces du public* (Damascus: Ifpo, 2005).

Cobb, Paul M., 'Virtual Sacrality: Making Muslim Syria Sacred before the Crusades', *Medieval Encounters* 8(1) (2002): 35–55.

Colla, Elliott, 'On the Iconoclasm of ISIS', available at: http://www.elliottcolla.com/blog/2015/3/5/on-the-iconoclasm-of-isis, last accessed 15 September 2016.

Colla, Elliott, 'Preservation and Destruction', available at: http:// www.elliottcolla.com/blog/2015/3/27/pm0t4j35d00plvir68mk 6fyquh0, last accessed 15 September 2016.

Commins, David, *The Wahhabi Mission and Saudi Arabia* (London: I. B. Tauris, 2006).

Commins, David, 'From Wahhabi to Salafi', in Bernard Haykel, Thomas Hegghammer and Stéphane Lacroix (eds), *Saudi Arabia in Transition: Insights on Social, Political, Economic and Religious Change* (New York: Cambridge University Press, 2015), pp. 151–66.

Comolli, Virginia, *Boko Haram: Nigeria's Islamist Insurgency* (London: Hurst, 2015).

Cook, David, *Studies in Muslim Apocalyptic* (Princeton, NJ: Darwin Press, 2002).

Cook, Michael, 'On the Origins of Wahhābism', *Journal of the Royal Asiatic Society* 3rd Series, 2(2) (1992): 191–202.

Cook, Michael, *Commanding Right and Forbidding Wrong in Islamic Thought* (Cambridge: Cambridge University Press, 2004).

Creswell, K. A. C., *The Muslim Architecture of Egypt* (New York: Hacker, 1979).

Crooke, Alastair, 'You Can't Understand ISIS if You Don't Know the History of Wahhabism in Saudi Arabia', *Huffington Post*, 27 August 2014, available at: www.huffingtonpost.com/alastair--crooke/isis-wahhabism-saudi-arabia_b_5717157.html, last accessed 4 September 2016.

Cuffel, Alexandra, 'From Practice to Polemic: Shared Saints and Festivals as "Women's Religion" in the Medieval Mediterranean', *Bulletin of the School of Oriental and African Studies* 68(3) (2005): 401–19.

Daoud, Kamel, 'Saudi Arabia, an ISIS That Has Made It', *The New York Times*, 20 November 2015, available at: https://www.nytimes.com/2015/11/21/opinion/saudi-arabia-an-isis-that-has-made-it.html, last accessed 4 September 2016.

DeLong-Bas, Natana J., *Wahhabi Islam: From Revival and Reform to Global Jihad* (Oxford: Oxford University Press, 2004).

Dieste, Josep L. M., *Health and Ritual in Morocco: Conceptions of the Body and Healing Practices* (Boston, MA: Brill, 2012).

Doumato, Eleanor Abdella, *Getting God's Ear: Women, Islam, and Healing in Saudi Arabia and the Gulf* (New York: Columbia University Press, 2000).

Dudoignon, Noack, *Allah's Kolkhozes: Migration, De-Stalinisation, Privatisation and the New Muslim Congregations in the Soviet Realm (1950s–2000s)* (Berlin: Klaus Schwarz, 2014).

Dumbe, Yunus, 'The Salafi Praxis of Constructing Religious Identity in Africa: A Comparative Perspective of the Growth of the Movements in Accra and Cape Town', *Islamic Africa* 2(2) (2011): 101–4.

Early, Evelyn A., *Baladi Women of Cairo: Playing with an Egg and a Stone* (Boulder, CO: Lynne Rienner, 1993).

Eickelman, Dale F., *Moroccan Islam: Tradition and Society in a Pilgrimage Center* (Austin, TX: University of Texas Press, 1976).

Eickelman, Dale F. and James Piscatori (eds), *Muslim Travellers: Pilgrimage, Migration, and the Religious Imagination* (London: Routledge, 1990).

Elias, Jamal J., '(Un)Making Idolatry: From Mecca to Bamiyan', *Future Anterior: Journal of Historic Preservation, History, Theory, and Criticism*, 4(2) (2007): 12–29.

Encyclopaedia of Islam (*EI2*), P. Bearman, Th. Bianquis, C. E. Bosworth, E. van Donzel and W. P. Heinrichs (eds), 2nd edn (Leiden: Brill, 1960–), available at: http://referenceworks.brillonline.com/browse/encyclopaedia-of-islam-2.

Exnerová, Věra, 'The Veneration and Visitation of the Graves of Saints in Soviet Central Asia: Insights from the Southern Ferghana Valley, Uzbekistan', *Archiv orientální* 83(3) (2015): 501–36.

Fartacek, Gebhard, *Pilgerstätten in der syrischen Peripherie: Eine ethnologische Studie zur kognitiven Konstruktion sakraler Plätze und deren Praxisrelevanz* (Vienna: Verlag der Österreichischen Akademie der Wissenschaften, 2003).

Fierro, Maribel, 'The Treatises against Innovations (*kutub al-bidaʿ*)', *Der Islam* 69(2) (1992): 204–46.

Fishman, Brian, 'The First Defector: Abu Sulayman al-Utaybi, The Islamic State, and al-Qaʿida', *Combating Terrorism Center*, 23 October 2015, available at: https://ctc.usma.edu/posts/the-first-defector-abu-sulayman-al-utaybi-the-islamic-state-and-al-qaida, last accessed 4 September 2016.

Flemming, Barbara, 'Die Vorwahhabitische Fitna im osmanischen Kairo 1711', in *Ismail Hakkı Uzunçarşılı'ya Armağan* (Ankara: Türk Tarih Kurumu, 1976), pp. 55–65.

Flood, Finbarr Barry, 'Between Cult and Culture: Bamiyan, Islamic Iconoclasm, and the Museum', *The Art Bulletin* 84(4) (2002): 641–59.

Flood, Finbarr Barry, 'Idol-Breaking as Image-Making in the "Islamic State"', *Religion and Society: Advances in Research* 7 (2016). 116–38.

Frank, Allen J. and Jahangir Mamatov, *Uzbek Islamic Debates: Texts, Translations, and Commentary* (Springfield, VA: Dunwoody Press, 2006).

Frank, Constance, 'Funeral Practices at Tell Masaikh (Syria): Late Roman and Islamic Graves', *Studies in Historical Anthropology* 3 (2006): 93–120.

Frenkel, Yehoshuʿa, 'Baybars and the Sacred Geography of *Bilad al-Sham*: A Chapter in the Islamization of Syria's Landscape', *Jerusalem Studies in Arabic and Islam* 25 (2001): 153–70.

Gamboni, Dario, *The Destruction of Art: Iconoclasm and Vandalism since the French Revolution* (London: Reaktion, 1997).

Gaborieau, Marc, 'A Nineteenth-Century Indian "Wahhabi" Tract against the Cult of Muslim Saints: *Al-Balagh al-Mubin*', in Christian W. Troll (ed.), *Muslim Shrines in India: Their Character, History and Significance* (Delhi: Oxford University Press, 1992), pp. 198–239.

Gardner, Katy, *Global Migrants, Local Lives: Travel and Transformation in Rural Bangladesh* (Oxford: Clarendon Press, 1995).

Geertz, Clifford, *Islam Observed: Religious Development in Morocco and Indonesia* (Chicago, IL: University of Chicago Press, 1971).

Gellner, Ernest, *Saints of the Atlas* (Chicago, IL: University of Chicago Press, 1969).

Gillsenan, Michael, *Saint and Sufi in Modern Egypt: An Essay in the Sociology of Religion* (Oxford: Clarendon Press, 1973).

Gladney, Dru C., *Muslim Chinese: Ethnic Nationalism in the People's Republic* (Cambridge, MA: Harvard University Press, 1996).

Goldziher, Ignaz, 'Le sacrifice de la chevelure chez les Arabes', *Revue de l'Histoire des Religions* 14 (1886): 49–52.

Goldziher, Ignaz, 'On the Veneration of the Dead in Paganism and Islam', in I. Goldziher, *Muslim Studies*, ed. Samuel M. Stern, trans. from German C. R. Barber and S. M. Stern (Chicago, IL: Aldine, 1967), vol. 1, pp. 209–38.

Goldziher, Ignaz, 'Veneration of Saints in Islam', in I. Goldziher, *Muslim Studies*, ed. Samuel M. Stern, trans. from German C. R. Barber and S. M. Stern (Chicago, IL: Aldine, 1971), vol. 2, pp. 255–341.

Grabar, Oleg, 'The Umayyad Dome of the Rock in Jerusalem', *Ars Orientalis* 3 (1959): 33–62.

Grabar, Oleg, 'Islam and Iconoclasm', in Anthony Bryer and Judith Herrin (eds), *Iconoclasm: Papers given at the Ninth Spring Symposium of Byzantine Studies* (University of Birmingham: Centre for Byzantine Studies, 1977), pp. 45–52.

Grehan, James, *Twilight of the Saints: Everyday Religion in Ottoman Syria and Palestine* (Oxford: Oxford University Press, 2014).

Grütter, Irene, 'Arabische Bestattungssitten in frühislamischer Zeit', *Der Islam* 31 (1954): 147–73.

Grütter, Irene, 'Arabische Bestattungssitten in frühislamischer Zeit', *Der Islam* 32 (1957): 79–193.

al-Hajiri, Yusuf, *Al-Baqiʿ: qissat tadmir Al Suʿud lil-athar al-islamiyya fi al-Hijaz* (Beirut: Muʾassasat al-Baqiʿ li-ihyaʾ al-turath, 1990).

Halevi, Leor, *Muhammad's Grave: Death Rites and the Making of Islamic Society* (New York: Columbia University Press, 2011).

Hamès, Constant, 'Deux aspects du fondamentalisme islamique: Sa signification au Mali actuel et chez Ibn Taimîya', *Archives de sciences sociales des religions* 50(2) (1980): 177–90.

Hammond, Andrew, *The Islamic Utopia: The Illusion of Reform in Saudi Arabia* (London: Pluto Press, 2012).

Harder, Hans, *Sufism and Saint Veneration in Contemporary Bangladesh: The Maijbhandaris of Chittagong* (London: Routledge, 2011).

Hardy, Samuel A., 'Pornographic Iconoclasm in Terrorist Propaganda: Islamic State Cinema and Audience Reactions', European Union National Institutes for Culture (EUNIC), 9 April 2016, available at: http://washington-dc.eunic-online.eu/?q=content%2Fpornographic-iconoclasm-terrorist-propaganda-islamic-state-cinema-and-audience-reactions-0, last accessed 15 September 2016.

al-Harigi, Fahad an-Nwisser, 'The Relationship between the Prophet's Mosque and its Physical Environment, al-Madina, Saudi Arabia', unpublished PhD thesis, University of Edinburgh, 1989.

al-Harithy, Howayda, 'The Four Madrasahs in the Complex of Sultan Hasan (1356–61): The Complete Survey', *Mamlūk Studies Review* 11(2) (2007): 49–76.

Harmanşah, Ömür, 'ISIS, Heritage, and the Spectacles of Destruction in the Global Media', *Near Eastern Archaeology* 78(3) (2015): 170–7.

al-Hashimi, Muhammad Ali, *The Ideal Muslimah* (Riyadh: International Islamic Publishing House, 2005).

Hawting, Gerald R., *The Idea of Idolatry and the Emergence of Islam: From Polemic to History* (Cambridge: Cambridge University Press, 1999).

Haykel, Bernard, 'A Zaydi Revival?' *Yemen Update* 36 (1995): 20–1.

Haykel, Bernard, *Revival and Reform in Islam* (Cambridge: Cambridge University Press, 2003).

Haykel, Bernard, 'On the Nature of Salafi Thought and Action', in Roel Meijer (ed.), *Global Salafism: Islam's New Religious Movement* (New York: Columbia University Press, 2009).

Haykel, Bernard, Thomas Hegghammer and Stéphane Lacroix (eds), *Saudi Arabia in Transition: Insights on Social, Political, Economic and Religious Change* (Cambridge: Cambridge University Press, 2015).

Hegghammer, Thomas, *Jihad in Saudi Arabia: Violence and Panislamism since 1979* (Cambridge: Cambridge University Press, 2010).

Hegghammer, Thomas and Stéphane Lacroix, 'Rejectionist Islamism in Saudi Arabia: The Story of Juhayman al-'Utaybi Revisited', *International Journal of Middle East Studies*, 39(1) (2007): 103–22.

Henninger, Josef, 'Pre-Islamic Bedouin Religion', in M. L. Swartz (ed.), *Studies on Islam* (New York: Oxford University Press, 1981), pp. 3–22.

Henninger, Josef, 'Zur Frage des Haaropfers bei den Semiten', *Die Wiener Schule der Völkerkunde. Festschrift anlässlich des 25-jährigen Bestandes des Instituts für Völkerkunde der Universität Wien (1929–1954)* (Vienna: F. Berger, 1956).

Henninger, Josef, 'Menschenopfer bei den Arabern', *Anthropos* 53(5/6) (1958): 721–805.

Higazi, Adam, 'Mobilisation Into and Against Boko Haram in North-East Nigeria', in Kadya Tall, Marie-Emmanuelle Pommerolle and Michel Cahen (eds), *Collective Mobilisations in Africa: Contestation, Resistance, Revolt* (Leiden: Brill, 2015), pp. 305–58.

Hillenbrand, Robert, *Islamic Architecture: Form, Function and Meaning* (Edinburgh: Edinburgh University Press, 1994).

Ho, Engseng, *The Graves of Tarim: Genealogy and Mobility across the Indian Ocean* (Berkeley: University of California Press, 2006).

Hourani, Albert, *Reason and Tradition in Islamic Ethics* (Cambridge: Cambridge University Press, 2007).

Hughes, Thomas Patrick, *A Dictionary of Islam* (New York: Scribner, Welford, 1885).

Hundhammer, Marianus, *Prophetenverehrung im Hadramaut: Die Ziyāra nach Qabr Hūd aus diachroner und synchroner Perspektive* (Berlin: Klaus Schwarz, 2010).

Hunwick, John, 'Sub-Saharan Africa and the Wider World of Islam: Historical and Contemporary Perspectives', *Journal of Religion in Africa* 26 (1996): 230–57.

al-Ibrashy, May, 'Death, Life and the Barzakh in Cairo's Cemeteries: The Place of the Cemetery in the Sacred Geography of Late Medieval Cairo', *JUSUR, UCLA Journal of Middle Eastern Studies*, available at: http://international.ucla.edu/institute/article/15501, last accessed 4 September 2017.

Idrissi, Aziz el Kobaiti, 'The Political Participation of Sufi and Salafi Movements in Modern Morocco: Between the "2003 Casablanca Terrorist Attack" and the "Moroccan Spring"', in Lloyd Ridgeon (ed.), *Sufis and Salafis in the Contemporary Age* (London: Bloomsbury, 2015), pp. 91–104.

Insoll, Timothy, *The Archaeology of Islam* (Oxford: Blackwell, 1999).

Jalabert, Cyrille, 'Comment Damas est devenue une métropole Islamique', *Bulletin d'Études Orientales* 53/4 (2001/2): 13–42.

Joffé, George (ed.), *Islamist Radicalisation in North Africa: Politics and Process* (London: Routledge, 2012).

Johnsen, Gregory, 'Profile of Sheikh Abd al-Majid al-Zindani', *Terrorism Monitor* 4(7) (2006): 3–5.

Johnsen, Gregory, *Last Refuge: Yemen, al-Qaeda, and America's War in Arabia* (New York: W. W. Norton, 2013).

Johnson, A., 'Saudis Risk New Muslim Division with Proposal to Move Mohamed's Tomb', *The Independent*, 1 September 2014, available at: www.independent.co.uk/news/world/middle-east/saudis-risk-new-muslim-division-with-proposal-to-move-mohameds-tomb-9705120.html, last accessed 4 September 2016.

Johnson, Casey Garret, Masood Karokhail and Rahmatullah Amiri, 'The Islamic State in Afghanistan: Assessing the Threat', *Peacebrief* 202, United States Institute of Peace, April 2016.

Jong, Frederic de, 'Cairene Ziyāra-Days: A Contribution to the Study of Saint Veneration in Islam', *Die Welt des Islams* 17(1/4) (1976/7): 26–43.

Jun, Sugawara and Rahile Dawut (eds), *Mazar: Studies on Islamic Sacred Sites in Central Eurasia* (Tokyo: Tokyo University of Foreign Studies Press, 2016).

Juynboll, Gautier H. A., *Muslim Tradition: Studies in Chronology, Provenance and Authorship of Early Ḥadīth* (Cambridge: Cambridge University Press, 1983).

Kaba, Lansine, *The Wahhabiyya: Islamic Reform and Politics in French West Africa* (Evanston, IL: Northwestern University Press, 1974).

Kabbani, Marwan, *Die Heiligenverehrung im Urteil Ibn Taymīyas und seiner Zeitgenossen* (Bonn: s.n., 1979).

Kane, Ousmane, *Muslim Modernity in Postcolonial Nigeria: A Study of the Society for the Removal of Innovation and Reinstatement of Tradition* (Leiden: Brill, 2003).

Kecia, Ali, *Imam Shafiʿi: Scholar and Saint* (Oxford: Oneworld, 2011).

Khalid, Adeeb, *Islam after Communism: Religion and Politics in Central Asia* (Berkeley: University of California Press, 2007).

Khosronejad, Pedram, *Saints and Their Pilgrims in Iran and Neighbouring Countries* (Wantage: Sean Kingston, 2012).

King, G. R. D., 'Islam, Iconoclasm, and the Declaration of Doctrine', *Bulletin of the School of Oriental and African Studies* 48(2) (1985): 267–77.

Kirkpatrick, David, 'ISIS' Harsh Brand of Islam is Rooted in Austere Saudi Creed', *The New York Times*, 24 September 2014, available at: http://www.nytimes.

com/2014/09/25/world/middleeast/isis-abu-bakr-baghdadi-caliph-wahhabi. html?_r=0, last accessed 4 September 2016.

Kister, M. J., 'You Shall Only Set Out for Three Mosques: A Study of an Early Tradition', *Le Muséon* 82 (1969): 173–96.

Kobo, Ousman M., 'Wahhabi Reforms in Ghana and Burkina Faso, 1960–1990: Elective Affinities between Western-educated Muslims and Islamic Scholars', *Comparative Studies in Society and History* 51(3) (2009): 502–32.

Kobo, Ousman M., *Unveiling Modernity in Twentieth-Century West African Islamic Reforms* (Leiden: Brill, 2012).

Kostiner, Joseph, *The Making of Saudi Arabia, 1916–1936: From Chieftaincy to Monarchical State* (New York: Oxford University Press, 1993).

Krawietz, Birgit, 'Ibn Qayyim al-Jawziyah: His Life and Works', *Mamlūk Studies Review* 10(2) (2006): 19–64.

Krehl, Ludolf, *Über die Religion der vorislamischen Araber* (Leipzig: Serig, 1863).

Kressel, Gideon M., Sasson Bar-Zvi and 'Aref Abu-Rabi'a, *The Charm of Graves: Perceptions of Death and After-Death among the Negev Bedouin* (Brighton: Sussex Academic Press, 2014).

Lacroix, Stephane, *Awakening Islam: The Politics of Religious Dissent in Contemporary Saudi Arabia* (Cambridge, MA: Harvard University Press, 2011).

Laffan, Michael, 'National Crisis and the Representation of Traditional Sufism in Indonesia: The Periodicals Salafy and Sufi', in Martin van Bruinessen and J. D. Howell (eds), *Sufism and the 'Modern' in Islam* (London: I. B. Tauris, 2007), pp. 149–62.

Lambton, Ann K. S., *Continuity and Change in Medieval Persia: Aspects of Administrative, Economic, and Social History, 11th–14th Century* (Albany, NY: Bibliotheca Persica, 1988).

Lamm, Maurice, *The Jewish Way in Death and Mourning* (New York: J. David, 2000).

Lancaster, W. and F. Lancaster, 'Observations on Death, Burial, Graves and Graveyards at Various Locations in Ra's al-Khaimah Emirate, UAE, and Musandan *wilayat*, Oman, Using Local Concerns', in L. Weeks (ed.), *Death and Burial in Arabia and Beyond: Multidisciplinary Perspectives* (Oxford: Archaeopress, 2010).

Lane, E. W., *Arabic–English Lexicon* (London: Williams & Norgate, 1863).

Laoust, Henri, *Essai sur les doctrines sociales et politiques de Taki-d-Din Ahmad b. Taimiya* (Cairo: l'Institut français d'archéologie orientale, 1939).

Lauzière, Henri, *The Making of Salafism: Islamic Reform in the Twentieth Century* (New York: Columbia University Press, 2016).

Layish, A., 'Ulama and Politics in Saudi Arabia', in M. Heper and R. Israeli (eds), *Islam and Politics in the Modern Middle East* (London: Croom Helm, 1984), pp. 29–63.

Leisten, Thomas, 'Between Orthodoxy and Exegesis: Some Aspects of Attitudes in the Shariʿa toward Funerary Architecture', *Muqarnas* 7 (1990): 12–22.

Leisten, Thomas, *Architektur für Tote: Bestattung in Architektonischem Kontext in den Kernländern der Islamischen Welt zwischen 3./9. und 6./12. Jahrhundert* (Berlin: D. Reimer, 1998).

Lav, Daniel, *Radical Islam and the Revival of Medieval Theology* (Cambridge: Cambridge University Press, 2013).

Levtzion, Nehemia and John O. Voll (eds), *Eighteenth-Century Renewal and Reform in Islam* (Syracuse, NY: Syracuse University Press, 1987).

Lia, Brynjar, 'Understanding Jihadi Proto-States', *Perspectives on Terrorism* 9(4) (2015): 31–41.

Litvak, Meir, *Shiʿi Scholars of Nineteenth-Century Iraq: The 'Ulama' of Najaf and Karbala'* (Cambridge: Cambridge University Press, 1998).

Litvak, Meir, 'Encounters between Shiʿi and Sunni ʿUlamaʾ in Ottoman Iraq', in Ofra Bengio and Meir Litvak (eds), *The Sunna and Shiʿa in History: Division and Ecumenism in the Muslim Middle East* (New York: Palgrave Macmillan, 2011), pp. 69–86.

Loimeier, Roman, 'Islamic Reform and Political Change: The Example of Abubakar Gumi and the Yan Izala Movement in Northern Nigeria', in Eva Evers Rosander and David Westerlund (eds), *African Islam and Islam in Africa: Encounters between Sufis and Islamists* (London: Hurst, 1997).

Louër, Laurence, 'The State and Sectarian Identities in the Persian Gulf Monarchies: Bahrain, Saudi Arabia, and Kuwait in Comparative Perspective', in Lawrence G. Potter (ed.), *Sectarian Politics in the Persian Gulf* (London: Hurst, 2013), pp. 117–42.

Lymer, Kenneth, 'Rags and Rock Art: The Landscapes of Holy Site Pilgrimage in the Republic of Kazakhstan', *World Archaeology* 36(1) (2004): 158–72.

Mabrouk, Mehdi, 'The Radicalisation of Religious Policy', in George Joffé (ed.), *Islamist Radicalisation in North Africa: Politics and Process* (London: Routledge, 2012), pp. 48–70.

Makdisi, George, 'Ibn Taimiya: A Sufi of the Qadiriya Order', *American Journal of Arabic Studies* 1 (1973): 118–29.

Makdisi, George, *Ibn Aqil: Religion and Culture in Classical Islam* (Edinburgh: Edinburgh University Press, 1997).

Massignon, Louis, 'La Cité des morts au Caire', *Bulletin de l'Institut Français d'Archéologie Orientale* 57 (1958): 25–79.

Masud, Muhammad Khalid, Brinkley Messick and David S. Powers (eds), *Islamic Legal Interpretation: Muftis and Their Fatwas* (Cambridge, MA: Harvard University Press, 1996).

Masud, M. K., B. Messick and D. S. Powers, 'Muftis, Fatwas, and Islamic Legal Interpretation', in Muhammad Khalid Masud, Brinkley Messick and David S. Powers (eds), *Islamic Legal Interpretation: Muftis and Their Fatwas* (Cambridge, MA: Harvard University Press, 1996), pp. 3–32.

Mathews, Charles D., 'A Muslim Iconoclast (Ibn Taymiyyeh) on the "Merits" of Jerusalem and Palestine', *Journal of the American Oriental Society* 56 (1936): 1–21.

McCants, William, *The ISIS Apocalypse: The History, Strategy, and Doomsday Vision of the Islamic State* (New York: Palgrave Macmillan, 2015).

Meijer, Roel, 'Politicising *al-jarh wa-l-taʿdil*: Rabiʿ b. Hadi al-Madkhali and the Transnational Battle for Religious Authority', in Nicolet Boekhoff-Van der Voort, Kees Versteegh and Joas Wagemakers (eds), *The Transmission and Dynamics of the Textual Sources of Islam: Essays in Honour of Harald Motzki* (Leiden: Brill, 2011), pp. 375–99.

Melčák, Miroslav and Ondřej Beránek, 'ISIS's Destruction of Mosul's Historical Monuments: Between Media Spectacle and Religious Doctrine', *International Journal of Islamic Architecture* 6(2) (2017): 389–415.

Memon, M. Umar, *Ibn Taymiyya's Struggle against Popular Religion* (The Hague: Mouton, 1976).

Meri, Josef W., *The Cult of Saints among Muslims and Jews in Medieval Syria* (Oxford: Oxford University Press, 2002).

Mernissi, Fatima, 'Women, Saints, and Sanctuaries', *Signs* 3(1) (1977): 101–12.

Mouline, Nabil, *The Clerics of Islam: Religious Authority and Political Power in Saudi Arabia* (New Haven, CT: Yale University Press, 2014).

Mulder, Stephennie, *The Shrines of the ʿAlids in Medieval Syria: Sunnis, Shiʿis and the Architecture of Coexistence* (Edinburgh: Edinburgh University Press, 2014).

Müller, Dominik, 'Sharia Law and the Politics of "Faith Control" in Brunei Darussalam: Dynamics of Socio-Legal Change in a Southeast Asian Sultanate', *Internationales Asienforum: International Quarterly for Asian Studies* 46(3/4) (2015): 313–45.

Muminov, Ashirbek, 'Fundamentalist Challenges to Local Islamic Traditions in Soviet and Post-Soviet Central Asia', in Uyama Tomohiko (ed.), *Empire, Islam, and Politics in Central Asia* (Sapporo: Slavic Research Center, Hokkaido University, 2007), pp. 255–8.

Munson, Henry, *Religion and Power in Morocco* (New Haven, CT: Yale University Press, 1993).

Munt, Harry, *The Holy City of Medina: Sacred Space in Early Islamic Arabia* (Cambridge: Cambridge University Press, 2014).

Musil, Alois, *The Manners and Customs of the Rwala Bedouins* (New York: American Geographical Society, 1928).

Musil, Alois, *V posvátném Hedžázu* (*In the Sacred Hijaz*) (Prague, 1929).

Musil, Alois, *V zemi královny Zenobie* (*In the Land of the Queen Zenobia*) (Prague, 1930).

Musil, Alois, *V biblickém ráji: Z mých cest při středním Eufratu a Tigridu* (*In the Biblical Paradise: From My Travels to the Central Euphrates and Tigris*) (Prague, 1930).

Musil, Alois, *Mezi Šammary* (*Among the Shammars*) (Prague, 1931).

Nafi, Basheer M., 'Salafism Revived: Nuʿmān al-Alūsī and the Trial of Two Aḥmads', *Die Welt des Islams* 49(1) (2009): 49–97.

Nakash, Yitzhak, *The Shiʿis of Iraq* (Princeton, NJ: Princeton University Press, 2003).

Nevo, Joseph, 'Religion and National Identity in Saudi Arabia', *Middle Eastern Studies* 34(3) (1998): 34–53.

Newton, Lynne S., 'Shrines in Dhofar', in Lloyd Weeks (ed.), *Death and Burial in Arabia and Beyond: Multidisciplinary Perspectives* (Oxford: Archaeopress, 2010), pp. 329–40.

Niezen, R. W., 'The "Community of Helpers of the Sunna": Islamic Reform among the Songhay of Gao (Mali)' *Africa*, 60(3) (1990): 399–424.

Noyes, James, *The Politics of Iconoclasm: Religion, Violence and the Culture of Image-Breaking in Christianity and Islam* (London: I. B. Tauris, 2016).

Obaid, Nawaf and Saud al-Sarhan, 'A Saudi View on the Islamic State', in Julien Barnes-Dacey, Ellie Geranmayeh and Daniel Levy (eds), *The Islamic State*

Through the Regional Lens (London: European Council on Foreign Relations, 2015), pp. 79–83.

Olcott, Martha Brill, 'Roots of Radical Islam in Central Asia', *Carnegie Papers* No. 77, Washington, DC: Carnegie Endowment for International Peace, 2007, p. 11, available at: http://carnegieendowment.org/files/olcottroots.pdf, last accessed 7 September 2016.

Olesen, Niels Henrik, *Culte des saints et pèlerinages chez Ibn Taymiyya* (Paris: P. Geuthner, 1991).

Osiander, Ernst, 'Studien über die vorislämische Religion der Araber', *ZDMG* 7 (1853): 463–505.

Patel, Abdulrazzak, *The Arab Nahda: The Making of the Intellectual and Humanist Movement* (Edinburgh: Edinburgh University Press, 2013).

Peake, Arthur S., *A Commentary on the Bible* (New York: Nelson, 1920).

Peirce, Leslie, *Morality Tales: Law and Gender in the Ottoman Court of Aintab* (Berkeley: University of California Press, 2003).

Penault, David, *The Shiites: Ritual and Popular Piety in a Muslim Community* (New York: St. Martin's Press, 1992).

Peters, Rudolph, 'The Battered Dervishes of Bab Zuwayla: A Religious Riot in Eighteenth-Century Cairo', in Nehemia Levtzion and John O. Voll (eds), *Eighteenth-Century Renewal and Reform in Islam* (Syracuse, NY: Syracuse University Press, 1987), pp. 93–115.

Petersen, Andrew, 'The Archaeology of Death and Burial in the Islamic World', in S. Tarlow and L. Nilsson Stutz (eds), *The Oxford Handbook of the Archaeology of Death and Burial* (Oxford: Oxford University Press, 2013), pp. 241–58.

Prager, Laila, ''Alawi Ziyāra Tradition and its Interreligious Dimensions: Sacred Places and their Contested Meanings among Christians, Alawi and Sunni Muslims in Contemporary Hatay (Turkey)', *The Muslim World*, 103 (2013): 41–61.

Preckel, Claudia, 'Wahhabi or National Hero? Siddiq Hasan Khan', *ISIM Newsletter* 11(2) (2002): 31.

Preckel, Claudia, 'Screening Siddiq Hasan Khan's (1832–1890) Library: The Use of Hanbali Literature in 19th-Century Bhopal', in Birgit Krawietz, Georges Tamer and Alina Kokoschka (eds), *Islamic Theology, Philosophy and Law: Debating Ibn Taymiyya and Ibn Qayyim al-Jawziyya* (Berlin: De Gruyter 2013), pp. 162–219.

Raghib, Y., 'Les prémiers monuments funéraires de l'Islam', *Annales Islamologiques* 9 (1970).

al-Rasheed, Madawi, *Contesting the Saudi State: Islamic Voices from a New Generation* (Cambridge: Cambridge University Press, 2007).

al-Rasheed, Madawi, 'The Shared History of Saudi Arabia and ISIS', *Hurst*, 28 September 2014, available at: www.hurst-publishers.com/the-shared-history-of-saudi-arabia-and-isis, last accessed 4 September 2016.

al-Rasheed, Madawi and Robert Vitalis (eds), *Counter-Narratives: History, Contemporary Society, and Politics in Saudi Arabia and Yemen* (New York: Palgrave Macmillan, 2004).

Ro'i, Yaacov, *Islam in the Soviet Union: From the Second World War to Gorbachev* (London: Hurst, 2000).

Ruggles, D. Fairchild, *Islamic Gardens and Landscapes* (Philadelphia, PA: University of Pennsylvania Press, 2008).

Şahin, Kaya, *Empire and Power in the Reign of the Süleyman: Narrating the Sixteenth Century Ottoman World* (Cambridge: Cambridge University Press, 2013).

Salamé, G., 'Political Power and the Saudi State', in A. Hourani et al. (eds), *The Modern Middle East: A Reader* (London: I. B. Tauris, 1987).

Sarró, Ramon, *The Politics of Religious Change on the Upper Guinea Coast: Iconoclasm Done and Undone* (Edinburgh: Edinburgh University Press, 2009).

al-Saud, Abdullah Saud, 'Central Arabia during the Early Hellenistic Period, with Particular Reference to the Site of al-'Ayun in the Area of al-Aflaj in Saudi Arabia', unpublished PhD thesis, University of Edinburgh, 1991.

Sauvaget, Jean, *La mosquée omeyyade de Médine: étude sur les origines architecturales de la mosquée et de la basilique* (Paris: Vanoest, 1947).

Scherberger, Max, 'The Confrontation between Sunni and Shi'i Empires: Ottoman–Safawid Relations between the Fourteenth and the Seventeenth Century', in Ofra Bengio and Meir Litvak (eds), *The Sunna and Shi'a in History: Division and Ecumenism in the Muslim Middle East* (New York: Palgrave Macmillan, 2011), pp. 51–67.

Schöller, Marco, *The Living and the Dead in Islam: Studies in Arabic Epitaphs, vol. II: Epitaphs in Context* (Wiesbaden: Harrassowitz, 2004).

Schulze, Reinhard, 'La *da'wa* saoudienne en Afrique de l'ouest', in René Otayek (ed.), *Le radicalisme Islamique au sud du sahara: Da'wa, arabisation et critique de l'occident* (Paris: MSHA, 1993), pp. 21–36.

Seesemann, Rüdiger, 'Ziyara: Funktionen und Bedeutungen in der Tiganiya (Westafrika)', *Der Islam*, 83(1) (2006): 157–69.

Shahin, Emad Eldin, *Political Ascent: Contemporary Islamic Movements in North Africa* (Boulder, CO: Westview Press, 1997).

Shinmen, Yasushi, Sawada Minoru and Edmund Waite (eds), *Muslim Saints and Mausoleums in Central Asia and Xinjiang* (Paris: Jean Maisonneuve successeur, 2013).

Shoemaker, Stephen J., *The Death of a Prophet: The End of Muhammad's Life and the Beginning of Islam* (Philadelphia, PA: University of Pennsylvania Press, 2012).

Shoshan, Boaz, *Popular Culture in Medieval Cairo* (Cambridge: Cambridge University Press, 2002).

Sirriyeh, Elizabeth, *Sufis and Anti-Sufis: The Defence, Rethinking and Rejection of Sufism in the Modern World* (Richmond: Curzon, 1999).

Smith, William R., *Lectures on the Religion of the Semites: The Fundamental Institutions* (London: Adam & Charles Black, 1889).

Smith, William R., *Kinship and Marriage in Early Arabia* (London, 1885).

Speckhard, Anne and Ahmet S. Yayla, 'Eyewitness Accounts from Recent Defectors from Islamic State: Why They Joined, What They Saw, Why They Quit', *Perspectives on Terrorism* 9(6) (2015): 95–118.

Stark, Freya, *Seen in the Hadhramaut* (London: John Murray, 1938).

Steinberg, Guido, 'Ecology, Knowledge and Trade in Central Arabia (Najd) during the 19th and Early 20th Centuries', in Madawi al-Rasheed and Robert Vitalis (eds), *Counter-Narratives: History, Contemporary Society, and Politics in Saudi Arabia and Yemen* (New York: Palgrave Macmillan, 2004), pp. 77–120.

Stewart, Alexander Blair, *Chinese Muslims and the Global Ummah: Islamic Revival and Ethnic Identity among the Hui of Qinghai Province* (London: Routledge, 2017).

Stewart, Pamela J. and Andrew Strathern (eds), *Contesting Rituals: Islam and Practices of Identity-Making* (Durham, NC: Carolina Academic Press, 2005).

Subtelny, Maria Eva, 'The Cult of Holy Places: Religious Practices among Soviet Muslims', *Middle East Journal* 43(4) (1989): 593–604.

Suleman, Fahmida (ed.), *People of the Prophet's House: Artistic and Ritual Expressions of Shi'i Islam* (London: Azimuth Editions in association with the Institute of Ismaili Studies, in collaboration with the British Museum's Department of the Middle East, 2015).

Swartz, Merlin, *A Medieval Critique of Anthropomorphism: Ibn al-Jawzi's Kitab akhbar al-sifat* (Leiden: Brill, 2002).

Takim, Liyakat, 'Charismatic Appeal or Communitas? Visitation to the Shrines of the Imams', in Pamela J. Stewart and Andrew Strathern (eds), *Contesting Rituals: Islam and Practices of Identity-Making* (Durham, NC: Carolina Academic Press, 2005), pp. 181–203.

Talmon-Heller, Daniella, *Islamic Piety in Medieval Syria: Mosques, Cemeteries and Sermons under the Zangids and Ayyūbids (1146–1260)* (Leiden: Brill, 2007).

Tapper, Nancy, '*Ziyaret*: Gender, Movements, and Exchange in a Turkish Community', in Dale F. Eickelman and James Piscatori (eds), *Muslim Travellers: Pilgrimage, Migration, and the Religious Imagination* (London: Routledge, 1990).

Tapper, Richard and Nancy Tapper, '"Thank God We're Secular!" Aspects of Fundamentalism in a Turkish Town', in Lionel Caplan (ed.), *Studies in Religious Fundamentalism* (London: Macmillan, 1987).

Tassy, Garcin de, *Muslim Festivals in India and Other Essays* (Delhi: Oxford University Press, 1995).

Taylor, Christopher S., 'Reevaluating the Shi'i Role in the Development of Monumental Islamic Funerary Architecture: The Case of Egypt', *Muqarnas* 9 (1992): 1–10.

Taylor, Christopher S., *In the Vicinity of the Righteous: Ziyāra and the Veneration of Muslim Saints in Late Medieval Egypt* (Leiden: Brill, 1999).

Thurston, Alexander, *Salafism in Nigeria: Islam, Preaching, and Politics* (Cambridge: Cambridge University Press, 2016).

Traboulsi, Samer, '"I Entered Mecca . . . And I Destroyed All the Tombs": Some Remarks on Saudi–Ottoman Correspondence', in Asad Q. Ahmed, Behnam Sadeghi and Michael Bonner (eds), *The Islamic Scholarly Tradition: Studies in History, Law, and Thought in Honor of Professor Michael Allan Cook* (Leiden: Brill, 2011), pp. 197–217.

Tritton, Arthur S., 'Muslim Funeral Customs', *Bulletin of the School of Oriental and African Studies* 9(3) (1938): 653–61.

Turner, Victor and Edith Turner, *Image and Pilgrimage in Christian Culture* (New York: Columbia University Press, 2011).

Valentine, Simon Ross, *Force and Fanaticism: Wahhabism in Saudi Arabia and Beyond* (London: Hurst, 2015).

Van Asselt, Willem, Paul van Geest, Daniela Müller and Theo Salemink (eds), *Iconoclasm and Iconoclash: Struggle for Religious Identity* (Leiden: Brill, 2007).

Vloeberghs, Ward, 'Worshipping the Martyr President: The *Darih* of Rafiq Hariri in Beirut', in Baudouin Dupret, Thomas Pierret, Paulo G. Pinto and Kathryn Spellman-Poots (eds), *Ethnographies of Islam: Ritual, Performances and Everyday Practices* (Edinburgh: Edinburgh University Press, 2012), pp. 80–92.

Vogel, Frank E., 'The Complementarity of *Ifta'* and *Qada'*: Three Saudi Fatwas on Divorce', in Muhammad Khalid Masud, Brinkley Messick and David S. Powers (eds), *Islamic Legal Interpretation: Muftis and Their Fatwas* (Cambridge, MA: Harvard University Press, 1996), pp. 262–9.

Vogel, Frank E., *Islamic Law and Legal System: Studies of Saudi Arabia* (Leiden: Brill, 2000).

Voll, John, 'Muḥammad Ḥayyā al-Sindī and Muḥammad Ibn ʿAbd Al-Wahhab: An Analysis of an Intellectual Group in Eighteenth-Century Madīna', *Bulletin of the School of Oriental and African Studies* 38(1) (1975): 32–9.

Voll, John, 'Hadith Scholars and *Tariqa*s: An ulama Group in the 18th Century Haramayn and Their Impact in the Islamic World', *Journal of Asian and African Studies* 15(3/4) (1980): 264–73.

Wagemakers, Joas, 'Framing the "Threat to Islam": *al-Wala' wa al-Bara'* in Salafi Discourse', *Arab Studies Quarterly* 30(4) (2008): 1–22.

Wagemakers, Joas, *A Quietist Jihadi: The Ideology and Influence of Abu Muhammad al-Maqdisi* (Cambridge: Cambridge University Press, 2012).

Wagemakers, Joas, 'Salafism', *Oxford Research Encyclopedia, Religion*, available at: http://religion.oxfordre.com/view/10.1093/acrefore/9780199340378.001.0001/acrefore-9780199340378-e-255?rskey=ntOZG8&result=14, last accessed 4 September 2016.

Wahba, Hafiz, 'Wahhabism in Arabia: Past and Present', *Journal of the Central Asian Society* 26(4) (1929): 458–67.

Weeks, Lloyd (ed.), *Death and Burial in Arabia and Beyond: Multidisciplinary Perspectives* (Oxford: Archaeopress, 2010).

Weismann, Itzchak, *The Naqshbandiyya: Orthodoxy and Activism in a Worldwide Sufi Tradition* (London: Routledge, 2007).

Westermarck, Edward, *Ritual and Belief in Morocco* (London: Macmillan, 1926).

Wheeler, Brannon, *Mecca and Eden: Ritual, Relics, and Territory in Islam* (Chicago, IL: University of Chicago Press, 2006).

Wheeler, Brannon, 'Gift of the Body in Islam: The Prophet Muhammad's Camel Sacrifice and Distribution of Hair and Nails at his Farewell Pilgrimage', *Numen* 57(3) (2010): 341–88.

Wiktorowicz, Quintan, 'Anatomy of the Salafi Movement', *Studies in Conflict and Terrorism* 29 (2006): 207–39.

Woldeselassie, Zerihun A., '*Wali* Venerating Practices, Identity Politics, and Islamic Reformism Among the Siltie', in Patrick Desplat and Terje Østebø (eds), *Muslim Ethiopia: The Christian Legacy, Identity Politics, and Islamic Reformism* (New York: Palgrave Macmillan, 2013), pp. 139–61.

Al-Yassini, A., *Religion and State in the Kingdom of Saudi Arabia* (Boulder, CO: Westview Press, 1985).

Zaman, Muhammad Qasim, 'Death, Funeral Processions, and the Articulation of Religious Authority in Early Islam', *Studia Islamica* 93 (2001): 27–58.

Zaman, Muhammad Qasim, *The Ulama in Contemporary Islam: Custodians of Change* (Princeton, NJ: Princeton University Press, 2002).

Zarabozo, Jamaal al-Din M., *The Life, Teachings and Influence of Muhammad ibn Abdul-Wahhaab* (Riyadh: International Islamic Publishing House, 2010).

Zarcone, Thierry, 'Pilgrimage to the "Second Meccas" and "Kaʻbas" of Central Asia', in Alexandre Papas, Thomas Welsford and Thierry Zarcone (eds), *Central Asian Pilgrims: Hajj Routes and Pious Visits between Central Asia and the Hijaz* (Berlin: Klaus Schwarz, 2012), pp. 251–77.

Index

al-ʿAbbad, ʿAbd al-Muhsin, 149
al-ʿAbbas al-Mahdi li-din Allah, 74
ʿAbd al-ʿAziz ibn ʿAbd al-Rahman Al Saʿud *see* Ibn Saʿud
ʿAbd al-Latif ibn ʿAbd al-Rahman ibn Hasan Al al-Shaykh, 87–8, 94
ʿAbd al-Majid Salim, 141
ʿAbd al-Qadir al-Jilani, 35, 75, 81
ʿAbd al-Rahman ʿAbd al-Khaliq, 151
ʿAbduh, Muhammad, 12, 13, 95, 96, 116, 141
Abdülhamit II, 92, 110
ʿAbdullah (Saudi king), 159
Abraham, 48, 49, 51, 52, 86, 87, 89, 153, 176
Abu Bakr, 2, 23, 75, 76, 130, 185, 187
Abu Hanifa, 26, 34–6, 54, 140, 141
Abu Shama al-Maqdisi, Shihab al-Din, 28

al-Afghani, Jamal al-Din, 12, 13
ʿAfifi, ʿAbd al-Razzaq, 147
Ahl al-hadith, 6, 12, 41, 43, 87, 89, 91, 93, 120n, 149, 151, 162, 165, 201
Ahl-i hadith, 162, 203
ʿAʾisha, 23, 24, 29, 139, 143
al-Albani, Nasir al-Din, 7–8, 45, 126, 127, 135, 136–45, 146, 147–9, 152, 154, 155, 156, 165, 194–5, 197, 206
Ali Bey al-Abassi *see* Badía y Leblich, Domingo
ʿAli ibn Abi Talib, 23, 77–8, 85–6, 98, 199, 201
al-Alusi, Abu al-Thanaʾ, 12, 93
al-Alusi, Mahmud Shukri, 7, 12, 93, 94–6
al-Alusi, Nuʿman Khayr al-Din, 12, 92
Amina bint Wahb, 108, 186
Annesley, George, 103
ansāb, 19–20

Ansar Dine, 195
Ansar al-islam, 174
Ansar al-sharia, 191, 192
Ansar al-sunna al-muhammadiyya, 96, 98, 116, 153, 162
'aqida, 11, 146, 148, 158
al-Aqsa Mosque, 22, 49–50
al-Ash'ari, Abu al-Hasan, 10, 44–5, 222
Ash'arism, 9, 10, 31, 41, 44–5, 59, 73, 96, 115, 116, 132, 139, 147, 222
al-'Asqalani, Ibn Hajar, 77, 118n
Atta, Muhammad, 173–4
Ayyubids, 31, 33, 221
al-Azhar, 87, 88, 162, 196

Badía y Leblich, Domingo, 102
Badr, 105
al-Baghdadi, Abu Bakr, 175, 177, 185
al-Baghdadi, Abu 'Umar, 175, 181
Bahrain, 148, 179, 189
Bangladesh, 204–5
al-Banna, Hasan, 145
al-Baqi' cemetery (Baqi' al-gharqad), 2, 23, 24, 36, 58, 105–7, 109, 111, 144, 186
Barelvi, Ahmad, 203
Basra, 30, 80, 98, 99
Bevan, Robert, 15

bid'a, 27, 28, 42, 47, 109, 131, 159, 202, 220
al-Bin'ali, Turki ibn Mubarak, 179
Board of Senior Ulama, 135, 157–9, 161, 192
Boko Haram, 198
Browne, William George, 102
Brunei, 206
al-Bukhari, 29, 49, 57, 138, 139, 221, 222
Burckhardt, Johann Ludwig, 100–1, 104, 105, 107
Burton, Francis, 104–5

Caucasus, 200, 201
China, 14, 173
Cook, Michael, 76
Corancez, Louis Alexandre Olivier de, 102

Dabiq, 1, 176, 179
Daraqutni, 57
Dome of the Rock, 31, 48, 50, 51
Doughty, Charles Montagu, 105

Ethiopia, 198
Eve (Hawa), 113, 186, 187

Fatima, 29, 107, 109
Faysal (Saudi king), 134, 145, 157–8, 163, 165

al-Fiqi, Muhammad Hamid, 96, 97
fitna, 15n, 72, 84, 85, 144, 155, 160, 220
fitnat al-qubūr, 1, 55, 84, 85, 145, 220

Gardner, Katy, 205
Geertz, Clifford, 194
Germany, 164, 173
al-Gharyani, Sadiq, 192
al-Ghazali, Abu Hamid, 136
ghurabā', 119n, 179
Goldziher, Ignaz, 18, 19–20, 104
Grehan, James, 37
Guinea, 207–8
Gumi, Abubakar, 197

Hadramawt, 100, 189
Ha'il, 105
Haji Shariatullah, 204–5
hajj, 3, 39, 48–51, 73, 104, 108, 114, 160, 173, 203, 205, 221
Hajj 'Umar Ibrahim, 197
al-Halabi, Sun'allah, 88
al-Harakan, Muhammad, 135
Hasan II, 194
al-Hasan ibn 'Ali, 36, 101, 105, 106, 107
al-Hawali, Safar, 147
Haykel, Bernard, 77, 79
al-Haytami, Ibn Hajar, 27
al-Hilali, Taqi al-Din, 194
Hizb al-tahrir, 162

al-Husayn ibn 'Ali, 98–9
al-Huzaymi, Nasir, 152, 154

Ibn 'Abd al-'Aziz, Mish'al, 132
Ibn 'Abd al-Muttalib, Hamza 24, 105
Ibn 'Abd al-Wahhab, Muhammad, 5, 7, 12, 45, 71–2, 73, 76–95, 97, 99, 100, 102, 108, 115–16, 129, 132, 144–8, 155–6, 165, 176, 178, 179, 192, 223
Ibn 'Abd al-Wahhab, Sulayman, 86
Ibn 'Aqil, 34, 42, 88
Ibn 'Arabi, 35, 46, 73, 137
Ibn al-Athir, 179
Ibn 'Atiq, Hamad, 88–9, 156
Ibn Battuta, 106
Ibn Baz, 7, 126, 127, 135–6, 144–5, 146, 149, 150, 151, 155, 157, 159, 160, 162, 167n, 192, 197
Ibn Bishr, 98, 107
Ibn Bulayhid, 'Abdullah, 111
Ibn Fawzan, Salih, 135, 145, 149, 157
Ibn Ghannam, 71
Ibn Hanbal, Ahmad, 10, 26, 30, 36, 42, 57, 73, 142, 143, 164, 208, 222
Ibn al-Jawzi, 36, 67n, 96
Ibn Jibrin, 'Abdullah, 135, 145, 157, 179

Ibn Jirjis, Da'ud, 94
Ibn Jubayr, 36, 106
Ibn Kathir, 86, 152
Ibn Qayyim al-Jawziyya, 45,
    46–8, 59, 67n, 73, 76, 77, 78,
    84–91, 93, 94, 97, 100, 115,
    132, 139, 140, 141, 152, 165,
    178, 179, 203
Ibn Qudama al-Maqdisi, 42, 58,
    141
Ibn Sab'in, 46
Ibn Sa'di, 152
Ibn Sahman, Sulayman, 76, 88,
    95, 97
Ibn Sa'ud, 74, 77, 78, 108, 129
Ibn al-Shutaywi, Sulayman, 152
Ibn Suhaym, Sulayman ibn
    Muhammad, 80–1
Ibn Taymiyya, 4–5, 6, 7, 9–13,
    29, 40–59, 72, 73, 76, 77–9,
    82, 84–6, 88–97, 100, 104,
    108, 115, 126, 129, 132, 136,
    138–41, 147, 149, 152, 178,
    179, 181, 188, 198, 200, 202,
    222–3
'ibra, 56, 143
al-Idrisi, al-Khatib, 192
Ihsanullah, Munshi, 113
ijtihād, 10, 43–4, 59, 73, 74,
    78, 92, 93, 95, 141, 158,
    222, 223
Ikhwans, 97, 130–1, 148, 150,
    154, 163, 173
Indonesia, 148, 150, 205–6

irjā', 147–8
ISIS (Islamic State), vii, 1, 2, 8,
    15, 83, 126, 152, 155, 172,
    174–86, 199, 201, 207, 225
Islamic University of Medina,
    135, 138, 149, 151, 152, 155,
    162, 163, 179, 188, 195, 197
i'tibār see *'ibra*
i'tizāl, 153, 154
izālat al-qubba, 149

Ja'far al-Sadiq, imam, 107, 186
jāhilīya, 7, 74, 75, 85, 86, 94
al-Jama'a al-salafiyya al-
    muhtasiba, 151–2
al-jarh wa al-ta'dīl, 138
al-Jaza'iri, Abu Bakr, 151
al-Jaza'iri, Tahir, 12, 138
Jerusalem, 22, 25, 31, 48–52
jihad, 7, 76, 86, 90, 94, 147, 154,
    161, 185
al-Jilani, 'Abd al-Qadir, 35, 75,
    81
Jirjis (Prophet), 182–3

Ka'ba, 3, 19, 48, 49, 50, 51, 55,
    81, 150, 199
al-Kattani, Sidi Muhammad bin
    Ja'far, 193
kawalan akidah, 206
keramat, 206
Khadija, 81, 103, 108, 110, 111–12,
    130, 132, 133, 134, 187
Khalidiyya order, 93

Kharijis, 78, 147, 154, 185
Kitab al-tawhid, 13, 81, 152, 178, 192
Kufa, 30

Laoust, Henri, 47
Lauzière, Henri, 11, 13
Libya, 191–2
al-Luhaydan, Salih ibn Muhammad, 159, 192

Ma Wanfu, 173
madhhab system, 9–10, 59, 73, 93, 138, 140, 154, 222–3
al-Madkhali, Rabiʿ ibn Hadi, 149
Makdisi, George, 9, 57
Malaysia, 206
Mali, 195–6
Malik ibn Anas, 26, 36, 56, 105
al-Maliki, Nuri, 175
Mamluks, 10, 28, 31, 33, 41, 43, 44, 57, 59, 71, 98, 149, 188, 221, 222
al-Manar (journal), 96, 102, 136
al-Manar (publishing house), 97, 116
al-Maqdisi, Abu Muhammad, 8, 152, 155–6, 176, 179, 225
Marwan I, 81, 105
Massignon, Louis, 21
Maymuna bint al-Harith, 81, 82
al-Mazruʿi, ʿAli, 151
mazār, 39, 199, 200, 203, 205
Meijer, Roel, 161

Mengin, Félix, 103
Meri, Josef, 39, 221
millat Ibrāhīm, 87, 89, 156, 176
Morocco, 193–5
Mosul, 1, 174, 179–86
Mouline, Nabil, 129
al-Muʿalla cemetery, 108, 111–12, 132–3
Muhammad ibn Ibrahim Al al-Shaykh, 7, 127, 132–5, 138, 162, 178, 223
Muhammad's grave, 2, 23–5, 27, 28, 52–3, 58, 62n, 104, 179
Mujaddidiyya, 200
Mulay Sulayman, 193
Munson, Henry, 193
Murji'a, 147
Musil, Alois, 18, 20, 70
Muslim (hadith collector), 49, 57, 138, 139, 142, 181, 221
Muslim Brotherhood, 141, 145–6, 150, 154, 155, 162
Muslim World League, 135, 157, 162, 163, 198
al-Mutawakkil, 77–8
Muʿtazila, 9, 13, 95

Nadwatul Ulama, 162
al-Najdi, ʿUthman Ahmad, 145
Naqshbandiyya order, 73, 92, 93, 94, 96, 201
Nasiriyya order, 193
Niebuhr, Carsten, 101, 102, 103
Nielsen, Ditlef, 18

Nigeria, 197–8
Nineveh, 179
niyāḥa, 20, 30, 144
al-Nuʿmi, Husayn ibn Mahdi, 73, 74, 88

Ottomans, 12, 34–5, 71, 88, 92, 93, 100, 109–10, 163, 173, 221

Peirce, Leslie, 34
Permanent Committee (for Scholarly Research and Fatwas), 135, 158–61
pīr, 203–5
Pococke, Edward, 18

Qadiriyya order, 35, 73, 75, 199, 201
al-Qaeda, 172, 176, 178, 188, 195
al-Qahtani, Muhammad ibn Saʿid, 147
al-Qahtani, Muhammad (supposed Mahdi), 155
al-Qarafa cemetery, 31
al-Qasimi, Jamal al-Din, 12, 93–4
Qasimis, dynasty, 74, 77, 78
Quba' Mosque, 56, 107, 144
qubba, 19, 36, 40, 108, 111, 141, 149
Qubbat al-sulaybiyya, 31
Qutb, Muhammad, 146–7

Qutb, Sayyid, 145, 146–7, 153, 154, 155, 178

al-Raqqa, 179
Rashidis, 105, 224
Rida, Rashid, 12, 95–7, 102, 116, 136
Rutter, Eldon, 108–9
Ryckmans, Gonzague, 18

Sabiq, al-Sayyid, 141, 144, 152
SADUM, 200
Safavids, 35, 221
salaf, 8–10, 26, 43–5, 85, 86, 93, 95, 99, 142, 196, 222, 223
Salah al-Din al-Ayyubi, 31
Samarra, 31, 34, 174
ṣanam, 45, 75
al-Sanʿani, al-Amir, 73–7, 88, 90, 139, 141, 143, 152
Sanusiyya order, 191
Sarajevo, 15
Sayon, Asekou, 207
Seljuqs, 34, 221
al-Shabab, 198
shafāʿa, 52–4, 55, 94, 100
al-Shafiʿi, 26–7, 28, 31, 32, 36, 55, 74, 139, 140
Shah Waliullah, 12, 72, 89, 93, 202–3
al-Shawkani, Muhammad, 7, 12, 47, 73, 74, 76–80, 88, 89–90, 91, 93, 139, 141, 143, 149, 152, 178, 182, 188, 203, 223

al-Shaybani, Muhammad, 140
Shu'aybi School, 178
al-Shuhada' cemetery, 144
Siddiq Hasan Khan, 7, 89–92, 93, 203
Sidi Muhammad bin 'Abdullah, 193
Somalia, 198–9
Soviet Union, 15, 172, 199, 200–1
al-Subki, Taqi al-Din, 30, 57–8
Surur, Muhammad, 145, 155
Su'ud ibn 'Abd al-'Aziz, 98, 100
Suyuti, Jalal al-Din, 57, 77

Tabligh, 151, 162
ṭāghūt, 45, 87, 128, 148, 163, 176, 177, 196
al-Ta'if, 75, 79, 108, 134
takfīr, 76, 86, 95, 116, 132, 147, 154, 155–6
taksīr al-ṣuwar, 151
Taliban, 1, 162, 199
Tamisier, Maurice, 103
taqlīd, 10, 44, 73, 74, 92, 93, 94, 95, 116, 222–3
tarbiya, 148
al-Tartusi, Abu Basir, 185
taṣfiya, 148
taswiyat al-qubūr, 1, 14, 25, 55, 76, 91, 140
tawassul, 53–4, 56, 79, 97
tawḥīd, 8, 11, 42, 45, 81, 87, 96, 116, 130, 134, 146, 148, 156, 196

Thalib, Ja'far Umar, 206
Tijaniyya order, 194, 197
al-Tirmidhi, 23, 139
Touré, Sekou, 207
Tunisia, 192
Turkey, 173
al-Turtushi, 28

Uhud, 24, 56, 58, 107, 111
'Umar ibn al-Khattab, 2, 23, 28, 51, 53, 55, 80, 90, 187
Umayyads, 24, 50, 51, 81, 131, 136, 137, 147, 179
Umm 'Atiyya, 21, 29
Umm al-Qura University, 146, 162
Umm Salama, 84, 140
Usama bin Ladin, 146
al-'Utaybi, Juhayman, 8, 150–5, 176, 178, 179, 225
al-'Uthaymin, Muhammad ibn Salih, 82, 131, 135, 136, 149, 150, 157
'Uthman ibn 'Affan, 105
Uthman ibn Fudi, 72
'Uthman ibn Maz'un, 105

Vogel, Frank E., 158

al-Wadi'i, Muqbil ibn Hadi, 148–50, 188, 206
Wagemakers, Joas, 8, 223
al-walā' wa al-barā', 7, 89, 147, 153, 177

al-Walid ibn ʿAbd al-Malik, 24, 54, 149
al-Waqidi, 30
Wavell, Arthur J. B., 109, 113
Weismann, Itzchak, 93
Wellhausen, Julius, 18
Wiktorowicz, Quintan, 11

Yan Izala movement, 197–8
al-Yusi, ʿAli al-Hasan, 193

Zaman, Muhammad Qasim, 128
Zayd ibn al-Khattab, 80, 81, 99
Zaydis, 74, 76, 77–8, 148, 150
Zinu, Muhammad ibn Jamil, 163–4

EU representative:
Easy Access System Europe
Mustamäe tee 50, 10621 Tallinn, Estonia
Gpsr.requests@easproject.com

www.ingramcontent.com/pod-product-compliance
Lightning Source LLC
Chambersburg PA
CBHW061709300426
44115CB00014B/2620